Routes and Realms

Routes and Realms

The Power of Place in the Early Islamic World

ZAYDE ANTRIM

OXFORD
UNIVERSITY PRESS

OXFORD
UNIVERSITY PRESS

Oxford University Press is a department of the University of Oxford.
It furthers the University's objective of excellence in research, scholarship,
and education by publishing worldwide.

Oxford New York
Auckland Cape Town Dar es Salaam Hong Kong Karachi
Kuala Lumpur Madrid Melbourne Mexico City Nairobi
New Delhi Shanghai Taipei Toronto

With offices in
Argentina Austria Brazil Chile Czech Republic France Greece
Guatemala Hungary Italy Japan Poland Portugal Singapore
South Korea Switzerland Thailand Turkey Ukraine Vietnam

Published in the United States of America by
Oxford University Press
198 Madison Avenue, New York, NY 10016

First issued as an Oxford University Press paperback, 2015.

Library of Congress Cataloging-in-Publication Data
Antrim, Zayde.
Routes and realms : the power of place in the early Islamic world / Zayde Antrim.
p. cm.
Includes bibliographical references and index.
ISBN 978-0-19-991387-9 (hardcover : alk. paper); 978-0-19-022715-9 (paperback : alk. paper)
1. Geography, Arab. 2. Geography—Philosophy.
3. Geography—Religious aspects—Islam. 4. Place attachment—Islamic Empire. I. Title.
G93.A67 2012
910.17'4927—dc23
2012003180

For Roger

CONTENTS

ACKNOWLEDGMENTS

The path to this book began when I was a graduate student at Harvard University. Roy Mottahedeh introduced me to the wonderful complexity of Islamic history and modeled his wide erudition, intellectual curiosity, and generosity of spirit. Nasser Rabbat's combination of trenchant critique and openness to theoretical experimentation pushed me to be ambitious, disciplined, and creative. Although I have left the Mamluk Syria of my dissertation behind, I am every day grateful to Roy and Nasser for setting me down this path and for helping me so much on the way.

After finishing my PhD, I have been fortunate to find new sources of intellectual support and inspiration, most prominently Paul Cobb, Suleiman Mourad, Dana Sajdi, and Steve Tamari. They have been incredibly generous with their help, advice, and encouragement, and I have learned as much about excellence from their work as I have from their collegiality. As I traveled to archives and conferences over the past several years, I benefited immensely from the expertise and warmth of Emilie Savage-Smith, Boris James, Keith Lilley, Wen-Chin Ouyang, Frédéric Bauden, Nancy Khalek, Fred Donner, Bruce Craig, Kristen Stilt, Sarah Bowen Savant, Afshan Bokhari, Ghada Al Siliq, Ahmed Kanna, and Ahmed Ragab.

At Trinity College, Rob Corber, Kathleen Kete, and Vijay Prashad all read and commented on portions of the manuscript, and I am thankful not only for that help, but also for their sage advice on every step of this process and for their friendship. Likewise, conversations with Sean Cocco, Kifah Hanna, Gary Reger, and Jonathan Elukin have both stimulated and buoyed me. Lou Masur, Alex Manevitz, Susan Pennybacker, and Joan Hedrick gave me invaluable guidance to the worlds of academic publishing and fellowships.

I simply could not have written this book without the ACLS fellowship I held in 2009–2010. It provided me with that rarest of commodities: quiet time. I drafted the manuscript from start to finish during that fellowship year, and though

I have revised it considerably since then, it remains a product of the space made possible by the ACLS. Thanks also to the Faculty Research Committee and the Office of the Dean of Faculty at Trinity College for making possible a final round of archival research and conference travel in 2010–2011, which vastly improved the book. I must acknowledge the kindness and hard work of the staffs of the Topkapı Palace Museum Library, the Süleymaniye Library, and Hakan Özkan in Istanbul, the staff of The Bodleian Library and Colin Wakefield in Oxford, and the staffs of the British Library, the Leiden University Library and the Bologna University Library. It has been an unparalleled privilege to work in Harvard's Widener Library over the past decade. May its open stacks and skilled librarians long flourish! Closer to home, the Trinity College Library, particularly staff in its interlibrary loan, acquisitions, and information technology divisions, has been a lifesaver on many occasions. I am indebted to Yuksel Serindag for a timely Turkish translation.

The Department of History at Notre Dame University played an important role in the production of this book. During a lecture there in the winter of 2009, Thomas Noble and Gail Bederman provided me with feedback that transformed my thinking. I am grateful to them, as well as to Olivia Remie Constable, Li Guo, and Deborah Tor, for their interest in the project and their overwhelming graciousness.

The final form of this book bears the strong imprint of Susan Ferber, my editor at Oxford University Press. She is an exceptional reader, brilliant, perceptive, and uncompromising. She pushed me to express my ideas with the confidence and clarity to which I have always aspired. Revising the manuscript under her guidance was an intense and rewarding process.

Although the direct path to this book began in graduate school, my love for history began when I was an undergraduate at the University of Virginia. I can never thank Joe Miller enough for teaching me to think historically, challenging me to write precisely, and taking me seriously when I showed up in his office one day in the fall of 1992 saying I wanted to be a historian. Although my first love was the African history I learned from him, I also discovered a love for the Arabic language at the University of Virginia, which made it possible for me to move on to the MPhil program in Modern Middle Eastern Studies at Oxford under the guidance of Eugene Rogan and Ronald Nettler. Eugene encouraged me to be ambitious and unconventional in my approach to the region, and Ronald pushed me to refine my close reading and analysis of Arabic texts.

It is because of Eugene Rogan that I ended up working after graduation in Amman, Jordan, at the Royal Institute for Inter-Faith Studies under the leadership of Kamal Salibi. Professor Salibi was an original, a true humanist and intellectual, a paragon of generosity and civility, and even though I had not been in touch with him for years I felt his recent death as a personal loss. Mona Deeb,

Baker Hiyari, and John Gay Yoh also made my time in Amman, and my subsequent visits, special. They have been wonderful colleagues and friends, and I miss them more than they know.

The time I spent in Jordan and the visits to Damascus and Jerusalem I made while there motivated me to write a doctoral dissertation on the region of Bilād al-Shām, or Greater Syria, during the medieval period. As a PhD student, I lived in Syria, studied classical Arabic at the Institut français du Proche-Orient in Damascus, and discovered a love for that country and its people that has stayed with me to the present day. Back at Harvard, Wolfhart Heinrichs and Stephanie Thomas gave me the linguistic tools I needed to embark on the analysis of early Islamic texts that has formed the backbone of my intellectual work ever since. The Arabic Table at Williams College, and in particular Bill Darrow, Leyla Rouhi, and Chris Stone, kept my love for the language and my spirits high as I was writing my dissertation.

While these experiences shaped me as an intellectual, they are inextricably intertwined with the people who have shaped me as a person. My mother, Zayde Child, first inspired me to pursue a PhD as I grew up watching her pursue her own. She, along with my stepfather, Edwin, always encouraged me to be an intellectual and a communicator. Dinners at their table are as notable for the intensity of discussion as for the quality of food and drink. I endured the death of my father, Joe Antrim, while finishing this book. Although his career was not one usually associated with texts, he was a writer and a lover of literature. He was also one of the clearest analytical thinkers I have known. My stepmother, Phoebe, shared with my father his passion for landscapes and territory. While he was the compass, she is the artist and continues to keep his memory alive in her strong connection with the natural environment and with my brother and me. My brother, Taylor Antrim, is a gifted writer. Our conversations about writing and books are always a source of nurture and insight. He has been my ally for so long that I would be lost without him. His wife Liz has become another source of support. Her sense of humor, intelligence, and energy are a pleasure and inspiration. My closest friends, Jennifer Husbands, Stefanie Chambers, Katja Zelljadt, and Stephanie Kuttner, are brilliant, beautiful people who have made my life richer and more fun. They have always supported me unconditionally, even in my darkest moments, and their friendship is one of the blessings of my life. Finally, this book is dedicated to Roger Kittleson, my partner and my favorite historian. He lived with its conception, research, and writing, start to finish, and has been a touchstone for every idea in it—and for many of its sentences. His wisdom and wit bring me joy every day. It is with him and our amazing son August that I have experienced the most profound sense of belonging.

NOTE ON TRANSLATIONS, TRANSLITERATIONS, AND DATES

All English translations in this book are my own unless explicitly identified otherwise in the notes. Although I routinely translate geographical terms, many of which would have had connotations inadequately expressed by an English word or phrase, I provide the transliterated original in parentheses for the benefit of readers who know Arabic or Persian. For transliteration, I use the *International Journal of Middle East Studies* system. Names of dynasties and many toponyms, however, have been anglicized or translated. I retain transliterated toponyms when there is no commonly used English equivalent, but where possible I have included modern territorial referents for unfamiliar toponyms. I have also supplied a glossary that explains key toponyms and other terms and phrases used frequently in the book. Names from Arabic and Persian are given in full form at the first mention and in a simplified form that follows common usage in secondary scholarship in subsequent mentions and in notes. They are also alphabetized by this simplified form in the bibliography. I use Common Era (CE) dating throughout the book except when providing significant dates, such as the foundation of a city or the death date of an individual, when I list the Islamic (*hijrī*) date followed by the Common Era date, as in ʿUmar b. al-Khaṭṭāb (d. 23/644). I have not included any modern maps of the Islamic world, since the point of the book is to examine the ways in which early Muslims imagined territory in texts, including maps, several examples of which are reproduced as figures in chapter five.

GLOSSARY

Abbasids dynasty of caliphs that ruled the Islamic world from their base in Iraq between 750 and 1258; the Abbasid Caliph al-Maʾmūn founded the city of Baghdad as a capital in 145/762

adab standards for conduct in cultural/social or moral/religious terms, involving expectations for oral agility, wide-ranging erudition, and proper etiquette

ʿAlī b. Abī Ṭālib the son-in-law and first cousin of the Prophet Muḥammad who claimed the title *Amīr al-Muʾminīn*, or "Commander of the Believers," between 656 and his death in 40/661; Sunni Muslims consider him to have been the fourth caliph of the Muslim community, whereas Shiite Muslims consider him to have been the first in the line of imams who inherited the right to leadership of the Muslim community from Muḥammad

Andalusia al-Andalus, or areas of the Iberian Peninsula ruled by Muslims or dominated by cultural forms associated with Islam and the Arabic language between the eighth and fifteenth centuries

"Balkhī School" group of tenth-century geographers, including al-Iṣṭakhrī, Ibn Ḥawqal, and al-Muqaddasī, whose works subdivide the *Mamlakat al-Islām* ("Realm of Islam") into regions and depict them through maps and written commentaries in the manner of a no longer extant work by Abū Zayd Aḥmad b. Sahl al-Balkhī (d. 322/934)

bedouin nomadic or seminomadic Arabic-speaker, usually associated with life in the Arabian Peninsula or other desert areas

caliph title claimed by the heads of the Umayyad and Abbasid dynasties, which meant "deputy" of God on earth; by the ninth century the majority of Muslims considered the first four leaders of the Muslim community after Muḥammad (Abū Bakr, ʿUmar, ʿUthmān, and ʿAlī) to have been the *Rāshidūn*, or "rightly guided," caliphs

Fatimids Ismāʿīlī Shiite dynasty that ruled Egypt and most of North Africa between 909 and 1171, founding the city of Cairo as a capital in 359/969; the head of the dynasty claimed descent from Ismāʿīl, believed to be the seventh imam after ʿAlī b. Abī Ṭālib, and, in assuming the titles of imam as well as caliph, directly challenged the legitimacy of the Abbasid Caliphate

faḍāʾil "merits," usually used to describe a genre of work that enumerates the "merits" of a city or region; such treatises were also composed on other topics, such as the Qurʾān, the Prophet, Arabian tribes, days of the week, or certain foods

Fārs territory in southwestern Iran centered on the city of Shiraz

hajj the annual pilgrimage to Mecca, which takes place between the eighth and the twelfth day of the lunar month Dhū l-Ḥijja and consists of a series of ritual activities in the village of Minā and on the plain of ʿArafa (or ʿArafāt), about fifteen miles outside the city; may or may not be combined with an *ʿumra,* often translated as "lesser pilgrimage," which can take place at any time of the year and consists of circumambulation of the Kaʿba and other ritual activity within the bounds of the Meccan sanctuary

Ḥadīth the corpus of traditions about the words and deeds of the Prophet Muḥammad preserved orally by a chain of transmitters, assembled in authoritative written compendia in the ninth and tenth centuries, and considered, by that time, the second most important source of guidance for Muslims after the Qurʾān; each individual tradition (*ḥadīth*) contained two parts, the *isnād,* or chain of transmitters stretching back to the Prophet Muḥammad, and *matn,* or the actual words or description of a deed of the Prophet himself

"al-ḥanīn ilā l-awṭān" "longing for homelands," or homesickness, a theme to which poetry and literary anthologies were frequently dedicated in the early Islamic world

al-Ḥijāz territory along the western coast of the Arabian Peninsula, including the cities of Mecca and Medina

Ifrīqiyya territory along the North African coast, centered on present-day Tunisia

imam the title associated with a line of descendants of ʿAlī b. Abī Ṭālib and the Prophet's daughter Fāṭima, who are believed to be the highest religious, and sometimes political, authorities among Shiite Muslims; one of the titles claimed by the Fatimid caliphs in North Africa

iqlīm "clime," or more generally "region"; may refer to the latitudinal clime system associated with Hellenistic geographical traditions

Īrānshahr the ancient name for the area dominated by Persian imperial culture that stretched loosely from the Euphrates River in the west to the Oxus River in the east

isnād "chain of transmission," or list of individuals who passed down a particular *ḥadīth* or historical report orally over the centuries

iʿyān "direct experience," a methodology claimed by some geographers to highlight their firsthand knowledge of the territories they describe

al-Jazīra Upper Mesopotamia, straddling parts of northern Iraq and northeastern Syria, including the city of Mosul and sometimes Aleppo

al-Jibāl/al-Jabal territory in west-central Iran that includes the cities of Isfahan, Hamadan, and Qom

Kaʿba black rectangular structure at the heart of the sanctuary in Mecca, which Muslims believe to have been built by Abraham and his son Ishmael on a cosmologically significant site to house a stone from heaven

Khurāsān territory stretching from northeastern Iran through present-day Turkmenistan, including parts of northwestern Afghanistan

al-Maghrib territory in western North Africa, centered on present-day Morocco

Mamlakat al-Islām "Realm of Islam"

al-Masjid al-Aqṣā "Farthest Mosque"; may refer either generally to the sanctuary around the Dome of the Rock in Jerusalem or specifically to the mosque lying at the southern end of that sanctuary

al-Masjid al-Ḥarām "Sacred Mosque"; refers to the sanctuary around the Kaʿba in Mecca

Muḥammad the Prophet of Islam who is believed to have received God's direct revelation in the form of the Qurʾān in the Arabian cities of Mecca and Medina over two decades or so before his death in 11/632

qibla prayer direction for Muslims toward the Kaʿba in Mecca

Qurʾān the Islamic scripture, believed by Muslims to be a direct transcript of God's revelation to the Prophet Muḥammad in the early seventh century

al-Sawād old Arabic toponym for the territory covering the central southern portions of present-day Iraq, emphasizing the fertile agricultural lands between the Tigris and Euphrates Rivers; sometimes used in the discourse of place as a synonym for al-ʿIrāq, including the cities of Baghdad, Samarra, Wāsiṭ, Kufa, and Basra

Shiism term for a variety of beliefs that emerged in the late seventh century concerning the issue of legitimate political and religious authority in Islam; Shiites believed that the Prophet Muḥammad had designated his son-in-law ʿAlī b. Abī Ṭālib as his successor and that the leadership of the Islamic *umma* should be passed down a line of descendants of ʿAlī and the Prophet's daughter Fāṭima

Shuʿūbiyya movement that challenged the perceived supremacy of Arabic-speaking Muslims who could trace their lineage back to the Arabian

Peninsula; usually associated with the Persian-speaking secretarial class in the early Abbasid Caliphate, but can also refer to other groups, such as the Berbers of North Africa and Andalusia

sīra shorthand term for the biography of the Prophet Muḥammad, a literary tradition that took shape by the eighth century

Transoxiana territory on the eastern side of the Oxus River, spanning most of present-day Uzbekistan

udabāʾ practitioners of *adab*, courtiers and literati

ʿulamāʾ religious scholars, responsible for shaping the *sīra* tradition, for preserving and circulating the Ḥadīth, and for developing the methods of Islamic jurisprudence (*fiqh*) by the ninth and tenth centuries

ʿUmar b. al-Khaṭṭāb the second *Amīr al-Muʾminīn*, or "Commander of the Believers," after the death of the Prophet Muḥammad; supervised the expansion of the Muslim community into Syria, Iraq, Iran, and Egypt between 634 and his death in 23/644

Umayyads dynasty of caliphs who ruled from Damascus between 661 and 750; an offshoot of this dynasty began consolidating control in Andalusia in the late eighth century and declared a caliphate from their base in Cordoba that lasted from 929 to 1031

umma the worldwide community of Muslims

waṭan "homeland," or in modern usage, "nation"

Routes and Realms

Introduction: The Discourse of Place

Two travelers meet in a crowded inn on the outskirts of al-Manṣūra, a city along the lower Indus River, in the 960s. They discover a mutual interest in charting territories, itineraries, and cities. One pulls from his luggage a map he has drawn of the region, known at the time as al-Sind, and the other suggests some corrections. They settle in and exchange maps of southwest Iran, Azerbaijan, upper Mesopotamia, Egypt, and northwest Africa, each complimenting and critiquing the other's work. Several hours pass, and the older of the two travelers reveals that he has sketched such regional maps, with accompanying commentaries, for the entire "Realm of Islam" (*Mamlakat al-Islām*), and asks the younger to undertake a revision. When they part ways, the younger traveler determines not simply to revise the other work but to compose his own comprehensive geography of the *Mamlakat al-Islām*, designing the maps, writing the commentaries, and drawing from his long-standing passion for the topic, knowledge of the relevant literature, and extensive travels. His name was Ibn Ḥawqal, and he tells this story in the resulting work, variously titled *Ṣūrat al-arḍ* (Image of the earth) or *al-Masālik wa-l-mamālik* (Routes and realms), to justify his status as author.[1] His qualifications for the task derive from encounters with the territories he describes and other experts in the field, both in texts and on the ground. His account of this meeting with a fellow mapmaker points to the complex relationship between land, textuality, and authority in the early Islamic world.

Ibn Ḥawqal's work participated in a "discourse of place" that flourished from North Africa to South Asia between the ninth and eleventh centuries, the first two centuries of intensive written production by Muslims. The discourse of place is a conceptual framework I use to bring together a wide variety of formal texts committed to the representation of territory in and of itself, rather than as a setting or backdrop for something else. Land mattered in these texts; it stimulated the geographical imagination and acted as a powerful vehicle for articulating desire, claiming authority, and establishing belonging. Representing a plot of land in a text could be a way of earning a living, legitimizing a king, facilitating a homecoming, and meriting a blessing. The shared concern with land did not mean, however, that these texts all emerged from the same genre or disciplinary background. The discourse of place includes works that have been classified separately as world and regional geographies, literary anthologies, topographical histories, religious treatises, travelogues, and poems. While recognizing these categories is useful for the purpose of comparison, a single work might reflect methods and conventions from a number of fields. As a conceptual framework, then, the discourse of place resists adhering too rigidly to classifications based on genre or discipline, which might obscure the parallels and intersections between works and mute their collective testimony to the importance of land in the early Islamic world.

Texts participating in the discourse of place all claimed authority at least in part by reference to and in imitation of each other. Like Ibn Ḥawqal, authors often mentioned or recreated within their works encounters with different works, authors, or audiences. These references suggest that similar encounters took place outside of texts and provide clues as to the multiple modes of reproduction and reception of knowledge about land in this period. In addition, even though they hailed from a variety of fields, these texts overlapped in a subset of methods and material that lent itself to the representation of territory and brought the texts into dialogue with each other. With only a handful of exceptions, they were originally written in Arabic, and all of the authors were Muslim, or were not identified otherwise. They used similar vocabulary to talk about land; they invoked similar historical and religious sources; and they represented territory at similar scales and in similar forms. In particular, they tended to envision plots of land as homes, cities, or regions, each of which associated some notion of attachment or belonging with land. Despite their similarities, these visions were transformed in subtle and nuanced ways over time. Understanding the complex and fluid ways in which texts from the ninth to the eleventh centuries represented territories as homes, cities, and regions—as land-based categories of belonging—and what they accomplished by doing so is the central project of this book.

That it is possible to identify a discourse of place at all in this period is evidence of the significance of land to early Muslims. However, this is not a book about land per se. It is a book about books, or rather about texts in a variety of forms, only the most recent of which resemble the closed, printed objects that are now called books. Nonetheless, its analysis of representations of territory in texts presumes that maintaining a recognizable relationship to "real" territory was essential to the ability of participants in the discourse of place to communicate with each other and their audiences and that the very visibility and omnipresence of land in people's lives made it a useful and compelling way to frame claims to authority and belonging. The importance of the recognition of a real territory in its textual representation implies a process of interaction between text and land and between author and audience. The way in which an author imagined land had to resonate with preexisting activities on and attitudes toward land to make sense to an audience but also had the power to shape, even to transform, them. Thus, this book's analysis resists privileging those works that seem to furnish the most reliable and straightforward evidence for the reconstruction of the physical environment of their era, such as geographical and travel literature, and affords equal weight to more historical, anthological, and artistic works.[2] Whatever their genre, texts in the discourse of place did not simply reflect or explain territoriality; they produced it. They were acts of creativity that "made a difference" in complicated ways that can only be understood by considering a wide array of texts over a substantial period of time, reading them closely with an eye to comparison, and assessing the contexts and modes in which they were composed, consumed, and circulated.[3]

This project necessitates attention to what can be thought of as "textual performance," defined as written or graphic acts of representation, and "extratextual performance," defined as cognitive, oral, and physical acts prompted by a text.[4] Because many of the works written in the early Islamic world were intended for oral recitation in group settings, textual and extratextual performances were very closely intertwined.[5] Texts were performances that anticipated extratextual responses by readers, reciters, viewers, or listeners. Such responses might be simple acts of recognition. For instance, a religious treatise describing the history and layout of Jerusalem's ritual topography might cause an audience to visualize the city or to experience a burst of pious devotion toward it. Indeed, the widespread recognition of plots of land less famous than Jerusalem would have been highly likely in the peripatetic societies of this period, in which people regularly traveled long distances for commerce, statecraft, and pilgrimage, facilitated by the lingua franca of Arabic and a common culture of worship. A text might also spark a desire to reproduce or revise its performance, either orally or in writing. Ibn Ḥawqal's narrative testifies to this kind of reaction, as his encounter with another text and its author inspired him to compose his own geography of the "Realm of Islam," intended both as a continuation of and improvement on previous work. Finally, these texts might motivate travel, pilgrimage, or immigration; they might cause people to pledge loyalty to the political regime associated with a territory or persuade that regime to invest money in its development or rehabilitation.

It is difficult, however, to document conclusively the reception of and responses to texts composed between the ninth and eleventh centuries given the absence of circulation figures, best seller lists, and book reviews. What percentage of the population was literate is unknown, though even that would be of limited use, since so many works were recited orally in public places. Texts were consumed in a variety of settings—in solitude, in small gatherings or study groups, in open lectures, at home, at mosques, at the courts of princes and caliphs—but very little is known about the context in which one particular text was actually consumed, by whom, and with what result. The practice of including "reader certificates" (*samāʿāt*) with manuscripts, which trace the circulation of a work within a certain, usually scholarly, milieu, did not become widespread until the eleventh century. What can be gleaned about the reception of texts, therefore, comes predominantly from the texts themselves—stories such as Ibn Ḥawqal's and references, implicit or explicit, to intended audiences or desired responses. In this regard, knowing the circumstances of an author's life can be helpful, and quite a bit of information about individual intellectuals exists thanks to the popularity of biographical dictionaries in this period. However, establishing authorship is not always a straightforward proposition, since so many works have been handed down without attribution to a particular author (or with unlikely or disputed attributions). Moreover, given the emphasis on compilation and the citation of previous authorities in these works and the process of transmitting and copying manuscripts over the centuries, authorship is best seen as a collaborative venture, thus reducing the decisive impact of any one life on a work. What matters is that texts in the discourse of place were intentionally and purposefully crafted, not that they were authored by a single, known individual.

The texts available for analysis in this book are the product of a largely random and serendipitous process by which manuscripts of some works rather than others have survived until the present day.[6] Very few extant manuscripts can be dated to the ninth through the eleventh centuries, and even fewer of them are "originals," i.e., autographed by the author. Thus, works composed in this period are almost always in the form of manuscript copies, sometimes abridged, revised, or translated, dating from later centuries. Moreover, the process by which scholars have located and compared surviving manuscript copies, subjected them to linguistic and paleographic analysis, and published them as a single work in a printed critical edition has shaped, perhaps even distorted, the more recent reception of these texts.[7] These considerations raise a number of questions: first and foremost, to what extent are the works analyzed here representative, in both form and content, of intellectual production between the ninth and the eleventh centuries, rather than of the interests and preferences of later generations?

While this question cannot be answered definitively, texts purportedly authored in this period can nonetheless be rewardingly approached through methods of close reading, taking into account their use of language, conventions, and source material and cross-referencing them with other texts. Fortunately, there is no evidence for a conspiracy of silence or selectivity that can be generalized to all the centers of manuscript production and reproduction over the centuries. The manuscripts of the works analyzed in this book exist today thanks to patrons, scribes, and libraries stretching from Spain to India and dating from the eleventh through the nineteenth centuries. While one ninth-century work might have been preferred, and thus preserved, over another in thirteenth-century Cairo, quite the opposite might have been occurring in thirteenth-century Bukhara. Moreover, while some works that were considered unpopular, minor, or subversive at the time of their composition might have disappeared, others might have survived by virtue of sheer chance or the changing tastes of later generations. What is left then is happily random and thus more likely to be representative of the range of intellectual production between the ninth and the eleventh centuries than it is of the preferences of any single group of patrons, scribes, or libraries. We may also accommodate—indeed welcome—the mediating function of critical editions of these works published over the past two centuries, while remaining aware of the ways in which they efface traces of the serendipitous, collaborative, and nonlinear process by which manuscripts were handed down over the centuries.

The chronological parameter for this project is the loose period of the ninth through the eleventh centuries. The ninth century represents the beginning of intensive written production in the Islamic world and the stage at which the representation of land in texts acquires the critical mass necessary to be seen as a discourse. The twelfth century marks an intensification and localization of participation in the discourse of place as well as a systematization of the transmission of manuscripts. Due perhaps to the success of the discourse of place up to that point in establishing the link between land and belonging in a broadly comprehensible and meaningful way, a much larger number of texts written in a greater diversity of languages and reflecting concerns distinct to different parts of the Islamic world appeared—and have been preserved—from the twelfth century on.[8] Thus, it is both possible and preferable to situate works from this period more closely in the known variables of their composition and circulation than can be done for the ninth through the eleventh centuries. However, to understand the ways in which later authors invoked earlier authorities to legitimize their visions of home, city, and region, it is necessary to understand the way the discourse of place developed across the Islamic world in its foundational period.

Nevertheless, since the process of manuscript transmission and redaction, which has made these early works available for analysis, extended for centuries thereafter, this chronological parameter is in some ways necessarily open-ended. The works discussed in this book are perhaps best seen as textual traditions originating between the ninth and eleventh centuries but persisting even up to the present day. That said, I have not systematically considered works from this period that survive only in small fragments or as quotations in later texts. The act of composition was purposeful and creative, even when it consisted primarily of compiling material from previous authorities. It is thus impossible to differentiate between quotations from a ninth-century text and the thirteenth-century act of composition that preserved them. In other words, the ninth-century material cannot be seen on its own terms, which are, in any case, obscured twofold: once by the processes of manuscript transmission and redaction, which I accommodate with caution, and a second time by the "strategies of compilation" employed in the later work, which is where I draw the line.[9] In a similar manner, quotations from poetry, famous religious or political figures, and scripture are interpreted as participating in the discourse of place only when they are presented in the context of a larger work that is devoted to the representation of territory. For instance, when an excerpt from a poem evoking nostalgia for a particular landscape appears under the entry for its author in a biographical dictionary, it functions primarily to portray an aspect of the author's life or an example of his intellectual production; however, when the same excerpt appears in an anthology of quotations on the topic of longing for homelands, it participates in the discourse of place.

A further category of texts excluded from this analysis are those focusing on territories that were generally unfamiliar or considered exotic, such as parts of India, Russia, and China, which lay outside of direct Muslim control during this period, as well as texts that approached land primarily in terms of the marvelous or the supernatural. The plots of land these works represented were characterized chiefly by difference; they were territorial "others" that may have acted as foils for the self, but did not always do so by evoking a contrasting territorial category of belonging. Even when they employed methods and vocabulary well established in the discourse of place, they did so in sufficiently different contexts and to sufficiently different ends as to merit consideration in a separate study.[10] This work is focused on the ways in which early Muslims imagined the territories where they lived and traveled, or might relatively easily travel as a pilgrim, merchant, or soldier. It is about their recognition of these territories in texts—whether they had been there or not—as familiar and compelling categories of belonging. In the discourse of place, the text was not the same thing as the territory, but the text was about territory as such, not as a curiosity or metaphor for something else.

The central project of this book, identifying the discourse of place as a body of diverse but interrelated texts, establishes the key role the geographical imagination played not only in intellectual endeavors, but also in everyday debates about political and religious authority. Participating in the discourse of place was a powerful way of intervening in such debates, because it provided a range of useful strategies for associating widely comprehensible images of land with loyalty and belonging. This loyalty and belonging might be connective and universalist on the one hand, or bounded and particular on the other. Texts often construct belonging in universalist terms, but tie it to the particularities of a plot of land.

Alternatively, they construct belonging in particularist terms, but project it onto an expansive and accessible territory. At times they admit ambiguity, ambivalence, or tension between loyalty to land and loyalty to someone or something else: family, rulers, the Islamic community (*umma*), God. Structurally, the discourse of place itself can be seen as both connective and bounded, universalist and particularist: as a corpus it transcends and complicates bounds of genre, but its texts often depend on the intellectual authority of particular methods of scholarly inquiry to substantiate their claims.

The simultaneously universalist and particularist dynamics of the discourse of place have two broad implications for historians of the early Islamic world. First, the frequent evocation of some form of inclusivity and connectivity in the construction of categories of belonging is striking in light of the traditional political narrative of this period, which stresses rivalry and fragmentation as the Baghdad-based Abbasid Caliphate lost economic and political control over its territories. In other words, plots of land at various scales were imagined as connective and inclusive categories of belonging, even when they were differentiated in terms of claims to the political legitimacy of one "successor" regime over another or in terms of the Abbasid dynasty's own contested claims to authority. Second, perhaps because of this sense of the capaciousness of territorial categories of belonging, the discourse of place seemed to make room for or to neutralize the threat of heterodox beliefs, particularist agendas, or alternative visions of the origins of Islam and its relationship to non-Muslims. Land was a topic that enabled authors to express pluralist, but nonetheless unified, visions of the Islamic *umma*.

While this book is directly concerned with the early Islamic world, it also engages with discussions about the significance of territory to Arabs and Muslims in the more recent past. The role played by land in conceptions of community and polity among these groups has generally been seen as secondary to the roles played by kinship and religion. Similarly, a conflation of the categories of "Arab" and "nomad" has contributed to the sense that Arabic speakers do not possess strong ties to any particular plot of land. These assumptions have produced, among other things, an interpretation of nineteenth- and twentieth-century nationalist ideologies in the Middle East that emphasizes their essential "foreignness" and their departure from past conceptualizations of belonging. While certainly nationalist ideologies and the political movements they helped shape were products of a particular time and place, marked by the experience of European colonialism and transformations in the way texts were produced, circulated, and consumed, they were also new chapters in a long history of the power of the geographical imagination to motivate, shape, and justify political and religious claims in the Middle East. The discourse of place sheds light on the many ways in which intellectuals in this region have drawn from a variety of sources over the centuries to assert attachment to land.

This book is organized in three parts focusing on the most significant categories of belonging constructed by participants in the discourse of place between the ninth and eleventh centuries: home, city, and region. Part One argues that homes were imagined as land-based categories of belonging that provided physical, social, material, political, or spiritual nurture. This idea of "homeland" was both geographically and conceptually flexible and allowed a wide variety of people to use attachment to land as a means of petitioning a prince, winning a patron, or expressing religious or political loyalty. Part Two focuses on cities, constructed in the discourse of place by means of textual strategies that included naming and locating, assembling a foundation or conquest narrative, and describing the built environment. These strategies emphasized the plurality of identities associated with urban areas and their inclusivity, both past and present, as categories of belonging. Part Three considers the question of regions, often dismissed as territorial entities too vague or contingent to have been meaningful or durable categories of belonging for early Muslims. In the discourse of place, however, regions were clearly and consistently represented as plots of land both bounded and connective. They were associated with the particularities of their inhabitants or rulers, but they were also accessible to outsiders both physically and symbolically as sources of religious merit and objects of political loyalty. The book concludes by considering the proliferation and diversification of texts participating in the discourse of place after the eleventh century, as more exclusive and bounded categories of belonging emerged, foreshadowing the dynamics of territorial nationalism in the modern Middle East.

***

Land mattered to early Muslims. It was a platform for places of prayer, monumental architecture, and humble dwellings. It was the raw material with which cities were built and the terrain across which people, animals, and goods moved. But land was also the stuff of the geographical imagination. It inspired people to write books and to draw maps—and in so doing to inscribe themselves, their pasts, their religious beliefs, and their political loyalties in landscapes and cityscapes at once widely familiar and wholly particular. Land was highly visible and lent itself to visible performances of commemoration and allegiance, in stone and wood, and in word and image. Plots of land at different scales and in different shapes were transformed in texts, just as they were on the ground, into places—homes, cities, regions—and made both recognizable and meaningful in the process. No matter how peripatetic the social group or how open the territory, land was not considered an undifferentiated mass. In the early Islamic world, from the Iberian Peninsula to the river valleys of the Indus and Oxus, land was an object of desire and a category of belonging.

PART ONE

HOME

1

Home as Homeland

The works most centrally occupied with crafting home as a category of belonging in the discourse of place were Arabic literary anthologies dedicated to the theme of homesickness, or *al-ḥanīn ilā l-awṭān* ("longing for homelands"). In order to associate the idea of home with land, these anthologies adopt the term *waṭan* (plural: *awṭān*), or "homeland," as their organizing principle and elaborate on it with a lexicon of other terms designating some form of territoriality. The literary materials anthologized within these works feature images of landscapes, soil and sand, mountains and rivers, stone and wood. These images appear at times to be symbols for relationships, states of mind, and times past, but this does not render the choice of a plot of land—often described, and named, in detail—insignificant. Home had to do with location, with being in, or imagining oneself in, a place in the world, even if it also had to do with feeling a certain way or interacting with certain people. Home was not, however, necessarily fixed in one location. The anthologies make it clear that the idea of home, and the attachment to a plot of land it entailed, was geographically transferable over a lifetime. The important thing was that identifying home had to do with identifying a particular plot of land, not that it always had to be the same plot of land.

This chapter argues that the distinguishing feature of early Arabic literary anthologies on the topic of homesickness was their construction of a universally compelling, yet multivalent and complex, concept of *waṭan*, of home as homeland. The material collected in the anthologies tends to imagine home as a plot of land that provided physical, social, material, political, or spiritual nurture, but that need not be coterminous with the site of birth or fixed in one location or at one scale. Although this material often likens the homeland to the body of a mother, it expresses attachment to the homeland in universal terms, establishing it as a category of belonging that crossed divides of gender and culture. Desire for this kind of belonging frequently manifests itself in terms of longing for a past home or hopes for a future home. The prominence of temporal distance, sometimes, but not always, linked to physical distance—home is frequently past, sometimes future, and rarely present—in these anthologies highlights their concern with nostalgia (*ḥanīn*). However, what sets them apart from anthologies on related topics, such as travel, longing, or alienation (*safar*, *shawq*, or *ghurba*), is their emphasis on the centrality of land to ideas about physical, social, material, political, or spiritual belonging. This construction of home as tightly bound up with the geographical imagination, but flexible enough to encompass a wide range of territories and experiences, made it a broadly resonant category of belonging in the early Islamic world.

The Territoriality of the *Waṭan*

Home was the category in the discourse of place shaped most distinctively by the world of *adab*, often restrictively translated as "belles-lettres." This translation privileges the written word in its most style-conscious form, while missing the broader sensibility cultivated by the *udabāʾ*, or practitioners of *adab*. The *udabāʾ* were concerned not only with composing eloquent works, but also with acquiring oral agility and mastering "correct" behavior in both social/cultural and moral/religious terms. They exchanged hospitality, attended court or dinner parties at the homes of notables, sang or played a musical instrument (especially in the case of women), and engaged in impromptu poetry recitations, debates, and other kinds of verbal sparring. The world of *adab* is most closely associated with urban areas, especially Baghdad, the capital of the Abbasid Caliphate, in the ninth and tenth centuries, and was peopled by courtiers, caliphs, and concubines; soldiers, scholars, and scribes; in short, anyone who hoped to use their wits and savoir faire to accumulate cultural and political clout.[1]

Underpinning the *adab* sensibility was an omnivorous intellectual appetite, encompassing fields of study from philology to history to geography to poetry to philosophy to religion to etiquette. The *udabāʾ* were polymaths whose interests were as wide-ranging as their words and conduct were consciously refined and collectively scrutinized. Composing anthologies was one way of showcasing the breadth and flexibility of their erudition, as well as their deference to established authorities. These works might bring together a selection of the writings of an individual author or quotations from a variety of sources on a particular topic. While anthologies on a particular topic sometimes stood alone, they more often appeared as chapters of larger works dedicated to a wide range of topics or areas of debate, from those that might seem mundane or frivolous, such as insects or drinking vessels, to those of more obvious political or religious import, such as justice or prayer. These larger works were sometimes arranged explicitly in terms of debate, as in the pros and cons of leaving home or the advantages and disadvantages of pride. In addition to recognizing authorities in the selection of source material, such anthologies reproduced the culture of *adab* by acting as textbooks for fledgling *udabāʾ*, who would be expected to produce an apt quotation for every occasion or to debate any topic presented at the frequent literary salons (*mujālasāt*), both formal and informal, held in cities across the Islamic world.[2]

The world of *adab* was also a political world, most obviously in terms of competition for access and patronage. Access to the caliph's inner circle was the best opportunity to win over the ultimate patron, the caliph himself, the titular head of the Islamic world. Moreover, the family and friends of the caliphs, as well as other administrative, military, or religious authorities, were all potential practitioners or patrons of *adab*. However, the practice of *adab* was political in a more subtle way in that it involved interaction with the heritage of the Arabic language, a heritage closely tied up with the scriptural authority of Islam and its political and legal representatives, most prominently the caliph, who claimed to be God's deputy on earth, and a loosely knit body of *ʿulamāʾ*, or religious scholars. Central to this linguistic and literary heritage were the two most important guides to living a righteous life as a Muslim: the Qurʾān, believed by Muslims to be a direct transcript of God's revelation to the Prophet Muḥammad in the early seventh century, and the Ḥadīth, or corpus of traditions about the words and deeds of Muḥammad transmitted orally over the generations and assembled in authoritative written compendia in the ninth and tenth centuries by the *ʿulamāʾ*. This heritage also included a body of early Arabic poetry, celebrated despite its testimony to what was known as the *Jāhiliyya*, or era of "ignorance" before the coming of Islam, as a key to the sometimes obscure or archaic language of the Qurʾān, and a variety of historical, para-Biblical, and legendary narratives, which were used to contextualize stories and allusions in the Qurʾān or to buttress the authority of the caliph or the *ʿulamāʾ*. Although knowledge of the literatures and areas of inquiry opened up through contact with the Greek, Syriac, Hebrew, Persian, and Sanskrit heritages was also prized among *udabāʾ*, there was simply no way to succeed in the world of *adab* without a firm command of this Arabic heritage.[3]

These political dynamics were probably the reason that the concepts of home and homesickness emerged as topics of interest between the ninth and eleventh centuries. The peripatetic life led by most members of the political, military, and religious elite in an era of territorial expansion and decentralization made the experience of leaving home or establishing a new home a preoccupation for the most frequent patrons of the *udabāʾ*. The mobility of potential patrons often resulted in the mobility of the *udabāʾ* themselves, who might harbor similar preoccupations. Finally, the Arabic literary heritage was itself rich in images of prophets, caliphs, warriors, and desert nomads whose mobility caused them to miss or replace homes. Thus, *adab* anthologies on the topic of *al-ḥanīn ilā l-awṭān* often portray home as a point of departure or a point of arrival. Home was somewhere one left, or contemplated leaving; or home was somewhere one found, or hoped to find. In either case, mobility or anticipated mobility was involved in locating home. As the author of the earliest surviving anthology put it in his introduction:

> Truly, the reason for gathering together bits from the reports of the bedouin on the topic of their longing for their homelands (*awṭān*), and their yearning for their grounds (*turāb*) and their countries (*buldān*), and their description in their poetry of the kindling of fire in their hearts—is that I had a discussion with one of those kings who has moved around on the topic of abodes (*diyār*) and attachment to homelands (*awṭān*).[4]

This passage functions as a textual reenactment of an encounter with a king, a figure of political authority, whose mobility inspires the author to collect material featuring Arabian nomads (the bedouin), figures of authority in the Arabic literary heritage, and the homesickness prompted by their mobility. Whether or not this encounter actually took place, the author uses it, and the authoritative experiences it invokes, to justify his decision to dedicate an *adab* anthology to the ideas of home and homesickness.

The frequent images of mobility in these anthologies have caused scholars to see them primarily as expressions of alienation and nostalgia caused by the rapid change and widespread displacement of the first two centuries after the coming of Islam, as well as continuing pressures to travel to fulfill religious and political obligations or to search for patronage.[5] However, they must also be seen as expressions of the centrality of land to ideas about physical, social, material, political, or spiritual belonging. This preoccupation with land might come from the experience of displacement, but it need not. One might collect literary material that expresses the feelings of homesickness as a way of emphasizing the importance of attachment to land, regardless of personal experience. Since other anthologies were dedicated to the themes of nostalgia, alienation, and longing, using the Arabic terms *shawq*, *ghurba*, or even *ḥanīn* itself, it is the idea of home and the territorial connotations of the *waṭan*, or "homeland," that set the anthologies on *al-ḥanīn ilā l-awṭān* apart.[6]

To be sure, the term *waṭan* had extraterritorial connotations in the Arabic written record by this period, especially in the fields of philosophy and mysticism.[7] Thus, another way of interpreting its role in these *adab* anthologies is as a reference to other sources of physical, social, material, political, or spiritual nurture, such as relationships with kin, patrons, lovers, or the divine. In this interpretation, homeland becomes a metaphor for a "real" home in other people, or in God. While this could certainly be true of much of the anthologized material if taken out of the context of the anthology, the concentration of material in these anthologies featuring a lexicon of terms relating specifically to land makes it clear that the concern with territory is not merely symbolic or figurative. This "lexicon of territoriality" consists of such terms as *dār* (plural: *diyār*), "abode"; *turba* (plural: *turab*), "soil, ground"; *manzil* (plural: *manāzil*), "encampment, dwelling"; *balad/bilād* (plural: *buldān*), "country"; *maḥall,* "site, residence"; *arḍ,* "land"; and *masqaṭ al-ra'́s,* "birthplace." Although these words all connote some form of territoriality, they do not necessarily imply immobility or a settled life; a *manzil* might be a moveable tentlike dwelling, but for the duration of its use it is rooted in the earth. Especially when combined with urban or regional toponyms and descriptions of topography, this lexicon is highly suggestive of a literal preoccupation with territory in the literary quotations that make up the anthologies. The implicit association of the term *waṭan* and its variants, deployed primarily in the titles and subheadings of the anthologies and in periodic insertions of authorial commentary, with the more varied lexicon of territoriality, deployed throughout the anthologized material, produces the idea of home as homeland and justifies the inclusion of these works in the discourse of place.

These anthologies were not, therefore, random or neutral compilations of Arabic literary fragments from the pre-Islamic and early Islamic period that can be used straightforwardly to reconstruct the experience of displacement in this era. Rather, they were carefully crafted products of a series of authorial acts, or "strategies of compilation," such as the choice of a theme or title for the anthology and the selection, organization, and framing of the anthologized material.[8] They bring together three levels of textual performance: first, the performance of the author of the anthology, which employs strategies of compilation that emphasize the term *waṭan*; second, the earlier performances of the authors of the anthologized material, which feature the lexicon of territoriality; and third, the performances of those *udabā'* who revised, composed, or recited from anthologies on the same topic. Evidence for this third level of performance can be found in the introduction to Ibn al-Marzubān's tenth-century anthology on *al-ḥanīn ilā l-awṭān* in which he makes explicit the relationship between his work and an earlier anthology on homesickness by his teacher Mūsā b. ʿĪsā al-Kisrawī: "I have taken from his book what I deemed appropriate, added to it what I have heard, and divided it into chapters so that it will not deviate from the path of my goal for my book."[9] This acknowledgment of a conscious intertextuality at work in the compilation of *adab* anthologies is an example of the active and often collaborative performances that produced and reproduced the discourse of place.

Of the extant anthologies on the topic of homesickness, two have been attributed to one of the most famous prose stylists in the Arabic literary tradition, Abū ʿUthmān ʿAmr b. Baḥr al-Jāḥiẓ (d. 255/868), often referred to as the "grandfather of *adab*."[10] Other anthologies on this topic that are no longer extant, but that appear in tenth- through twelfth-century bibliographical and biographical citations, are attributed to some of the leading intellectuals of the age, among them Abū Ḥayyān ʿAlī b. Muḥammad al-Tawḥīdī (d. 414/1023), a great admirer of al-Jāḥiẓ.[11] The rest of the anthologies were compiled by well-known *udabā'* and experts in a variety of fields from the Iberian Peninsula to Central Asia. This star-studded and far-flung cast of authors suggests that the idea of home as a land-based category of belonging enjoyed as broad a currency in the world outside the text as it did in the discourse of place. The perception that the concept of homeland was widely compelling made anthologies on the topic of *al-ḥanīn ilā l-awṭān* popular and powerful vehicles for expressing loyalty to land.

The Universalism of the *Waṭan*

These anthologies portray the *waṭan* as a universal source of physical and social nurture through material that anthropomorphizes landscape and emphasizes an inextricable link between land and body.[12] The two are joined in images of the intake of food, drink, and air native to the homeland, the sheltering of the body in the contours of its landscape, and the eventual burial of the body in its soil, dust, or sand. The anthologies compare attachment to land to attachments between humans, generally the kind that spring from some bond perceived as physical or natural, such as parent-child relationships or those between lovers. Moreover, rites of passage or stages of life are often invoked when remembering the homeland from a temporal distance. These memories embed the human life cycle in a landscape and render the two inseparable. Despite the fact that social relationships and life cycle rituals are frequently understood as gender- and culture-specific, the anthologists stage performances within the anthology in which both men and women from a variety of walks of life act as reciters or narrators for the literary fragments, regardless of the identity of their original authors or the nature of their content. This range of performers means that entitlement to the physical and social belonging provided by the homeland is not restricted, at least in the context of the anthology, to men or to nomads, nor is the bond with homeland imagined as necessarily forged between a male subject and a female object, even when the homeland is likened to a mother or female lover. Textual performances in which, for instance, women recite poetry about coming-of-age rituals generally associated with Arabian boys or men narrate anecdotes about the homesickness felt by women after leaving their families for marriage reinforce the message that such belonging transcended sexual and cultural difference.

The anthologies forge a strong link between body and homeland by comparing the homeland to an animal's natural habitat, and attachment to the homeland to an animal's instincts for survival. Although the term *waṭan* appeared infrequently in early Arabic poetry, when it did occur it connoted the relationship between camels and the water sources so vital to surviving the harsh desert conditions of the Arabian Peninsula.[13] One tenth-century anthology on the topic of *al-ḥanīn ilā l-awṭān* uses such subheadings as "Description of the homeland (*waṭan*) in terms of sweetness and pleasure," "What has been said about trees, mountains, lightning, etc.," and "What has been said about the longing of camels," to bring together fragments of poetry that detail the landscape of the Arabian Peninsula, especially its flora, fauna, and water sources, but do not necessarily include the term *waṭan*.[14] Indeed, the introduction to the earliest surviving anthology on *al-ḥanīn ilā l-awṭān* asserts that kings long for their homelands in the same way that camels long for their watering holes (*aʿṭān*, a term that has the poetic virtue of rhyming with *awṭān*).[15] Many scholars have noted the recurring images in these anthologies of the animals of the Arabian Peninsula, such as camels, doves, bulls, lions, and lizards, closely associated with or dependent upon their homelands or habitats.[16] Just as animals are weakened or endangered by straying too far from the nourishment provided by their habitats, so too humans who have fallen sick abroad yearn for the salutary effects of the food of their homelands, often literally the meat of those animals, as in roasted lizard, an Arabian delicacy.[17] A variety of interlocutors in these anthologies, from Hippocrates to the Abbasids, identify the healing powers of the scents, air, water, or soil of their homelands, as in the verses: "A stranger in Marj weeps, longing for/ loved ones who are absent.// When a caravan approaches from the direction of his land (*arḍ*),/ he inhales its scent seeking a cure."[18] Several anthologies even list a series of anecdotes about historical figures, such as Alexander the Great, Joseph, and Moses, who advocate burial in one's homeland, the final intermingling of body and *waṭan*.[19]

One of the most clearly gendered ways in which these anthologies "embody" the homeland is by portraying it as a mother or wet nurse. The homeland gives up its milk, or its water, and physically nourishes those born on (to) it: "the country (*balad*) that suckled you with its water"; "the birthplace (*masqaṭ al-raʾs*) and site (*maḥall*) of suckling"; "the country (*balad*) that gave you the milk you suckled."[20] Sometimes the contours of the landscape are likened to those of a pregnant or nursing woman's body, as in "I was an embryo in its dunes and a suckling infant in its clouds; its river valleys nursed me and its water catches suckled me" or "its ground gave birth to me and its air nourished me."[21] At other times the equation between homeland and wet nurse is made explicit, as in "a man's land (*arḍ*) is his wet nurse" and "just as your wet nurse has the right of milk over you, so your land (*arḍ*) has the right of homeland (*waṭan*) over you."[22] This last saying implies not only that people receive nourishment from their homelands, but also that they are legally bound by such a relationship. Indeed, given the acceptance of the use of wet nurses in the Qurʾān (2:233), early Muslim jurists went to some lengths to establish the legal ramifications of "milk" relationships as parallel to those of "blood" relationships, especially in terms of marriage prohibitions.[23] While such prohibitions against marriage between people who shared a breast were not applicable to those who shared a homeland, it does suggest both a physical and a social link between a person and the *waṭan*.

Although homeland is portrayed vividly as a maternal figure in its capacity to physically nourish its offspring, it is also portrayed in relation to both mother and father, or to an extended kinship network, in the context of nurturing and protecting its sons and daughters. One saying attributes the physical sustenance of the embryo to both parents, who are in turn sustained by the homeland: "According to the Indians, you owe your country (*balad*) the same respect you owe your parents; when you were an embryo your nourishment came from them both, just as their nourishment came from it."[24] This may have resonated with beliefs among Muslims about the father's seminal fluid joining the mother's milk at conception to nourish the young, as well as expectations about the social and legal relationships among those who have shared such fluids.[25] Moreover, present in both fluids is the nourishment the parents have received from the homeland, either through their own parents' milk and semen or through the water and foods they have consumed throughout their lives. This accentuates the physical, even genealogical, nature of the attachment between humans and their homelands.

The experience of leaving a homeland and becoming a stranger in a foreign land is likened to that of becoming an orphan, "bereaved of both parents, with no mother to caress him and no father to care for him."[26] This sentiment often emerges from the mouth of a woman who has left her homeland as well as her parents and kin for marriage, as in a verse composed by Nāʾila bint al-Farāfiṣa after having been taken to Medina to wed ʿUthmān b. ʿAffān (d. 35/656): "God willed that I be a stranger/ in Yathrib, neither mother nor father beside me."[27] This suggests that women were considered as likely as men to become physically separated from the shelter of the homeland and the social network associated with it, especially because of the virilocal nature of most marriages among early Muslims.[28] In Ibn ʿAbd al-Barr's eleventh-century anthology, ʿAbd Allāh b. Muṣʿab al-Zubayrī (d. 184/800), governor of Medina under Abbasid Caliph Hārūn al-Rashīd, narrates an anecdote in which he encounters a woman living in a palace in Syria who recites to him the following verses penned by al-Ḥārith b. Khālid al-Makhzūmī (d. 85/704): "How could I get used to living in Syria (*al-Shām*)/ when I lived elsewhere only yesterday?// Truly, even life in a palace is no substitute for my homeland (*waṭan*);/ rather in Mecca, just yesterday, were my family and my homeland (*waṭan*)."[29] Pairing the word for family (*ahl*) with *waṭan* and contrasting it with the life of luxury implied by the image of a palace suggests that homeland and kin are more important to both men (as in the original author of the poem) and women (as in the reciter of the verses) than wealth. While the relative importance of wealth and homeland was debated in these anthologies, the key issue here is that the social nurture of kinship networks was closely linked to land, and physical separation from that land often meant physical separation from that source of belonging for both men and women.[30]

Memories of childhood among family and friends and rites of passage are also closely related to the homeland in these anthologies. The following saying likens physical separation from homeland and family to temporal separation from the time of youth: "Among the signs of the dignity of man and the nobility of his disposition is his longing for his homelands (*awṭān*), his love for his brothers before him, and his mourning for what has passed of his time."[31] A set of verses by ninth-century poet Ibn al-Rūmī quoted in many of the anthologies emphasizes the close connection between childhood, memory, and homeland. For example, "The homelands (*awṭān*) of men are dear to them/ because of the goals they achieved there in youth.// When they remember their homelands (*awṭān*) they are reminded/ of the time of childhood spent there, and for that they yearn."[32] In other poetic renditions of such memories, the human life cycle is portrayed as inseparable from the landscape. Just as the embryo or infant receives sustenance, so too do children and adolescents receive protection and a sense of belonging from the landscape of the *waṭan*. One of the most quoted pair of verses sets the bestowal of amulets, a well-known practice among the bedouin intended to protect an infant or child from the evil eye, against the backdrop of a specific landscape: "The most beloved of God's countries (*bilād*) lies between Ṣāra/ and Ghaṭafān during a cloudburst,// a country (*bilād*) in which my amulets were fastened on,/ and the first land (*arḍ*) whose soil (*turāb*) touched my body."[33] This rite of passage involves not only the bestowal of amulets, which would have been performed by a family member, but also physical contact between the body and the soil, dust, or sand of the land itself. Thus, the homeland is both setting for and actor in the rites of passage associated with childhood.

Despite the specificity of the Arabian toponymy and the image of amulets often associated with the bedouin in these anonymously authored verses, the anthologists put them in the mouths of a variety of reciters, including the ninth-century litterateur Ḥammād b. Isḥaq al-Mawṣilī, a prototypical male bedouin (*aʿrābī*), a young girl from the Arabian region of the Ṭayyiʾ, and a slave-girl leading a goat.[34] In this way, the author of the anthology stages a textual performance of the anthologized material in which the identity of the reciter is as important as the content of the performance itself. Moreover, by virtue of being included in an *adab* anthology, these verses were made available for extratextual performance by the *udabāʾ* of cities from Isfahan to Kairouan.[35] Any number of men and women who had never been anywhere near the Arabian Peninsula may have recited the verses and thus laid claim to the kind of attachment to land expressed therein. This possibility suggests that the significance of the connection between land, body, and the social network invested in the protection of a child—the physical and social nurture of the homeland—extended to both boys and girls, both on the Arabian Peninsula and beyond, whether or not the places and practices described in the verses were literally meaningful to their reciters.[36] The tendency among *udabāʾ* in the ninth through eleventh centuries to embrace the bedouin as the personification of the Arabic literary heritage to which they were dedicated meant that the homesickness of the bedouin could be seen as the most authentic and authoritative expression of that noble sentiment.[37]

Highlighting the applicability of such sentiments to people far removed from the Arabian Peninsula and the desert-bound life of the bedouin, al-Ḥuṣrī al-Qayrawānī, the eleventh-century North African author of the *adab* compendium *Zahr al-ādāb wa-thamar al-albāb* (The flower of culture and the fruit of insight), introduces a subsection of an anthology on *al-ḥanīn ilā l-awṭān* entitled "words of the people of [our] age on remembering the homeland (*waṭan*)" with the following commentary: "One country (*balad*) cannot be substituted for another, and you cannot renounce it ever. It is the nest in which you grew and from which you departed. It is the place where your kin gather and the place where your umbilical cord was severed, the country (*balad*) whose soil (*turba*) gave birth to you, whose air nourished you, whose breezes reared you, and in which your amulets were unfastened."[38] Such an intervention on the part of the anthologist, incorporating imagery from centuries-old poetry about the desert, communicates a perception of the universality of the physical and social link between body and homeland by representing acts of nurture and rites of passage, whether literal or figurative, as performed by or on the land.

In these anthologies, erotic love, with its obvious physical and social dimensions, also served as a human metaphor for attachment to land. Much scholarly attention has been paid to the conventional opening of the traditional Arabic ode, known as the *nasīb*, in which the narrator remembers a past love affair while gazing on the ruins of a former dwelling.[39] When fragments of poetry of this type are anthologized under the heading of *al-ḥanīn ilā l-awṭān*, land is not merely symbolic of memories of times or loves past but is a concrete, even corporeal link to the idea of homeland. Just as the body and its physical and social connection with parents and kin makes land into a homeland, the body of the beloved possesses transformative power in the following examples: "I was delighted to see one whose place (*makān*)/ is tall dunes, black and white sand as far as the eye can see,// and to reach the water that Sulaymā/ drank, when night travel had tired every long-striding camel.// I pressed my guts to its cold soil (*turāb*)/ even if it was mixed with snake venom."[40] Although Sulaymā is not identified explicitly as a former paramour, the narrator is moved to make a physical connection with the same landscape that had once nourished her by lying belly down on the ground in what could be seen as a sexual gesture. The name Sulaymā, among others, recurred in early Arabic poetry, conjuring images of timeless bedouin female beauty.[41] Such physical presence had the power to make even the harshest desert landscape beloved: "I love the land (*arḍ*) where Sulaymā dwells/ even if it is surrounded by barrenness.// It is not my fate to love the soil (*turāb*) of a land (*arḍ*),/ but rather the beloved who resides on it."[42] In this example the association of land (*arḍ*) with the physical and social nurture of erotic love acts as *waṭan*, rather than soil (*turāb*) as an attribute of the land itself. Indeed, the presence of a beautiful female body makes barren soil fertile and poisonous soil worth risking one's life to touch.

Sometimes temporal distance from the time of youth overlaps with physical distance from the beloved to associate the homeland with both childhood and first love, as in these verses attributed to the ninth-century poet Abū Tammām: "Let your heart wander wherever you wish out of desire,/ but love was only for the first beloved.// How many dwellings (*manzil*) on the earth (*arḍ*) has the youth become familiar with,/ but his longing is only for the first."[43] In verses attributed to eighth-century poet Bashshār b. Burd, the narrator remembers the territory of his youth and a woman who once lived there: "When were you acquainted with the abode (*dār*) whose people departed/ with Suʿdā? Indeed, it was very recently.// The breezes remind you of when you were an adolescent/ there, and her villa (*maghnā*) remains to you a beloved."[44] Here the dwelling place (*maghnā*) rather than Suʿdā herself is identified as the beloved. The implication is that the overlap between temporal distance from the time of adolescence and physical distance from Suʿdā renders the land itself and the dwellings upon it the only remaining object for the narrator's affection and attachment.

In most of the material invoking erotic love, the homeland is associated with a female beloved, and the authors, reciters, and narrators are either explicitly male or anonymous in the context of the anthologies. These examples suggest that it was men who were considered the agents of *al-ḥanīn ilā l-awṭān* and women the *awṭān* themselves—passive, often absent, recipients of love and devotion—which would resonate with modern Middle Eastern nationalist discourses that tend to gender citizenship male and make loyalty to a female *waṭan* a matter of heteronormative desire or duty.[45] However, in the far more numerous examples from these anthologies in which the homeland is embodied as a mother or parent, it commands the loyalty of its sons and daughters equally. While there may be enough material to make the case that *waṭan* was constructed in the early discourse of place as a kind of motherland, attachment to homeland was not the prerogative, or burden, solely of men. The primary argument of these anthologies is that attachment to a *waṭan* was universal and natural, associated frequently with the place of birth or family and with the importance of physical and social nurture.

The Transferability of the *Waṭan*

Waṭan in these anthologies is also characterized as a source of material, political, and spiritual nurture and, as such, might take a person far from his or her birthplace and family. Although attachment to homeland might coincide, or conflict, with social or legal norms about filial loyalty or marriage, it was in its capacity as a source of material, political, and spiritual nurture that homeland most directly coincided, or conflicted, with obligations to patrons or the divine. And it is in this capacity that *waṭan* should be seen as territorial attachment that was transferable over the course of a lifetime. Thus, the category of home in the discourse of place might entail more than one plot of land, each of which might be called a *waṭan,* and a person might owe loyalty to any of them depending on the circumstances. The fact that the term *waṭan* appeared most often in early Arabic poetry in the plural form suggests that the concept of territory as a source of nurture necessitated familiarity with a plurality of plots of land or, more precisely, water sources, given the arid conditions of the Arabian Peninsula. In short, a person had to have more than one *waṭan,* because no single site in the desert could sustain human, or animal, life for long.[46] This poetic tendency is borne out in *adab* anthologies, as images of the *waṭan* as the place of birth, implicitly singular, are juxtaposed with images of the *waṭan* as the place of family or the beloved, potentially movable, and of *waṭan* as a place of wealth, livelihood, prestige, or piety, often movable. The reality that people moved away from their families and their beloveds inspired the longing or nostalgia (*ḥanīn*) that figures so prominently in the anthologies.[47] However, the reasons for moving away are not always portrayed as bad; the moving away is often related to the gaining of a new homeland, a new source of social and material nurture or political and spiritual belonging, even if an old one is lost along the way.

Most of these anthologies present a tension between the virtue of loyalty to one's place of birth or family and the possibility that one's place of birth or family might not provide sufficient material resources to enable one to live a life of dignity. Thus, Ibn ʿAbd al-Barr includes a second anthology containing a variant plural form of *waṭan* in its title, "A chapter on renouncing homelands (*mawāṭin*) of baseness," which directly follows "A chapter on travel (*safar*) and displacement (*ightirāb*)."[48] Ibn al-Marzubān includes subsections entitled "Those who choose wealth over *waṭan*" and "Those who choose *waṭan* over wealth" in his anthology on *al-ḥanīn ilā l-awṭān,* and al-Rāghib al-Iṣfahānī includes subsections in his anthology on displacement entitled "Preference for ease abroad (*fī l-ghurba*) over hardship in the *waṭan*" and "Preference for hardship in the *waṭan* over ease abroad (*fī l-ghurba*)."[49] Part of this tension stems from the fact that much of the material associating *waṭan* with place of birth or family portrays images from the bedouin life on the Arabian Peninsula, a life idealized, if also mocked, in urban *adab* circles as one of hardship and simplicity.[50] The following saying highlights this association: "One cannot be familiar with the homeland (*waṭan*) without also being familiar with scarcity of water (*ʿaṭan*)."[51] Some of the anthologized material maintains that attachment to the *waṭan* is so natural, even divinely foreordained, that it does not depend on the quality of life provided by the *waṭan*, as in the saying variously attributed to ʿUmar b. al-Khaṭṭāb (d. 23/644) and the Prophet Muḥammad: "If not for love of homeland (*waṭan*), then bad countries (*balad*) would fall to ruin."[52] Thus, attachment to the *waṭan* naturally maintains equilibrium among all the lands that God created, both the "good" or fertile and prosperous ones and the "bad" or arid and destitute ones.

Nevertheless, people could and often did trade in a "bad" country for a "good" one. Other examples from the anthologies suggest that if the homeland does not provide sufficient material, political, or spiritual nurture, then leaving it is justified.[53] Most of the anthologies on *al-ḥanīn ilā l-awṭān* include material representing the homeland as flexible and transferable, such as: "Ease abroad (*ghurba*) is like being in the homeland (*waṭan*), and hardship in the homeland (*waṭan*) is like being abroad (*ghurba*)."[54] Similarly, the following verses indicate that possibilities for material nurture make lands into homelands, not their status as place of birth or family: "Poverty in our homelands (*awṭān*) is like being abroad (*ghurba*)/ and wealth abroad (*ghurba*) is like being in the homelands (*awṭān*).// The land (*arḍ*) is something indivisible,/ and one group of neighbors follows another."[55] According to these verses, what constitutes homeland is a land (*arḍ*) that provides opportunities for material nurture, while social nurture in the form of neighbors can be found anywhere. A set of verses attributed to Abū Tammām implies that it is possible to combine love of family and homeland with the search for a life of ease: "The inclination of the soul toward family and homeland (*awṭān*)/ should not prevent the life of ease you seek!// In every country (*balad*), if you settle there, you will meet/ family to replace family and neighbors to replace neighbors."[56] Here the linked concepts of homeland and social belonging are portrayed as geographically transferable in the service of material nurture.

Al-Rāghib al-Iṣfahānī inserts himself into his anthology on displacement, which immediately precedes his anthology on *al-ḥanīn ilā l-awṭān*, by describing an encounter with a prince in which he recites the following verses and is rewarded with "a large sum of money": "When you are powerful in a land (*arḍ*), even if it is far away,/ do not let it increase your attachment to the homeland (*waṭan*)!// For it is nothing but a place (*balda*), like any other place (*balda*),/ and the best of them is that which buttresses you against the vicissitudes of time."[57] While these verses fix the *waṭan* in space and urge movement away from it, they also suggest that when another plot of land provides better opportunities for social, material, or political nurture, it should command the same kind of attachment as a homeland. Moreover, by staging an autobiographical performance within the anthology in which the anthologist's own recitation of poetry acts as a kind of "mirror for a prince," al-Rāghib al-Iṣfahānī draws attention to the realities of mobility for both the *udabāʾ* and the political elite. The extratextual performance of such literary material featuring the widely resonant concept of *waṭan* might also bridge the two experiences and, as in al-Rāghib al-Iṣfahānī's textual performance, act as a successful bid for patronage.

Ibn ʿAbd al-Barr was a scholar from an old Cordoban family who had every reason to embrace mobility and a more flexible concept of homeland. Forced to leave his family's seat in the wake of the Berber uprising of 399/1008–1009, he composed his *adab* compendium late in life for one of the "party kings" (*mulūk al-ṭawāʾif*) under whose rule the Muslim-controlled territories of the Iberian Peninsula, otherwise known as Andalusia or al-Andalus, were fragmented in the eleventh century. His anthology on renouncing "homelands (*mawāṭin*) of baseness" is unique among the anthologies for containing only material that urges Muslims to leave any land in which they are humiliated or debased or, in the words of the Prophet, in which "they are subjected to unbearable trials."[58] The overall message is not, however, that certain homelands, such as those in impoverished or arid territories, are inherently humiliating or debasing, but that lands in which one's condition is humiliating or debased for a variety of reasons are not true homelands, as in the following verses by ninth-century poet ʿAbd al-Ṣamad b. al-Muʿadhdhal: "If a homeland (*waṭan*) makes me uneasy,/ then every country (*bilād*) is a homeland (*waṭan*)."[59] Verses attributed to seventh-century poet Mālik b. al-Rayb express the desire to adopt a new homeland: "If the family of Marwān treats us justly, we will come close/ to you, even if they urge us to stay away,// leaving an abode (*dār*) of humiliation on the earth (*arḍ*)./ Every country (*bilād*) can become a homeland (*ūṭinat*) like my country (*bilād*)."[60] By setting as a condition for immigration the justice of the Umayyad dynasty ("the family of Marwān"), the poet associates political power with possibilities for mobility, although the phrase "even if they urge us to stay away" suggests either an undertone of rebelliousness, which would not be out of place given that Ibn al-Rayb was considered one of the "brigand poets," or desperation due to circumstances in the old homeland, which would fit the theme of the anthology.[61] In either case, the overall message, that "every country can become a homeland," highlights the transferability of the *waṭan* in the search for a life of dignity and plenty. Ibn ʿAbd al-Barr himself experienced the kind of reversal of fortune that makes a homeland intolerable and, like al-Rāghib al-Iṣfahānī, inserts himself into the anthology by quoting a set of verses he composed upon leaving Seville: "He whom we were delighted to be near changed beyond recognition,/ turning into poison when he had been cool fresh water.// A neighbor recognizes when a neighbor no longer agrees with him/ and when an abode (*dār*) is no longer suitable for him, so he goes roaming."[62] While he is not explicit about what went wrong in Seville, the implication from these verses (and from Ibn ʿAbd al-Barr's personal history of mobility in a decentralized political environment) is that opportunities for political favor and patronage made a land into a homeland and that a lack of such resources justified leaving in search of a new homeland.

On the other hand, some of the anthologized material suggests that political favor and patronage might conflict with attachment to homeland. Just as mobility in the search for livelihood or wealth might justify leaving home, so does mobility in the service of the caliph, though much of the anthologized material implies that a just ruler recognizes the pain that such mobility might cause. Al-Bayhaqī includes two anecdotes in his anthology set during the time of the Abbasid Caliph al-Maʾmūn that feature the sensitivity of the regime toward attachment to homeland. In the first, while Abū Dulaf (d. 226/840–841) is serving as al-Maʾmūn's governor in Syria, he writes a poem expressing his homesickness and sends it to a friend. Somehow the poem reaches the caliph, and when he hears it he declares: "Al-Qāsim b. ʿĪsā is longing for his homeland (*waṭan*)!" At that, al-Maʾmūn orders him to leave.[63] Although the poem never mentions the word *waṭan*, the Caliph recognizes the poem as an example of *al-ḥanīn ilā l-awṭān* and immediately acts to reconcile his servant with his homeland by imperial dictate. In the second anecdote, the poet Saʿīd b. Ḍamḍam approaches his patron, al-Maʾmūn's vizier al-Ḥasan b. Sahl (d. 236/850–851), and recites a poem in which he longs for the hardship of the desert and asks the vizier for a favor. Moved by the poem, Ibn Sahl offers to give him whatever he wants. Saʿīd says: "Buy me some sheep, and return me to the desert." Ibn Sahl exclaims: "You are longing for the place you described in the poem! The homeland (*waṭan*)! The homeland (*waṭan*)!" With that realization, the vizier buys him a thousand sheep, gives him a large sum of money, and returns him to the desert.[64] Although the term *waṭan* does not occur in the poem, al-Maʾmūn's vizier realizes that the territory evoked so poetically is none other than the poet's homeland and that the poet should be reunited with that territory.

Similarly, in an anecdote taken from Ibn ʿAbd al-Barr's anthology the chief jurist of Mecca, ʿAbd al-Malik b. ʿAbd al-ʿAzīz b. Jurayj (d. 150/767–768), travels to collect a debt from the governor of Yemen, Maʿn b. Zāʾida (d. 152/769–770), appointed by the Abbasid Caliph al-Manṣūr. During his sojourn in Yemen, the jurist sees a caravan preparing to leave for the pilgrimage to Mecca, and his eyes fill with tears. When the governor of Yemen asks him what is wrong, he replies by reciting some verses by the turn-of-the-eighth-century poet ʿUmar b. Abī Rabīʿa. Although the verses do not mention the term *waṭan*, the governor responds: "Are you determined to travel and return to your homeland (*waṭan*)?" When the jurist replies in the affirmative, the governor gives him gifts, pays his debt, and wishes him well on his return trip to Mecca.[65] In all of these examples, service to the caliph, or to one of his appointees, causes separation from the homeland, and the caliph or a member of his regime is the one who makes possible a return.[66] Thus, the wisdom and justice of a ruler may ease the tension between attachment to homeland and the political and religious obligation of serving the caliph. These anecdotes each feature a textual performance, the recitation of poetry, which is represented as a strikingly effective way of making a demand of a political or religious authority. This likely reflected the uses—and usefulness—of *adab* anthologies in the competition for patronage and resources in the world outside the text.[67] The fact that the political or religious authority always recognizes the concept of *waṭan* in the performance, even though it is not uttered explicitly, reinforces the dominant message that *waṭan* was a widely comprehensible and compelling territorial category of belonging.

Another way in which traveling abroad might outweigh clinging to the homeland, or might actually act as a substitute homeland, is if it offered opportunities for the fulfillment of religious obligations or the attainment of wisdom or piety. One saying attributed to "the philosophers" urges people to seek their livelihoods abroad, for "even if you do not gain wealth, you will come away with much insight."[68] Ibn al-Marzubān's inclusion of the Qurʾānic verse 67:15, enjoining people to roam throughout the world enjoying God's bounty, in his chapter on "Those who choose wealth over *waṭan*" suggests that such a divine injunction is more important than homeland, or might be a substitute for homeland.[69] Similarly, the inclusion of Qurʾānic verses 2:246 and 4:66 in several of these anthologies, illustrating people's reluctance to leave their abodes (*diyār*), even if ordered by God to do so, suggests that though attachment to homeland is natural, it is less important or virtuous than mobility in the service of God.[70] While these verses set homeland and service to God in tension with one another, they can also be seen as justifying mobility as a form of spiritual nurture.

To a limited extent, the later anthologies suggest easing this tension by the adoption of Mecca as a universal homeland of spiritual nurture. Composed in the far western reaches of the Islamic world, Ibn ʿAbd al-Barr's collection on the topic of *al-ḥanīn ilā l-awṭān* is dominated by material in which Mecca or the Ḥijāz, a regional toponym referring to the western part of the Arabian Peninsula, features as the *waṭan*.[71] Other anthologies include a *ḥadīth* in which the Prophet longs for Mecca after being forced to leave for Medina in what became known as the *hijra* (migration, flight) of 622.[72] Although the Prophet's own longing might be interpreted as a justification for characterizing the *waṭan* as the place of birth and family, since Mecca was certainly that to him, it could also be interpreted as an exemplary longing for an ideal *waṭan*, Mecca, which all pious Muslims should adopt as their own.

Just as one might ask whether a place of birth and family, a place of wealth and patronage, or a place of piety and ritual like Mecca is the true homeland, so too do the anthologies exhibit a tension between the bedouin longing for the homelands of the Arabian Peninsula and the longing of a variety of other figures for the settled centers of the Islamic world. Some have seen this tension as a reflection of the battle lines drawn by the movement known as the *Shuʿūbiyya*, which questioned the privileged place of the Arabic linguistic and literary heritage, and its iconic images of Arabian life, in Islamic civilization.[73] The earliest extant anthology, a freestanding work attributed to al-Jāḥiẓ, is the most explicit in its construction of the nomadic bedouin lifestyle as the archetypal experience of *al-ḥanīn ilā l-awṭān*. In his introduction, the anthologist compares the longing of the king whose homesickness inspired him to compose the work to the longing of a camel.[74] Other authorial commentary reinforces the sense that the inhabitants of the Arabian Peninsula, both animal and human, demonstrate a kind of primordial attachment to territory, as in the following statement: "If we were to collect all the anecdotes and poetry of the bedouin on this topic, it would take forever."[75] With the exception of a handful of pre-Islamic kings and prophets and a brief reference to the Abbasid-era Iranian family of viziers the Barmakids, the vast majority of the material in this anthology features images from the Arabian Peninsula. The bedouin emerges from the anthology as the hero of *al-ḥanīn ilā l-awṭān*, even if that heroism could be mocked in some of the anecdotes that emphasize the coarseness of desert life.[76]

While material featuring the bedouin and Arabia never disappears from the anthologies, there is a marked trend in the later anthologies toward the inclusion of material featuring contemporary city folk and, in particular, itinerant members of the *udabāʾ* like the anthologists themselves.[77] Some anthologies create this effect by privileging material from ninth- through eleventh-century sources and urban and regional toponyms from outside of the Arabian Peninsula. Al-Bayhaqī's anthology includes a number of examples of what have been called graffiti, verses of poetry etched upon doors or walls of caravanserais, in cities like Baghdad and al-Ahwāz.[78] These graffiti testify to the longing inspired by mobility in an urban world, a longing that was inscribed literally in the built environment. Ibn al-Marzubān quotes a set of verses in which the following line represents not a city but a region as a *waṭan*: "He left Iraq (*al-ʿIrāq*), which had been to him a homeland (*waṭan*),/ and there is nothing good in life having moved away from the homeland (*waṭan*)."[79] Regional toponyms, like those of cities or descriptions of landscapes, were another way of associating the *waṭan* with territoriality. Ibn al-Marzubān uses the subheading "those for whom displacement (*ghurba*) is a perpetual cycle" to introduce a set of oft-quoted verses by Abū Tammām in which he compares himself to the ever-wandering pre-Islamic prophet and legendary figure al-Khiḍr: "I am the successor to al-Khiḍr. Others fix their homeland (*waṭan*)/ in a place (*balda*), but my homelands (*awṭān*) are the backs of camels.// My people are in Syria (*al-Shām*), my desire is in Baghdad, and I/ am in al-Raqqatayn, while my brothers are in al-Fusṭāṭ."[80] Even though this is one of the few examples in which the *waṭan* is specifically defined extraterritorially ("the backs of camels"), the toponyms in these verses celebrate the cities and regions of the Abbasid empire, each plot of land taking on one of the attributes of homeland, so that only by moving between them all can the poet truly be at home.

In certain cases, the anthologists stage encounters between bedouin and urban literati in which the composition or recitation of poetry on the topic of homeland acts as a test or a competition for the audience's approval. In al-Rāghib al-Iṣfahānī's anthology, one anecdote has litterateur Abū Dulaf, a noted patron of *adab*-style gatherings, criticizing a bedouin for indifference toward loved ones after hearing him recite the following verse: "In every country (*bilād*), if I settle there, I meet/ people to replace people and brothers to replace brothers."[81] Here, the bedouin's recitation, and its celebration of a nomadic life, is portrayed as an unsuccessful performance, both within the text and, it is implied, without, in that it fails to win over its urban and urbane audience. Al-Ḥuṣrī al-Qayrawāni presents an anecdote in which the well-known Baghdad-born poet Ibn al-Rūmī brings a friend one of his odes that includes lines likening longing for the homeland to nostalgia for the time of youth and asks him to judge between it and the verses recited by a bedouin describing "a country (*bilād*) in which my amulets were fastened on,/ and the first land (*arḍ*) whose soil (*turāb*) touched my body." His friend explains that Ibn al-Rūmī's verses are better because "they mention the homeland (*waṭan*) and love for it and the pain that affirms it."[82] The conclusion of this anecdote suggests that one of the ways in which city folk like Ibn al-Rūmī had improved upon the expressions of attachment to homeland attributed to the archetypal bedouin is by consciously using the word *waṭan*. This word allows Ibn al-Rūmī to express in more universal terms what the bedouin could only accomplish by describing a specific desert landscape. Thus, the text contains a performance validating the project of the text itself, the construction of a concept of *waṭan* as a territorial category of belonging that was comprehensible and compelling across divides of class, culture, and gender, just as it was transferable across space and scale—from desert to city to region—in a highly mobile world.

The signal contribution of *adab* anthologies on the topic of *ḥanīn ilā l-awṭān* to the discourse of place was their construction and deployment of the universal, yet flexible, concept of *waṭan*, or homeland. The very flexibility of this concept had political resonance in the ninth to eleventh centuries, as it justified the mobility of the *udabāʾ* themselves and their patrons in the political elite. If loyalty to a *waṭan* was transferable, so too was loyalty to a patron. Conversely, if a client's loyalty to a *waṭan* conflicted with loyalty to a patron, it might be the duty of the patron to reconcile the client with his or her *waṭan*; or, if a believer's loyalty to a *waṭan* conflicted with loyalty to God, it might be the believer's duty to adopt a new *waṭan*. In any of these cases, the mobility justified by the flexibility of the concept of *waṭan* was always *to* or *from* a plot of land that was either explicitly styled a *waṭan* or had the characteristics of a *waṭan* in terms of providing physical, social, material, political, or spiritual nurture. Even if the *waṭan* was, as Abū Tammām claimed, the back of a camel, it was only so that it could move the rider between plots of land that provided different kinds of belonging.

This emphasis on geographically locating belonging makes these anthologies eloquent testimony to land as an object of desire among Muslims in this period. Although *adab* anthologies on the topic of *al-ḥanīn ilā l-awṭān* mount the most focused and textured representations of home as homeland, echoes of these representations reverberate throughout the discourse of place, facilitated by the capacity of the *waṭan* to encompass plots of land of very different sizes and locations and by the ability of the individual to choose and change the *waṭan* depending on circumstance.[83] For instance, when al-Khaṭīb al-Baghdādī, author of the eleventh-century city-based biographical dictionary *Taʾrīkh Baghdād* (History of Baghdad), quotes the religious scholar al-Shāfiʿī (d. 204/820) saying, "I never entered a country without counting it a place of sojourn, except for Baghdad, for when I entered it I counted it a homeland (*waṭan*)," he is making a gesture to the authoritative corpus of material on *al-ḥanīn ilā l-awṭān* assembled and performed in these anthologies.[84] Moreover, he is emphasizing the flexibility of the *waṭan*, enabling someone like al-Shāfiʿī, likely born in Syria or Yemen, to adopt Baghdad as a homeland and, conversely, enabling Baghdad to lay claim to al-Shāfiʿī, as well as other illuminati, which was, after all, the goal of such a biographical dictionary. Similarly, when Ibn ʿAbd Rabbih in his tenth-century *adab* anthology on "comparing the merits of countries" (*tafāḍul al-buldān*) describes Kufa as "the homeland (*waṭan*) of ʿAlī, may God be pleased with him, and his abode (*dār*)," he is anticipating an audience that understands the *waṭan* as a transferable territorial allegiance, in this case from ʿAlī's place of birth and residence in Mecca and Medina, where his claim to leadership of the Islamic community was contested, to Kufa, where he found social and political belonging among the supporters of his claim.[85] The geographical transferability of this idea of home and the universalism of its gravitational pull made it a powerfully flexible vehicle for associating land and belonging and for expressing diverse and changing loyalties, both in *adab* anthologies and elsewhere in the discourse of place.

PART TWO

CITY

2

Cities and Sacred History

One of the most visible ways in which early Muslims expressed their values and aspirations was by claiming and transforming urban space or by founding new cities. Processes of transformation in old cities were often gradual, punctuated by the erection or renovation of monumental architecture, such as the Dome of the Rock in Jerusalem, the Umayyad Mosque in Damascus, or the Kaʿba in Mecca. The foundation of new cities also unfolded in stages, shaped by organic forces as much as by imperial dictate. Even the storied acts of creation that established Baghdad and Cairo as the political capitals of the Abbasid and Fatimid Caliphates respectively were mere preambles to centuries of expansion and reorganization in response to commercial and cultural trends, military conquest, and the movement of peoples.

Another powerful way in which early Muslims expressed their values and aspirations was by representing their cities in texts. Like the cities themselves, works in the discourse of place devoted in whole or large part to representing urban areas acquired critical mass slowly and from multiple directions. They incorporated scriptural, legendary, and literary material from both the pre-Islamic and Islamic periods and proliferated between the ninth and eleventh centuries in an increasingly familiar, if flexible, set of forms that reimagined earlier forms and communicated messages to a broad audience. These texts can be grouped loosely into two categories: *faḍāʾil* ("merits") treatises praising a city, which resemble *adab* anthologies by bringing together quotations, poetry, and anecdotes from a variety of sources, but sometimes exhibit a pious orientation by favoring material from the Qurʾān and Ḥadīth;[1] and topographical histories, which represent cities through historical reports, as well as para-Biblical and legendary material, documenting changes in their built environments, administration, and residence patterns over time.[2] In practice, these categories overlapped considerably. For instance, Ḥadīth-based *faḍāʾil* treatises may be joined with topographical histories to act as introductions to biographical dictionaries of the early generations of Muslims and later members of the *ʿulamāʾ* associated with a particular city.[3] Alternatively, what might be thought of as mini-*faḍāʾil* treatises favoring poetry and legend in content and the *adab* tradition of debate in form recur in world geographies, as well as in some topographical histories.

Despite their variations in form and content, these works not only share a preoccupation with an urban area, but also, taken together, suggest certain "family resemblances" among cities in the geographical imagination in this period.[4] It was not a simple formula, such as "Friday mosque + public bath + market = Islamic City," nor a formal definition a lexicographer might compose for a particular term, such as *madīna*, one of the most common Arabic words for "city."[5] Indeed, a lexicon of urbanism would include a host of terms, many of which were used in very different ways depending on context: *madīna* (plural: *mudun*), *miṣr* (plural: *amṣār*), *qaṣaba* (plural: *qaṣabāt*), *balda/balad* (plural: *bilād*), *kūra* (plural: *kuwar*), *qarya* (plural: *qurā*).[6] Instead, authors employed a set of textual strategies to make plots of land recognizable as cities and distinguish them from homes and regions. Such strategies include naming and locating the city, assembling a foundation or conquest narrative, and describing its built environment. These recur frequently not only because they conjured legible images of cities in the minds of audiences, but also because they allowed authors to express a range of political and religious agendas. Although not every work engages all three of the strategies, most of them deploy more than one, with an eye to intertextuality, so that particular statements could be made about particular cities while maintaining their "family resemblance" to other cities in the discourse of place.

This chapter focuses on the strategies of naming and locating a city and assembling its foundation or conquest narrative, strategies primarily of the selection and ordering of diverse materials in *faḍāʾil* treatises and topographical histories. These strategies draw substantially from a reservoir of sources dealing with what might be called sacred history, and they are particularly effective in making proximate what otherwise might seem distant and disconnected, whether temporally or spatially, and therefore expanding in both time and space the bases for belonging in and to a city. What is striking about the claims to belonging and authority produced by each strategy is their overwhelming inclusivity and openness to heterogeneity. This suggests that cities in the early Islamic world were imagined more as sites of negotiation and compromise than as symbols of Islamic purity or triumphalism. Cities between the ninth and eleventh centuries remained remarkably "up for grabs," available to a wide range of people and, at least in the texts that made up the discourse of place, able to accommodate a variety of political and religious agendas. In a period that is often portrayed as dominated by the political fragmentation and religious rivalry caused by waning Abbasid power, cities loom large on the textual horizon as landmarks of connectivity and unity.

Naming and Locating Cities

Cities were consistently named and located in the discourse of place. This may not seem in itself surprising—two of the most seemingly self-evident and essential characteristics of cities on the ground are their names and locations—but the authorial acts of naming and locating cities were performed with an intensity and intentionality that telegraphed their meaningfulness. The first thing to notice about city names in the discourse of place is their multiplicity. Most cities were assigned more than one name, and the more names a city could claim, it seems, the better.[7] In one mid-tenth-century work on the history of Bukhara, today a city in southwest Uzbekistan, the author, Abū Bakr b. Jaʿfar al-Narshakhī, proudly declared: "In Khurāsān there is no other city with so many names."[8] Al-Narshakhī claimed that one reason for Bukhara's multiple names was the bilingualism of the region of Khurāsān, which stretched roughly from the northeastern part of present-day Iran to the Oxus River valley, as each of its prominent cities could boast at least one Persian and one Arabic name.[9]

Related to this bilingualism is the prominence accorded the name of a city's pre-Islamic antecedent, usually derived from a language other than Arabic, in the discourse of place. Except in the cases of cities like Damascus that had enjoyed uninterrupted status as large urban areas, most cities that came into being after the coming of Islam could claim additional names by linking their sites to a nearby settlement or stronghold founded by some notable figure in ancient or Biblical history. Works on Yemen from the tenth and eleventh centuries celebrate the city of Sanaa as the site of Ghumdān, a legendary castle constructed by Sām b. Nūh, or Shem the son of Noah, and the two names seem to be used interchangeably, especially in poetry, to evoke the long history and past grandeur of the city.[10] In an early-tenth-century world geography, Abū Bakr Aḥmad b. Muḥammad al-Hamadhānī, known as Ibn al-Faqīh, opens the section on his hometown of Hamadan, today a city in west-central Iran, by proposing two origins for its name: first, that the city was named after its founder, a great-grandson of the Biblical Noah; and second, that its name is an anagram of the Persian *nādhimah*, meaning "beloved."[11] The name "Baghdād," which was associated with the village or market town near which the Caliph al-Manṣūr founded the Abbasid capital in 145/762, could be derived from ancient Persian in a number of ways, among them the construction "bagh" referring to an "idol" and "dād" or "dādh" meaning "gift." The resulting translation "gift of the idol" was objectionable to some Muslims, who preferred the Arabicized and Islamized name "Madīnat al-Salām" ("City of Peace"), though it was never as widely used.[12] Even if a city name was controversial, a consciousness of the pre-Islamic antiquity claimed by way of that name was palpable in the discourse of place.

The ten names of Medina exemplify the way in which the virtue of a multiplicity of names is directly linked to the traces of a city's pre-Islamic past that linger in the discourse of place. The ninth-century *Ta'rīkh al-Madīna al-Munawwara* (History of Medina) by Abū Zayd ʿUmar b. Shabba al-Baṣrī includes a tradition reported to him by one Muḥammad b. Yaḥyā in which the Prophet declares that the city has ten names and enumerates eight of them: al-Madīna, Ṭayba, Ṭāba, Maskīna, Jabār, Maḥbūra, Yandad, and Yathrib. This tradition is followed immediately by a divine tradition (*ḥadīth qudsī*) in which ʿAlī b. Abī Ṭālib (d. 40/661) reports God's direct speech, dubbing Medina "al-Dār and al-Īmān." Muḥammad b. Yaḥyā then admits that he is not sure whether the ten names of Medina are the sum total of the eight mentioned by Muḥammad and the two mentioned by God, or whether they might be the ten names for the city revealed by God in the Torah: al-Madīna, Ṭayba, Ṭāba, al-Ṭayyiba, al-Miskīna, al-ʿAdhrāʾ, al-Jābira, al-Majbūra, al-Maḥabbaba, and al-Maḥbūba.[13] The association of Medina through its names with what Muslims considered to be God's earliest scripture, the Torah, inscribed the city in the annals of sacred history, or the unfolding of God's plan for humankind, punctuated by moments of divine intervention to guide the faithful or warn the disobedient, from the moment of creation to the end of time.[14] The Biblical significance of the number ten and the relationship between the city names and the authority of the Prophet Muḥammad on the one hand and God on the other suggest that the multiplicity of names for Medina was one of the city's clear virtues.

Or was it? The emphasis on the ambiguous and potentially controversial etymology of the name Baghdād suggests a preference, at least in some quarters, for the Arabicization or Islamization of city names. Early works in praise of Medina communicate a similar discomfort with a pre-Islamic name, in this case Yathrib. Despite the fact that both Yathrib and al-Madīna appear in the Qurʾān, the majority of the traditions assembled by ʿUmar b. Shabba propose the names Ṭāba or Ṭayba, neither of which makes a Qurʾānic appearance, as the best names for the city. Several of these traditions even exhort believing Muslims, if they call the city "Yathrib" by mistake, to beg forgiveness from God and then repeat the preferred name "Ṭāba" three times.[15] The source of this preference may be that the names Yathrib and al-Madīna are associated in the Qurʾān with "hypocrites" (*munāfiqūn*), those who pretended to follow Muḥammad but actually worked against him in Medina.[16] In this context, naming the city by using the Arabic root *ṭ-ī-b*, which connotes purity, assigns belonging to one group of its residents, the steadfast believers, rather than to another, the doubters and hypocrites.[17] Whatever the particular implications, the broader point is that debate about or negotiation of the multiplicity of names of a city, particularly among those on either side of the divide between the pre-Islamic and Islamic eras, is a prominent feature of the discourse of place. These textual debates and negotiations suggest the existence of parallel extratextual debates or negotiations, and when a text signals a preference for one name over another it should be seen as an intervention in contests for prestige and belonging in the world outside the text.

Not all works on cities were, or could afford to be, so dismissive of negative Qurʾānic associations with their names. For the many cities that do not make an appearance in the Qurʾān, some contortions, and the risk of bad press, might be necessary to forge a link to God's revelation. One of the clearest examples is the case of "Iram of the Columns," an ancient city destroyed for its people's arrogance and disobedience to God (Qurʾān 89:7). On first glance, this might not seem an auspicious name for any city. However, in an eleventh-century treatise on the merits of Damascus, Abū l-Ḥasan ʿAlī b. Muḥammad al-Rabaʿī claims the name Iram for Damascus in a section in which other Qurʿānic quotes are associated with the city, situating it along the trajectory of sacred history.[18] It follows that other works associate Iram with sites elsewhere: Alexandria in Egypt or the desert in central Yemen.[19] Just as cities might have multiple names, city names, especially those from the sacred past, might have multiple territorial referents to be claimed and contested in the discourse of place.

Mecca, of course, is the name of a city that does appear in the Qurʿān, though as "Makka" only once (48:24), and as the variant "Bakka" a second time (3:96), so the effort to link it with God's revelation was relatively straightforward. Moreover, alternate names for Mecca could be derived from its ritual importance in Islam, such as "al-Kaʿba," "al-Bayt," or "al-Masjid al-Ḥarām," all of which occur in the Qurʿān and are produced as virtually synonymous with Mecca in al-Azraqī's landmark ninth-century topographical history of the city.[20] In fact, the section of the work that contains the traditions related to the names of Mecca is called "What has been said on the names of the Kaʿba when it was not called the Kaʿba because a house [of worship] (*bayt*) had not [yet] been built to honor it."[21] Under this heading, both "Makka" and "Bakka" can be identified as the names that preceded the building of the house of worship, or *bayt*, that became known as the Kaʿba, as in: "Bakka was the site of the house (*bayt*) and Makka was the town (*qarya*)" and "Bakka was the site of the house (*bayt*) and Makka was the entire sanctuary (*ḥaram*)."[22] Other traditions in this section continue to suggest a certain equivalence between the names al-Kaʿba, al-Bayt, Bakka, and Makka, to which are added a litany of other names, such as al-Bayt al-ʿAtīq, al-Qarya al-Qadīma, Qādis, Bādir, Umm Ruḥm, Umm al-Qurā, Ṣalāḥ, Kūthā, al-Bāssa, and al-Ḥāṭima.[23] These names stress the antiquity, sanctity, and power of the city, as well as its precedence among cities. The names Umm Ruḥm ("Mother of Beneficence") and Umm al-Qurā ("Mother of Towns") in particular characterize Mecca as a progenitor, a "mother," which overlaps with the portrayals of *waṭan* as a mother. If *waṭan* is the mother territory, and Mecca is the mother of all territories, then Mecca might be considered the original *waṭan*. Indeed,

Mecca is assigned a cosmological role as progenitor in a tradition that explains the name Umm al-Qurā in terms of its status as God's original creation from which the rest of creation emanated.[24]

Just as the names of Mecca relate it to all other towns and even to the rest of creation, the multiplicity of names of other cities relate them to a network of dependent villages or rural areas. The concept of "city" in the discourse of place was not always circumscribed spatially by strict boundaries or city walls, and almost always included what might be thought of as suburbs or hinterlands. The well-known tenth-century geographer Shams al-Dīn Muḥammad b. Aḥmad al-Muqaddasī developed a hierarchy of terms for cities that reflected their administrative function. According to this hierarchy, cities earned the rank of metropolis (*miṣr*) or capital (*qaṣaba*) by claiming relationships with dependent cities (*mudun*), districts (*nawāḥin*), and rural areas (*rasātīq*).[25] In line with this concept, two eleventh-century works on Isfahan, today a city in west-central Iran, represent it as a territory that comprises multiple towns or villages (*qurā*), districts (*nawāḥin*), and rural areas (*rasātīq*), with walled twin cities known as Jayy and al-Yahūdiyya serving as its principal urban area.[26] The authors of both works stress the role played by ancient royalty, from Alexander the Great to various pre-Islamic Persian monarchs, in founding and constructing Jayy, and one of them even boasts that his own ancestor had a hand in building the walls of Jayy almost two centuries before the coming of Islam.[27] Jayy's claim to the semilegendary Iranian convert to Islam Salmān al-Fārisī (d. ca. 35/655), who is quoted in one of the works as stating "I am from the people of Isfahan, from Jayy," asserts the centrality of the name Jayy to any representation of Isfahan as a category of belonging.[28] The two names seem to be used synonymously in poetry, although the overall sense from the works is that Isfahan may refer either to a broader region or the city, whereas Jayy only refers to the city proper.[29]

In another eleventh-century example, the well-watered gardens and orchards of the oasis known as the Ghūṭa were so closely associated with the city of Damascus that "al-Ghūṭa" and "Dimashq" seem synonymous. The city's association with such a sheltered, verdant area served not only to bolster claims to beauty and salubrity but also to connect the city with the Qur'ān, in this case by identifying the "high ground" (*rabwa*) where Mary and Jesus took refuge in Qur'ān 23:50 as, variously, the Ghūṭa or Damascus.[30] Whether "al-Ghūṭa" was located on the outskirts or within the bounds of "Dimashq" is never made absolutely clear in this text. However, in the cases of both Damascus and Isfahan, a multiplicity of plots of land, separately named but related at the textual level, if not also at the extratextual level, project an image of the city as a category of belonging capacious enough to include all possible sources of prestige and to confer the prestige of its parts on its whole.

Locating a city was not simply a matter of relating it to a range of dependent or constituent plots of land and co-opting their various claims to fame. Many cities were distinguished for their centrality and connectivity in terms of their location on the earth's surface or in the cosmos. That is to say, locating a city in a text, especially locating it in a way that made possible a claim to geographical or cosmological centrality and connectivity, was a means of establishing it as a particularly inclusive category of belonging. Sometimes the authorial act of naming the city doubles as an act of locating the city, especially when the name asserts its geographical centrality or connectivity, as in "Wāsiṭ," literally "the center" of Iraq or "the midpoint" between Kufa and Basra, and "al-Mawṣil" (Mosul), literally "that which connects" Syria and upper Mesopotamia or the Tigris and the Euphrates.[31] One tradition invoked in praise of residing in Wāsiṭ in the introduction to Aslam b. Sahl Baḥshal's late-ninth-century city-based biographical dictionary emphasizes its centrality and connectivity: "If you want to settle somewhere between the frontier fortresses (al-Thughūr) and Mecca and Medina (al-Ḥaramayn), don't settle anywhere except at Wāsiṭ."[32] Implicit in this tradition was the tension between proponents of *mujāhada,* or the pursuit of military campaigns at the frontiers of the lands controlled by Muslims, and *mujāwara,* or the pursuit of a life of prayer and piety in Mecca or Medina.[33] Wāsiṭ offered the perfect middle ground between the two extremes, accessible to both the frontier and the holy cities.

Other works in the discourse of place evoke the geographical centrality and connectivity of cities by locating them at an economically or strategically significant crossroads. The best example of this is Baghdad. In almost every representation of the city, the connective role of the Tigris River is celebrated for facilitating the convergence of people and goods from the furthest corners of the world, enriching Baghdad materially and intellectually, as in the following excerpt from the *Kitāb al-buldān* (Book of countries), by the ninth-century historian and geographer Aḥmad b. Abī Yaʿqūb, known as al-Yaʿqūbī:

> The two great rivers, the Tigris and the Euphrates, run along either side of [Baghdad], and merchandise and provisions come to it by water and by land because of the ease of the effort, such that every piece of merchandise carried to it from the eastern and western parts of the land of Islam (*arḍ al-Islām*) and that which is outside of the land of Islam reaches it. For [merchandise] is carried to [Baghdad] from India (*al-Hind*), al-Sind, China (*al-Ṣīn*), Tibet, [the land of] the Turks, al-Daylam, [the land of] the Khazars, Ethiopia (*al-Ḥabasha*), and the rest of the countries until there are more goods from [these] countries in [Baghdad] than there are in the countries that exported them. This [process] is so easy and certain that it is as if all good things on earth are conveyed to [Baghdad] and gathered there are the treasures of the world and completed there are the blessings of the universe.[34]

This passage focuses on the economic and cultural benefits of the connectivity established by rivers and roads, but other works describe Baghdad's centrality and connectivity as a political boon. The geographer Ibn al-Faqīh quotes Yazdadjird al-Kisrawī, a principal source for his section on the city of Baghdad, observing that the Umayyad capital city of Damascus had been located too far west on the east-west axis of the Islamic world. According to this interpretation, Baghdad occupied a central position that enabled it to connect with, and thus to gain the support of, the population of the eastern regions of the Islamic world, support that was vital to the Abbasid victory over the Umayyads in the middle of the eighth century.[35]

While Baghdad was celebrated for its geopolitical centrality and connectivity, Jerusalem and Mecca were celebrated for their cosmological centrality and connectivity, often using the same epithets as Baghdad: *surrat al-dunya* ("navel of the world"), *surrat al-arḍ* ("navel of the earth"), *wasaṭ al-dunya* ("center of the world"), or *wasaṭ al-arḍ* ("center of the earth").[36] Representations of Jerusalem focus on the cosmological significance of its Rock (*ṣakhra*), located on the summit of Mount Moriah and believed to be a rock of paradise, underneath which paradisiacal rivers of sweet water run.[37] Several works cite the Torah as an authority on sacred history to describe the Rock as God's throne from which he created heaven and earth, making Jerusalem the point of origin of all creation and the junction between the terrestrial and celestial realms.[38] Mecca's Kaʿba is also associated with cosmological connectivity in the discourse, sometimes with reference to the Torah, as in the following tradition: "The house [of worship] (*bayt*) in heaven is called *al-Ḍurāḥ* and its structure is the same as that of *al-Bayt al-Ḥarām* [in Mecca]. If [*al-Ḍurāḥ*] falls, it will fall upon [*al-Bayt al-Ḥarām*]."[39] The implication is that the two houses of worship are not only mirror images of each other but are actually physically connected, linking heaven to earth. While other traditions stress the cosmological precedence of Mecca over Jerusalem at the beginning of time, Jerusalem's centrality and connectivity is distinguished from that of Mecca at the end of time, since the Rock is depicted as the portal to paradise and the Wādī Jahannam, a valley lying just to the east of Mount Moriah, as the portal to hell.[40] Thus predictions about God's final judgment of humanity emphasize Jerusalem's connectivity, not only between heaven and earth but between this world and the next.

City locations were also made meaningful in the discourse of place by their centrality and connectivity in regional or comparative rather than geopolitical or cosmological terms. Mecca and Jerusalem were both located at the physical center of a regional entity designated as a sacred or blessed land.[41] Some cities were deemed central in a particular region by epithets such as *surrat al-ʿIrāq* ("navel of Iraq") for Isfahan, *ʿayn al-ʿIrāq* ("eye of Iraq") for Basra, *ʿayn Khurāsān* ("eye of Khurāsān") for Nishapur, *quṭb al-Yaman* ("axis of Yemen") for Sanaa, and *qalb al-ʿIrāq* ("heart of Iraq") for Baghdad.[42] The geographer al-Muqaddasī uses epithets like "the Baghdad of Yemen" for Zabīd or "the Umm al-Qurā (Mecca) of

Khurāsān" for Merv to establish the regional centrality of more geographically or symbolically peripheral cities and to emphasize the common "city-ness" shared by plots of land separated by long distances.[43] One of the ways in which Andalusian cities were represented in medieval Arabic literature was by juxtaposing their names with eastern toponyms that could be seen as more symbolically—as well as geographically—central.[44] Similarly, eleventh-century litterateur Abū Muḥammad ʿAlī b. Ḥazm (d. 456/1065), in a *faḍāʾil* treatise on the merits of Andalusia, compares his hometown of Cordoba with Samarra in Iraq, since they both lie in the same "clime" (*iqlīm*) according to the widely endorsed latitudinal seven-clime system.[45] These strategies established more peripherally located cities as central both regionally and comparatively in the Islamic world.

The tradition of regional mapping that accompanied a handful of world geographies from this period was the primary way in which cities were portrayed as central or connective within the context of a region. Occasionally in these maps, a prominent city is located at the physical center of a region, such as Hamadan in al-Jibāl or Shiraz in Fārs, regions occupying west-central and southwestern portions of present-day Iran respectively.[46] However, all of these maps depict cities in their connective capacity, portraying them along simple lines that indicated rivers, roads, or coastlines. This kind of map would have been more valuable for the seasoned travelers of the period than one that represented cities in terms of, for instance, precise latitude and longitude measurements.[47] The iconographic depiction of al-Mahdiyya, a coastal North African city located in present-day Tunisia, from the anonymous eleventh-century geography *Kitāb gharāʾib al-funūn wa-mulāḥ al-ʿuyūn* (Book of curiosities of the sciences and marvels for the eyes) includes embedded text listing distances between anchorages from al-Mahdiyya itself to Palermo in Sicily. This use of writing within an image establishes a seafaring connectivity for al-Mahdiyya that belies or complicates the seeming impenetrability of the thick, dark walls that are depicted separating the city from the Mediterranean (see Figure 2.1).[48] Locating cities in texts—both written and graphic—endowed them with meaning in terms of the functional connectivity that could be represented between them along a variety of routes.

The textual strategy of naming and locating cities shaped them as inclusive categories of belonging in the discourse of place. Cities were imagined in terms of a multiplicity of names that stood for the different languages, the different pasts, and the different regional relationships that enriched them and their inhabitants. Cities were located in terms of regional relationships, but also in terms of geopolitical or cosmological centrality and connectivity, asserting a link between the city and the rest of the world or God's creation. When a work celebrates a city as connecting disparate peoples and territories over time and across space, it asserts the belonging of those territories and peoples in the Islamic community (*umma*) past or present. This connectivity had the effect of making the

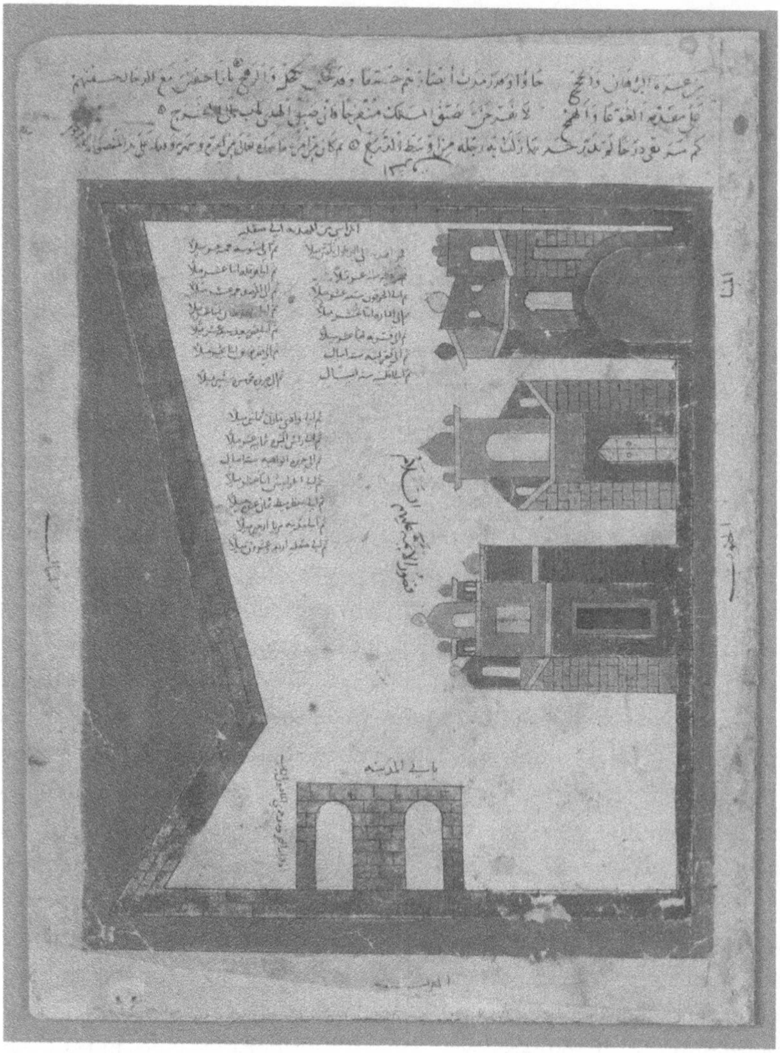

Figure 2.1 The city of al-Mahdiyya (oriented east), located in present-day Tunisia. Source: *Kitāb gharāʾib al-funūn wa-mulāḥ al-ʿuyūn*, Ms. Arab c. 90, fol. 34a. Dept. of Oriental Collections, The Bodleian Library, University of Oxford.

representation of cities in texts an effective way of staking a variety of claims to political or religious authority.

Assembling a Foundation or Conquest Narrative

Assembling a foundation or conquest narrative was a textual strategy that built on the acts of naming and locating to connect a city to its ancient or sacred past.

Although these narratives always conclude with a city's incorporation into the Islamic community—its Islamization—neither the process nor the end result is portrayed as unproblematic or absolute.[49] Since such narratives were always assembled from a reservoir of earlier sources, including legendary and para-Biblical material, historical reports (*akhbār*), and Ḥadīth, composing them can be seen as an act of negotiation, bringing together discrete textual units of very different provenance and organizing them into a more or less linear account of a city's original foundation or its conquest by Muslim armies. Thus, both the form and the content of these narratives emphasize heterogeneity and accommodation in the production and reproduction of urban space.

Landmark works representing Mecca, Jerusalem, and Baghdad present different ways in which narratives of origins, whether of foundation or conquest, construct the city as an inclusive category of belonging. These three cities were each associated with powerful and mainstream claims to religious and political authority in the Islamic world between the ninth and eleventh centuries. Mecca and Jerusalem were premier destinations for Muslim pilgrimage and beneficiaries of ample scriptural testimony to their sanctity. Baghdad was the seat of the Abbasid Caliphate and a city founded well after the coming of Islam. It might not be surprising when the conquest of a city like Isfahan is represented as contested and, in terms of the related processes of Islamization and Arabicization, gradual or incomplete because of its strong association with the pre-Islamic Persian past and its relative marginality in Muslim understandings of sacred history.[50] However, even the foundation and conquest narratives of three of the most politically and religiously symbolic centers of the early Islamic world—Mecca, Jerusalem, and Baghdad—are not presented in the discourse of place as straightforward accounts of the triumph of Islam over what came before.[51] Foundation and conquest narratives represented cities as "Islamic" but in a process marked by continuity and negotiation, rather than by rupture, with the past.

Mecca

The landmark contribution to the discourse of place on Mecca before the eleventh century was the *Akhbār Makka*, a history of Mecca composed by Abū l-Walīd Muḥammad b. ʿAbd Allāh al-Azraqī (d. ca. 241/855 or 250/864) largely from topographical information that had been passed down to him by his grandfather. The foundation narrative with which he introduces the work, however, is compiled of material often attributed to seventh- and eighth-century sources considered authorities on para-Biblical lore and pre-Islamic history, such as the semilegendary "convert" from Judaism Kaʿb al-Aḥbār (d. 34/654–655) and the Umayyad-era scion of a prominent Yemeni family Wahb b. Munabbih (d. 110/728 or 114/732), as well as from the growing corpus of

Ḥadīth. Al-Azraqī's first set of sources, sometimes referred to as *qiṣaṣ al-anbiyā'* ("stories of the prophets") or, later, *isrāʾīliyyāt*, but including stories about such extra-Biblical figures as Alexander the Great and the mysterious al-Khiḍr, seems to have emerged from the heterogeneous religious and cultural context of the Hellenistic, Arabian, and Persian worlds that predated the coming of Islam. Such material was circulated widely in his period, both among religious scholars to contextualize or explain elliptical Qurʾānic passages and among more diverse audiences to edify and entertain.[52] The corpus of Ḥadīth, by contrast, was carefully shaped, vetted, and circulated among *ʿulamāʾ* according to increasingly strict methods of analysis designed to establish guidelines both for participating in Ḥadīth studies as a scholarly field and for evaluating the authenticity of individual traditions.[53] Thus, al-Azraqī's method of compilation can be characterized as a negotiation between more inclusive and more exclusive approaches to historical and religious source material current in his era. In this way, the form of the foundation narrative mirrors its content: a negotiation between varying sources of authority that produces both the text itself and the representation of the city of Mecca within the text.

The content of al-Azraqī's foundation narrative can be divided into four stages: 1) the Kaʿba exists prior to the rest of creation; 2) Adam builds the Kaʿba; 3) Abraham and Ishmael (re)build the Kaʿba; and 4) the Quraysh rebuild the Kaʿba. The narrative conflates the foundation of the city of Mecca with the foundation of "al-Kaʿba" or "al-Bayt," both of which were synonyms for the Qurʾānic "Makka" or "Bakka" and references to the central feature of the city's ritual topography.[54] While Mecca was the hometown of the Prophet Muḥammad, most of the narrative predates his birth, and his direct agency in the final stage is minimal. However, certain episodes echo topoi in Muḥammad's biography, which crystallized as a literary tradition known as the *sīra* ("way" or "path") around the same time that al-Azraqī composed his work.[55] Despite its association with Muḥammad and the paradigm of prophethood offered up by the *sīra* tradition, Mecca does not emerge from al-Azraqī's narrative as a site of unproblematic or absolute Islamization, but rather a site of compromise and continuity with the past.

Al-Azraqī opens his topographical history of Mecca with a set of traditions establishing the Kaʿba as existing *prior* to God's act of creation.[56] The following tradition related on the authority of Kaʿb al-Aḥbār represents the Kaʿba as part of the stuff of creation—water—mentioned in Qurʾān 21:30: "The Kaʿba was the froth on the water forty years before God Almighty created the heavens and the earth; from it the earth was spread out."[57] Thus, the Kaʿba not only preceded creation, but has cosmological significance as the point of origin from which the creation of all celestial and terrestrial bodies emanated. The next stage in the foundation narrative comes after Adam's fall from heaven for disobedience to God. To compensate (for his disobedience or for his loss, depending on the version), God orders Adam to build a "house [of worship]" (*bayt*) on earth and to circumambulate it in the same manner that the angels circumambulate God's throne in the heavens.[58] After a period of wandering, during which his giant footsteps form the contours of the earth's surface, Adam arrives at Mecca and builds *al-Bayt al-Ḥarām* ("the Sacred House") with help from God and the angels who sink its foundations to the depths of the earth and endow it with treasures from the heavens.[59] Thus, the story of Adam's construction of the Kaʿba resonates with traditions that establish it as the point of origin for the creation of the heavens and earth, since its physical shape and material endowments link the lowest level of earth with the highest level of heaven.[60]

Another instance of human disobedience to God, however, prompts the flood, during which Adam's *Bayt* was lifted up to heaven and/or its site destroyed, according to variant traditions.[61] This ushers in the third stage of the foundation narrative, during which Abraham and his son Ishmael (re)build the Kaʿba, a stage in the narrative that was documented in the Qurʾān itself (2:125–127, 22:26, verses that neither mention the prior structure built by Adam nor discount its existence).[62] In the traditions al-Azraqī collects, this third stage includes a period of wandering before identifying the site for the construction of *al-Bayt al-Ḥarām*. This period emphasizes the special status of Mecca as the site for the Kaʿba, since no other site on earth was found satisfactory. In one tradition, Abraham is raised up to heaven so that he can see the whole earth, "its east and its west, and he picked the site of the Kaʿba."[63] In other versions, he, his infant son Ishmael, and Ishmael's mother Hagar, who is still nursing, leave Syria to find the sacred site, and they are carried by the winged steed Burāq or guided by the angel Gabriel to Mecca.[64]

Although Abraham leaves Hagar and Ishmael shortly thereafter to return to his wife Sarah, Hagar is visited by miracles that strengthen her and that associate her son and the city of Mecca with prophecy. In one set of traditions an angel visits Hagar, shows her a spot on a plot of raised land, and says: "Here is the first house [of worship] (*bayt*) on the earth established for the people, and it is the ancient house [of worship] (*bayt*) of God. Know that Abraham and Ishmael, peace be upon them both, will erect it for the people."[65] This prophecy prefigures the revelation of Qurʾān 3:96 and resonates with the prophecies issued about Muḥammad to his biological mother Āmina and to his wet-nurse Ḥalīma in the *sīra* literature.[66] Hagar appears to be the counterpart to Ḥalīma, both of them given signs of the greatness that will be made possible by the child-prophet they are nurturing. Moreover, just as Ḥalīma experiences the miraculous flowing of her breast milk when entrusted with the infant Muḥammad, Hagar quenches the thirst of her son Ishmael with the miraculous discovery of the spring of Zamzam.[67] In the case of Ishmael, when his mother can no longer feed him, the substitute nourishment comes from the earth of Mecca itself, the ultimate mother territory, echoing the characterizations of *waṭan* as a mother and the epithets for Mecca that include the Arabic term for "mother" (*umm*).

The emphasis on divine and miraculous intervention in the lengthy litany of traditions describing the third stage of the foundation narrative, the (re)building project of Abraham and Ishmael some years later, foreshadows a similar emphasis in the even lengthier set of traditions that comprise the fourth stage in the narrative, the rebuilding of the Kaʿba by the Quraysh during the lifetime of Muḥammad. The miracles that punctuate the third stage include a mystical presence, called the *Sakīna*, arriving in Mecca from the direction of Syria or Armenia, to identify and hallow the building site for Abraham and Ishmael;[68] God's transformation of the barren land of Mecca with a proliferation of fruits and other foodstuffs in response to Abraham's plea for sustenance, quoted in Qurʾān 2:126;[69] and assistance from the angel Gabriel, who places the Black Rock (*al-ḥajar al-aswad*), originally one of the heavenly materials used by Adam to construct the Kaʿba, at a corner of the structure.[70] Parallel miracles occur in the fourth stage of the narrative, when the elders of the tribe of the Quraysh, centuries later serving as guardians of the Kaʿba in Mecca, decide to demolish the existing structure, deeming it too insecure and/or damaged, and replace it with a more secure, roofed structure. In this project, they make use of the timber provided by a Greek merchant ship (*safīna*) that had wrecked at the coast near Jidda and of the presence of a skilled carpenter of Greek or Syrian origin.[71] The use of the term *safīna* and its association with the Christian north echoes that of the mystical *Sakīna* from Armenia that helped Abraham mark out the site for the Kaʿba and represents Mecca as a place of convergence and mutual aid between those who worship the God of Abraham.

During the rebuilding process itself, the Quraysh discover inscriptions on the foundation stones they uncover "documenting" the miraculous bounty that God granted Abraham in stage three of the narrative. These inscriptions reproduce God's speech and combine some version of the cosmological significance of the Kaʿba with the worldly benefits promised Mecca's inhabitants, as in: "I am the God of Bakka. I created it the day I created the heavens and the earth and fashioned the sun and the moon. I surrounded it with seven territories of *Ḥanīfs*. It will never cease to exist, even if its timbers cease to exist. Its people are blessed with milk and water."[72] In two of the traditions relating the discovery of the inscriptions, the Quraysh must seek help deciphering or translating the texts, in one version from a Yemenite and a Christian monk and in the other from a Jew who reads Syriac.[73] The discovery of prophetic inscriptions in urban areas recurs in foundation narratives in the discourse of place, as does the search for someone, usually a Christian or Jew, capable of translating the ancient inscription.[74] In these cases, the inscription testifies to the importance of the site in sacred history, and the fact that only a member of one of the pre-Islamic Abrahamic religious communities can translate such testimony suggests the persistent need for negotiation among different groups in representations of cities as part of the sacred past.

In the final episode of the fourth stage of the foundation narrative, when the Quraysh argue among themselves as to who will place the Black Rock in the new structure, they decide the only solution is to ask an outsider to help. It is here that al-Azraqī's history of Mecca intersects directly with the *sīra* tradition.[75] The thirty-five-year-old Muḥammad, not yet aware of his prophetic mission, steps in to help, wraps the stone in his robe, and moves it to its site at one corner of the rebuilt Kaʿba. In this he plays the role previously played by the Angel Gabriel in the third stage of the foundation narrative. Moreover, this episode shows Muḥammad in a role that he reprises elsewhere in the *sīra* tradition, that of mediator, as he asks representatives from each of the squabbling clans to hold a corner of his robe during the transfer, symbolically bringing them together around the Black Rock. Similarly, the Kaʿba, or Mecca itself, is represented as a mediator, a transcender of particularist loyalties, through the participation in its foundation narrative of representatives not only of different families but also of different lands and different religions. The Black Rock also acts as a mediator between heavenly blessing and human fallibility, a symbol of accommodation that continues to hallow the site even though it, like the site itself, has been marked by disobedience and error.

Traditions throughout al-Azraqī's foundation narrative attribute the blackening of the Rock from its original state as a jewel dropped from heaven in the period after Adam's construction of the Kaʿba to human ignorance or impurity.[76] In many traditions, its blackening is caused by a fire, and the fire about which al-Azraqī assembles the most material is the one that destroyed a portion of the Kaʿba during the war between ʿAbd Allāh b. al-Zubayr (d. 73/692) and the forces of the Umayyad Caliph Yazīd I in 64/683, a fire that not only blackened, but also fractured, the Rock.[77] In some ways, this episode is a continuation of the fourth stage of the foundation narrative, as all the major players are members of the Quraysh and the end result of the episode is a restoration of the Kaʿba to the same form it had when it was rebuilt by the tribesmen in the early seventh century. After a temporary ceasefire in the hostilities between his followers and the Umayyad army, Ibn al-Zubayr decides to rebuild the Kaʿba in its entirety.[78] He bases this decision on the authority of his aunt, ʿĀʾisha (d. 58/678), who had heard her husband the Prophet Muḥammad criticize the Quraysh for reducing the size of the structure in their rebuilding project and thus for neglecting a portion of the foundation laid by Abraham. It was only the importance of his role as a mediator that kept the Prophet himself from rectifying their error, as he explained to his wife: "Had your people not recently been unbelievers, I would have demolished the Kaʿba and restored it to [the foundations] they neglected."[79]

Thus, Muḥammad's sensitivity to the amount of change that believers of such recent vintage could tolerate prevented him from correcting the mistakes of the past. Instead, when circumambulating the Kaʿba, he simply included in his circuit the unbuilt area to the northwest of the structure that, according to ʿĀʾisha's report, comprised the neglected portion of the Abrahamic site.[80]

ʿĀʾisha's testimony to this practice makes up one of a set of traditions that are not only recorded in al-Azraqī's work but also preserved in the canonical works of Ḥadīth from the eighth and ninth centuries.[81] The multiple transmitters of these traditions suggest that it was not only Ibn al-Zubayr who perceived the shortcomings of the Kaʿba but that others in Mecca at the time supported Ibn al-Zubayr's project, at least after a period of initial hesitation and trepidation during the demolition.[82] Despite this, when Yazīd's successor, the Umayyad Caliph ʿAbd al-Malik, sends al-Ḥajjāj b. Yūsuf (d. 95/714) to defeat Ibn al-Zubayr and take control of the Ḥijāz once and for all, he permits al-Ḥajjāj to destroy the Kaʿba and to restore it to its smaller form on the assumption that Ibn al-Zubayr had fabricated his aunt's testimony. Later, however, ʿAbd al-Malik discovers that others could corroborate ʿĀʾisha's report, and he repents: "By God, I wish I had left Ibn al-Zubayr and what he undertook in the way of [the rebuilding of the Kaʿba] alone."[83] Although al-Azraqī recounts no further rebuilding—only beautification—projects after this, it is evident from other sources that a detached semicircular wall was later built along the Abrahamic foundation to the northwest of the Kaʿba, an area known as the *Ḥijr*, so that pilgrims might follow Muḥammad's example and skirt its perimeter in circumambulation.[84]

In addition to the clear anti-Umayyad politics of the traditions narrating this episode in al-Azraqī's work, the partial exoneration of ʿAbd al-Malik for his repentance notwithstanding, this postscript to Mecca's foundation narrative represents the city as a site of compromise. The structure of the Kaʿba remains marked by the *Jāhiliyya*, or era of "ignorance" before the revelation of Islam. Moreover, ritual practice on its site emphasizes Muḥammad's willingness to accommodate and negotiate rather than to confront and reject the ignorance of the past. In each stage of this foundation narrative, the city of Mecca is shaped by compromise, the currency of a prophet in his role as a mediator, carefully balancing the human fallibility of his followers and the perfection of the divine guidance he has received.[85] Mecca and Muḥammad are both "human" *and* touched by the divine, the inner contradiction of prophethood in the Islamic tradition superimposed on its most ritually significant city.

Jerusalem

Jerusalem's foundation narrative in the discourse of place also represents the city as marked by compromise, though it is less because of a prophet's accommodation of the fallibility of his followers than because of the fallibility of the prophets themselves. Perhaps as a result, Jerusalem is imagined simultaneously as a place of judgment and absolution, of reversal and restoration. Two *faḍāʾil* treatises on Jerusalem from the early eleventh century, Abū Bakr Muḥammad b. Aḥmad al-Wāsiṭī's *Faḍāʾil al-Bayt al-Muqaddas* (The merits of Jerusalem) and Abū l-Maʿālī al-Musharraf b. al-Murajjā al-Maqdisī's *Faḍāʾil Bayt al-Maqdis wa-l-Khalīl wa-faḍāʾil al-Shām* (The merits of Jerusalem and Hebron, and the merits of Syria), resemble al-Azraqī's history of Mecca by focusing Jerusalem's foundation narrative on the central feature of its ritual topography, another "house [of worship]" (*bayt*), from which came two of its Arabic names, al-Bayt al-Muqaddas and Bayt al-Maqdis ("Holy House" and "House of Holiness").[86] Despite the fact that these authors lived almost two centuries after al-Azraqī, they structure their foundation narratives in a very similar way, emphasizing the city's cosmological significance, its role in sacred history, and the relationship between the city and prophethood. While neither work mentions al-Azraqī's history of Mecca, the city of Mecca hovers at the margins, occasionally making its way into the text itself, as a foil for Jerusalem's prominence in sacred history, and the same authorities on para-Biblical lore that al-Azraqī so often cites—Wahb b. Munabbih and Kaʿb al-Aḥbār—appear repeatedly in the eleventh-century works.

Abū l-Maʿālī's treatise presents Jerusalem's foundation narrative as a coherent whole at the beginning of the work, and it too can be divided into four stages: 1) Bayt al-Maqdis was among God's first creations; 2) David and Solomon build Bayt al-Maqdis; 3) ʿUmar b. al-Khaṭṭāb conquers Bayt al-Maqdis; 4) ʿAbd al-Malik builds the Dome of the Rock.[87] Although Muḥammad does not participate directly in any of these stages, the account of his "Night Journey," an episode in which God transported the Prophet in his sleep from Mecca to Jerusalem and then to heaven, appears in both treatises to associate Jerusalem, a city that Muḥammad never visited "in the light of day," as it were, with the last prophet in the Abrahamic line. Although the "Night Journey" is not presented as part of Abū l-Maʿālī's foundation narrative, the multiple references to it throughout (as well as the lengthy engagement with it in separate sections of both eleventh-century works) remind the audience of the city's intersection with the *sīra* tradition. Even if Jerusalem's foundation narrative does not mirror the biography of Muḥammad as clearly as does Mecca's, it nonetheless represents the city as a geographical manifestation of the struggle between sin and repentance with which the prophets of the Abrahamic tradition were engaged.

The first stage of Jerusalem's foundation narrative makes explicit a comparison with Mecca, which is implicit throughout most of the rest of the narrative, in traditions that establish a chronology of creation. The first *ḥadīth* has Abū Dharr asking the Prophet Muḥammad, "Which mosque was established first?," to which the Prophet answers, "al-Masjid al-Ḥarām." When he is asked which was established second, he answers, "al-Masjid al-Aqṣā," and explains that forty years spanned the two acts of creation.[88] *Al-Masjid al-Aqṣā* ("The Farthest Mosque") is to Jerusalem what *al-Masjid al-Ḥarām* ("The Sacred Mosque") is to Mecca: a term for both the city as a whole and one of the central features of its ritual topography, a place of prayer (the literal translation of *masjid* or "mosque") located today just south of the Dome of the Rock in the old part of the city. The term appears in Qurʾān 17:1 as the destination of Muḥammad's "Night Journey" and was designated in the canonical body of Ḥadīth, the *sīra* literature, and the *faḍāʾil* treatises considered here as a reference to Jerusalem.[89] The second tradition inserts Medina between Mecca and Jerusalem in the chronology: "God Almighty created Mecca and surrounded it with angels before he had created anything else on the entire earth at that point by 1,000 years. Then he joined [Mecca] to Medina and joined Medina to Jerusalem, and then he created the entire earth after 1,000 years in a single gesture."[90] The idea that the creation of the earth in its entirety (*al-arḍ kullahā*) followed the creation of Mecca, Medina, and Jerusalem by 1,000 years suggests the absolute precedence of the three cities in cosmological terms. Finally, the third tradition maintains the order of creation from Mecca to Medina to Jerusalem but adds the city of Kufa, a city of particular importance to Shiites, in fourth place.[91] Though these traditions unequivocally sustain al-Azraqī's image of Mecca as the original creation, they attribute to Jerusalem a cosmological significance if not equivalent to Mecca's then at least comparatively distinct from the rest of creation.[92]

The second stage in the foundation narrative of Jerusalem echoes that of Mecca by featuring another father-son team of pre-Islamic prophets, David and Solomon. Rather than acting together as Abraham and Ishmael did in constructing the Kaʿba, however, David chooses the site of Jerusalem and then Solomon erects the central feature of its ritual topography, a *bayt,* the Biblical Temple. The foundation narrative explains this division of labor by quoting God's direct speech to David when he was hoping to erect a place of worship atop the rocky summit of Mount Moriah, in one version: "This is a holy house (*bayt muqaddas*), and, verily, your hands are stained with blood. Therefore, it is not for you to build it, but for a son of yours [who will come] after you and whom I will name Solomon and whom I will protect from bloodshed."[93] Different traditions give different reasons for David's unsuitability for the task of building the Temple, but all of them highlight the tension caused by the human limitations of prophets in their relationship with the divine. Even Solomon cannot complete the construction of the Temple without the help of the *jinn,* or spirits, granted to him by God.[94] In fact, the narrative of the construction of the Temple is as touched by the spirit world as the narrative of the construction of the Kaʿba is touched by the angels. Both construction projects must conform to preexisting, divinely ordained foundations, and just as Adam and Abraham needed the guidance of angels to find the proper site for the Kaʿba in Mecca, Solomon struggles with the depth of the ancient foundations of the Temple and only succeeds in filling them with superhuman help.[95]

Despite his access to the spirit world and the splendor of the finished Temple, described in the narrative as "an accomplishment that cannot be described and that no one is able to fathom," Solomon is portrayed as no less susceptible to human fallibility than his father.[96] In one tradition, Solomon finds himself locked out of the Temple, even though he possessed the only key:

> One day [Solomon] arrived to open [the Temple], but it was difficult for him, so he asked some people to help him with it, to no avail. Then he asked the *jinn* for help, again to no avail. He sat down dejected and saddened, thinking his Lord had prohibited him from his house [of worship]. As he was sitting there, a *shaykh*, advanced in years and leaning on a stick, who had been one of the companions of David, peace be upon him, approached, and [Solomon] said: I went to this house [of worship] to open it, but I had difficulty with it, so I asked some people to help, but it would not open. Then I asked the *jinn* to help, but it would not open. The *shaykh* said: Do you not know the words that your father David said in his distress when God had prevented him from that? [Solomon] said: No. [The *shaykh*] said: "Oh God, by your light I am guided and by your grace I am sustained. I am with you morning and evening. My sins are in your hands. I ask your forgiveness and I turn to you in repentance, oh Compassionate One, oh Beneficent One!" When he said this, the door opened for him. Thus, it is recommended that this supplication be uttered upon entering the door of the Rock or the door of the mosque.[97]

Solomon is therefore likened to David, two prophets whose sins kept them from the Temple, David from constructing it and Solomon from entering it, at least until he repented. The conclusion of this tradition suggests Islamic-era ritual practice, and the representation of continuity from the days of David and Solomon to the Islamic era emphasizes the association of repentance with the site.[98] When the construction of the Temple is complete, Solomon asks God to bestow a series of blessings on those who pray there, among them the absolution of sins. While this blessing appears once in the foundation narrative, references to it and to its continued benefits for Muslim penitents at the site recur throughout the two works.[99] These episodes in the foundation narrative serve as a reminder of the fallibility and sinfulness that may afflict all of God's creatures, even as they represent the central feature of its ritual topography as purified—and purifying.

The third stage in the narrative diverges from that of Mecca by featuring a moment of conquest rather than foundation. Although references to the Prophet

Muḥammad's conquest of Mecca appear sporadically throughout al-Azraqī's topographical history, it is only dealt with directly in a short section dedicated to Muḥammad's destruction of the idols in the Kaʿba.[100] On the other hand, Jerusalem's conquest by the Muslims in the year 16/637 or 17/638 is represented as the climax of the city's foundation narrative.[101] Preceded by a lengthy account of the destruction of Jerusalem at the hands of Nebuchadnezzar as divine punishment for the disobedience and self-aggrandizement of its inhabitants, ʿUmar b. al-Khaṭṭāb's conquest of Jerusalem is portrayed as the reclaiming of the city for God, collapsing the intervening centuries in obscurity. Though some historical reports included in this stage of the narrative indicate that the reclaiming of Jerusalem involved the rejection of the past, others present it more as a negotiation and restoration. In either case, ʿUmar does not ride at the head of a victorious army demanding the surrender of the city's inhabitants, but walks into the city, having reached an agreement with Jerusalem's Byzantine leadership to avoid bloodshed and win the support of the primarily Christian population. In this, ʿUmar is cast as having learned a lesson from David in approaching the "holy house" with clean hands, repentant and accommodating.[102]

Several reports feature lengthy exchanges between ʿUmar and his generals, principally Abū ʿUbayda, in which he urges restraint in the conquest of Jerusalem. In one, he recalls the Prophet Muḥammad's prophecy that he would conquer Jerusalem "without combat" and orders his armies to hold off the siege they had been staging from the top of the Mount of Olives to the east of the city.[103] In others, the leadership of the city is said to have preempted strife by asking for a settlement, and lengthy exchanges between the two sides ensue, aided by translators and signs of mutual recognition. The conditions of the settlement are detailed at varying lengths in the different reports, but generally include the payment of a tax (*jizya*) by the city's Christian inhabitants in return for the protection of life and property.[104] Although at one point this settlement is described as more generous than any the Muslims had yet offered in newly conquered territories, it resonates with the conquest narrative presented about the city of Damascus in another eleventh-century *faḍāʾil* treatise in which Muslims and Christians agree to share the Church of St. John the Baptist as a place of prayer, an agreement that is maintained by both sides for almost seventy years until the Umayyad Caliph al-Walīd I demolishes the church to make room for the Great Mosque in 87/706.[105] Negotiation and accommodation, therefore, may be hallmarks not only of the foundation but also of the conquest of cities in the discourse of place.

In general, the "conquest" of Jerusalem is presented as a very harmonious process, stumbling only when ʿUmar asks the Patriarch of the city to take him to the *Masjid Dāwūd* ("Place of Prayer/Mosque of David"), most likely a reference to the Rock upon which David had offered supplications to God before Solomon built the Temple. The Patriarch takes ʿUmar instead to two different churches, claiming each one as the Mosque of David. ʿUmar is not fooled, however, having been present when the Prophet Muḥammad described Jerusalem in detail after his "Night Journey." When ʿUmar's delegation finally arrives at the proper site, they find a ramshackle structure so filled with debris that they can only enter on their hands and knees. After crawling through the wreckage, they finally reach Jerusalem's Rock.[106] It is a moment of utmost humility, the Muslims on their hands and knees beneath the destruction wrought by centuries of neglect and ignorance. In a different account, ʿUmar heads for the site of the *Miḥrāb Dāwūd* ("Tower of David"), most likely a reference to the citadel on the perimeter of the city, and recites the *Sūrat Ṣād,* a chapter of the Qurʾān that not only warns humans against disobedience and self-aggrandizement but also makes reference to the sins and repentance of David.[107] Thus, ʿUmar uses the moment of conquest, of claiming Jerusalem for God and Islam, to emphasize the fallibility of humans, even prophets. Although in another tradition he bans prayer at the Rock until three rains cleanse it, this is not a reversal so much as a restoration of the site to the simple place of prayer it was during the reign of David and a cautionary tale for the future.[108]

One moment of reversal can be seen, however, in an oft-quoted tradition that appears in Abū l-Maʿālī's conquest narrative in which ʿUmar enters the city after the conquest and asks Kaʿb al-Aḥbār to guide him to the Rock. After clearing the debris from the site, ʿUmar asks his companion whether he should build a mosque to the north or the south of the Rock. Kaʿb replies that he should build to its north, thus combining the *qibla* ("prayer direction") of Moses, toward the Rock of Jerusalem, with that of Muḥammad, toward Mecca. ʿUmar retorts angrily, "By God, you are imitating Judaism!" and proceeds to build a mosque on the south side.[109] This tradition resonates with the Qurʾānic verses 2:143–145 and related traditions included in both works explaining God's command to Muḥammad to change the *qibla* from Jerusalem to Mecca as a test for those among the "Peoples of the Book" (Christians and Jews) who wished to join his community. Those who were reluctant to change their prayer direction were deemed hypocrites or insufficiently convinced of Muḥammad's message from God.[110] Thus, ʿUmar's refusal to build a mosque to the north of the Rock, which would not, after all, have compromised God's command to pray toward Mecca, should be seen as Islamic Jerusalem turning its back on Jewish Jerusalem. Other traditions suggest less dramatic or complete moments of exclusion, such as those warning Muslims not to call Jerusalem by its ancient name Īliyāʾ or to pray in various Christian sites.[111] Similarly, the images of Jews bringing on the destruction of the Temple and Christians letting its site become a trash pit provide a contrast to those that emphasize accommodation and absolution.[112] Nevertheless, continuities between the foundational era of David and Solomon and ʿUmar's conquest of the city dominate both works, suggesting restoration rather than rejection. Moreover, it is in the final episode of the narrative, the construction of the Dome of the Rock, that the process of restoration initiated by ʿUmar comes full circle.

Although he makes every effort to claim the city with clean hands, ʿUmar is not portrayed as the one who restores the Temple of Solomon to its former glory. Instead, these two works credit the Umayyad Caliph ʿAbd al-Malik with erecting on its site the kind of monumental architecture that would recall the splendor of the Temple.[113] Only, unlike Solomon, ʿAbd al-Malik has no *jinn* to help him—merely the blessing of the Muslim community far and near and a surfeit of tax revenue. At first his goals are presented as a simple matter of facilitating already existing ritual practice at the site: "to build a dome over the Rock that would protect Muslims from the heat and cold and [to build] a mosque." Despite this seemingly uncontroversial proposal, he sends letters to representatives of every city in his empire requesting feedback on the matter, since "he would not want to proceed without the counsel of his subjects." When he receives responses endorsing his proposal, he starts by assembling a group of builders who mark the foundations on the ground for his approval. Satisfied, he appoints two supervisors and has a treasury built for the funds that he puts at their disposal before returning to Damascus. When the structure is finally erected in 72/692, the supervisors write to ʿAbd al-Malik announcing its completion under budget and declaring that "there is nothing left to be said about it."[114] This declaration may have been intended to preempt the kinds of criticisms that had been lodged against other Umayyad building projects, but it may also have been intended to act as a conclusion to, and thus an acknowledgement of, the conversation that ʿAbd al-Malik had opened with his subjects on the topic of the construction, reinforcing the image of community consensus behind the project.[115] Jerusalem is portrayed here as belonging to all Muslims, further evidenced by their rush to take advantage of the new prayer site as soon as it is opened.[116]

Although ʿAbd al-Malik's original plan was described as a simple matter of protecting the Rock from the elements, the adornment of the final structure and the elaborate purification ceremony performed before its opening recall the splendor of Solomon's Temple and its association with purity. ʿAbd al-Malik puts to use the funds remaining in the treasury after the completion of construction, funds that the building supervisors piously refuse to accept as a reward, by ordering them melted down to coat the dome in gold. The effect was so brilliant that "no one was able to gaze directly at it." Moreover, elaborate purification rituals anointing the Rock with precious oils and filling the air with costly incense herald its opening for worshippers, such that those returning from a visit to the Dome of the Rock could be identified by their scent.[117] Further reinforcing these images reminiscent of the splendor and purity of Solomon's Temple are the prophetic words recited by Kaʿb "from one of the scriptures (*baʿḍ al-kutub*)" at the end of the narrative: "*Īrūshalāīm*, which means Bayt al-Maqdis, and the Rock, which is called the Temple (*al-haykal*), I send to you my servant ʿAbd al-Malik to build you and to adorn you. Truly, I will restore to Bayt al-Maqdis its first kingdom, and I will crown it in gold, silver, and pearls. Truly, I will send to you my creatures, and I will establish my throne upon the Rock. For I am the Lord God, and David is the king of the Israelites."[118] This prophecy repeated by a known, if not uncontroversial, authority on sacred history identifies the Dome of the Rock with the Temple and identifies its builder, ʿAbd al-Malik, with the restoration of the kingdom of David and Solomon. Apart from the obvious pro-Umayyad message of this tradition, it also acts as the seal on the foundation narrative presented in these two eleventh-century works. The conclusion of the narrative is a restoration not only of the house of worship built by Solomon but also of the political sovereignty once held by David in Jerusalem. The political authorities of early Islam, beginning with ʿUmar and ending with ʿAbd al-Malik, restore Jerusalem to its rightful place in sacred history. While this may accomplish the Islamization of the city, it does so by resurrecting the prophetic past and reinscribing it in urban space.

Baghdad

Baghdad's foundation narrative, by contrast, does not directly engage sacred history. Rather, it combines indirect references to prophecy and divine intervention with direct emphasis on political, military, and economic strategy in justifying and celebrating its origins. One obvious reason for this contrast is that Baghdad's foundation by the Abbasid Caliph al-Manṣūr in 145/762 postdated the coming of Islam by over a century and thus could not be seen as a sign of the antiquity of the Abrahamic tradition or of its culmination in Muḥammad's prophetic career. Nonetheless, in the 150 years that had passed since Muḥammad started receiving revelations from God, dissent, civil war, and revolution had divided the Islamic world. Some of these crises of political and religious authority find their way into the foundation narratives of Jerusalem and Mecca in the form of anti- and pro-Umayyad traditions. However, the foundation narrative for Baghdad represents it as a city that will finally unite Muslims under the Abbasid Caliphate both because of its physical centrality and connectivity and because of its founder's political authority. Thus, of the three cities under discussion, Baghdad's foundation narrative most clearly aspires to a break with the past, only this past is a state of Muslim disunity rather than unbelief. Even so, Baghdad's unifying power is attributed in the narrative to its ability to include rather than to exclude both what came before it and what lies outside of it, and al-Manṣūr is not portrayed as infallible, benefitting as much from negotiation and accommodation as from foresight and inspiration in founding his city.

The landmark work on Baghdad in the discourse of place is the *faḍāʾil* treatise cum topographical history that opens the *Taʾrīkh Baghdād*, a multi-volume city-based biographical dictionary by the well-known Baghdad resident and religious scholar Abū Bakr Aḥmad b. ʿAlī al-Khaṭīb al-Baghdādī (d. 463/1071). Al-Khaṭīb al-Baghdādī brings the methods of the field of Ḥadīth studies as it had evolved by the eleventh century to the work as a whole, including in his introductory representation of the city of Baghdad multiple variants of traditions, each with a complete chain of transmission (*isnād*), and largely excluding the kinds of para-Biblical and legendary material that could not be subjected to such methods. This sets al-Khaṭīb al-Baghdādī's representation of Baghdad apart from those of Mecca and Jerusalem, which engage directly and substantially with such material. A de-emphasis on material attesting to the pre-Islamic, cosmological, or eschatological dimensions of sacred history is also characteristic of other foundation narratives for the city of Baghdad in the discourse of place, even those that do not bear the imprimatur of the Ḥadīth scholar, likely because such material was simply not in circulation about the city or its site.[119] For instance, the relatively lengthy treatments of Baghdad in the late-ninth- and early-tenth-century world geographies by Ibn al-Faqīh and al-Yaʿqūbī share al-Khaṭīb al-Baghdādī's focus on historical reports and Ḥadīth from the Islamic era that evoke the political centrality and connectivity made possible by the foundation of Baghdad as an Abbasid capital city in this world rather than the next. Works on Baghdad in the discourse of place therefore do not reflect as much of a negotiation in form—between different categories of sources with varying claims to authority—as do those for Mecca and Jerusalem.

In terms of content, however, the foundation narrative assembled by al-Khaṭīb al-Baghdādī certainly emphasizes processes of negotiation. He opens his foundation narrative, and the *Taʾrīkh Baghdād* as a whole, with historical reports representing the initial Muslim conquest of the region between the Tigris and Euphrates rivers, known as al-Sawād, as neither absolute nor uncompromised.[120] Instead, it is presented as a legal matter that seems to have provoked considerable debate. Did the Muslims first acquire the land of the Sawād by force (*ʿanwatan*) or by settlement (*sulḥan*)? If by force, as the better part of its territory seems to have been, was the land of the Sawād in its entirety designated an endowment (*fayʾ* or *waqf*) for the use of all Muslims or was it divided between them as spoils? Or did ʿUmar b. al-Khaṭṭāb decide to leave the land in the hands of its preconquest inhabitants, subject to taxation, as a gesture of goodwill and/or as a safeguard against competition between Muslims? These complex legal questions must have remained open among eleventh-century *ʿulamāʾ*, as attested by al-Khaṭīb al-Baghdādī's lengthy litany of historical reports representing all different angles on the subject.[121] However, one of his goals in presenting the material seems to have been to support the view that ʿUmar had used his prerogative as

Commander of the Believers (*Amīr al-Muʾminīn*) to leave the land in the hands of its preconquest inhabitants, an act of accommodation that had the effect of legitimating all subsequent acts of buying and selling of the land, including al-Manṣūr's acquisition of the site upon which he would build the city of Baghdad.[122] It also allows him to criticize those scholars, the controversial ninth-century jurist Aḥmad b. Ḥanbal prominent among them, who considered the foundation of Baghdad to be not only an illegal appropriation of land that under the terms of the conquest could not be bought or sold, but also—and perhaps consequently—a land of impiety where everything had a price and the lingua franca was that of the *dīnār*.[123] Though these positions emerge from a close reading of the content of each of the reports he assembles, it is the debate, rather than al-Khaṭīb al-Baghdādī's position in it, that occupies the foreground, and his chief goal in this section may simply have been to demonstrate his expertise in the methods and sources of the scholarly field of *fiqh* (legal reasoning).

He soon switches to the methods of the field of Ḥadīth studies, the field to which his biographical dictionary stands as a monument, and launches a much more direct attack on those who would cast doubt on the righteousness of the foundation of Baghdad. His immediate target in this section appears to be those *ʿulamāʾ* who transmit a *ḥadīth* in which the Prophet Muḥammad predicts the downfall of a city of overreaching arrogance to be built on the Tigris. Although he clearly disagrees with the content of these traditions, his criticism, as a good Ḥadīth scholar, focuses on dissecting the weaknesses of each *isnād*, or the list of individuals who passed a tradition down over the centuries.[124] In other words, by introducing a set of traditions that defame Baghdad, he sets up his own performance of the proper methods of Ḥadīth analysis, which prove these traditions forgeries. In fact, his zeal for these methods even leads him to defend the continuing circulation of such inauthentic traditions, as long as they are accompanied by an explication of their inauthenticity. Al-Khaṭīb al-Baghdādī thus advocates the future reproduction, both textual and extratextual, of the very performance of *isnād* analysis he has staged in this foundation narrative. The endorsement of the circulation and analysis of Ḥadīth furnishes a platform for him to assert the central argument of the work as a whole: "The people of Baghdad are the most enthusiastic, serious, and prolific collectors and recorders of Ḥadīth [in the world]."[125] The first half of al-Khaṭīb al-Baghdādī's introduction to the *Taʾrīkh Baghdād*, therefore, investigates two questions, one about the postconquest legal status of the Sawād, future site of the city of Baghdad, and another about the authenticity of a body of Ḥadīth prophesying Baghdad's downfall, to establish his own authority, and that of his fellow Baghdadis, in religious scholarship. What it does not do so straightforwardly is portray the foundation of the city as an accomplishment of unquestionable—or unquestioned—virtue.

These debates, and the doubts they hint at, are wholly lacking in the geographers' accounts of Baghdad's foundation, probably because they do not self-consciously situate their work within the same fields of religious scholarship as does al-Khaṭīb al-Baghdādī. Moreover, Ibn al-Faqīh and al-Yaʿqūbī lived two centuries earlier, when the parameters of such fields were still inchoate. Nevertheless, the rest of the foundation narrative presented in the *Taʾrīkh Baghdād* bears strong similarities to those presented in the ninth- and tenth-century geographies and emphasizes processes of negotiation and accommodation. The authors all describe the extensive deliberations by which al-Manṣūr chooses the optimal site for his new city, characterizing Baghdad's founder as practical and politically astute. One account has al-Manṣūr bringing together a group of local village chiefs and heads of monasteries to counsel him on the region around Baghdad: "[Al-Manṣūr] questioned them about their sites and what they were like in the heat, the cold, and the rain. Each of them told him what they knew about their sites. Then he sent men from his own retinue to spend a night in each of the villages around Baghdad, and when they returned they agreed that the most pleasant site with the most salubrious climate was that belonging to the chief of Baghdad." The chief is then summoned, and he agrees that his village is the best site for the city because of the Tigris River and the local canal system that makes it easy to provision and to defend.[126] This image of consultation with locals, including representatives of Christian communities, functions to legitimize the choice of the site of Baghdad, both in terms of its strategic conditions and in terms of its role, even in its as yet unbuilt state, as a unifier of al-Manṣūr's subjects, Muslim and non-Muslim alike, around his imperial project. While it provides a strong contrast to the accounts of divine intervention leading Abraham and Ishmael to Mecca or David and Solomon to Jerusalem, it mirrors the acts of accommodation by ʿUmar b. al-Khaṭṭāb after the conquests of Jerusalem and Iraq and the consultative process engaged by ʿAbd al-Malik before the construction of the Dome of the Rock.

Nevertheless, the works also include prophecies that inject divine intervention into the foundation narrative and make possible both a parallel between the Abbasid Caliph and the Prophet Muḥammad and a further emphasis on the unifying function of the city of Baghdad. Al-Khaṭīb al-Baghdādī includes a series of traditions predicting the power and legitimacy of the first three Abbasid caliphs and an account of a vision that visited al-Manṣūr's mother while pregnant foreshadowing his greatness, similar to the visions that visited the mother of the Prophet Muḥammad in the *sīra* literature and the mother of Ishmael in the foundation narrative of Mecca.[127] A further echo of the *sīra* is furnished by the prophecy uttered by a Christian monk attributing the founding of the city of Baghdad to one "Miqlāṣ," which is revealed to have been al-Manṣūr's childhood nickname.[128] Another version of the prophecy from the lips of a Christian doctor not only predicts the identity of the founder as al-Manṣūr but also the outcome of the foundation itself as creating political unity and legitimacy for the Abbasids:

> A man called "Miqlāṣ" will build a city between the Ṣarāt canal and the Tigris that will be called "al-Zawrāʾ." When he has laid its foundation, a crack will appear in the Ḥijāz, so he will interrupt the construction to repair the crack. When he has just about repaired it, another crack will arise in Basra, which will be bigger than the first. It will not be long before he will repair both of them and then he will return to [the city's] construction and will complete it. Then he will live a long life, and sovereignty will rest with his progeny.[129]

This prediction incorporates into Baghdad's foundation narrative a reference to pre-Islamic scripture, an additional name of ancient pedigree, and a clear statement of political allegiance, in this case pro-Abbasid.[130] The two "cracks" that al-Manṣūr must repair most likely refer to Shiite rebellions in Medina and Basra, and the prediction that he will prevail in both cases and that sovereignty will rest with his progeny serves to legitimize the Abbasid claim to the caliphate and to represent the completion of the city of Baghdad as the end to further assaults on that claim and further disunity among Muslims.[131]

Reinforcing this image of Baghdad ushering in a new era of unity, the works portray al-Manṣūr summoning engineers and builders from near and far before personally participating in the laying of the city's foundations in the shape of a circle.[132] Although al-Manṣūr is credited with innovating by designing Baghdad as a round city, "the like of which is not known in all the corners of the world," the significance of the shape of the city is represented not simply in terms of its originality but also in terms of its capacity to connect the ruler to his city and the city to its ruler.[133] One source explains: "a round city has an advantage over a square city. If the ruler is at the center of a square city, parts of it are closer to him than others, whereas if he is at the center of a round city, however it is divided, he is equidistant from all its parts."[134] The emphasis on this connectivity may have been intended to reinforce al-Manṣūr's strategic priorities for the city, as proximity strengthens control, but it also seems intended to associate the caliph with his subjects on a more intimate and equitable basis. Nevertheless, when the Byzantine emperor during a state visit to Baghdad questions the security of a city in which commercial activity takes place so close to the seat of government, al-Manṣūr responds by moving the civilian population and the markets outside of the city walls and into a southern suburb called al-Karkh.[135] Although this has the effect of making the caliph less accessible to his subjects, it connects Baghdad's urban space more fully with its surrounding hinterland and sustains the image of a city fashioned by a series of consultations with a diverse array of people.

Despite these images of convergence and consultation, Baghdad's foundation narratives in the discourse of place suggest more of a rupture with the past, both Islamic and pre-Islamic, than do those of Jerusalem and Mecca. Al-Yaʿqūbī repeatedly celebrates Baghdad as a city unmarred by the mistakes or sins of previous princes, particularly the Sasanians and the Umayyads; in other words, it was a clean slate, politically suitable for the righteousness and legitimacy of the unifying project of the Abbasids.[136] Both al-Khaṭīb al-Baghdādī and Ibn al-Faqīh include in their foundation narratives anecdotes that suggest an attempt to erase the legacy of Persian sovereignty, the traces of which could still be seen in Baghdad's hinterland. In an exchange reminiscent of the one between Kaʿb al-Aḥbār and ʿUmar b. al-Khaṭṭāb after the conquest of Jerusalem, al-Manṣūr asks Khālid b. Barmak (d. 165/781–782), one of his advisors, whether or not he should demolish the *Īwān Kisrā*, a majestic palace of the former Sasanian Empire located twenty miles southeast of Baghdad on the Tigris, in order to use its materials for the construction of Baghdad. Khālid counsels him to leave the palace standing as a reminder to Muslims of what Islam had vanquished. Al-Manṣūr does not like this answer, accusing Khālid of harboring Persian sympathies, and proceeds with the demolition. Only its great expense convinces him to abort the project, again against the advice of Khālid, who urges him to complete the demolition lest anyone think he had been defeated in his purpose.[137] The end result is an incomplete erasure, and the partially ruined palace remains standing both as a testimony to what came before and as a symbol of ambivalence about the continuity with the pre-Islamic past that recurs in foundation and conquest narratives in the discourse of place.[138]

The authors of the works on Mecca, Jerusalem, and Baghdad drew upon the pre-Islamic or the more recent Islamic past in the same way that al-Manṣūr drew upon the *Īwān Kisrā* in this anecdote, to help them construct their cities. Their textual constructions, like al-Manṣūr's real-life construction, did not rely solely upon these pasts, and the use to which they put these pasts was selective and sometimes communicated with uncertainty or ambivalence. Nevertheless, assembling foundation narratives allowed them to situate their cities in the *longue durée* of sacred history, marching toward salvation for the faithful at the end of time. In this context, the cities could be seen as spatial manifestations of prophethood, bearing witness to the divine will and revealing signs of its fulfillment, or lack thereof, in their stones, just as prophets did in their words and deeds. Even if these pasts spoke of ignorance or error, they were never banished or reversed completely in the discourse of place. Rather, they remained close at hand, just like the partially ruined *Īwān Kisrā*, reminders of the persistence of sin or disunity and of the need for absolution or unity on that march to salvation.

3

The Image of the City

The debate over using building materials from the ruins of an ancient Persian palace for the construction of Baghdad suggests the importance of the built environment, particularly politically or religiously symbolic structures, to the representation of the city in the discourse of place. Indeed, the foundation and conquest narratives of Mecca, Jerusalem, and Baghdad all make descriptions of construction on the ground central to the construction of the city in the text. From the building and rebuilding of the Kaʿba to the building of Solomon's Temple and the Dome of the Rock to the laying of the foundations for the Round City of Baghdad, each narrative features builders, both human and superhuman, and structures of wood, metal, and stone, the conception, erection, and decoration of which are frequently described in detail. Recent scholarship has addressed questions about the form and function of early Islamic architecture in many nuanced and complex ways, but less often have the texts describing this architecture been analyzed on their own terms.[1] In addition to preserving valuable factual information, these texts were carefully constructed representations intended to conjure a mental image of a city that would have been meaningful to their audience.

This chapter focuses on the textual strategy of describing the urban built environment, a strategy that depended on the visual in a more direct way than foundation or conquest narratives.[2] By engaging the visual imagination, this strategy stimulated, ideally, the recognition of that which was being described as a cityscape; in other words, it registered the "city-ness" of the mental image formed by the text and differentiated it from the other landscapes represented in the discourse of place. This does not mean that the authors had necessarily seen the cities they were describing, although many of them had, but that they were describing the cities in terms of what could be seen, i.e., the architecture and location of structures in the built environment. Describing this environment was intended to make cities legible, or comprehensible in terms of their written representation, and thus to make them compelling as categories of belonging for people whether or not they had firsthand experience of the city.[3]

A legible city in the discourse of place usually featured a description of a monumental structure, one that dominated the cityscape because of its great size, lavish adornment, powerful patrons, or ritual function.[4] Such structures clearly commanded the visual imagination and were often explicitly associated with claims to political and religious authority. For instance, in an iconographic representation of al-Mahdiyya, first capital of the North African Fatimid Caliphate, from an eleventh-century world geography, the space within the walls of the city is taken up primarily by two oversized, ornate, and colorful structures labeled "Palaces of the Imams, peace be upon them" (see Figure 2.1, p. 42).[5] As an actual graphic depiction rather than written description—an unusual feature of surviving texts from the ninth through the eleventh centuries—this cityscape is particularly visually compelling and its caption ensures that the link it makes between the city and the power and prosperity of the Fatimids, as well as to their legitimacy as infallible "imams" in the Ismāʿīlī Shiite tradition, cannot be misunderstood.[6] In this way, describing or depicting monumental architecture was a legible and effective means of establishing cities as categories of belonging that depended on certain notions of political and religious authority.

Insider Knowledge and Belonging in the City

Al-Azraqī's ninth-century topographical history of Mecca is critical to any discussion of the way in which a description of monumental architecture makes a city legible in the discourse of place and shapes it as a category of belonging. An astounding collection of information about Mecca's built environment, this work has been seen as serving an explanatory function for visitors to the city, thousands of whom flocked there every year for the annual pilgrimage, or hajj, who might have questions about various structures in its ritual topography.[7] However, if one did not already know what to do on the hajj, one would not find the answer, or at least a clear, systematic answer, in al-Azraqī's book. This suggests that al-Azraqī did not intend to produce a pilgrimage guide per se, perhaps because he did not see the need, as pilgrims already knew what to do or got their information elsewhere. The author's primary goal for the work was rather to bear witness to the ongoing recognition and commemoration of sacred history uniquely possible for "insiders" in Mecca, those who belonged in the city, who paced and peered at its built environment on a day-to-day basis.

The first third of the work is devoted to a foundation narrative focusing on the Kaʿba, but after that al-Azraqī moves from a chronological to a spatial organization, beginning with the Kaʿba and then radiating outward to describe the surrounding sanctuary and city, concluding with a brief enumeration of the mountains and valleys in its hinterland. Each structure is thus approached in order of decreasing proximity to the Kaʿba at the center.[8] One effect of this ordering is the relative minimization of Minā and ʿArafa, localities in Mecca's immediate hinterland, which are arguably more central to the rituals of the hajj than the Kaʿba, but to which al-Azraqī only assigns a series of short sections toward the end of the work, as their relative distance from the Kaʿba dictates.[9] This contributes to a sense that while ritual informs his interest in Mecca's built environment, it is not exclusively or even primarily the rituals of the hajj that endow al-Azraqī's Mecca with meaning.

To get a sense of what does endow his city with meaning, it is necessary to assess the three distinct kinds of material that al-Azraqī marshals to describe each structure of its built environment: first, para-Biblical and Ḥadīth material recalling an episode involving Abraham, Muḥammad, or one of his Companions engaging in some ritual activity at a particular site in Mecca; second, historical and contemporary reports attesting to an Abbasid caliph's intervention in reconstructing or transforming some aspect of Mecca's built environment; and third, firsthand observations of the location and measurements of various structures in that built environment. While the para-Biblical and Ḥadīth material frequently echoes that already produced as part of the opening foundation narrative, the ninth-century reports about Abbasid building projects and the firsthand catalogues of measurements conspicuously separate the spatially organized bulk of the work from the chronologically organized introduction.

What is most striking about al-Azraqī's compilation of contemporary and recent historical material about Mecca's built environment is the pivotal role of the Abbasid caliphs in transforming the cityscape in response to the needs of the faithful and the depredations of the physical environment. These include principally the successive expansions of *al-Masjid al-Ḥarām*, specifically the enclosed courtyard surrounding the Kaʿba, ordered by a series of caliphs from ʿUmar b. al-Khaṭṭāb to the early Abbasids al-Manṣūr and al-Mahdī. Episodes recounting caliphal involvement in the city tend to be lengthy and detailed, especially those that took place during al-Azraqī's lifetime, such as the renovations ordered by Caliph al-Mutawakkil after floods swept through the region in 240–241/854–855.[10] For al-Azraqī, dwelling on such interventions in the city's built environment seems to fulfill the dual purpose of emphasizing the religious authority of the caliphs and the piety of the residents of Mecca, many of whom, including al-Azraqī's own ancestors, agreed to the sale and destruction of their homes in order to enlarge the ritual space surrounding the Kaʿba.[11]

The importance of full-time residents of Mecca participating in the commemoration of sacred history by shaping Mecca's built environment is reinforced by the almost intimate meticulousness with which al-Azraqī records the measurements of every aspect of the ritual topography of the city in his own time. These sections recur throughout the final two-thirds of the work and are conspicuous for their lack of chains of transmission, indicating that the information was gathered and attested by al-Azraqī himself or his redactor, Abū Muḥammad Isḥāq al-Khuzāʿī (d. 308/921), who added updates on changes or renovations to the structures that postdate al-Azraqī's death.[12] In one of the longest of these sections, al-Azraqī provides the overall dimensions of *al-Masjid al-Ḥarām*, including the number and ornamentation of its columns, arcades, gates, and minarets, as well as distances between them. The following excerpt conveys the detail with which al-Azraqī evokes the built environment of this mosque and the way in which updates from al-Khuzāʿī are interwoven into the description:

> The third gate [of the southern wall of *al-Masjid al-Ḥarām*]: This is the Bāb al-Ṣafā, which has four columns separating five arches. The height of each arch at the top is thirteen and a half cubits, and the central arch is fourteen cubits. The façade and interior of each arch is decorated with mosaics. The two columns on either side of the middle arch are decorated and inscribed with gold. The distance between the two walls of the gate is thirty-six cubits. The two walls are covered in marble decorated with gold, and the marble is white, red, green, and azure. Twelve steps lead to the gate, and the limit [of the mosque] is on the fourth stair as you exit the mosque. The middle arch has a stone of lead in it. It is said that the Prophet stepped on its site when he exited in the direction of al-Ṣafā. Abū Muḥammad al-Khuzāʿī said: when the mosque and its vicinity, including al-Masʿā, the valley, and the road, were flooded in 281/894 during the caliphate of al-Mutaḍid Billāh, more steps to the gates appeared than were mentioned by al-Azraqī. The number of steps that appeared to the gates of the whole valley from the highest point of the mosque to its lowest was twelve steps for each gate.[13]

From here, al-Azraqī goes on to explain more about the piece of lead in the middle arch as well as the derivation of two alternate names for the gate. All of this is about only one of the twenty-three gates of the structure, to say nothing of the columns, cornices, parapets, and arcades!

The meticulous detail supplied in these topographical sections suggests a degree of intimacy with the Meccan built environment that could only be achieved through close scrutiny. While it seems certain that al-Azraqī intended to preserve a description of the mid-ninth-century cityscape for posterity, he also communicated a sense of belonging in Mecca that was not accessible to the one-time pilgrim.[14] Someone who knew the back story to every idiosyncrasy in the architecture, someone who had paced the length and width of the mosque many times over, someone who had counted every step to every gate; this person was and could only be a local, and it is this kind of local knowledge that al-Azraqī is almost ostentatiously displaying in his topographical history of Mecca. But he is also recognizing and commemorating the sacred in the same way the Abbasid caliphs he celebrates for shaping and beautifying *al-Masjid al-Ḥarām* were. In fact, by preserving a detailed record of its changing contours, al-Azraqī is accomplishing the textual equivalent of the erection and renovation of the structure itself; he is performing an act of recognition and commemoration in writing. If the Abbasids were creating a monumental shrine in Mecca on the level of the Dome of the Rock in Jerusalem, al-Azraqī was constructing it textually in an equally monumental way, cubit by cubit, step by step, stone by stone.[15]

Abū l-Maʿālī's eleventh-century *faḍāʾil* treatise on Jerusalem also includes a series of sections that conspicuously present "insider" knowledge of the city's loci of devotion, but instead of acting as the textual equivalent of the erection of monumental architecture these sections facilitate the interaction between individuals and the built environment through ritual.[16] That is, they function as a veritable pilgrimage guide for the pious visitation (*ziyāra*) of Jerusalem. As in al-Azraqī's work, these sections occur at the end of the opening foundation narrative and signal a transition from chronologically to spatially organized material. Also like al-Azraqī's measurements of the built environment, Abū l-Maʿālī's instructions for devotions in the built environment lack chains of transmission and therefore stand out in the context of the work as a whole, which relies heavily upon material that could be attested by earlier authorities.[17] Unlike al-Azraqī, however, Abū l-Maʿālī uses his "insider" knowledge of Jerusalem's ritual topography to make possible "outsider" interaction with that topography, not just textually but also physically. Each of the six sections in this pilgrimage guide begins with a straightforward physical directive, such as the opening of the first chapter on the *Masjid Bayt al-Maqdis* ("Mosque of Jerusalem"), also known as *al-Ḥaram al-Sharīf* ("The Noble Sanctuary"), which refers to the enclosed courtyard surrounding the Dome of the Rock: "It is recommended that when one enters the sanctuary (*Masjid Bayt al-Maqdis*) one should begin with the right leg and follow with the left and say what the Prophet, peace be upon him, said upon entering mosques." Only after this does Abū l-Maʿālī provide a chain of transmission to introduce a *ḥadīth*, which reproduces the words that Muḥammad intoned upon entering and exiting mosques.[18] The next section follows the same formula for the Dome of the Rock, and subsequent sections deal with nearby loci of devotion, such as the Dome of the Chain (*Qubbat al-Silsila*), the Dome of the Ascension (*Qubbat al-Miʿrāj*), and the Dome of the Prophet (*Qubbat al-Nabī*).[19]

The final section of the pilgrimage guide takes the visitor on a circuit of the perimeter of the sanctuary in a roughly counterclockwise direction and contains the most explicitly sequenced physical directions in the work.[20] The following excerpt, which moves from the perimeter gates to the congregational mosque located to the south of the Dome of the Rock, known today as *al-Masjid al-Aqṣā* or the Aqṣā

Mosque, conveys the importance of human interaction with Jerusalem's built environment as a form of recognition and commemoration of sacred history:

> Then [the visitor] comes to the rocks in the rear (northern) part of the sanctuary, adjacent to the Gate of the Tribes (*Bāb al-Asbāṭ*), and prays on the spot that is called the Chair of Solomon (*Kursī Sulaymān*), facing the *qibla*, and uses his independent judgment to offer an invocation, for this is the spot upon which Solomon, peace be upon him, offered an invocation when he finished building the Temple, an invocation that God Almighty answered. Then [the visitor] continues to the Gate of the Divine Presence (*Bāb al-Sakīna*) and does likewise there, as well as at the Gate of Pardon (*Bāb Ḥiṭṭa*). Then he enters the interior roofed mosque and heads to the prayer-niche (*miḥrāb*) of ʿUmar and prays and uses his independent judgment to offer an invocation there, as well as at the prayer-niche (*miḥrāb*) of Muʿāwiya and at all of the prayer-niches (*maḥārīb*) inside the mosque. Then [the visitor] descends to the Gate of the Prophet (*Bāb al-Nabī*), peace be upon him, and prays there, offering an invocation out of those we have mentioned before that have been handed down from the Prophet, peace be upon him. Then he heads to the Oratory of Mary (*Miḥrāb Maryam*), the site of her devotions, known for the cradle of Jesus, peace be upon him, and uses his independent judgment to offer an invocation, for invocations there are answered, and prays there, reciting the *Sūrat Maryam*, since it mentions her, and prostrates himself there.[21]

In this excerpt, Abū l-Maʿālī draws an explicit connection between the recommendations he makes for appropriate ritual behavior at each site and the role that site played in sacred history. Thus, the visitor to the Chair of Solomon is urged to recite an invocation inspired by the one Solomon made when he finished erecting the Temple, an invocation that is quoted in the foundation narrative that precedes the pilgrimage guide in Abū l-Maʿālī's work. Similarly, at the Oratory of Mary the visitor should recite the *Sūrat Maryam* ("Chapter of Mary") from the Qurʾān because it tells the story of the birth of Jesus and his miraculous speech from the cradle.[22] With these recommendations, Abū l-Maʿālī can be seen as commemorating sacred history at two different levels, textually through his description of ritual in the built environment of Jerusalem, and extratextually by facilitating future ritual activity in that built environment.

While both Abū l-Maʿālī and al-Azraqī participate in the discourse of place by showcasing "insider" information about the built environment of their cities, descriptions of structures of religious or political significance were produced by "outsiders" as well, to prove that they had travelled to or had knowledge of a city, to multiply the spiritual benefits of pilgrimage, or to communicate loyalty to the founders or patrons of the structures. It could be argued that the whole purpose of the tenth-century geography by Jerusalem native al-Muqaddasī was to prove his own knowledge, primarily by means of what he celebrates as "direct experience" (*ʿiyān*), of the cities of the Islamic world by describing, delineating, and classifying them in writing.[23] Though this work is not, strictly speaking, a travelogue, as it is organized neither chronologically nor spatially in terms of an itinerary, al-Muqaddasī highlights his bona fides as a traveler by producing firsthand information about urban built environments, in greater or lesser detail depending on the status of the city in the hierarchy he establishes for each region. For similar purposes, Ibn ʿAbd Rabbih, a tenth-century Andalusian litterateur, uses a section on cities and regions within his multivolume *adab* compilation, *al-ʿIqd al-farīd* (The unique necklace), to showcase three seemingly firsthand descriptions of monumental urban architecture, the sanctuary of Jerusalem, *al-Masjid al-Ḥarām* of Mecca, and the Prophet's Mosque of Medina.[24] These accounts stand out, in a work otherwise very anthological in character, as testimony to the thousands of miles the author trekked eastward on pilgrimage and, therefore, to his piety as a Muslim.[25]

One of the first formal travelogues to participate in the discourse of place, the mid-eleventh-century *Safarnāma* by Nāṣir-i Khusraw, a Persian-speaking bureaucrat from the region of Khurāsān, also makes claims to direct experience of cities along itineraries reaching from present-day Afghanistan to Egypt. For example, in Mecca the author bases his authority in describing the built environment on a six-month *mujāwara*, or extended stay in the holy city for the purposes of prayer and devotion, an experience that, it is implied, accords him quasi-"insider" status.[26] In Jerusalem, he emphasizes his own visual and physical interaction with the built environment, both as a pilgrim and as a keen observer and recorder of information. When he first enters *al-Ḥaram al-Sharīf*, he writes: "I wanted to measure the dimensions of the sanctuary, but I thought that first I should get a general idea of the plan and layout, after which I could make my measurements. For a long time I wandered about the area, looking at it from different vantages."[27] At the end of the lengthy description of the sanctuary, he reminds his audience of his firsthand authority: "This much I saw and sketched myself inside the Jerusalem sanctuary, and I made notes in a diary I had with me right there."[28] Nāṣir-i Khusraw's textual performance, a record of the sanctuary's measurements and layout, is therefore framed by reminders of his extratextual visual and physical interaction with Jerusalem's built environment. Within the description, he also notes his own ritual activity in the sanctuary and, in so doing, forges a direct link with the sacred history of the site. Of the Gates of Mercy and Repentance (*Bāb al-Raḥma* and *Bāb al-Tawba*) in the eastern wall, he informs us: "They say that David had scarcely crossed the threshold when an inspiration came to him to the effect that God has accepted his repentance. There he remained, occupying himself with acts of obedience. I, Nasir, prayed there and asked God for grace in piety and to be cleansed of the sin of disobedience."[29] His reenactment of sacred history in the world outside of the text is thus repeated inside the text as a testimony to, perhaps even as a multiplier of, the spiritual benefits accrued to him, and to those who might follow in his footsteps, by visiting Jerusalem.

Nāṣir-i Khusraw's description of the built environment of Cairo similarly focuses on ritual, but instead of invoking the sacred past he celebrates the present righteousness of the Fatimid Caliphate in its capital city. The portion of the *Safarnāma* afforded to his almost three-year stay in Cairo is dominated by lengthy accounts of official processions and festivals in which the Fatimid regime can be seen to occupy the urban built environment in a ceremonial show of power and prestige.[30] His evocation of the spectacle of these ceremonies emphasizes the visual and makes the city of Cairo legible as an imperial capital. When he describes the grand opening of the canals to mark the annual rise of the Nile, he depicts the caliph performing an act of connectivity in front of the greater urban population by leading a glittering parade along the major canal that connected the old city of al-Fusṭāṭ, founded in the seventh century for the first settlement of Muslims in Egypt, and the new city of al-Qāhira (literally "the victorious"), founded in 359/969 by the conquering Fatimids.[31] The textual recreation of this parade is itself a performance of loyalty to the regime and the Ismāʿīlī Shiism it espoused.[32] Moreover, Nāṣir-i Khusraw's description of the interior of the caliph's palace, to which he gained access as a guest at one of the biannual banquets, stresses the monumental scale of the architecture and its lavish adornment as a reflection of the power of the Fatimid dynasty.[33] This episode reinforces his more general observations about the prosperity of the Fatimid capital as evidenced in the quality of its infrastructure and its numerous shops, caravanserais, and mosques, all thronged with people.[34]

While the genre of travel writing generally presumes eyewitness authority, firsthand descriptions of urban built environments might also be injected into more historical and anthological works to communicate an author's sense of belonging in a city he had visited. Although ʿUmar b. Shabba spent most of his life in Iraq, his ninth-century representation of Medina reveals a pious commitment to follow in the footsteps, both literally and figuratively, of the first generation of Muslims who shaped and inhabited the city. His representation of Medina occupies a significant portion of the beginning of a larger work dedicated to the biographies of Muḥammad, ʿUmar, and ʿUthmān; thus, ʿUmar b. Shabba participates in the discourse of place by privileging a topographical description of the city of Medina as a means of introducing three of the earliest figures of political and religious authority in Islam.[35] Accordingly, he is primarily concerned with portraying Medina's urban space as it was apportioned and settled by Muḥammad and the *Muhājirūn*, or immigrants, who fled with him from Mecca to Medina in 622. Nonetheless, ʿUmar b. Shabba brings his information about the charitable estates (*ṣadaqāt*), houses (*duwar*), residences (*maḥāll*), and settlements (*manāzil*) administered or owned by the *Muhājirūn* up to date by consistently noting the current status of the structures, most of which remained in the hands of the descendants of the original owners or administrators.[36]

Even though ʿUmar b. Shabba was not a resident of Medina, it seems that he acquired his knowledge of the city's topography from physical visits, as he situates all the structures he describes in relation to neighboring structures, streets, and alleyways, often without reference to another source or text. In a remarkable passage, he lists the houses surrounding the Prophet's Mosque in a clockwise circuit starting and ending at the southern (*qibla*) side of the mosque, including details such as the number of cubits between each house that suggest he gathered his information by personally pacing the route.[37] Other directional details in the descriptions of the residential structures of the city reinforce a sense that ʿUmar b. Shabba conducted his fieldwork on foot, as in the entry for the house claimed by Qudāma b. Maẓʿūn: "It is at the mouth of Banū Ḍamra Lane and behind the Abu Dhayyab family's house, on your right as you are going toward Banū Ḍamra."[38] Despite his "outsider" status, ʿUmar b. Shabba's representation of Medina in these sections closely resembles the work of the "insider" *par excellence*, al-Azraqī, particularly the latter's lengthy description of the residential quarters (*ribāʿ*) of Mecca that occurs toward the end of his work.[39] Although ʿUmar b. Shabba and al-Azraqī each occasionally cite earlier sources for historical information about the residences—and ʿUmar b. Shabba even includes the texts of primary documents relating to the ownership or administration of properties in the early Islamic period—both authors present most of their topographical material, historical or contemporary, on their own authority.[40] This allows them to connect centuries-old information directly to their present-day experience of the cities, communicating their own sense of belonging in that early community of Muslims whose traces were still visible, and thus could be recognized and commemorated, in the built environments of Mecca and Medina.[41]

A work that draws directly on al-Azraqī's description of Mecca's built environment as a model for claiming belonging is Abū ʿAlī Aḥmad b. ʿUmar b. Rustih's *Kitāb al-aʿlāq al-nafīsa* (Book of precious and valuable things), a compilation of materials on a variety of topics, the extant portion of which appears to be devoted to world geography. One of the noteworthy features of this portion of the work is a detailed description of the Prophet's Mosque in Medina as observed during the Isfahan-born author's pilgrimage to the city in the year 290/903.[42] Here Ibn Rustih records the dimensions of the Mosque, a catalog of its accoutrements, and texts of its inscriptions, which he states he copied by hand, attesting to the pious works of various Abbasid caliphs in renovating and beautifying the structure.[43] Not only is this description detailed in the manner of al-Azraqī's description of *al-Masjid al-Ḥarām* in Mecca, but it follows a reproduction of much of al-Azraqī's own topographical data for Mecca.[44] Although Ibn Rustih does not attribute the Meccan data to al-Azraqī, his emphasis on his own authority as the source for the Medinan data suggests that either he did not make it to Mecca, and would have produced an explicitly firsthand description if he could, or he considered reproducing al-Azraqī's "insider" description to be the equivalent of, if not more credible than, producing his own.[45] The similarities in both form and content between his firsthand representation of Medina and the material he borrowed from al-Azraqī on Mecca suggest that al-Azraqī's work was already, only decades after his death, considered an exemplary expression of belonging in the most ritually significant city in the Islamic world and of loyalty to the Abbasid caliphs who had patronized it. Ibn Rustih's concern with lavishing attention on the monumental architecture of Mecca and Medina may have been a strategy to establish his bona fides among mainstream Muslims, which would make palatable his more controversial agenda for the work as a whole, including support for the *Shuʿūbiyya* and a sympathetic stance toward Shiism.[46] Whether consciously or not, and whatever his ulterior motives, Ibn Rustih crafted his descriptions of Mecca and Medina as a textual performance of city-ness that recalled earlier such performances—notably one by the ultimate Meccan "insider" and Abbasid loyalist al-Azraqī—highlighting the intertextual and interactive nature of the discourse of place.

Citational Performances and Longing for the City

The intertextual and interactive nature of the discourse of place can also be thought of as "citational," in the sense that earlier works were often used as templates for—if not also quoted or reproduced directly in—later works, enhancing the legibility of the cities they described to an audience for whom such earlier descriptions might have the ring of the familiar and the authoritative.[47] These works generally emerged from intellectual cultures—the worlds of *adab* and Ḥadīth studies, for instance—defined by the citational. In these worlds knowledge production was shaped by methods that privileged the citation of previous authorities over "original" observations, recollections, or ideas. While some participants in the discourse of place, such as al-Azraqī, used their access to firsthand information to communicate a sense of belonging and others, such as al-Muqaddasī, embraced "direct experience" (*ʿiyān*) as the best method for producing knowledge, many authors felt no compunction about employing citational methods to describe cities they had never visited, and some chose to employ such methods even when more direct access to information was possible. Thus, just because the authority of the visual was invoked to make a cityscape legible in the discourse, it did not necessarily mean that the author had seen that cityscape with, or would choose to describe it through, his own eyes.

The geographer Ibn al-Faqīh is a good example of an *adab*-inspired scholar who embraced the citational in his descriptions of built environments. While little is known about his life, in particular whether or how far he traveled from his hometown of Hamadan, many of his representations of cities imply that his information comes from secondhand sources.[48] Even if it was possible to know for sure that Ibn al-Faqīh did *not* visit the cities he describes in his world geography, one does not get the sense that he considered his choice of sources a last resort or born of mere necessity. Rather, the following description of the ritual topography of Jerusalem seems intended by its author to be not only fully authoritative but also as effective in recognizing the city's significance in sacred history as firsthand information derived from residence in or visitation of the city would be:

> It is said (*yuqāl*) that the length of the sanctuary of Jerusalem (*Masjid Bayt al-Maqdis*) is 1,000 cubits and its width is 700 cubits. In it are 4,000 beams of wood, 700 pillars, and 500 chains of brass. Every night 1,600 lamps are lit in it, and it has 140 servants. Every month it receives 100 jars of oil, and every year it receives 800,000 cubits of matting. In it are 25,000 pitchers of water and sixteen wooden cases that hold copies of the Qurʾān for pious use, some of which a man would not be able to lift. In it are four pulpits for volunteer preachers and one for the paid preacher. It has four basins for ablutions. Covering the roofs of the sanctuary, in the place of clay, are 45,000 sheets of lead.[49]

From here, the description continues at length, including detailed measurements of the Dome of the Rock and the locations of other structures in the sanctuary. The use of the phrase "it is said" to introduce the passage suggests that the information was not gathered by Ibn al-Faqīh himself, and yet he does not appear to be apologetic or defensive about relaying secondhand information, here or anywhere else in the work. It may be that reproducing a description of Jerusalem's built environment from another source was intended as a substitute for actually going there, a "virtual" act of pilgrimage every bit as legitimate as a physical one.[50] In this interpretation, the recognition and commemoration of sacred history that occupied visitors to the city and motivated political authorities past and present to build, appoint, and maintain its monuments might be performed equally effectively both textually and citationally.[51]

It is noteworthy that al-Muqaddasī's description of Jerusalem nearly a century later includes the same overall dimensions for the sanctuary and the same figures for the number of wooden beams, columns, jars of oil, cubits of matting, and sheets of lead therein—and presents them in roughly the same order—as in this excerpt from Ibn al-Faqīh.[52] Even though al-Muqaddasī celebrated the primacy of direct experience, possessed knowledge of the building trade, and, as a Jerusalem native, had certainly visited the sanctuary himself, it still seems likely that he saw fit to borrow this information from Ibn al-Faqīh's work, to which we know he had access because he criticizes it in the introduction to his own work. Like Ibn Rustih's unattributed reproduction of al-Azraqī's description of Mecca, al-Muqaddasī's unattributed reproduction from another text of a description of Jerusalem's built environment is evidence of the pervasive intertextuality of the discourse of place, as well as the wide acceptance of, even preference for, a citational approach to knowledge production, or at least presentation and dissemination, in this period.[53]

Likewise, al-Khaṭīb al-Baghdādī, a proud "insider" representing his hometown of Baghdad, preferred information mediated by earlier authorities over his own observations. Despite the fact that as a Ḥadīth scholar he was immersed in an intellectual environment that valued the citational, it is still striking that his description of Baghdad's built environment in the introduction to the *Taʾrīkh Baghdād* relies so heavily on sources that predate his birth in 392/1002 by a century or more.[54] Thus, the materials he assembles describe the palaces, canals, and suburbs constructed during the reigns of the early Abbasid caliphs in the late eighth and early ninth centuries. This has the effect of capturing the contours of the city at what was, according to al-Khaṭīb al-Baghdādī, a more glorious moment not only architecturally, but also politically, socially, and economically. In short, the Baghdad he described was a city he had never actually seen.

The textual construction of Baghdad as it looked in the late eighth and early ninth centuries was not unique to al-Khaṭīb. In true citational fashion, his eleventh-century description of Baghdad's built environment relies on evidence transmitted by earlier authorities and reproduces the emphasis in earlier works on construction that took place even earlier, during the first decades of the city's existence, rather than on up-to-date topographical information. The ninth-century scholar and Baghdad native al-Yaʿqūbī compiled a lengthy introduction to his world geography featuring descriptions of the built environments of Baghdad and Samarra, the two Abbasid capitals in Iraq. At the end of his description of Baghdad, he writes: "These land grants (*qaṭāʾiʿ*), avenues (*shawāriʿ*), streets (*durūb*), and lanes (*sikak*) that I have mentioned are according to what was described during the days of al-Manṣūr and the time of their foundation. They have changed."[55] Al-Yaʿqūbī gives little detail about how they changed in the period since the foundation of the city or how they looked during his own lifetime some decades later, except to say that as people come and go different areas of the city wax and wane. It is clear that for al-Yaʿqūbī the built environment worth describing in detail is that of late-eighth-century Baghdad. Since his sources emphasize the apportioning of urban space according to political allegiance in this period, particularly the palaces and villas built on land granted to Abbasid loyalists, it seems that it was the Baghdad associated with Abbasid power and patronage that mattered to him. While he claims that the transfer of the capital to Samarra in 223/838 did not damage Baghdad's economic prosperity, his more up-to-date topographical description of Samarra, from its foundation through construction projects commissioned by the Caliph al-Mutawakkil during his own lifetime, suggests the urban built environment took mental form—or was legible—for al-Yaʿqūbī only when and where it could be seen as shaped by the office of the caliphate.[56]

Like that of al-Yaʿqūbī, al-Khaṭīb al-Baghdādī's enumeration of land grants, palaces, and estates or suburbs (*arbāḍ*) in and around Baghdad doubles as an enumeration of names associated with the Abbasid bureaucracy, military, and ruling house in the first half century after the city's foundation. The following excerpt from his treatment of the western part of the city, preceded by a chain of transmission extending back to the Baghdad resident and judge Muḥammad b. Khalaf (d. 306/918), exhibits his use of earlier authorities to describe a city that predated even those earlier authorities:[57]

> The site of the new prison was a fief granted to ʿAbd Allāh b. Mālik, where Muḥammad b. Yaḥyā b. Khālid b. Barmak [later] settled and then during the reign of [Caliph] Muḥammad [al-Amīn] it became part of Umm Jaʿfar's building, which she called al-Qarār. The house of Sulaymān b. Abī Jaʿfar was [originally] a fief granted to Hishām b. ʿAmr al-Fazārī. The house of ʿAmr b. Masʿada was [originally a fief granted] to al-ʿAbbās b. ʿUbayd Allāh b. Jaʿfar b. al-Manṣūr. The house of Ṣāliḥ al-Miskīn was a fief granted to him by [Caliph] Abū Jaʿfar al-Manṣūr. [There is] the small market (*suwayqa*) of al-Haytham b. Shuʿba b. Ẓuhayr, the client of [Caliph] al-Manṣūr, who died in 156/772–773 while on the belly of a concubine. [There is] the house of ʿUmāra b. Ḥamza, one of the most eloquent and eminent secretaries. It is said that he was a descendant of Abū Usāma, the client of the Prophet of God, peace be upon him, and it is also said that he was a descendant of ʿIkrima. [There is] the palace of ʿAbdawayh of al-Azd, one of the notables of the dynasty, who undertook its building during the reign of [Caliph] al-Manṣūr.[58]

While this excerpt opens with a landmark—the "new prison"—seemingly familiar to the early-tenth-century source upon whose authority it is quoted, this building was destroyed in 350/961–962, well before the lifetime of al-Khaṭīb al-Baghdādī.[59] The rest of the landmarks in this passage are of even earlier vintage: fiefs, houses, and palaces granted, developed, or built between the founding of the city in 145/762 and the reign of the Abbasid Caliph al-Amīn (193/809–198/813). Not only does none of this information date from al-Khaṭīb al-Baghdādī's lifetime, but even the more recent early-tenth-century topographical detail is mentioned only in relation to the apportioning and shaping of the city's built environment a century earlier by the Abbasid ruling house and its supporters.

Al-Khaṭīb al-Baghdādī relies on these earlier reports to celebrate the city when it was most closely associated with the prestige and prosperity of the caliphate at its height. Accordingly, the structures that receive the most detailed descriptions are the Abbasid palaces, an architecture of power meant to reflect the ultimate political and religious authority in Islam. One of the most memorable passages, quoted from an earlier work compiled by Hilāl b. al-Muḥassin al-Ṣābi' (d. 448/1056), describes the visit of a Byzantine delegation to the city in 305/917.[60] As the delegates are led from chamber to chamber and courtyard to courtyard in the palace complex of Caliph al-Muqtadir Billāh on the east side of the Tigris River, they encounter ornamentation and ceremonial of greater and greater opulence, including 7,000 servants, 38,000 curtains, and 22,000 carpets.[61] This calculus of excess sketches the contours of a city of the past that had the capacity to awe representatives of a rival empire.[62]

To similar effect, al-Khaṭīb al-Baghdādī, also on the authority of earlier interlocutors, presents statistics about the features of Baghdad's infrastructure as a meditation on the city's past capaciousness, its ability, now significantly diminished, to accumulate and accommodate immigrants and visitors from among the many peoples of the Islamic world. For instance, he quotes Abū Bakr Muḥammad b. Yaḥyā al-Ṣūlī (d. 335/947) on the authority of a no longer extant topographical description of the city written by Aḥmad b. Abī Ṭāhir Ṭayfūr (d. 280/893) that establishes the number of public baths in late-ninth-century Baghdad as 60,000. Based on this figure, calculations as to the number of attendants needed in each bath, the number of mosques needed to accommodate that number of attendants, and the number of attendants needed to service that number of mosques result in a whopping 1.5 million men reportedly employed in Baghdad's baths and mosques alone.[63] By the late tenth century, however, the number of baths had dropped to anywhere between 3,000 and 10,000, according to an anecdote reported by Hilāl al-Ṣābi', a still impressive tally but significantly lower than the figures of a century before.[64] No statistics are reported from al-Khaṭīb al-Baghdādī's lifetime.

Statistics like these occur in other representations of Baghdad, and many of them are so inflated that it seems that accuracy may never have been the intended goal.[65] Instead, the repetition of such statistics acts almost as an incantation, conjuring a magical city of immense proportions—or a city of a more glorious past.[66] At the end of his section on statistics, al-Khaṭīb al-Baghdādī launches into a first-person manifesto of nostalgia for Baghdad's size and splendor "before our own time and prior to our era."[67] It is as if he cannot bring himself to describe the city that he himself knew, so diminished was it from its earlier proportions.[68] To describe the diminished city would also be to diminish the image of Abbasid power that is so clearly projected in the introduction to the *Taʾrīkh Baghdād*, from the foundation narrative stressing al-Manṣūr's inspiration and foresight to the topographical sections emphasizing the capaciousness of Baghdad's built environment and its ability, both physical and symbolic, to unite the Islamic world under Abbasid suzerainty.[69]

Al-Khaṭīb al-Baghdādī's nostalgia for a Baghdad of the past resonates with the evocations of loss that emerge from many representations of territories as homelands. The capaciousness and splendor of Baghdad's cityscape as portrayed in the introduction to the *Taʾrīkh Baghdād* made possible the physical, social, material, political, and spiritual nurture associated with the *waṭan*, not simply for residents like al-Khaṭīb al-Baghdādī's own ancestors, but for the entire Islamic world of an earlier era. Another intersection between nostalgic representations of territory and descriptions of the urban built environment between the ninth and eleventh centuries can be found in a genre of poetry known as "elegies for cities" (*rithāʾ al-mudun*). Like al-Khaṭīb al-Baghdādī, the authors of these elegies tend to portray images of a cityscape of a more glorious past, but unlike al-Khaṭīb al-Baghdādī they do not shy away from describing the diminished cityscape, evoking its ruin and decay in graphic detail.

The panegyric and the elegy were two of the longest-standing Arabic poetic forms in the early Islamic world, and they usually emerged from a direct connection with a figure of political power, who acted as patron, or would-be patron, of the poet.[70] Elegies associated their authors with the past beneficence of the figure being mourned, and were sometimes used to curry favor with or motivate the right action of successors or heirs. Correspondingly, the elegy for a city aligns its author with the past power of its rulers as manifested in the past prosperity of the city, though it tends less to curry favor than to demand restitution from the present or future rulers of the city.[71] The ruins of the cityscape are a reflection of the failures of a city's stewards, guardians, and governors, and meditation on those ruins often moves the poet to invoke them directly—to demand a return to vigilance, righteousness, or unity in their administration of the city and its inhabitants.

One of the earliest extant Arabic elegies for cities was the cri de coeur for Baghdad composed by Abū Yaʿqūb Isḥāq al-Khuraymī (d. ca. 206/821) during the civil war between the sons of the Abbasid Caliph Hārūn al-Rashīd, al-Amīn and al-Maʾmūn. He contrasts the past capaciousness and prosperity of the city, evoked by images of its built environment, particularly its extensive suburbs and the ferries and bridges that connected the sprawling city on both banks of the Tigris River, with its current desolation:

At Zandaward and al-Yāsiriyya,
  and on the two river banks, where the ferries have ceased,
At the mills of Ruḥā al-Baṭrīq and at upper al-Khayzurāniyya,
  whose bridges were lofty,
And at the Palace of ʿAbdawayh, there is a lesson and guidance
  for every soul whose inner thoughts have become pure.
Where is their protection, and where is their protector?
  Where is their restoration, and where is their restorer?
Where are their eunuchs and their servants?
  Where are their inhabitants and their builder?[72]

This excerpt from the 135-verse poem reminds the audience of the city's pathways (bridges over the Tigris), districts (the east-side neighborhood of al-Khayzurāniyya known for its famous cemetery), and landmarks (the Palace of ʿAbdawayh, mentioned earlier in a passage from the *Taʾrīkh Baghdād*)—in other words, the features of Baghdad's built environment that made legible its past success as a city.[73] The series of questions that follow this poetic topography suggest the depopulation of the city and thus the end of its success, while also focusing attention on the absence or neglect of its political personnel. The figure of the protector, restorer, and builder refers to the Abbasid caliph and his administration, and the related processes of protection, restoration, and construction to the duties that al-Khuraymī implies are owed to the beleaguered city of Baghdad.[74]

Ibn al-Rūmī's famous elegy for Basra after the rebellion of the Zanj, the slaves of East African origin who wrested control over southern Iraq from the Abbasid caliphs between 255/869 and 270/883, includes a similar evocation of a built environment, now destroyed, that made legible its past success as a city:

Turn aside, my two comrades, at Basra the brilliant,
  As one wasted with sickness, turns aside,
And enquire of her—but answer is not to be found in her
  To any question, and who is there to speak for her?
Where is the clamor of them that dwelt in her?
  Where are her jostling markets?
Where is any ship sailing from her or sailing to her—
  Ships raised up in the sea like landmarks?
Where are those palaces and mansions that were in her?
  Where is that well-secured edifice?

Those palaces have been changed into rubbish-mounds
  Of ashes and heaped dust;
Flood and fire have been given authority over them,
  And their columns have crumbled down in utter destruction.[75]

Ibn al-Rūmī opens this passage with the conventional opening of the pre-Islamic ode (*qaṣīda*), in which the itinerant poet pauses in the company of traveling companions to ponder the ruins of a past campsite or stopping place and to reminisce about the good times enjoyed there. In the case of this excerpt, occurring midway through the eighty-three-verse poem, Ibn al-Rūmī contrasts his own unsought-after itinerancy, having been rendered homeless by the destruction of his native Basra, with that of the footloose bedouin poet of yore, and ponders the ruins of a city, a more permanent and thus devastating loss, it is implied by the description of its "well-secured edifice," than the ruins of a campsite. The good times Ibn al-Rūmī remembers here have to do with the economic prosperity that had been visible in the cityscape of the past, which for this port city included ships "raised up ... like landmarks"—not unlike the ferries of al-Khuraymī's riverine Baghdad. Also as in al-Khuraymī's Baghdad, there seem to be no political personnel to rehabilitate Basra's built environment, since "flood and fire have been given authority" over it. The Arabic verb here, "to be given authority," is *sulliṭa*, from the same root as *sulṭān*, or "political power," reinforcing the sense that only active and strong political mobilization will restore Basra's former flourishing.

While both al-Khuraymī and Ibn al-Rūmī conclude their elegies with verses in the form of direct address, exhorting the powerful to rescue their cities, Abū ʿĀmir Aḥmad b. Shuhayd (d. 426/1035) in his elegy for Cordoba after the civil war of the early eleventh century turns his grief inward, though he clearly associates strong and unified political leadership with his city's past glory. Ibn Shuhayd portrays this past glory through images of its built environment, as in the following excerpt:

And the palace—that of the Umayyad clan—so abundant
  With everything, but the Caliphate was even more abundant.
And the Zāhiriyya with its boats that shone brightly
  And the ʿĀmiriyya given life by the stars.
And the Grand Mosque overflowing with all who
  Recited, heard, and looked on at anything they wished to.
And the streets of the markets bearing witness that
  The marketplace was never empty of shopping throngs.[76]

Even more clearly than al-Khuraymī and Ibn al-Rūmī before him, Ibn Shuhayd associates the landmarks of Cordoba's cityscape with the strength and unity of the Umayyad Caliphate of Andalusia, an architecture of power evoked by the names of two of its palaces, the Zāhiriyya and the ʿĀmiriyya, built by the Umayyad official Muḥammad b. Abī ʿĀmir during a period of stability in the late tenth century.[77] However, instead of calling for the restoration of that strength and unity, he seems to accept, sadly, its passing. Ibn Shuhayd is the only one of the three poets examined here who does not describe the built environment in ruins; perhaps, like al-Khaṭīb al-Baghdādī, he simply cannot bring himself to do so—for to do so would be to complete the city's destruction, reducing its memory to rubble just as marauding troops had done to its built environment.[78]

Nostalgia in Arabic literature has been interpreted in the past as a passive posture—a mood of reverie rather than a vehicle for making claims or demands on religious and political authorities.[79] By contrast, these elegies for cities, just like al-Khaṭīb al-Baghdādī's nostalgic representation of Baghdad in the introduction to the *Taʾrīkh Baghdād*, were products of active textual strategies that were at times explicitly critical or subversive of existing power structures.[80] Descriptions of the urban built environment that did not turn on nostalgia, such as those by al-Azraqī or Abū l-Maʿālī of their hometowns of Mecca and Jerusalem or those by geographers and travelers as they "visited" the cities of the Islamic world, were equally active, aimed at promoting a variety of agendas: the commemoration or recognition of sacred history in a city; the celebration of the special role played by locals in that commemoration or recognition; the accumulation of the spiritual benefits of pilgrimage by (re-)inhabiting a city's loci of devotion in writing; and the expression of loyalty to authority figures by documenting their transformation of the cityscape as a reflection of their regime's power and legitimacy and their subjects' prosperity and unity. Describing a city's built environment was therefore a textual strategy that was adopted with particular frequency to make cities legible in the discourse of place and to shape them as categories of belonging.

The Power of Cities

If naming and locating cities, assembling their foundation and conquest narratives, and describing their built environments were useful and compelling textual strategies, in a broader sense cities themselves were useful and compelling objects of representation in texts. Their visibility and durability on the ground—their rootedness in land—is one of the reasons images of cities were especially resonant with audiences in the Islamic world. The rootedness of cities not only encouraged their representation but also contributed to the flourishing of the entire discourse of place, which was, after all, about translating attachment to land into a persuasive textual idiom for expressing loyalty and belonging. Moreover, since cities were clearly associated with politics in the world outside the text, they could very easily be associated with politics inside texts. Works about certain cities, especially capital cities like Abbasid Baghdad or Umayyad Cordoba, can be read as pledging loyalty to or making demands on the associated regimes. Similarly, the frequent allusions to city rivalries in the discourse of place reflected the realities of not only political, social, and economic competition, but also intellectual competition as it was understood in the worlds of *adab* and Ḥadīth studies from which most of the authors emerged.

These two kinds of competition—between cities and between scholars—correspond to two levels at which textual performances had extratextual political ramifications. On the one hand, composing a *faḍāʾil* treatise celebrating the preeminence of one city—over another or over all others—can be seen as a textual performance intended to encourage a response from its audience in the form of political, economic, or religious investment in that city on the ground. On the other hand, the composition of a *faḍāʾil* treatise praising a city might not be intended necessarily or primarily to encourage an extratextual response for the benefit of the city itself, but to encourage an extratextual response for the author's own benefit. For instance, some authors might participate in the discourse of place to establish their bona fides as *udabāʾ* through word play that riffed on popular city rivalries but did not necessarily communicate their own allegiances in these rivalries.[81] Others might participate in the discourse of place to establish their bona fides as *ʿulamāʾ* through the assembly of scriptural, legendary, and historical material about cities that could be seen as having contributed to sacred history, whether because of their cosmological or eschatological significance or because of their association, past or present, with prophets, caliphs, scholars, or pilgrims. These textual performances served as evidence of the performers' erudition and linguistic agility or of their religious authority and piety—and sometimes of both—and might yield prestigious or lucrative opportunities for patronage or employment. Vying to represent cities in the discourse of place was, therefore, a competitive textual performance with potential political, social, and economic benefits in the world outside the text.

The city rivalry about which the most material from the ninth to the eleventh centuries has been preserved is the competition for the status of holiest city in Islam.[82] Mecca and Jerusalem are often compared in terms of cosmological and eschatological precedence, and a variety of cities are ranked according to the relative value of pilgrimage to or prayer in them. Many works quote what has become known as the "*ḥadīth* of the three mosques" in which Muḥammad exhorts his followers not to set out on pilgrimage to any site other than *al-Masjid al-Ḥarām* in Mecca, the Prophet's Mosque in Medina, and *al-Masjid al-Aqṣā* in Jerusalem.[83] This *ḥadīth* has the virtue of not ordering the three cities in any explicit sequence of precedence and could thus be combined with other material that emphasized the merits of one of the three while maintaining the exclusivity of the triad. Thus, the eighth-century religious scholar al-Ḥasan al-Baṣrī, in one of the earliest *faḍāʾil* treatises, urges a friend not to move away from Mecca, as the spiritual benefits of *mujāwara*, or full-time residence within a holy city for pious purposes, outweigh the benefits of living anywhere else in the Islamic world. He quotes the "*ḥadīth* of the three mosques," but follows it up quickly by reporting Muḥammad's saying: "A prayer in my mosque [in Medina] is worth 1,000 prayers in any other mosque, with the exception of *al-Masjid al-Ḥarām*, for a prayer there is worth 100,000 prayers anywhere else. A prayer in *al-Masjid al-Aqṣā* is worth 500 prayers elsewhere."[84] Despite this nod to the cities of Medina and Jerusalem, al-Ḥasan al-Baṣrī is concerned with impressing upon his audience Mecca's unequaled gravitational pull on the pious. Throughout the treatise, he uses the rhetorical strategy of repeating the comparative construction, "There is no town (*balda*) on the face of the earth more _____ than Mecca," thus rejecting any other claimants or aspirants to Mecca's status as the territorial epicenter of sanctity for Muslims.[85]

Not surprisingly, works devoted to Medina and Jerusalem tend to strike a more defensive tone, relying on frequent comparisons with Mecca to fulfill the more modest goal of establishing their city on the same, or close to the same, level. For instance, both al-Wāsiṭī and Abū l-Maʿālī quote the "*ḥadīth* of the three mosques" in the introductions to their *faḍāʾil* treatises on Jerusalem, though other traditions admit to Mecca's precedence as the destination for hajj, while maintaining Jerusalem's related, though lesser, status as a pilgrimage city, as in: "[Performing] the hajj is preferable to [performing] two *ʿumra*s, and [performing] an *ʿumra* is preferable to a trip to Jerusalem."[86] Occasionally, the implication is that Medina or Jerusalem surpasses Mecca in one or another category of holiness, such as Jerusalem's claim to be the gathering place of the faithful on Judgment Day, to which even the Kaʿba would be conducted at the end of time, or Medina's claim to be the city (and place of death) of the Prophet Muḥammad.[87] Al-Janadī, in his tenth-century *faḍāʾil* treatise on Medina, assembles traditions that exhort their audience not to neglect Medina, as even if Mecca could be associated with Abraham, Medina could be associated with Muḥammad, God's last messenger whose revelation superseded all that came before.[88]

The "*ḥadīth* of the three mosques" notwithstanding, other cities occasionally entered the fray. For instance, al-Rabaʿī's eleventh-century *faḍāʾil* treatise on Damascus proclaims that a prayer in Mecca is worth 100,000 prayers elsewhere; a prayer in Medina is worth 50,000 prayers elsewhere; a prayer in Jerusalem 40,000 prayers elsewhere; and a prayer in Damascus 30,000 prayers elsewhere.[89] Moreover, the next tradition asserts that a prayer on a certain spot within the Umayyad Mosque is worth the same as a prayer in Jerusalem.[90] Kufa, associated with reverence for ʿAlī and the Shiite tradition, occasionally appears as a fourth destination for pious visitation in variants of the "*ḥadīth* of the three mosques" and is sometimes linked to Mecca, Medina, and Jerusalem in legends establishing the order of creation.[91] Hebron too, as the burial place of Abraham, receives its own tributes as a destination for pilgrimage.[92] Moreover, world and regional geographies represent a wide range of cities by listing their *mazārāt,* or such places of pious visitation as shrines, tombs, and sites associated with figures in sacred history or the wonders (*ʿajāʾib*) of God's creation, that attracted travelers, pilgrims, and curiosity seekers.[93]

The reason these rivalries, especially over the question of sanctity, mattered was because they implied that loyalty to a city or cities was a universalist and normative expectation for Muslims. For example, the geographer al-Muqaddasī repeatedly uses the possessive, *baladunā,* "our town," in praising Jerusalem to a skeptical group of scholars in Basra:

> I was asked: "What town is the most glorious?" I said: "Our town." It was then said: "Which is the most pleasant?" And I said: "Our town." It was then said: "Which is the most meritorious?" And I said: "Our town." It was then said: "Which is the most beautiful?" And I said: "Our town." It was then said: "Which has the most treasures?" And I said: "Our town." It was then said: "Which is the largest?" And I said: "Our town." Those at the assembly were astonished at that.

Al-Muqaddasī's responses to the questions put to him in this passage could be interpreted as an assertion of local pride, since Jerusalem was his hometown. However, when he defends his claims to the "astonished" assembly, he expresses loyalty to Jerusalem in universalist terms:

> As for my saying that it is the most glorious, it is because it is a town that joins this world with the next. Whoever is of the sons of this world but wants to go to the next will find impetus to it there; whoever is of the sons of the next world but whose spirit calls for the blessings of this world will find them there. As for the pleasantness of its climate, there is no bite to its cold, nor harm in its heat. And as for its beauty, you will not see more beautiful nor cleaner than its buildings, nor more revered than its mosque. As for the abundance of its treasures, God has gathered in it fruits from the valleys, from the plain, and from the mountains, as well as the opposite kinds of things, such as citrons and almonds, dates and walnuts, figs and bananas, as well as an abundance of milk, honey, and sugar. As for its merits, it is the theatre of the [final] judgment and the site of congregation and resurrection [on Judgment Day]; even if Mecca and Medina are more meritorious because of the Kaʿba and the Prophet, on Judgment Day they will both be conducted

> in solemn procession to Jerusalem, and then all merits will be revived there. As for the great size of Jerusalem, all of creation will congregate there [on Judgment Day], so what land could be more spacious?[94]

Al-Muqaddasī thus stages a performance within a text representing the virtues of the city of Jerusalem as relevant to all Muslims, linked to its role as the site of the Final Judgment. This performance, in which the author distinguishes himself in front of an audience of Iraqi scholars, recalls the popularity of *adab*-style oral debate in this period and suggests that staging similar performances in the world outside of the text was a recognized way to accumulate cultural, economic, and political capital.

Performing loyalty to cities was advantageous not only for the performers but also for the cities themselves, both of which might benefit from increased attention and patronage. Even if the material used to communicate the virtues of a city could be seen as controversial, the expectation that people had strong attachment to cities may have neutralized the controversy, or the material itself may have become more mainstream in its reproduction over time. For instance, the original circulation of *ḥadīth*s praising Medina may have been initiated by its inhabitants as a challenge to the Abbasids, who were wary of the potential threat to their authority posed by descendants of the Prophet living there, or as a fund-raising tool for a city that was beset by economic woes and emigration. However, the proliferation of texts drawing from this material over the centuries was motivated by its widely understood usefulness for establishing the intellectual and religious authority of the authors, most of whom were not residents of the city.[95] Similarly, even if the circulation of *ḥadīth*s praising Jerusalem was instigated by the Umayyad regime in late-seventh-century Syria for the polemical purpose of deflecting attention from their rivals in the Ḥijāz, later works, such as the *faḍāʾil* treatises by Abū l-Maʿālī and al-Wāsiṭī and Nāṣir-i Khusraw's travelogue, were composed in the context of well-established practices of pilgrimage to the city and can be seen as encouraging the continuation of this practice and exhibiting the piety of the authors to a broad audience.[96]

Expressing attachment to cities less closely associated with Islamic cosmology, eschatology, and religious authority than Mecca, Medina, and Jerusalem might also be a useful method of gaining recognition and asserting belonging in universalist terms. The introductory representation of Isfahan in Abū Nuʿaym's eleventh-century biographical dictionary, which opens with multiple variants of a *ḥadīth* in which the Prophet praises the semilegendary Iranian Salmān al-Fārisī as the ideal Muslim, must be understood as a vehicle for inserting the city, rather than some more particularist or separatist concept of the Persian people, into a salvation history of Islam.[97] This text makes Isfahan legible as a city through name, conquest narrative, and built environment, combining an emphasis on the antiquity and complexity of the city's past with its close, and ongoing, relationship to the caliphate.[98] Abū Nuʿaym's opening claim to the symbolic figure of Salmān and emphasis on Isfahan's proximity, both physical and symbolic, to the Abbasid regime represent the city as a category of belonging in universalist and inclusive terms.

This use of the particularities of a plot of land to assert belonging in universalist and inclusive terms is suggestive of a broader aspiration to a heterogeneous, but nonetheless unified, vision of the Islamic *umma*, or worldwide community of Muslims. This aspiration emerges prominently in the discourse of place from the tenth century on, when the strength of the caliphate and unity of the Islamic world had suffered sustained blows with the emergence of semi-independent "successor" states on its peripheries and the assumption of day-to-day control over its center by a dynasty of Persian-speaking warrior-kings, the Buyids, whose authority was only nominally subject to the Abbasid caliph in Baghdad. The normative expectation of some form of urban loyalty among Muslims in this period meant that representing cities could be an acceptable and nonthreatening method of making unconventional voices heard and incorporating them into the *umma*. The strategies of naming and locating a city, assembling a foundation or conquest narrative, and describing an urban built environment emphasized connectivity and facilitated diverse claims to allegiance and authority in a proliferation of texts—*faḍāʾil* treatises, topographical histories, and geographies—that may have neutralized otherwise controversial material. More than ever at a time of political fragmentation and decentralization, attachment to land made possible the expression and legitimization of pluralist forms of belonging.

PART THREE

REGION

4

Dividing the World

The larger scale of the region allowed for an even greater degree of inclusivity and heterogeneity in crafting territorial categories of belonging in the discourse of place. While it was more expansive than a city, the region could still be distinguished from the world as a whole by a degree of particularity and boundedness. The region thus offered the perfect size at which to imagine land as a category of belonging at once particular and universal, linked to a certain claim to religious or political authority but at the same time open and available to anyone willing to support that claim. Although regions were less visible than cities on the ground, their treatment in texts indicates that they were imagined and widely recognized as coherent and meaningful geographical entities not reducible to a major urban area and its hinterland. Regional toponyms and their territorial referents did not remain constant in this period, but they were also not entirely contingent on the administrative decisions or political pretensions of the regime in power. The discourse of place both produced and reflected patterns of regional thought that testify to the persistence of land-based categories of belonging at a variety of scales in the early Islamic world.

Authors who composed works representing regions hailed from the same variety of backgrounds as those who represented cities, and many of them wrote about both. In fact, representations of regions almost always included representations of cities (though the converse was not true). For this reason, one possible definition for a region would be a plot of land that could lay claim to more than one city. However, a region was not simply the sum of its cities. It was a meaningful territorial entity that bound together and transcended its urban nodes. Moreover, a region was brought into relationship with the entirety of the world in the discourse of place in a way that only occasionally happened with cities. To be sure, certain cities—namely Jerusalem and Baghdad—were described as the "navel of the earth," implying cosmological precedence and proximity to the heavens in the case of the former and a central location on the earth's surface in the case of the latter. By contrast, regions were almost always portrayed in terms of their location on the earth and their alignment with the cosmos, but they also enjoyed coherence independent of calculations of longitude and latitude.

Because of their relationship to the world as a whole, regions were most explicitly represented in the discourse of place by geographical works, especially those associated with the emerging field of "human geography." This field of thought, which flourished between the ninth and eleventh centuries, brought together the best of two broad intellectual orientations: the omnivorous sensibilities of the world of *adab*, and the scientific inquiry into the size and shape of the earth's surface encouraged by the Abbasid caliphs in order, among other things, to facilitate the administration of the vast territories under their control.[1] Thus, the category of region, in contrast to the categories of home and city, was often the product of an intersection between technical and administrative considerations, on the one hand, and humanist interests, such as history and *adab*, on the other.

This chapter examines the textual practice of dividing the world in the geographical literature of this period. From the latitudinal clime system, to the circular *kishwar* system, to systems of dividing the world based on more overtly Islamic criteria, the resulting regions were endowed with meanings that differentiated peoples as well as plots of land. The two most common textual strategies for representing regions—locating them along routes and demarcating them as realms—set up an expectation of interactivity, recreating movement along routes and between realms that anticipated movement from the audience, both on the ground and in the imagination. These strategies, like those used to evoke cities, crafted regions as categories of belonging in open-ended and universalist terms while maintaining the particularity of their political and religious associations.

From the World to the Region

Thus far this book has not dealt directly with ideas of the world (*ʿālam, dunyā*) or the earth (*arḍ*) as a whole, though of course an assumption of such ideas underpins the very notion of attachment to land. It is clear that early Muslims understood the world both as a wonder of God's creation and as a set of physical realities that contained the conditions of their earthly existence.[2] The necessity of navigating by the stars in the desert-seas of Arabia as well as the importance of determining the prayer direction toward Mecca ensured that the earliest Muslims possessed knowledge of their position on the earth and its interrelation with the cosmos.[3] Moreover, in the great intellectual ferment that sprang from the intensification of encounters between peoples during the expansion of Muslim rule in the seventh and eighth centuries, the scholarly classes of the Umayyad and early Abbasid Caliphates developed competing notions of how to measure and divide the world. Thanks to the Abbasid Caliph al-Maʾmūn's patronage of scholarship and the "translation movement" he sponsored, texts from Indo-Persian and Hellenistic traditions of learning were translated into Arabic, revised, and in many cases improved in Baghdad beginning in the first half of the ninth century.[4] At the same time the culture of *adab* was on the ascendant, embracing simultaneously the polyphonic literary heritage of the early Islamic world and the importance of performing it in Arabic. Add to this the administrative requirements of controlling the vast territories claimed by the Abbasids, and it is clear that the cultivation of knowledge about the nature of the world and the identification and interrelationship of its constituent parts was fed from a variety of wellsprings and put to a variety of purposes from the ninth century on.

One of the fruits of the translation movement was the dissemination of the oeuvre of the second-century Greek scholar Claudius Ptolemy. In particular, the theories he advances in the *Almagest*, a work on astronomy, and the *Geography*, a practical guide to cartography, contributed greatly to efforts to determine the shape and size of the earth and to bring the contours of its surface into relationship with celestial bodies. Ptolemy's presentation of preexisting theories of a geocentric universe and a spherical world divided into inhabited (or known) and uninhabited (or unknown) portions were widely consumed and regurgitated in various forms in ninth- and tenth-century Arabic geography and cosmography. However, it was his division of the world into latitudinal "climes" parallel to the equator, based in large part on the earlier work of Marinus of Tyre, that captured the attention of Baghdad's intellectuals. The Arabic term for clime (*iqlīm*, pl. *aqālīm*) would become a frequent signifier for regional entities in the discourse of place, regardless of whether the regional entity so signified had the remotest resemblance to the Ptolemaic system. The coordinates of the climes into which Ptolemy divided the inhabited world were calculated on the basis of the longest day, with the length of daylight at each parallel differing by a set interval from the twelve-hour equatorial day. In his *Geography*, Ptolemy calculated the boundaries of twenty-three climes, twenty-one above and two below the equator, beyond which, it was believed, human life was impossible.[5] It followed that the central clime, equidistant from both extremes, enjoyed the greatest benefits of temperate climate, seasonal variation, and generally salubrious conditions. Conveniently for the scholars of the early Abbasid Caliphate, the coordinates of the city of Baghdad placed it at the center of this system.

Despite its popularity in the discourse of place, the clime system only features in Ptolemy's *Geography* when he is giving instructions for preparing a world map at the start of the work. Moreover, the system he presents is noteworthy for its departure from earlier conventions that divided the inhabited world into only seven climes. In the rest of the *Geography*, which is dominated by latitude and longitude tables for well-known cities, rivers, mountain ranges, and other features of the earth's surface, not only does Ptolemy eschew the clime system completely, but he uses, at least in part, what seem to have been the administrative boundaries of the provinces of the Roman and Parthian Empires to organize his data.[6] Thus, the seven-clime system that is invoked repeatedly in the discourse of place is only very loosely Ptolemaic in origin. It is perhaps not surprising that no Arabic translation of Ptolemy's *Geography* survives, if one was ever made. It may have been that Ptolemy was a name, like al-Jāḥiẓ in the world of *adab*, more useful for conferring the authority of an ancient tradition on systems of dividing the world than it was for shaping the particulars of those systems.

Similarly elusive is the world atlas commissioned by the Caliph al-Maʾmūn, known as "al-Ṣūra al-Maʾmūniyya," in which Ptolemy's principles and data were allegedly applied and revised. However, a handful of scholars assembled Arabic tables of longitude and latitude that may have been taken from or used in the preparation of just such an atlas, the earliest surviving example of which is the *Ṣūrat al-arḍ* (Image of the earth) by the ninth-century Muḥammad b. Mūsā al-Khwārazmī.[7] While the latitudes of numerous locations in this work are identical to those in Ptolemy's *Geography*, longitudes were calculated differently, many locations added, and all coordinates organized in terms of the seven-clime system rather than in terms of Ptolemy's politico-administrative regions.[8] A half-century later, an obscure scholar known simply as Suhrāb compiled a similar work, *Kitāb ʿajāʾib al-aqālīm al-sabʿa ilā nihāyat al-ʿimāra* (Book of the wonders of the seven climes up to the limits of civilization), which opens with a diagram for a world map in which the seven parallel climes are stacked one atop the other within a rectangular frame.[9] The tables of longitude and latitude for cities that follow this diagram are organized by clime, each of which is introduced by a capsule description associating it with one or two particular toponyms, a celestial body, and two signs of the zodiac, as in the following for the fourth, or central, clime: "It is Babylon (*Bābil*) and Iraq and for celestial bodies it has the sun and for zodiac signs it has Taurus and Libra."[10] The climes thus presented were more than products of mathematical calculations; they were entities that gained meaning from terrestrial (and celestial) focal points. Given that Suhrāb's table of coordinates for the fourth clime includes cities as far west as Tangiers, located in present-day Morocco, and as far east as Herat, located in present-day Afghanistan, his opening identification of the clime with Babylon and Iraq cannot be taken as merely descriptive.[11] He is symbolically associating the fourth clime with particular plots of land rather than others, even though he is technically acknowledging its broader, mathematically determined, territorial expanse. Thus, even at its most technical, the practice of dividing the world in the discourse of place endowed its subdivisions—regions—with meanings, meanings that may be indirectly, if at all, related to the technical accomplishments on display.

The Ptolemaic, or pseudo-Ptolemaic, system was not the only way of seeing and dividing the world in the ninth century. Another system, derived most likely from Indo-Persian traditions of geography, replaced the latitudinal clime with a circular region (*kishwar*), six of which were arrayed around a central circle, usually associated with "Īrānshahr," the ancient name for the area dominated by Persian imperial culture that stretched loosely from the Euphrates River in the west to the Oxus River in the east.[12] The early-eleventh-century polymath Abū al-Rayḥān Muḥammad b. Aḥmad al-Bīrūnī provides the most straightforward description of this system, including a diagram assigning to each *kishwar* a set of toponyms and indicating which toponyms refer to border areas between regions.[13] Al-Bīrūnī is adamant that this was a system devised for purely political purposes:

> The reason for this division is that the great kings were natives of Īrānshahr, which consists of Iraq, Fārs, al-Jibāl, and Khurāsān. During the dawn of creation and before the spread of mankind over various regions, some of those great kings subjugated all these kingdoms. Such kings had to come down on the central region to satisfy their own ambitions and to take freely whatever they wanted. Some did not rule over it, in particular, those who reigned after Alexander. However, any one of these kings was regarded with considerable reverential fear. His menace was warded off by annual tributes, and by propitiation with gifts and gestures of friendship. He was in need of a definite settlement of the demarcation lines between the kingdoms of others and his own. He also needed a prevailing influence to get what he wanted, and to instill in all those surrounding him a state of fear of his might and a desire for his friendship. Those partitions were called *keshvar*, which is derived from the Persian word (*keshettah*) for line, to signify that each partition is distinguishable from the others, like what is bounded by lines.

In this passage, al-Bīrūnī is invoking a long history of dividing the world into regions that could be clearly separated one from the other by borderlines. These borders reflected political reality and were reinforced by the necessity of regulating relations between polities. Indeed, he protests, "This partition has nothing to do with natural climatic conditions, nor with astronomical phenomena. It is made according to kingdoms which differ from one another for various reasons—different features of their peoples and different codes of morality and customs." He goes on to attribute to the Greeks, "who invariably adopted pragmatic and realistic methods in their work," the more technical method of dividing the world into latitudinal climes.[14]

Despite al-Bīrūnī's differentiation between the *kishwar* and clime systems, and by implication the Indo-Persian and Hellenistic approaches to dividing the world, many authors seemed to blend the two and generally used the term "clime" (*iqlīm*) to refer to regional entities of different size, shape, and provenance.[15] For instance, the tenth-century historian ʿAlī b. al-Ḥusayn al-Masʿūdī clearly favors a system of seven circular "climes" in his abridged world geography and history, *Kitāb al-tanbīh wa-l-ishrāf* (Book of admonition and supervision), although he admits to differences of opinion on the issue. According to "the sages and philosophers of [various] peoples":

> The division into climes of the northern part of the inhabited world has been made in a circle, and the fourth clime, which is the clime of Babylon, has been made the center and the [other] six in a circle around it. Each clime is 700 *farsakh*s or thereabouts. The first is India, the second is the Ḥijāz and Ethiopia, the third is Egypt (*Miṣr*) and North Africa (*Ifrīqiyya*), the fourth Babylon and Iraq, the fifth Byzantium (*al-Rūm*), the sixth Gog and Magog, and the seventh Yawamārīs and China.[16]

The explicit circular organization of these climes distinguishes them from the latitudinal clime system, but al-Masʿūdī equates each clime with the same "snapshot" toponyms as Suhrāb in his tables of longitude and latitude, as well as al-Bīrūnī in his avowedly geopolitical *kishwar* diagram.[17] Further confusing the issue, al-Masʿūdī gives the last word to the Hellenistic tradition in the conclusion to the section: "I have seen these climes portrayed in multicolored illustrations in a number of books, and the best that I have seen among them is the *Geography* by Marinus—'geography' meaning sections of the earth—and 'al-Ṣūra al-Maʾmūniyya,' commissioned by the Caliph al-Maʾmūn."[18] This general overlap between systems produces a sense that the seven climes were at times no more than a convenient numbering system for divisions of the world already understood in terms of particular names and meanings and having little to do with the ancient geographical traditions being invoked explicitly or implicitly as authorities.

Helping to clarify these meanings, al-Masʿūdī waxes descriptive on the topic of the fourth and central clime in his system, which he identifies with the toponym Babylon. First he explains his use of this toponym to refer to a region comprising a much broader territorial expanse than would normally be associated with the ancient city, an expanse stretching from the Oxus River in the northeast to the Arabian Peninsula in the southwest:

> If what comprises this clime all together is known as "Babylon," it is only because of the excellence of its site and the splendor of its area, as people of learning tend to associate things with the most excellent and famous [among them]. If Babylon were not thus, they would not

> associate it with this clime, which has su… nt of land and is comprised of such splendid countries.

Thus, the toponym Babylon is a metonym for the fourth clime as a whole, a word that conjures ancient glory and conveys the positive light in which the wider region should be regarded. Next he describes one of the reasons for that regard, the salubrious conditions it enjoys by virtue of its central location:

> This clime is the center of the seven climes; it is the most temperate and the best. The country (*balad*) of Iraq is at its center; it is the noblest and choicest on earth. Life there is easy and the air is fresh; neither hot nor cold are excessive there. It is located on a site in which time is apportioned in four parts. Its inhabitants do not move from winter to summer without experiencing the season of spring, nor from summer to winter without experiencing the season of fall.[19]

Centrality, however, has other, more profound, repercussions for what makes this region distinctive in his world system of climes, repercussions that hearken back to the connotations of the toponym Babylon. Al-Masʿūdī explains that it is this centrality that has made the fourth clime the headquarters of great empires since ancient times:

> As we have mentioned, its centrality was what caused the kings of ancient peoples to settle there, since the relationship of a king to a kingdom is as the heart to the body it is in. Just as God almighty in his considerable wisdom created the heart as the noblest of the organs and accordingly situated it in the center of the body, so kings take up residence in this manner in their kingdoms. The monarchs of old used to say that a great king is the center of the circle of his kingdom, so that his distance from its circumference is the same everywhere; he is a fixed pole and a hoisted standard, from which administration emanates and to which all matters return. For this reason, it is said that a great king and a mighty administrator must take up a central residence in this, the fourth, clime.

Al-Masʿūdī stipulates that this central residence should be in Iraq, "where the Tigris and Euphrates come together and the surrounding Sawād, an area that has for limits the two Zābs (tributaries of the Tigris River) north of Samarra, including [the towns of] al-Sinn and Tikrīt, and the district (*nāḥiya*) of Ḥulwān, including [parts of] al-Jabal, and the district (*nāḥiya*) of Hīt, including [parts of] the Euphrates and Syria (*al-Shām*)."[20] This vision of Iraq, which is fairly precisely delineated, is conceived as but a part, though the most politically important one, of the extensive territories comprised by the fourth clime. Thus, in constructing this region, al-Masʿūdī has identified three concentric circles of land, one focusing on the site of the ancient city of Babylon but symbolically conjuring the virtues of the fourth clime as a whole; another comprising the "country" (*balad*) of Iraq, in which the political center of the clime, if not the world, should be situated; and finally, another more broadly encompassing the entire fourth clime, a circle at the center of the inhabited world.

This description combines what can be thought of as more technical considerations of climate and location on the earth's surface with more theoretical and practical considerations of history and politics. It also seems to combine insights derived from the Greek and Indo-Persian literatures disseminated during the translation movement, and certainly the focus on Mesopotamia as an ancient imperial center suggests a Persian orientation.[21] However, all of these ideas were so mutually reinforcing as to be inseparable in terms of their influence on the representation of regions in the discourse of place. Not only did Ptolemy make use of well-known politico-administrative regions to organize some of his technical data, but theories of astrology and climatic determinism brandished by Greek historians and geographers centuries before Ptolemy obviously endow the divisions of the world described in al-Masʿūdī's oeuvre with ethnographic and geopolitical meaning.[22] By the coming of Islam, many thinkers had endorsed the idea that the relationship between a technically identifiable location on the earth's surface and a celestial body had the capacity to produce physical conditions of heat, cold, humidity, or aridity that imprinted themselves upon its inhabitants, influencing not only their appearance but also their temperament and aptitudes for different pursuits, including statecraft.

Al-Masʿūdī provides an extensive discussion of such climatic determinism at the beginning of the *Kitāb al-tanbīh wa-l-ishrāf*.[23] First, he divides the world into four quarters, each of which lies at one of the four compass points. The eastern and southern quarters enjoy closer proximity to the sun than the western and northern, and the eastern and western quarters enjoy more temperate conditions than the southern and northern. Thus, the eastern quarter profits most from both proximity to the sun and temperate conditions: "It is a male quarter, indicating longevity, both in years and in duration of sovereignty, memory, strength of character, disinclination to secrecy, straightforwardness, pride, and all that relates to it, and these are [due to] the imprint of the sun [on its people], whose knowledge is of history, chronology, biography, statecraft, and astronomy." Al-Masʿūdī's discussion of the west, by contrast, invokes the influence of the moon, which he associates with the feminine: "Its inhabitants are secretive, religious, godly, and variable in terms of the espousal of opinions and creeds, and all that relates to it, because they are under the sway of the moon." The peoples of the north are described at the greatest length and with the greatest distaste: "Their bodies are strong; their characters are weak; their manners are uncouth; their comprehension is dull; and their tongues are heavy. Their skin is so white it is almost blue, and their skin is delicate, their flesh weak; their eyes are also blue, like the color of their skin, and their hair is lanky and reddish because of the humid vapors." Finally, in the south, "they are black-skinned and red-eyed, and their spirits are wild because the air is scorching."[24] The north and the south clearly represent extremes, inhospitable and tending towards the uninhabitable, their peoples adapting as best as possible to oppressive conditions. But the difference between east and west has to do with the character of the governing celestial body, a character al-Masʿūdī expresses here in gendered terms, associating the masculine with steadfastness and sovereignty and the feminine with variability and religiosity. It is clear that al-Masʿūdī's fourth clime, whatever its shape or parameters, is situated in the masculine eastern quarter, and the association of that quarter with the sun also resonates with the capsule description of the fourth clime in the more technical Ptolemaic work of his contemporary Suhrāb.[25]

Ideas reminiscent of climatic determinism were expressed, often with reference to Hippocrates and Galen, in making the connection between the human body and the soil, water, air, and food of the *waṭan*. Moreover, the humanistic spirit of *adab* encouraged a particular enthusiasm for connecting personality traits or cultural practices to different peoples or to different parts of the world, and sometimes to both, as in the famously stingy inhabitants of Khurāsān described by al-Jāḥiẓ in his landmark work *al-Bukhalāʾ* (The misers). Even the *ʿulamāʾ*, often assumed to be opposed to, or simply uninterested in, such profane considerations, understood regional and cultural difference in similar terms, often citing Qurʾān 49:13, which highlights God's purposeful division of the world into multifarious "peoples and tribes, that they might learn about each other."[26] These strands of thought were inextricably intertwined by the ninth century, and it made the division of the world an exercise not only in geography but in ethnography as well, an exercise that ideas about climatic determinism seemed to facilitate. Regions were thus frequently understood in terms of peoples (and vice versa), and regionalism emerged as a language for making claims to belonging or for mounting contests for religious or political authority by portraying the connection between particular groups of people and particular lands in the discourse of place. If in speaking the language of regionalism participants in the discourse of place availed themselves of Greek and Persian ideas, it was because they were useful and widely understood methods of compiling a catalog of regions and peoples and in ranking those regions and peoples. These ideas were easily adapted to, if not tailor-made for, the project of representing a regional entity that included the seat of the Abbasid Caliphate as the center of the inhabited world and of associating its people with political power and righteousness. However, later authors found these ideas flexible enough to reflect shifts in centers of power, as in the Ptolemaic work, *Kitāb gharāʾib al-funūn wa-mulāḥ al-ʿuyūn*, most likely authored in early-eleventh-century Egypt, which promotes the virtues of the third clime, that of Fatimid-ruled Egypt and North Africa, and its people in language that is very similar to that used for the fourth, while Baghdad and Iraq, toponyms associated with the Abbasid rivals to the Fatimids, go unmentioned.[27]

Methods of dividing the world that produced similar results could be expressed in terms of what might be called a more self-consciously Islamic form. In some works, the shape of the earth was conceived not as a sphere but as a bird, with each of its body parts corresponding to various regions and peoples. The image of the world as a bird is of unknown origin, but the following version quoted by Ibn al-Faqīh is attributed to ʿAbd Allāh b. ʿAmr b. al-ʿĀṣ (d. 63/683), son of the legendary Muslim conqueror of Egypt:

> The image of the world (*ṣūrat al-dunyā*) is made up of five parts, like the head of a bird, its two wings, its chest, and its tail. The head of the world is China, and beyond China is a people called Wāq-Wāq and beyond the Wāq-Wāq are peoples of whom only God knows the number. Its right wing is India and beyond India the sea, beyond which is nothing. Its left wing is al-Khazar, and beyond al-Khazar are two peoples, one of whom is called Manshak and the other Māshak, and beyond Manshak and Māshak is Gog and Magog full of peoples known only to God. The chest of the world is Mecca, the Ḥijāz, Syria, Iraq, and Egypt. Its tail is from Dhāt al-Ḥumām to al-Maghrib, and the worst part of a bird is its tail.[28]

This division of the world places at its center, or rather at its heart, the territories in which Muslim control had been consolidated during the lifetime of its late-seventh-century source, with the city of Mecca and the surrounding land of the Ḥijāz mentioned specifically in addition to the toponyms for Egypt, Syria, and Iraq. Curiously, it portrays the head and wings as areas that had yet to fall under Muslim suzerainty at the time of ʿAbd Allāh b. ʿAmr b. al-ʿĀṣ, and that were only partially known by Muslims at the time of Ibn al-Faqīh. Moreover, it consigns the North African coastline, an area ruled, if unevenly, by Muslims from an early period, to the "worst part of a bird ... its tail." What this suggests is an orientation generally eastward, privileging the heartlands of the Islamic world but reflecting, perhaps, an understanding of the differences between the character of peoples residing in the east, west, north, and south not unlike that expressed by al-Masʿūdī in his discussion of climatic determinism. A more local version of the world-as-bird tradition, this time on the authority of the Companion of the Prophet Qatāda b. Diʿāma, has Syria as the head, Egypt as the tail, and Iraq as the wing.[29] This seems to privilege the head of the bird, as it is quoted in an eleventh-century *faḍāʾil* treatise on Syria, and to thus make Iraq and perhaps especially Egypt peripheral, but it is noteworthy for not including any part of the world not ruled by Muslims. These divisions of the world are more obviously adversarial than the clime and *kishwar* systems and suggest a view of the earth as host to regions and peoples that are interrelated but unequal.

In al-Masʿūdī's longer world geography and history, *Murūj al-dhahab wa-maʿādin al-jawhar* (Meadows of gold and mines of jewels), he presents a division of the world into regions and peoples in the context of the seventh-century migration out of the Arabian Peninsula to settle territories newly brought under Muslim rule. In the following historical anecdote, ʿUmar b. al-Khaṭṭāb, asks a wise man to counsel him as to the character of the different areas advisable for settlement. The wise man responds first by laying out the principles of climatic determinism and then by describing the specific conditions of a series of regions and the characteristics of their peoples: Syria, Egypt, Yemen, al-Ḥijāz, Iraq, al-Jibāl, Khurāsān, Fārs, Khūzistān, and al-Jazīra.[30] Here is a representative extract:

> In Syria, clouds accumulate, swell, and burst, moistening bodies, dulling intelligence, and purifying complexions, especially the territory of Homs, which beautifies the body and purifies the complexion, even though comprehension is dull, attention wanders, dispositions are coarse, happiness is washed away, and minds are carried away. Despite what I have described, oh Commander of the Believers, in Syria pastures are fertile, rains pour forth, trees are abundant, rivers flow, and revenue is plentiful. It is host to the dwelling places of the prophets and Jerusalem the Elect. The nobility of God's creation, the righteous and the devout, have settled there. Its mountains are the residences of saintly hermits.[31]

Like Syria, each region is assigned both positive and negative attributes, reminiscent of the vogue for debate in the world of *adab*, and no region is represented by means of exact geographical coordinates or boundaries. The toponyms are simply assumed to be self-explanatory, except in the case of the Ḥijāz, which is clarified etymologically as a "barrier (*ḥājiz*) between Syria, Yemen, and al-Tahāʾim," and Khūzistān, which is glossed as "the districts (*kuwar*) of al-Ahwāz."[32] In general, however, the emphasis on climate and rural landscape and the occasional mention of constituent cities suggests that these territorial entities should be understood as regions. At the end of the list, the wise man makes a point of excluding India, China, and Byzantium as "there is no use my describing them to you, since they are remote and distant, countries of infidels and despots."[33] Thus, while there are definite disadvantages to settling in any of the territories under Muslim control, those not under Muslim control are perceived as beyond the pale, unworthy even of description.[34]

The patriarch of the world of *adab*, al-Jāḥiẓ, supports a generally hierarchical division of the world by arguing that the earth's regions and peoples must be ranked according to universal Islamic principles rather than according to human nature, which tends to regard the homeland (*waṭan*) as the best of all countries. In the introduction to his *Kitāb al-buldān* (Book of countries), a partially extant geographical essay, he explains:

> If it were not incumbent on us to put first what God put first and to put last what he put last, the majority would mention the homelands (*awṭān*) [first], because of the place they occupy in the human heart. It used to be said: "God populated the countries (*buldān*) by means of love of homeland (*ḥubb al-awṭān*)." And Ibn al-Zubayr said: "There is nothing in people's lots more satisfying to them than their homelands (*awṭān*)." If it were not for the desire that God stirs up in each generation for that which they possess and his casting in a positive light that which is in their power, and were that not implanted in their minds and in the preferences of their spirits, the peoples of jungles and thickets would not dwell in the damp and the mud, nor would they live with the mosquitoes and the gnats; the peoples of the countryside would not dwell on the summits of mountains; the peoples of the desert would not stay among the wolves and the vipers where "he who overcomes takes the spoil"; the peoples of the outermost parts would not stay among the perils and the dangers; and the peoples of caves and the bottoms of valleys would not be content with these dwellings. All would seek to live at the center, in the heart of the Arabs, in a secure and well-defended abode.[35]

This passage combines the rhetoric of climatic determinism with the language of the *waṭan* and attributes them both to the divine will. It makes clear that the surface of the earth is apportioned between peoples unequally, but God's consolation is instilling love of the homeland in all hearts, which causes attachment even to the meanest of terrestrial conditions and avoids overcrowding in the most comfortable and privileged of places. It also unequivocally equates centrality and precedence with "the heart of the Arabs … a secure and well-defended abode," which is an allusion to a Qurʾānic epithet for Mecca, the "city of security" (14:35, 95:3). Accordingly, al-Jāḥiẓ proceeds from here first to representations of Mecca and Medina and then continues with representations of the Banū Hāshim, the clan named for an ancestor of the Prophet Muḥammad, and the Banū Abī Ṭālib, the subclan named for the father of the Prophet's first cousin ʿAlī. In so doing, al-Jāḥiẓ relates these two "peoples," represented here as kinship groups, with a region that includes the cities of Mecca and Medina, "the heart of the Arabs." It is noteworthy that he does not call this region the heart of Islam, as he is associating a particularly privileged land with a particularly privileged people, rather than representing it as a category of universal Muslim belonging.[36]

Divisions of the world focused on the *qibla* did, however, represent the territory of Mecca as a lodestone for all Muslims, as the faithful were supposed to turn toward the Kaʿba in prayer no matter where they were located on the earth's surface. Thus, *qibla* charts, diagrams in which a circular world was partitioned along radii extending from the central Kaʿba, united people in sacred communion with Mecca even as they distinguished people regionally.[37] The first known division of the world according to the *qibla* comes from Abū l-Qāsim ʿUbayd Allāh b. ʿAbd Allāh b. Khurradādhbih's early ninth-century *Kitāb al-masālik wa-l-mamālik* (Book of routes and realms):

> The prayer direction (*qibla*) of the people of Armenia, Azerbaijan, Baghdad, Wāsiṭ, Kufa, al-Madāʾin, Basra, Ḥulwān, al-Dīnawar, Nihāwand, Hamadan, Isfahan, al-Rayy, Ṭabaristān, and Khurāsān, all of them, and the countries (*bilād*) of the Khazars and Kashmir in India, which extend to the left of the north pole [along the arc of the horizon] to the midpoint of the east, is toward the wall of the Kaʿba in which its door is located. As for Tibet, the countries (*bilād*) of the Turks, China, and al-Manṣūra, which extend eight degrees beyond the midpoint of the east, their prayer direction (*qibla*) is close to the Black Rock. As for the prayer direction (*qibla*) of the people of Yemen, their prayer is toward the *Yamānī* (southern) corner, and they face in prayer the people of Armenia. As for the prayer direction (*qibla*) of the people of al-Maghrib, Ifrīqiyya, Egypt, Syria, and al-Jazīra, which is to say the midpoint of the west, their prayer is toward the *Shāmī* (northern) corner, and they face in prayer the people of al-Manṣūra.[38]

Ibn Khurradādhbih thus divides the world into four general groups of peoples, territories, and cities, which have in common a prayer direction but little else to unite them as a region. Nonetheless, the emphasis in this passage on the action of each group turning in prayer toward its designated portion of the Kaʿba can be read as a textual performance of regionalism. The implication is that the inhabitants of each region are united in ritual five times a day, a practice that entails both their awareness of a common position on the earth's surface and their imagination of a common focal point—a particular wall or corner of the Kaʿba. In another sense, however, the Kaʿba, and with it Mecca and the land of the Ḥijāz, stands at the center of the world, just as the kings of al-Masʿūdī's schema stand at the center of their circular regions, equidistant from—or equally present to—all of the faithful. What regionalism can be discerned here is subordinated to the universal magnetism of the Kaʿba, reinforced by the depiction of people of different regions facing each other, as well as the Kaʿba, during prayer.

Three tenth-century world geographies also privilege the Arabian Peninsula, home of Mecca and the Kaʿba, by presenting it first in the context of their works as a whole. At the same time, they each craft a greater regional category of Muslim belonging, called the *Mamlakat al-Islām* ("realm of Islam"), which has no clear center or focal point, such as Mecca or Baghdad, but which loosely conforms to the territorial extent of Muslim suzerainty in the mid-tenth century.[39] This lack of a clear focal point reflects the reality of multiple political centers in the period.[40] It is noteworthy that al-Muqaddasī, the premier geographer of this trio in some estimations, mentions the coexistence of two "Commanders of the Believers" in the Islamic world at the time of the composition of his work in 375/985, the Abbasid al-Ṭāʾiʿ in Baghdad and the Fatimid al-ʿAzīz in Cairo. Moreover, in one of the extant manuscripts of this work, another name is inserted at the end of the same sentence, that of the Samanid ruler in Bukhara, Nūh b. Manṣūr, "client (*mawlā*) of the Commander of the Believers."[41] Similarly, the other two geographies by Abū Isḥāq Ibrāhīm b. Muḥammad al-Iṣṭakhrī and Abū l-Qāsim Muḥammad b. Ḥawqal exhibit marked emphases on the eastern and western reaches of the *Mamlakat al-Islām*.[42] While Baghdad is accorded reverence in these works, its presence is nowhere near as central as it is in the geographies composed by Abbasid administrators of a century earlier, such as Ibn Khurradādhbih and al-Yaʿqūbī.

Moreover, although the term *mamlaka* in the singular suggests a unified entity, the description of the *mamlaka* as a whole occupies only a few pages in these works, which are otherwise devoted to the many subregions into which that entity could and should be divided. What unity the *Mamlakat al-Islām* is assigned in these few pages stems from its exclusion of portions of the inhabited world not under Muslim control at the time, notably Byzantium, India, and China, rather than on its political centralization.[43] That said, the world maps that accompany al-Iṣṭakhrī's and Ibn Ḥawqal's works nowhere indicate the territorial extent of the *Mamlakat al-Islām* (nor does any such toponym appear on the maps), which diminishes a sense of its boundedness and separability from the rest of the inhabited world. Instead, the toponyms for subdivisions of the *Mamlakat al-Islām* are often inscribed in small boxes and juxtaposed with toponyms, often in the same style, for subdivisions of the rest of the world, producing a regionalism that seems to depend on something other than the presence or absence of a Muslim ruler.[44] Al-Muqaddasī replaces the world map of his predecessors with a circular *qibla* chart divided into eight parts, which has the effect of isolating the *Mamlakat al-Islām* more fully from the rest of the world, but at the same time the visual emphasis is on its subdivisions.[45] If there is a unifying factor in the representation of the *Mamlakat al-Islām* in the geographies by al-Iṣṭakhrī, Ibn Ḥawqal, and al-Muqaddasī, it is not the presence of a Muslim ruler or isolation from the rest of the world, but the sense that both geographer and audience belong in and to the entirety of the *Mamlakat al-Islām*.[46] When al-Muqaddasī explains that he is not describing lands outside of the *Mamlakat al-Islām* because he "did not enter them and saw no use in mentioning them," he is effectively saying that he had no basis upon which to claim belonging to or in these lands and could see no reason to make or facilitate that claim for his audience.[47]

To the extent that the *Mamlakat al-Islām* is considered an identifiable region, like the climes and other territorial divisions, it is because of a conception of the entire or inhabited world from which it can be singled out on the basis of a particular coherence or meaning. Thus, whether they used the term clime (*iqlīm*), country (*bilād*), or realm (*mamlaka*), participants in the discourse of place made regions legible as meaningful divisions of the world as a whole. Sometimes this legibility involved the description of frontiers or dividing lines determined by mathematical calculations or political realities past and present. Sometimes it involved the close association of land and people according to theories of climatic determinism, divine design, or the ethnographic impulse current in the world of *adab*. Sometimes it involved simply the evocation of belonging in or to a region. The resulting regionalism was flexible enough to reflect changing political realities and different authorial agendas, and generally involved some form of hierarchy or ranking that established belonging in or to regions on particular bases rather than others. This emphasis on belonging, at times overt and at times muted, is what made the textual practice of dividing the world a statement of regionalism, and, conversely, it made the conceptualization of regions dependent on an understanding of the world as divided into territories that could be associated with peoples and meanings and peoples and meanings that could be associated with territories.

Itineraries and Nodes

If the concept of a region was dependent on, but distinct from, the concept of the world as a whole, it was also dependent on and distinct from the concept of a city. Representations of regions in the discourse of place often consist in large part of representations of cities. At first glance, some world geographies seem to treat regions as little more than convenient organizing mechanisms for their enumeration of cities. Others present cities in order of appearance along itineraries that traverse great stretches of territory and seem to ignore regional divisions.[48] On looking closer, however, it becomes clear that these works also communicate a sense of the areas between urban nodes and the boundedness of the regional entities in which they are located. Moreover, many world geographies relate cities to each other not only in terms of itineraries and networks of trade, administration, and communication but also in terms of regional claims to political and religious authority.

Among the earliest extant Arabic world geographies are two works that have been characterized as "administrative geographies" or "road books," since they are occupied primarily with recording distances between the cities controlled by the Abbasid Caliphate.[49] These late-ninth-century works, the *Kitāb al-masālik wa-l-mamālik* by Ibn Khurradādhbih and the *Kitāb al-buldān* by al-Yaʿqūbī, divide the world into quarters arrayed at compass points around Baghdad. Although Ibn Khurradādhbih opens with a division of the world centered on the Kaʿba, he quickly shifts his schema north and east to celebrate the centrality of the region of the Sawād, headquarters of the Abbasid caliph, whom he served as a director of postal and intelligence services (*ṣāḥib al-barīd wa-l-khabar*) and to whom the work may have been dedicated.[50] Similarly, al-Yaʿqūbī begins his work with lengthy descriptions of Baghdad and Samarra, "the two cities of the sovereign power, the two seats of the caliphate," and he too served the Abbasid caliph in administrative posts.[51] However, while both authors trace itineraries between cities located in quarters surrounding the same political and administrative center, they organize their routes in different ways, Ibn Khurradādhbih generally maintaining Baghdad as a central hub from which long-distance itineraries originate and al-Yaʿqūbī moving from one hub to another and charting shorter itineraries from each. This may have to do with the reality that al-Yaʿqūbī himself moved away from Baghdad, spending significant time in North Africa and ultimately composing his book in Cairo, while Ibn Khurradādhbih served his career mostly in the neighboring regions of Iraq and al-Jibāl.[52]

Despite this concern with establishing routes and distances between cities arrayed around an imperial center, both authors organize their data at least partially in terms of regions. Ibn Khurradādhbih opens his work not with the cities of Baghdad and Samarra, as does al-Yaʿqūbī, but with their region, the Sawād, which he describes as "what the kings of Persia called *dil Īrānshahr*, which is to say 'the heart of Iraq.'"[53] In this way, he immediately associates the Arabic toponym "al-Sawād" with the Persian toponym "Īrānshahr" and justifies it on the authority of pre-Islamic monarchs. He then divides the Sawād into twelve subregions, for which he uses the Arabicized term *kūra* linked with the Persian term *astān*, and then subdivides each of these further into entities to which he assigns the Persian term *ṭassūj* (pl. *ṭasāsīj*). By way of clarification, he writes: "The [Arabic] translation of *astān* is *iḥāza* (province), and the [Arabic] translation of *ṭassūj* is *nāḥiya* (district)."[54] After this lesson in Persian geographical nomenclature, he goes on to enumerate the Sawād's twelve subregions, using the composite term *kūra astān* to introduce each, and their constituent *ṭasāsīj*. Next, he lists each *ṭassūj*, its constituent rural areas (again, using a Persian term: *rustāq*, pl. *rasātīq*), the number of its threshing floors, and its annual land tax in wheat, barley, and silver coins.[55] This careful subdivision into territorial units of descending scale and markedly nonurban character is what constructs the Sawād as a region. Notably, the names of the principal cities that were located in these territorial units during Ibn Khurradādhbih's lifetime, including Baghdad, Samarra, Wāsiṭ, Kufa, and Basra, are nowhere to be found in this enumeration. Moreover, the emphasis on tax revenue in kind as well as in coin highlights the agricultural character of the region and deemphasizes the importance of urban areas to its representation. Finally, the use of Persian geographical nomenclature and, frequently, toponyms to identify each subdivision of the region also serves to diminish the aforementioned cities, all of which were founded in the Islamic era, as central to the representation of the region.

Ibn Khurradādhbih does not lavish the same attention on any other regional entity in his book, but he does intersperse sections enumerating provinces (*kuwar*) and rural areas (*rasātīq*) with sections supplying distances between cities on the long-distance itineraries he extends at compass points from Baghdad. As in the description of the Sawād, he ignores or minimizes urban areas in these enumerations. For instance, in his list of the provinces and rural areas associated with the toponym Isfahan, he does not include anything that can be clearly identified as the urban area by the same name, nor does he mention its alternate names "Jayy" or "al-Yahūdiyya." Instead, he writes of Isfahan: "The provinces (*kuwar*) of Isfahan are eighty farsakhs by eighty farsakhs, and it has seventeen rural areas (*rasātīq*) in each of which can be found 365 old villages (*qarya qadīma*), not counting the modern ones. Its land tax is seven million dirhams, and it is a large territory (*arḍ*), populous and thriving, with salubrious air."[56] This "Isfahan" is a regional entity, represented in terms of area rather than as a network of urban nodes.[57] In other works, cities are represented in relation to dependent or surrounding plots of land of various sizes. The region often acts merely as a textual catchment basin that enables the author to collect a wider range of material and associate it with the city.[58] By contrast, the territorial referents for many of Ibn Khurradādhbih's toponyms are represented as broad areas that must in turn be subdivided, a representation often reinforced by measurements of length and width, if not exact boundaries. These sections do not conjure an image of a central urban node exerting a kind of gravitational pull on dependent or surrounding plots of land. Instead, they emphasize the regional and rural character of the toponyms, even if terrain is not evoked in great detail.

As Ibn Khurradādhbih moves from the eastern to the western, northern, and southern quarters of the world, his regions lose some of their consistency and independence from representations of cities. Part of the reason for this may be that only the eastern quarter allows him to display the full range of his knowledge of pre-Islamic Persian administrative practice, which involved the division of regions into agricultural units for the purposes of taxation.[59] His interest in displaying such knowledge explains his overwhelming use of Persian geographical nomenclature and toponyms for this quarter, as well as his relative neglect of the big cities founded in the Islamic era or, as he puts it in his section on Isfahan, "modern" cities. Notably, his descriptions of the non-Islamic and non-Persian imperial capitals Rome and Constantinople are longer than any other description of a city in the work. Ibn Khurradādhbih's eastern regions are, therefore, platforms for the performance of a certain kind of authority, anchored in the Persian imperial past rather than the Islamic imperial present.

Al-Yaʿqūbī, on the other hand, clearly saw the representation of cities as central to the representation of the Islamic world and to an assertion of authority anchored in the imperial present. Accordingly, al-Yaʿqūbī's regionalism is both more city-centric and more concerned with the settlement and governance of cities and regions after the coming of Islam than is Ibn Khurradādhbih's. He generally appends thumbnail conquest or foundation narratives to the major cities he mentions along his itineraries, and the narratives are quite extensive for cities that could be associated with caliphal authority past or present, such as Baghdad, Samarra, and Kufa. He also almost always assesses what might be described loosely as the ascribed identity of the inhabitants of each plot of land traversed in his work, specifically whether they are "Arab" (*ʿarab*) or "non-Arab" (*ʿajam*), often modified by a phrase denoting specific genealogical or tribal affiliation. Thus, his concern with the inhabitants of territories is the same as with cities: how they were defined under Islamic rule, when the distinction between "Arab" and "non-Arab" became salient.[60] At times he distinguishes between subgroups of "Arabs" and "non-Arabs" by territory of origin, such as "Arabs" who hailed from Yemen. Similar examples arise when he wants to emphasize the status of the inhabitants of a particular plot of land as having emigrated from somewhere else, as in the "non-Arabs" of Khurāsān who settled in North Africa or the troops of the military-administrative districts (*jund*, pl. *ajnād*) of Syria who settled in the Iberian Peninsula after the fall of the Umayyad Caliphate.[61] In his representations of the cities along his routes and the peoples encountered along the way, al-Yaʿqūbī's emphasis is firmly in the categories of belonging constructed since the coming of Islam.

His representations of regions vary considerably depending on the part of the Islamic world being described. To the east of Baghdad, al-Yaʿqūbī sketches comparatively short itineraries, from one to ten days' journey, linking major cities. After "arriving" at each major city, he lists its dependent towns and settlements and the yearly land tax revenue. What regions emerge from these eastern lands, therefore, are generally termed "provinces" (*kuwar*) and identified by the names of their central cities. At the same time, he indicates broader regional designations that cut across or complicate the city-centered provinces that appear along his itineraries. For example, at the city of Ḥulwān he explains, "even though it is among the provinces (*kuwar*) of al-Jabal, its land tax is incorporated into the land tax of the districts (*ṭasāsīj*) of al-Sawād."[62] Thus, two regions, "al-Jabal" and "al-Sawād," apparently have claims on the city and/or subregion of Ḥulwān. Neither broader region, however, is represented directly by al-Yaʿqūbī. Further east, only the territories of Sijistān and Khurāsān receive direct attention as regions that transcend their urban nodes, but through enumerations of their governors (*wulāh*) since the mid-seventh century, rather than sketches of their districts, terrains, or boundaries.[63] Thus, al-Yaʿqūbī evokes these regions in terms of the authorities appointed by the caliphs to rule them, suggesting simultaneously their semi-independent status as territorial entities and the subordination of their political personnel to the caliphate.

In the west, this concern with the territorial manifestation of political authority is much clearer, and al-Yaʿqūbī's regionalism is, perhaps consequently, more pronounced. In particular, his representation of the region ruled semiautonomously by the Aghlabid dynasty in the name of the Abbasid caliph is both the most detailed in terms of its territorial expanse and the most clearly dependent on a claim to political power. He sketches a series of ten itineraries extending in all directions, like the spokes of a wheel, from the North African city of Kairouan, and, though he never formally names the regional entity thus sketched, repeated references to the Aghlabids suggests that the territorial extent of their sovereignty could be superimposed on the territorial extent of the itineraries.[64] For instance, coming upon the eastern limit of one of his routes marked by the city of Qabīs, he writes: "It is the seat of a prefect appointed by Ibn Aghlab, ruler (*ṣāḥib*) of Ifrīqiyya."[65] In this way the toponym "Ifrīqiyya" is slipped into the representation, as if its association with the area covered by these itineraries was so widely understood as to need no further explanation. As al-Yaʿqūbī makes his way along the rest of his routes, he conveys a wealth of politico-administrative information, such as the fact that the current Aghlabid ruler lives eight miles outside of Kairouan at al-Raqqāda and that his prefects reside in towns up to ten days journey from Kairouan.[66] In addition, he notes that in territories (*balad, bilād*) along these routes certain Berber tribes have either refused to pay fealty to the Aghlabid sovereign or are in outright rebellion against him.[67] Al-Yaʿqūbī terminates his tenth itinerary in one of these areas, at "the city of Arba, which is the last city of [the territory of] al-Zāb going west, in the last province (*ʿamal*) governed by the Aghlabids, beyond which Abbasid authority does not extend."[68] This description identifies a territorial and political frontier, one that was associated at least symbolically with the Abbasid Caliphate even though it was the practical manifestation of semi-independent Aghlabid governance, or the limits thereof. While al-Yaʿqūbī's lists of the governors of Sijistān and Khurāsān are appended to the itineraries he sketches through these regions, here al-Yaʿqūbī inscribes political authority directly in areas along his itineraries, emphasizing the coincidence of territorial and political meaning in this region, which he obliquely identifies with the toponym "Ifrīqiyya," though more directly with the central node of Kairouan and the land encompassed by the perimeter of its radii.[69]

In other territories, though he is less explicit about associating political authority with land, he nonetheless emphasizes what were most likely politico-administrative subdivisions centered on principal cities. He often uses the more generic terms for "province," such as *kūra* in the east or *ʿamal* in the west, but occasionally he substitutes regionally specific nomenclature associated with politico-administrative practices past or present, such as the *mikhlāf* in Yemen, the *jund* in Syria, or the *ṭassūj* in the Sawād.[70] Moreover, he pays periodic attention to boundaries in ways that suggest a broader, politically salient regional awareness, one that simultaneously transcends and determines the nature of these subdivisions. Moving along the route from Syria to Egypt, for instance, he writes of the frontier: "to Rafaḥ, which is the last of the provinces (*aʿmāl*) of Syria, to a site that is called 'Two Trees,' which is the beginning of the border (*ḥadd*) with Egypt, then to al-ʿArīsh, which is the first of the frontier outposts (*masāliḥ*) of Egypt and the first of its provinces (*aʿmāl*)."[71] What is interesting about this passage is his use of the nonurban site of "Two Trees" to mark the start of a buffer zone between two regions and his description of al-ʿArīsh as a "frontier outpost," with connotations of fortification and vigilance, indicating a clear sense of a border located in space and monitored in practice. While he does not frequently use the regional toponyms mentioned here, "al-Shām" and "Miṣr," they, like the aforementioned toponyms "Ifrīqiyya" or "Khurāsān," hover over his routes, suggesting a regionalism operating both above and through the politico-administrative, city-centric subregions he emphasizes and complicating a relegation of al-Yaʿqūbī's geography solely to the realm of "linear" or urban geography.

In their persistent return to itineraries, both Ibn Khurradādhbih and al-Yaʿqūbī earn for their works the sobriquet "road books," even though the routes they trace are various, multidirectional, and crosscut by descriptions of urban hinterlands, agricultural areas, and frontier zones. The label "administrative geography" is less apt, despite the administrative data both authors supply. If this is administrative geography, then it is of a symbolic stripe, occupied less with reflecting or regulating administrative practices than with displaying administrative knowledge as a way of associating land with political power, most often at the regional scale, with the notable exceptions of al-Yaʿqūbī's Baghdad, Samarra, and Kufa and Ibn Khurradādhbih's Rome and Constantinople.[72] Thus, the authors list the pre-Islamic Persian administrative divisions for the Sawād and the pathways of Aghlabid power in Ifrīqiyya. However, neither author provides a neat catalog of regional toponyms, or even subregional nomenclature. Regional toponyms come and go, and subregional nomenclature is unsystematically, if frequently, employed. Nevertheless, and despite an emphasis on movement along itineraries punctuated by urban landmarks along the way, these "road books" are also concerned with portraying regions as spatial manifestations of political power past or present.

Almost two centuries later, at the end of the eleventh century, the armchair Andalusian geographer Abū ʿUbayd al-Bakrī (d. 487/1094) also represents the regions of the Islamic world in a work dominated by itineraries. Al-Bakrī's *al-Masālik wa-l-mamālik* (Routes and realms) can certainly be thought of as a "road book," though one with a markedly historical bent, bringing to mind in this pairing of intellectual orientations the works of al-Masʿūdī, particularly his *Murūj al-dhahab*, which uses world geography as a preface to universal history. Al-Bakrī's concern with itineraries, especially short-distance ones, and the political systems of North Africa closely resembles that of al-Yaʿqūbī, though al-Bakrī's explicit interest in borders (*ḥudūd*) emphasizes his regional divisions more clearly. For most of the regional toponyms he mentions, al-Bakrī compiles mini-*faḍāʾil* treatises, including etymologies and other historical material that often bridges the pre-Islamic and Islamic periods, as well as descriptions of their borders. For instance, while al-Yaʿqūbī does not comment on the toponym Ifrīqiyya, al-Bakrī offers five different explanations for the derivation of the region's name and then identifies its limits in the east, west, north, and south, which generally conform to the territory covered by al-Yaʿqūbī's itineraries. From there, al-Bakrī furnishes a series of *ḥadīths* in which the Prophet predicts that Ifrīqiyya will be a privileged territory of struggle against infidelity, inserting it into sacred history as a region designated by Muḥammad for future merit.[73] Only then does he shift to the region's urban nodes and routes between them, providing brief political histories of dynasties that founded or ruled from major cities, such as the Fatimids of al-Mahdiyya or the Idrisids of Fez. While al-Bakrī's regionalism is no more consistent or systematic than that of Ibn Khurradādhbih or al-Yaʿqūbī, it is more pronounced. Moreover, like his predecessors, al-Bakrī endows his regions with meanings that stretch back into antiquity but that remain relevant as sources of prestige in the early Islamic world. In geographical literature produced between the ninth and eleventh centuries, regions were not only divisions of the world and collections of cities, but also compelling categories of belonging associated with particular peoples and political regimes. They were flexible and open-ended enough to remain meaningful to participants in the discourse of place over the centuries.

5

Routes and Realms

Ibn Khurradādhbih, al-Yaʿqūbī, and al-Bakrī were not the only authors of world geographies interested in roads and regions. Three tenth-century geographers, al-Iṣṭakhrī, Ibn Ḥawqal, and al-Muqaddasī, also recorded distances between cities along itineraries, but their routes are secondary to their concern with representing the Islamic world as systematically divided into bounded regional entities, each of which are assigned distinct political and religious meanings. One of the chief differences between these geographers and those discussed thus far is their integration of a series of regional maps into the written text. For this reason, they are associated with one Abū Zayd Aḥmad b. Sahl al-Balkhī (d. 322/934), eponym of the so-called "Balkhī school," whose no longer extant world atlas, its regional divisions, and mapping tradition they are believed to have reproduced and revised in their own works.[1] These maps add an important visual element to the representation of land in the discourse of place, and one that is crucial to any discussion of regionalism.

The "Balkhī school" geographers have been characterized as the first geographers to distance themselves from "foreign" influences and to focus solely on the Islamic world.[2] Their approach has been contrasted with the liberal use of administrative data reflecting pre-Islamic Persian imperial practice in Ibn Khurradādhbih's geography and with the Hellenistic orientation of the latitude and longitude tables compiled by al-Khwārazmī and Suhrāb. However, the attempt to separate "foreign" from Islamic or "Arab" elements in geographical literature from this period is a problematic enterprise. Whether making such a distinction leads to evaluating the "Balkhī school" geographies as reactionary in rejecting knowledge generated outside of an Arabo-Islamic frame of reference or revolutionary in proposing new knowledge generated by new methods, it misrepresents the many sources and preoccupations these geographers shared with others in the discourse of place. Nevertheless, the central and explicit methodological role played by *ʿiyān* ("direct experience") in their works contrasts with more historical and anthological methods, and their interest in contemporary conditions in the territories they visit makes their observations particularly helpful for reconstructing the geographical, social, and economic realities of the period.[3] In the context of the discourse of place, however, the most innovative contribution made by these three geographies lies in their systematic division of the "Realm of Islam" into regions represented through both word and map.[4]

Analyzing these works is complicated by issues of authorship, which are even more difficult to resolve than they are for other texts from this period. Various explanations have been proposed for the tangled relationship between the manuscripts attributed to al-Iṣṭakhrī and Ibn Ḥawqal, as well as their relationship with the no longer extant atlas by al-Balkhī himself. Almost nothing is known about al-Iṣṭakhrī, though he seems to have used a series of annotated maps prepared by al-Balkhī around 309/921 as the basis for an expanded commentary on the same, or a similar, series of maps.[5] Ibn Ḥawqal writes that he met al-Iṣṭakhrī over the course of his travels and then embarked on a series of revisions of al-Iṣṭakhrī's work between 350/961 and 378/988.[6] The extant manuscripts attributed to Ibn Ḥawqal reproduce much of the written material included in manuscripts attributed to al-Iṣṭakhrī, but add a significant amount of new information seemingly derived from Ibn Ḥawqal's personal experience. Thus, it is not only difficult to identify the passages originally authored by al-Balkhī, if any, in the written text attributed to al-Iṣṭakhrī, but it is also challenging to isolate al-Iṣṭakhrī's voice from that of Ibn Ḥawqal, not to mention later copyists and editors, in the manuscripts.[7] Moreover, the maps, which occur in most of the extant manuscripts of the geographies, many of which have been passed down as anonymous abridgements and/or Persian translations, are themselves products of the pens of a host of scribes and artists over the centuries, and it is even more difficult to pinpoint the form of the maps as they were originally prepared by al-Balkhī, al-Iṣṭakhrī, or Ibn Ḥawqal than it is to disentangle the written texts.[8] Al-Muqaddasī's geography presents slightly fewer complexities, as the written text is relatively independent from that of his predecessors, and the smaller number of surviving manuscripts means that the question of the form of the original maps included in the work has a more limited number of answers.[9]

In any case, just as the production of early Islamic written works was a performative and collaborative process, so too was the production of maps.[10] While Ibn Ḥawqal and al-Muqaddasī assert their own authorship fairly definitively within their works, their names, and that of al-Iṣṭakhrī, should be seen as shorthand references to what are really textual traditions, both written and graphic, originating in the tenth century but bearing the imprint of the wide array of influences, sources, and hands that went into producing the forty-some manuscripts dating from the eleventh to the nineteenth centuries that survive today.[11] Nevertheless, a basic consistency in form and content among the extant maps and commentaries associated with each geographer suggests a strong relationship with the tenth-century originals despite the collaborative process by which they were produced and reproduced over the centuries.[12] Thus, while details have been changed and ornamentation added by later copyists, the underlying map forms included in the numerous manuscripts attributed to al-Iṣṭakhrī, for instance, exhibit clear relationships with each other and clear distinctions from those in the less numerous manuscripts attributed to Ibn Ḥawqal and al-Muqaddasī.[13]

This chapter analyzes the way these works purposefully integrate word and map to reflect prevailing ideas about what constituted a region in the geographical imaginations of the early Islamic world. In writing commentaries and designing maps, al-Iṣṭakhrī, Ibn Ḥawqal, and al-Muqaddasī mounted textual performances of a regionalism that would have been legible to other participants in the discourse of place, not to mention the many readers, viewers, and users of their works over the centuries. By dividing the world into bounded but connected "realms" (*mamālik*) associated with particular religious and political meanings and by portraying them in written and graphic form, they construct regions as widely resonant and useful categories of belonging.

Subdividing the Realm of Islam

Despite the fact that all three works open with a description of a territorial entity termed the "Realm of Islam" (*Mamlakat al-Islām*) or the "country of Islam" (*Bilād al-Islām*), they devote the vast majority of their space to its subdivision into regions, each of which receives its own written commentary and accompanying map or maps. The works by al-Iṣṭakhrī and Ibn Ḥawqal include twenty such regional maps and commentaries, three of which are focused on seas and one on the Persian desert.[14] They also share an ordering system for the presentation of their regions, starting with the Arabian Peninsula and the neighboring "Persian Sea," today's Indian Ocean, and then moving from the far west with the region of al-Maghrib (literally, "the place where the sun sets," or northwest Africa and Andalusia) steadily eastward to conclude with a region in Central Asia located to the northeast of the Oxus River, known in Arabic as "Mā Warāʾ al-Nahr" (literally, "what is beyond the river," or Transoxiana).[15] Al-Muqaddasī's work is slightly differently organized, as he announces in the introduction his intention to divide the *Mamlakat al-Islām* into fourteen regions, six of which he describes as "Arab" and eight as "non-Arab" (*aqālīm al-ʿarab* and *aqālīm al-ʿajam*).[16] Like his predecessors, al-Muqaddasī begins with the Arabian Peninsula, but then inserts the other five "Arab" regions and the Arabian desert before embarking on the eight "non-Arab" regions and the Persian desert. He sequences each group of regions roughly from east to west, though the "non-Arab" regions might be better described as following a counterclockwise circuit starting in the east. One noteworthy difference between these organization and ordering systems is that whereas al-Iṣṭakhrī and Ibn Ḥawqal include separate chapters for three bodies of water—the Indian Ocean, the Mediterranean Sea, and the Caspian Sea—al-Muqaddasī addresses them as a group in a preliminary chapter. Al-Muqaddasī's deliberate enumeration of fourteen "regions" (*aqālīm*) excludes the seas and deserts, while al-Iṣṭakhrī and Ibn Ḥawqal make no such distinction.[17] Another difference is that whereas Ibn Ḥawqal separates three territories at each of the frontiers of the *Mamlakat al-Islām*—the Maghrib, Andalusia, and Sicily (*Ṣiqilliyya*) in the west and Sijistān, Khurāsān, and Transoxiana in the east—al-Muqaddasī groups these territories into single regional chapters and assigns them the toponyms "al-Maghrib" and "al-Mashriq" respectively.[18] However, what is striking overall is the consistency of toponyms and their basic territorial or maritime referents as portrayed in written and graphic form in the three works, though the portrayal of boundaries between regions varies among them.[19]

All three geographers employ the term *iqlīm* (pl. *aqālīm*) for their regions, but do not employ the latitudinal seven-clime system from which the term is derived. Moreover, they all make explicit their familiarity with previous methods of dividing the world, as well as their rejection of such methods as unequal to the task of producing regions that would be legible and meaningful to their audience.[20] At the beginning of his work, Ibn Ḥawqal stresses the limitations of the seven-clime system:

> I do not intend the seven climes (*aqālīm*) into which the earth (*arḍ*) has been divided, as I have seen the Indian Map (*al-Ṣūra al-Hindiyya*) in al-Quwādhiyān, and even if it is accurate it creates much confusion. Instead I have prepared for each section that I single out a shape and form that communicates the location of the region. Then I have mentioned what surrounds it in the way of places (*amākin*) and territories (*biqāʿ*); what belongs to it in the way of cities (*mudun*) and provinces (*aṣqāʿ*); what it has in the way of imposts and tributes; what it has in the way of rivers and seas; what is necessary to know of all that the region (*iqlīm*) comprises in the way of varieties of wealth, levies, tithes, taxes, and distances along the roads; and what it has in the way of exports and trade, since this is the knowledge with which reigning princes, people of consequence, and leaders of all classes are the only ones occupied.[21]

This explanation highlights the central role played by maps in Ibn Ḥawqal's conception and composition of his geography. His description of the so-called "Indian Map" as "accurate" (*ṣaḥīḥa*) but "creating much confusion" (*kathīrat al-takhlīṭ*) suggests his view of the seven climes as regional entities that were too broad in form and too diverse in content to be displayed graphically in a manner that was meaningful or legible to viewers.[22] Thus, his solution is to single out "sections" of territory that would be represented in both word and image in a way that responded to the needs and expectations of a particular audience associated with political and economic power. When in the last line he uses the verb *tafarrada bi-*, which means to be the only one occupied with something, he is describing the relationship between his intended audience, "reigning princes, people of consequence, and leaders of all classes," and the information he is supplying about each region. The resulting regionalism seems, thus, to be shaped solely by and for the exercise of this kind of power, a sense that is reinforced by the dedication of the work, in one version, to the tenth-century Hamdanid prince Sayf al-Dawla of Aleppo and, in another, to the unknown, but presumably powerful, Abū al-Sarīy al-Ḥasan b. al-Faḍl al-Iṣbahānī.[23]

In a passage found in some manuscripts of the work, however, Ibn Ḥawqal reveals that he also saw regions as meaningful and legible in a broader context. In this passage, inserted directly after the above-quoted one, he describes his own personal interest in regions, an interest that might be shared by anyone who has ever wondered about other people and other places:

> Among the things that incited me to write [this book] and prompted me to compose it and attracted me to record it was that in my youth I was always passionate about reading books of itineraries (*kutub al-masālik*) and curious about the method of differentiating among realms (*mamālik*) in terms of lifestyles and characteristics and distinguishing them one from the other in terms of religious schools of thought and rules of conduct and determining the amount of impact those have on aspirations, customs, fields of learning, sciences, particularities, and generalities.[24]

This, presumably, is the information that would make his regions legible or meaningful to those not immediately implicated in the exercise of power he refers to above. But it also suggests that his regions are distinguishable one from the other on both bases simultaneously; their distinctiveness in terms of the geographical, political, and economic factors that are of particular interest to the powerful coincides with their distinctiveness in terms of the cultural, religious, and social factors that might be of broader interest.[25] Moreover, this information was already in circulation and thus already shaping people's expectations of regions. Therefore, Ibn Ḥawqal situates himself and his interest in regions in the context of the discourse of place, a discourse that had reached him in his youth and in which he is self-consciously participating. He goes on to describe the extensive reading and traveling that over the years qualified him to participate.[26] These introductory passages establish Ibn Ḥawqal's work as a textual performance guided just as much by its audience's expectations of what constitutes a region as it is by its author's research on or experience of those regions, both of which were informed by a preexisting discourse of place.

Al-Muqaddasī's understanding of what constituted a region was clearly shaped by similar expectations. To an even greater extent than Ibn Ḥawqal, al-Muqaddasī boasts of his qualifications for participation in and unprecedented contribution to the discourse of place. These qualifications consist of a combination of citational authority and experiential authority, or authority deriving from previous authorities on the one hand and his own *ʿiyān* on the other. In the introduction to his work, al-Muqaddasī lists the works of his predecessors, including al-Jayhānī, Ibn Khurradādhbih, Ibn al-Faqīh, al-Jāḥiẓ, al-Balkhī, and al-Iṣṭakhrī, and finds each of them lacking in one way or another, thus authorizing, as well as justifying the need for, his own participation in the discourse of place.[27] This invocation of earlier authorities was not a slight of hand, intended to disguise the innovative nature of his enterprise in front of an audience uneasy with innovation.[28] Al-Muqaddasī seems sincere in his claim of continuity with earlier authorities, while at the same time staking out new ground, a balancing act performed by many scholars in this period. Like Ibn Ḥawqal, he sees his project as consistent in its aims and parameters with the projects of those who came before him, albeit improved in its methods and presentation. Therefore, his regions will be recognizable to his audience from their familiarity with earlier works in the discourse of place, but his particular mode of textual performance will be more successful in reaching and benefiting them than any that came before.

Al-Muqaddasī explains that his improvements correct two tendencies in earlier scholarship: first, he systematizes the gathering and presentation of material that had been gathered and presented in a haphazard way; and, second, in so doing he makes this material more effectively legible and meaningful to more people. The material with which he is concerned focuses on the territorial makeup of regions, or, more precisely, on the varieties of plots of land from which regions are constructed, a focus announced by the title of his work, *Aḥsan al-taqāsīm fī maʿrifat al-aqālīm* (Best divisions for knowledge of the regions). Key to the systematization of this material is the assignment of consistent nomenclature to each category of the territorial "building blocks" that together constitute regions. The introduction of a new territorial vocabulary applicable across the Islamic world contrasts with the approach taken by, among others, Ibn Khurradādhbih and al-Yaʿqūbī, who tended to use different terms, even different languages, for the subdivisions of each region they discuss.[29] Al-Muqaddasī thus intends his work to propose not simply a description, but a theory, of the region as constructed from a predictable, interdependent, and classifiable array of territorial "building blocks." Moreover, he vouches for the applicability of this theory by stressing his direct observation of the territories he classifies and his overriding concern with objectivity and accuracy in information gathering. Regions are not therefore constructed by locals for locals in a local language, but are a universally applicable category of territorial consciousness that al-Muqaddasī has observed across the *Mamlakat al-Islām*—by, to be sure, talking to locals and sometimes even assimilating to their ways, but also by subjecting the resulting body of knowledge to a disciplinary scrutiny and systematization.

According to al-Muqaddasī, the maps that accompany the written text are integral to his second goal, which is to make his theory of the region widely legible and meaningful. In the following passage, he suggests that representing the region by means not only of a consistent vocabulary, but also a consistent and clear method of graphic portrayal, increases the accessibility and educational potential of his book: "We divided each region (*iqlīm*) into provinces (*kuwar*), assigned them metropolises (*amṣār*), mentioned their capitals (*qaṣabāt*), and classified their chief cities (*mudun*) and military districts (*ajnād*). After that we depicted them and sketched their borders (*ḥudūd*) and internal boundaries (*khiṭaṭ*). We designated their well-known roads in red, and we made their golden sands yellow, their salt seas green, their well-known rivers blue, and their foremost mountains dust-colored. Thus would the portrayal be readily understandable and accessible to both a specialist and a general audience."[30] Here he explains his twin projects of classification and cartography, word and image joined to bring a clear understanding of regionalism to a broad audience. The maps are not intended as vehicles for his classification scheme but rather for displaying lines, whether those that follow the contours of the landscape, such as coastlines, rivers, or mountain ranges, or those that follow human arteries of communication and separation, such as borders and roads. This passage suggests that what many have observed as a disconnect between the (detailed and dense) written text and the (simple, not to say simplistic) maps in al-Muqaddasī's work may have to do with a deliberate distinction between the kinds of information most effectively communicated by the two different modes of representation. Thus, a region's complex hierarchy of plots of land is most effectively represented in writing, while its shape and contours are most effectively represented in graphic form, but both are necessary to achieve a full understanding of what constitutes a region in the Islamic world. Furthermore, his emphasis on presenting such information in readily understandable and accessible forms suggests an expectation that his book will interest and benefit a wide range of people. That al-Muqaddasī might have harbored such an expectation is reinforced by his habit of opening each section of his introduction with the imperative: "Know that ... " He perceives himself and his work as fulfilling an instructive function and impressing "the best divisions for knowledge of the regions" upon one and all.

Mapping the Region

Each of the three authors devotes the first of his regional chapters to the Arabian Peninsula (*Diyār al-ʿArab* for al-Iṣṭakhrī and Ibn Ḥawqal and *Jazīrat al-ʿArab* for al-Muqaddasī), a decision justified in the written texts by its importance as the crucible of Islam.[31] It is the precedence of the Arabian Peninsula, rather than Iraq or Īrānshahr, that has caused some scholars to interpret these works as a reaction against "foreign" influences in geographical writing. However, to my knowledge, all of the maps of the Arabian Peninsula in manuscripts attributed to al-Iṣṭakhrī and Ibn Ḥawqal actually include Baghdad, even though the toponym does not occur in the written description of the region (see Figures 5.1 and 5.2).[32] The

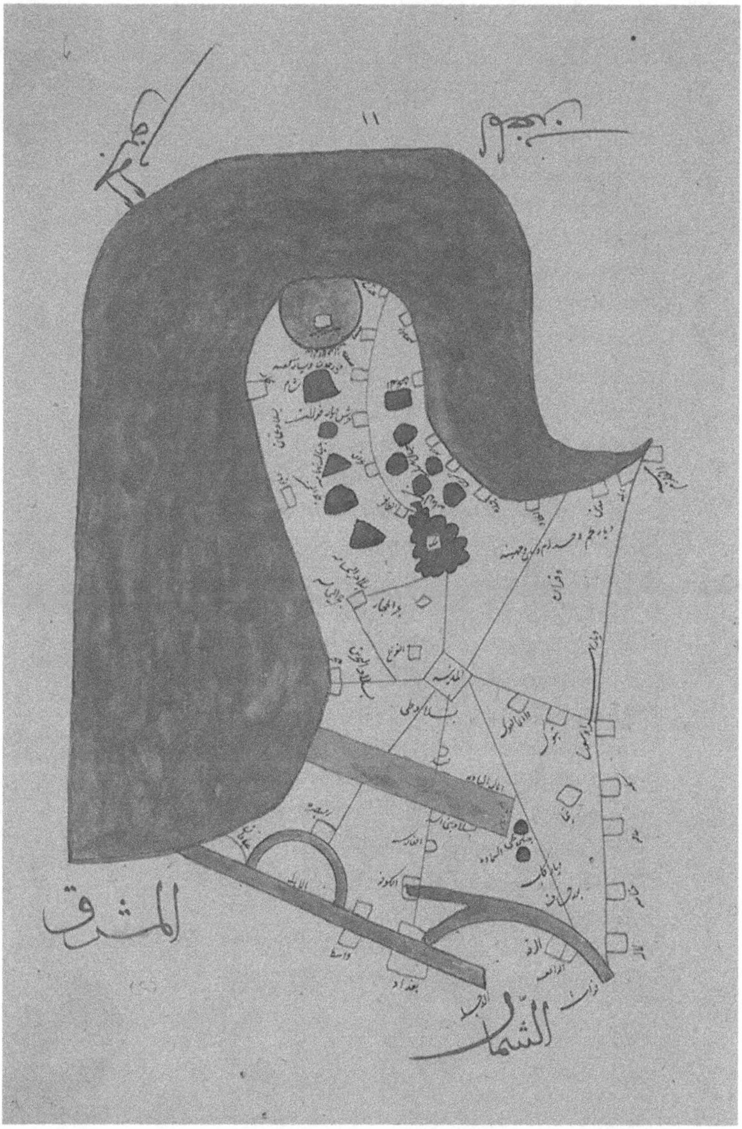

Figure 5.1 The Arabian Peninsula (oriented south). Source: al-Iṣṭakhrī, *al-Masālik wa-l-mamālik*, Ms. Ayasofya 2613, p. 11/fol. 6a. Süleymaniye Kütüphanesi, Istanbul.

Tigris and Euphrates Rivers also appear on the maps as a continuation of the waters encircling the peninsula and could be seen as constituting a northerly border for the region, even though the commentary fixes a land border in that direction stretching from Balīs in the north to Anbār and on to ʿAbadān in the southeast. These encircling waterways, particularly the Tigris and Euphrates, seem to reach outward to the edges of the map, like vectors extending in the

Figure 5.2 The Arabian Peninsula (oriented northwest). Source: Ibn Ḥawqal, *Ṣūrat al-arḍ*, Ms. III. Ahmed 3346, fol. 8b. Topkapı Sarayı Müzesi Kütüphanesi, Istanbul.

direction of the rest of the territories connected geographically and religiously with Arabia. Moreover, on several of the maps a straight line runs from Baghdad through Kufa and on to Medina and Mecca, symbolizing a direct connection between Baghdad and Mecca, even if the pilgrimage routes in the written text originate only at Kufa. These features of the maps are noteworthy not because they indicate a dissonance between word and image, attributable perhaps to copyist additions or revisions, but because they suggest that al-Iṣṭakhrī and Ibn Ḥawqal intended their maps to portray different information than their commentaries. Almost consistently throughout, when a map diverges from the written text it is by including neighboring areas, a visual expansiveness on the frontiers of regions not translatable as clearly into writing.[33] The inclusion of Baghdad and the Tigris and Euphrates River systems in the opening regional map suggests not an exclusion of earlier supposedly "foreign" or pro-Persian geographies but a graphic display of connectivity between the regions of the *Mamlakat al-Islām*.

An even more striking example of visual expansiveness not translated or translatable into writing can be found in Ibn Ḥawqal's treatment of the western frontier of the *Mamlakat al-Islām*. This treatment consists of three consecutive commentaries, addressing the Maghrib, Andalusia, and Sicily respectively, and one map, depicting them all simultaneously (see Figure 5.3).[34] Thus, the very nature of a written text—sequential and linear—separates, while the graphic text connects.[35] In addition to bringing together the three territories described in the commentaries, the map also brings together the *Mamlakat al-Islām* and its neighbors along the northern shores of the Mediterranean. In fact, the title at the top right corner of the map, whether originally inscribed by Ibn Ḥawqal or added by a copyist eager to clarify its contents, draws attention to the deliberate pairing of regional entities therein: *Ṣūrat al-Maghrib wa-Balad al-Rūm* (Image of the Maghrib and the Country of the Byzantines). While certainly the map exhibits the most detail on the North African coastline and the Iberian Peninsula, territories belonging to the *Mamlakat al-Islām* in the tenth century, enough detail graces the northern shores of the Mediterranean, especially the Italian peninsula, to suggest its intentional inclusion.[36] The only use of the term *ḥadd* (border, limit) on the map, a term that recurs in the maps that accompany all three geographies, is the inscription of the following phrases, positioned from south to north respectively, in a swath of empty territory at the eastern end of the Mediterranean: *ḥudūd Miṣr wa-aʿmālihā* (borders of Egypt and its provinces), *ḥudūd al-Shām* (borders of Syria), and *ḥudūd al-Thughūr* (borders of the "Frontier Fortresses").[37] The term *ḥadd*, with its connotation of definitive closure, is used here only to separate this composite Maghrib region from other regions *within* the *Mamlakat al-Islām*.[38]

Why does Ibn Ḥawqal design his map of the Maghrib to transmit a sense of connectivity with the non-Muslim world while the written text is dedicated to

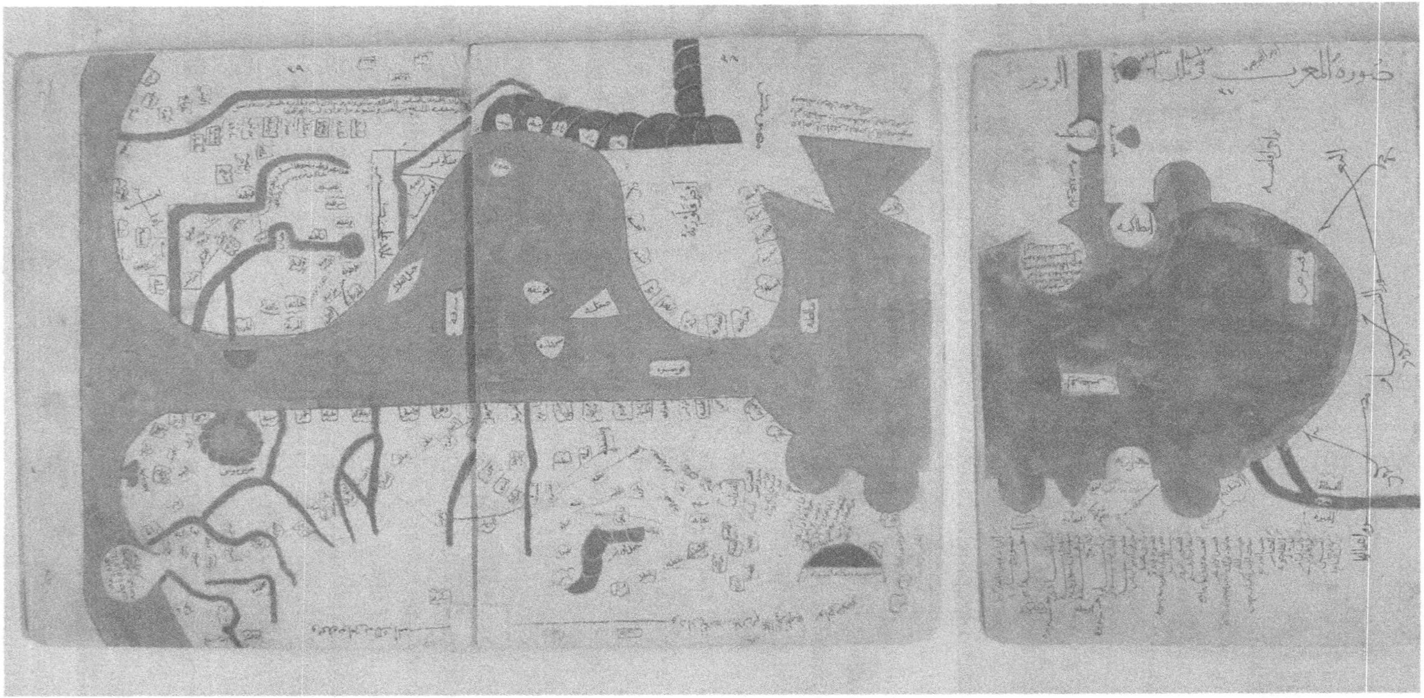

Figure 5.3 The region of al-Maghrib (oriented north), centered on the Mediterranean Sea. Source: Ibn Ḥawqal, *Ṣūrat al-arḍ*, Ms. III. Ahmed 3346, fols. 20a, 20b–21a. Topkapı Sarayı Müzesi Kütüphanesi, Istanbul.

describing subdivisions of the *Mamlakat al-Islām* alone? Is this evidence of an activist map copyist with particular interest in southern Europe making additions to Ibn Ḥawqal's original design? Ibn Ḥawqal's written text is actually much more engaged with land outside of the "Realm of Islam" than his regional divisions might suggest.[39] For instance, Ibn Ḥawqal's commentary on the Maghrib discusses the trade in slaves, metals, and fine fabrics that linked it to Iraq, Europe, and sub-Saharan Africa.[40] He also records stages along itineraries stretching southward from the North African coast into the Saharan desert and the cities beyond, most famously ancient Ghana, which was still dominated by non-Muslims in the tenth century, and mentions the territories of the Francs and other non-Muslims neighboring Andalusia.[41] Similarly, he uses his commentaries on the Indian Ocean, the Mediterranean Sea, and the Caspian Sea to describe the lands outside of the *Mamlakat al-Islām* that border these bodies of water and to describe the customs of and interaction between the various peoples on or near their shores.[42] Thus, the connectivity communicated by Ibn Ḥawqal's maps is actually consistent with emphases in his written text. Even though their writing does not go as far as Ibn Ḥawqal's in describing relations between the "Realm of Islam" and the rest of the world, maps from al-Iṣṭakhrī's and al-Muqaddasī's works also seamlessly portray the Muslim and non-Muslim lands arrayed around, and within, the Indian Ocean and the Mediterranean Sea.[43] Examining maps as integral parts of these works belies the supposed exclusion of the non-Muslim world from the gaze of the "Balkhī school" geographers.

Overall, however, al-Muqaddasī's map forms circumscribe the regions of the *Mamlakat al-Islām* more tightly than do those of his predecessors, maritime maps notwithstanding.[44] His map of the Arabian Peninsula, for instance, replaces the open-ended system of waterways in the maps by al-Iṣṭakhrī and Ibn Ḥawqal with a closed geometric shape that excludes territory at the Syrian and Iraqi frontiers (see Figure 5.4).[45] His maps of Syria, al-Jazīra, and Iraq display none of the overlapping territory at the frontiers that appears on the same maps by al-Iṣṭakhrī and Ibn Ḥawqal.[46] His map of the Maghrib depicts only the North African coastline and the Iberian Peninsula, with references to the other lands encircling the Mediterranean relegated outside the lines of the rectangular frame of the map.[47] This circumscription may have to do with his declared intention to control more tightly than his predecessors the assignment of territorial "building blocks" to each region, as well as their organization therein. Thus, if Baghdad has been assigned the status of metropolis (*miṣr*) for the region of Iraq, it cannot appear to belong to the Arabian Peninsula, even on the map. Instead, the cities of Yemen and southern Arabia are featured more prominently than on al-Iṣṭakhrī's and Ibn Ḥawqal's maps, and a triangle connecting the cities of Sanaa, Aden, and Zabīd, this latter city, according to the written text, sharing with Mecca the title of metropolis (*miṣr*) of the region, occupies one end of the map. Moreover,

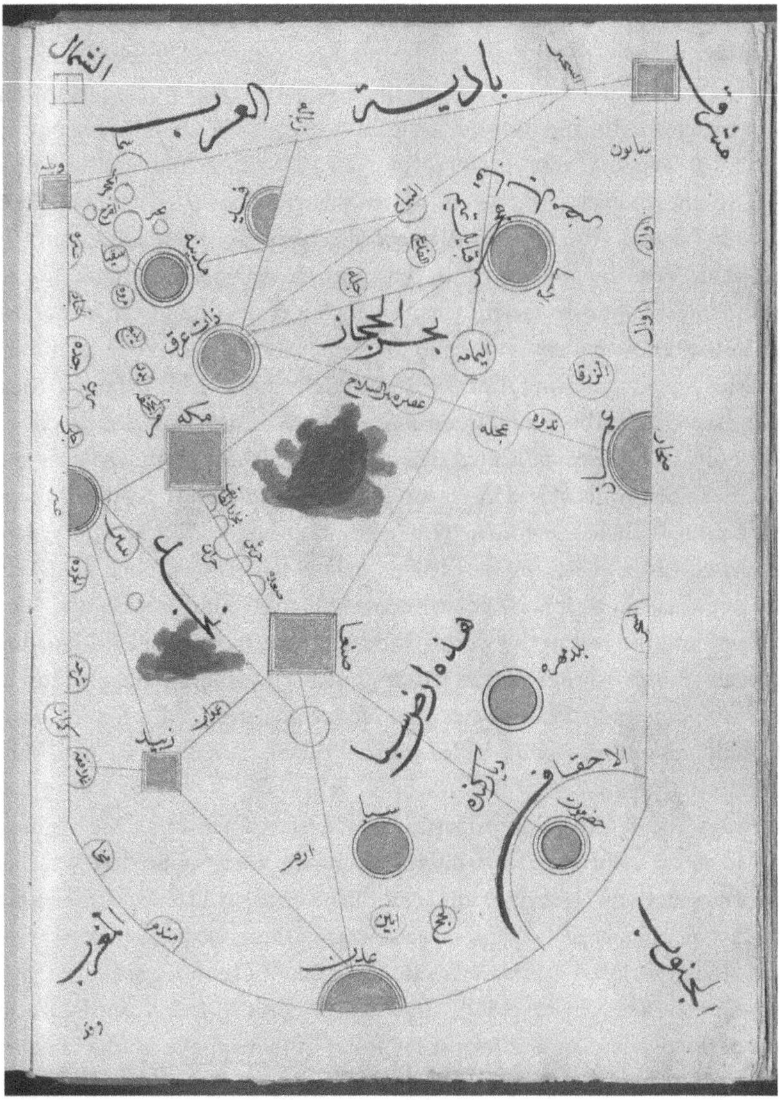

Figure 5.4 The Arabian Peninsula (oriented north). Source: al-Muqaddasī, *Kitāb aḥsan al-taqāsīm fī maʿrifat al-aqālīm*, Ms. Or. 1013, f. 65. Leiden University Library.

depicting the cities of al-Fusṭāṭ, Constantinople, or Ghana on the map of the Maghrib, as Ibn Ḥawqal does, would confuse not only al-Muqaddasī's isolation of each region for the purposes of subdivision into constituent cities and territories, but also his more deliberate exclusion of the lands outside of the *Mamlakat al-Islām* from his regionalism.

The decision to exclude extraneous territory may also spring from al-Muqaddasī's announced intention to design maps to convey different information than the written text in a readily accessible format. His maps depict cities portrayed as small boxes or circles along straight lines, presumably routes, with a toponym inscribed either in or beside them. The resulting simple geometric pattern does not communicate a complex urban hierarchy, which is the primary concern of the accompanying commentary. For example, it would be impossible to determine from the maps alone whether the cities of Mecca and Zabīd, twin metropolises for the Arabian Peninsula, or Kairouan and Cordoba, twin metropolises for the Maghrib, occupied more significant or central positions than any other box, circle, or toponym depicted therein.[48] Nor do his maps convey a sense of the religious or political meaning of the regions for Muslims, which the written introductions to each of his chapters do so effusively. It may be that al-Muqaddasī intended his maps to contribute to his theory of the region primarily by emphasizing the concept of boundedness; that is, without a basic understanding of boundedness, how is it possible to contain, mentally or physically, the territorial "building blocks" that make up or the meanings that distinguish each region? Thus, he translates the concept of boundedness into stark and simple graphic form at the expense of the map's ability to communicate the complexity of a region's contents or meanings, which is, in any case, the purpose of the written text.

However, boundedness does not necessarily imply disconnectedness in mapping. One striking feature of the maps for the eastern regions in all three works is the prominence of borderlines labeled by the toponyms for neighboring regions.[49] A good example is maps of the region of Fārs from manuscripts attributed to al-Iṣṭakhrī and Ibn Ḥawqal, most of which are a rectangular shape aligned in a southwesterly direction with a crescent-shaped Persian Gulf at the top (see Figures 5.5 and 5.6).[50] Written along the right side of al-Iṣṭakhrī's map is the phrase *ḥadd Khūzistān* (border of Khūzistān); written inside the indentation at the bottom right corner of the map is *hudūd Iṣfahān* (borders of Isfahan); written along the bottom side of the map is *mafāza bayn Fārs wa-Khurāsān* (desert between Fārs and Khurāsān); and written along the left side of the map is *ḥudūd Kirmān* (borders of Kirmān).[51] Ibn Ḥawqal's map has no borderlines per se, but rather the elongated lines of the Arabic script of these labels themselves act as the borderlines. The effect of these labeled borderlines (or, in the case of Ibn Ḥawqal's map, the toponym-borders) is to communicate a sense of the boundedness of the region but also of its connectedness to neighboring regions. These regional maps are clearly not intended to fit together like puzzle pieces to form a world map, as Ptolemy instructed the cartographer to accomplish in his *Geography*. However, they do lead a viewer on a visual journey from one to the other, similar to the way numbers on the edges of maps in modern atlases direct the viewer to the page depicting the adjoining region. Thus, flipping from the map of Fārs to the next map in the sequence for the region of Kirmān in both al-Iṣṭakhrī's and Ibn Ḥawqal's works reveals a protrusion at the bottom right corner of the map of Kirmān that recalls the indentation at the bottom left corner

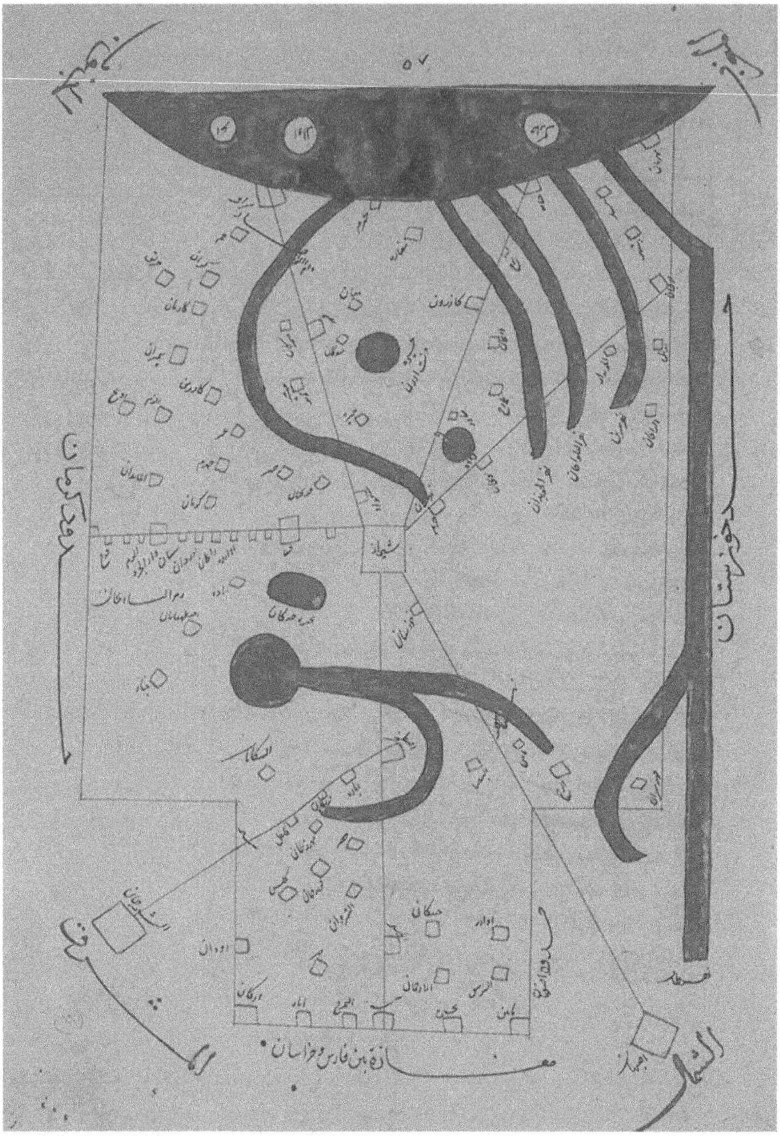

Figure 5.5 The region of Fārs (oriented southwest), located in present-day Iran. Source: al-Iṣṭakhrī, *al-Masālik wa-l-mamālik*, Ms. Ayasofya 2613, p. 57/fol. 29a. Süleymaniye Kütüphanesi, Istanbul.

of the map of Fārs (see Figure 5.7).[52] This communication between shapes and labels at the borders of successive maps makes it possible for an audience to perceive relationships between regions and to perform them in the act of reading.[53] The boundaries depicted on these maps are, therefore, simultaneously sites for the production of regional particularism and for the performance, both textual and extratextual, of regional connectivity in the discourse of place.

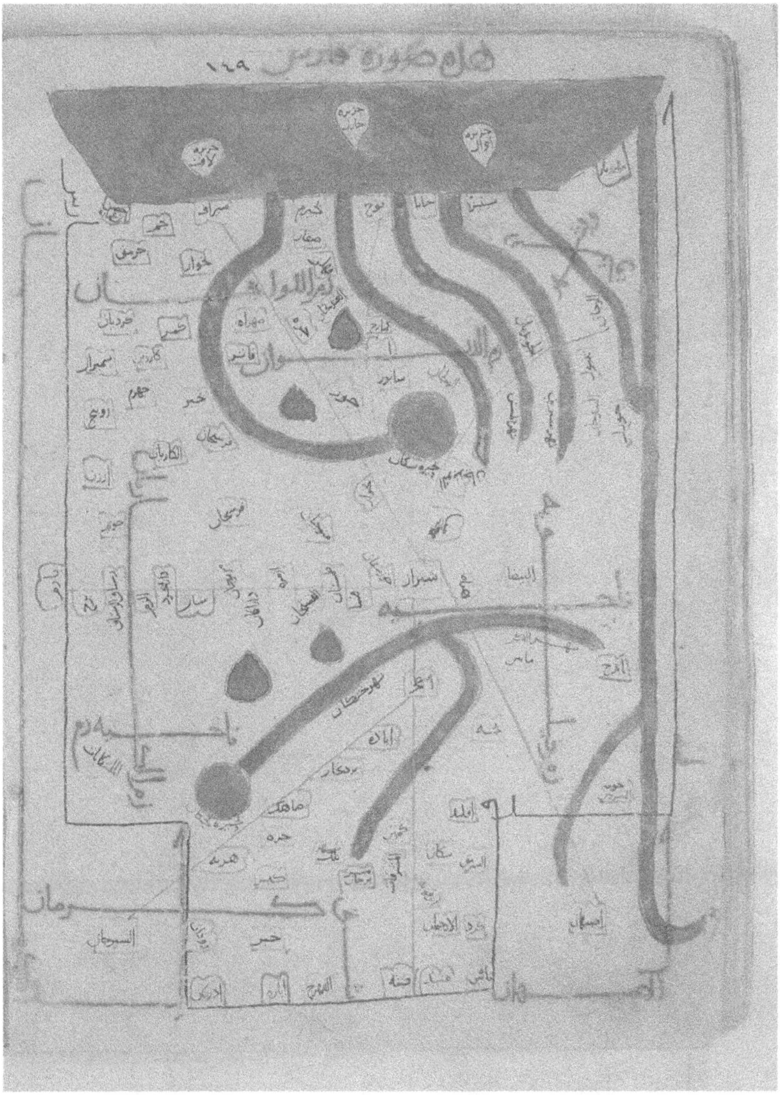

Figure 5.6 The region of Fārs (oriented southwest), located in present-day Iran. Source: Ibn Ḥawqal, *Ṣūrat al-arḍ*, Ms. III. Ahmed 3346, fol. 76b. Topkapı Sarayı Müzesi Kütüphanesi, Istanbul.

Recent scholarship has interpreted the portrayal of boundaries between regions in early Arabic geographical literature as a necessarily imprecise gesture toward the zones of transition, rather than "real borderlines," that separated polities on the ground.[54] This preoccupation with borderlines has resulted in a general emphasis on absence in studies of the Islamic world—the absence of boundaries, the absence of private property, the absence of religious or legal

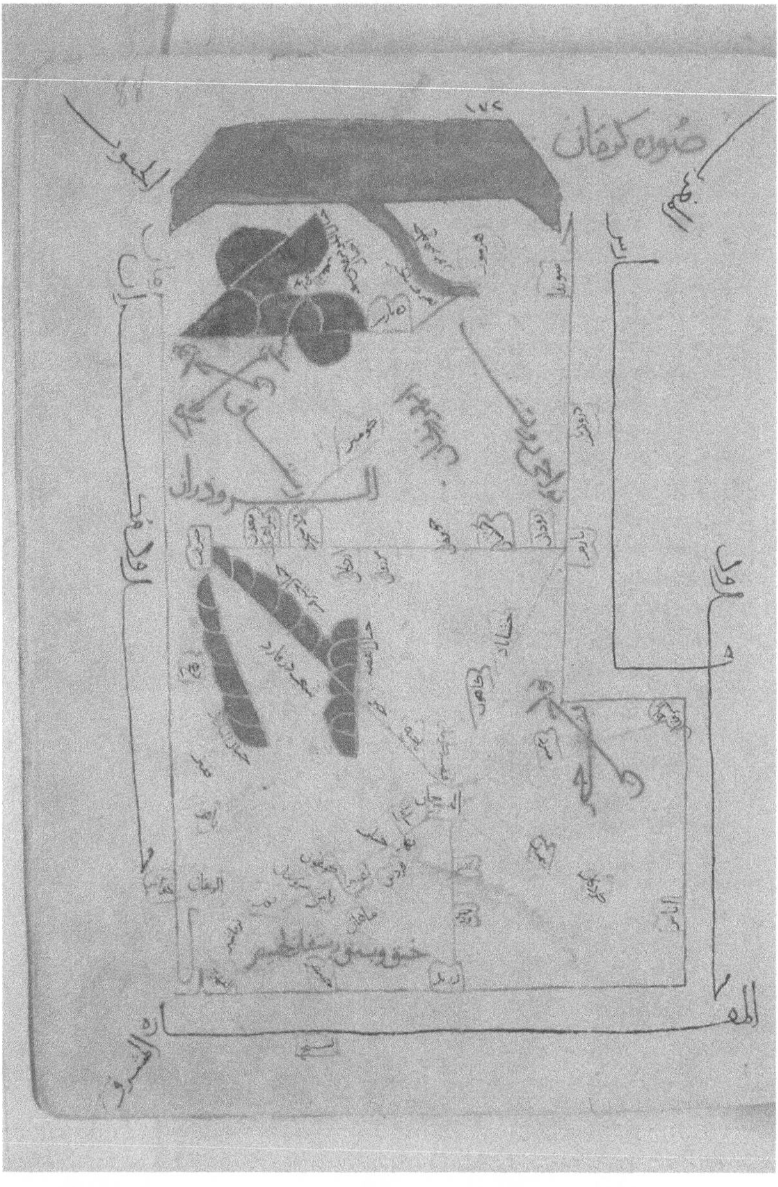

Figure 5.7 The region of Kirmān (oriented south), located in present-day Iran. Source: Ibn Ḥawqal, *Ṣūrat al-arḍ*, Ms. III. Ahmed 3346, fol. 88a. Topkapı Sarayı Müzesi Kütüphanesi, Istanbul.

discourses that imagined political jurisdiction in territorial terms, the absence of attachment to land. Not coincidentally, these "absences" were also articulated to justify and facilitate the colonization of the Middle East in the late nineteenth and early twentieth centuries. In fact, Middle Eastern responses to colonialism in this period often sought to answer these charges of "absence" with "presence," drawing a good deal of intellectual justification from the texts that make up the discourse of place. From a different perspective, however, even when and where "real borderlines" between neighboring polities can be shown to be present, people on the ground have not necessarily experienced them as such and, furthermore, may imagine them quite differently.[55] Similarly, in the context of the discourse of place, whether or not the borders portrayed on maps were "real" or corresponded to lines on the ground is less important than the way in which they were portrayed or the fact that they were portrayed at all.[56]

One of the clearest consequences of the representation of a bounded regionalism in the works by al-Iṣṭakhrī, Ibn Ḥawqal, and al-Muqaddasī is that it challenges views of early Islamic geography as linear or city-centric. It also distinguishes these geographies from those that came before by Ibn Khurradādhbih and al-Yaʿqūbī. The earlier works address frontiers, but do not systematically portray regions as bounded entities, a portrayal that makes possible the twin processes of naming and mapping.[57] It is impossible to divide the *Mamlakat al-Islām* into regions in the first place, not to mention naming and mapping them, without some concept of boundedness—some concept of where one region ends and the next begins. This boundedness does not have to be a function of "real borderlines" on the ground or areal measurements, but it does have to contain the geographical knowledge assigned to each region. The descriptions of towns, landscapes, and cultural characteristics and the lists of revenues, resources, and itineraries that distinguish one region from the other in the commentaries are contained mentally by boundaries, just as the inscription of toponyms and the iconographic representation of mountain ranges, waterways, and roads are contained by the boundaries of a map, even if those boundaries are simply the edges of the page. While boundedness did not imply disconnectedness, it nonetheless facilitated the expression of regional particularism in the discourse of place.

Invoking the Audience

The written texts of the geographies by al-Iṣṭakhri, Ibn Ḥawqal, and al-Muqaddasī no less consciously craft regions as bounded territorial entities than do the graphic texts. This boundedness contains the information about urban areas, tax revenue, and cultural practices that fills the pages of these works, and it also allows the geographers to endow each region with meanings that are both particular to that region and comprehensible to a wide range of people. Thus, al-Muqaddasī's introductions to chapters, like the borders on the maps that lead from one region to another, should be seen as interactive performances of regionalism that rely simultaneously on a sense of boundedness and a sense of connectivity. Whereas Ibn Ḥawqal and al-Iṣṭakhrī open each of their commentaries with a written description of the frontiers of the region as an introduction to the accompanying map, al-Muqaddasī opens with an invocation of the religious and cultural meanings of each region for Muslims. For example, here is al-Iṣṭakhrī's chapter opening on Syria:

> As for Syria, to its west is the Mediterranean Sea; to its east is the desert stretching from Ayla to the Euphrates and then from the Euphrates to the border (*ḥadd*) with the Byzantines; to its north is the Country of the Byzantines (*Bilād al-Rūm*); and to its south is Egypt and the Tīh of the Israelites. Its extreme limits (*ākhir ḥudūdihā*) are, in the direction of Egypt, Rafaḥ and, in the direction of the Byzantines, the Thughūr, which are Malatya, al-Ḥadath, Marʿash, al-Hārūniyya, al-Kanīsa, ʿAyn Zarba, al-Maṣṣīṣa, Adhana, and Ṭarsūs. In the direction of the east and the west are districts that we have already mentioned on the map of Syria, so their reiteration would be unnecessarily lengthy.[58]

This introduction is short and direct, highlighting the aforementioned priority of avoiding unnecessary repetition between commentary and map—of using the different forms to convey different information. By contrast, here is al-Muqaddasī's much lengthier introduction to the chapter on Syria:

> The region of Syria is of glorious prestige! It is the abode of the prophets, station of the righteous, source of the substitutes (*al-budalāʾ*), and desire of the meritorious. It is the first *qibla* and the site of congregation [on Judgment Day] and the Prophet's Night Journey (*al-masrā*). It contains the holy land (*al-arḍ al-muqaddasa*), the meritorious military outposts (*al-ribāṭāt*), the glorious frontier fortresses (*al-thughūr*), and the noble mountains. Here is the refuge of Abraham and his final resting place, the abode of Job and his well, the oratory of David and his gate, the wonders of Solomon and his cities, the grave of Isaac and his mother, the birthplace of Christ and his cradle, the village of Saul (Ṭālūt) and his river, the slaying ground of Goliath (Jālūt) and his citadel, the cistern of Jeremiah (Irmiyāʾ) and his prison, the mosque of Uriah (Ūriyyā) and his house, the dome of Muḥammad and his gate, the rock of Moses, the high ground (*rabwa*) of Jesus, the oratory of Zachariah, the baptismal font of John, the shrines of the prophets, the villages of Job, the stopping places of Jacob, the Masjid al-Aqṣā, the Mount of Olives, the city of Acre, the mosque of Ṣiddīqā, the tomb of Moses, the resting place of Abraham and his mausoleum, the city of Ascalon, the spring of Siloam, the home of Luqmān, the Valley of Canaan, the cities of Lot, the site

> of the Gardens, the mosques of ʿUmar, the *waqf* of ʿUthmān, the gate named by the two men, the assembly attended by the two disputants, the wall that separates the condemned from the pardoned [on Judgment Day], the near place (*al-makān al-qarīb*), the shrine of Baysān, the Gate of Pardon (*bāb ḥiṭṭa*), it of the power and the prestige, and the Gate of the Trumpet (*bāb al-ṣūr*), the site of Certainty (*al-yaqīn*), the tombs of Mary and Rachel, the meeting point of the two seas, the dividing point of the this world and the next (*al-dārayn*), the Gate of the Divine Presence (*bāb al-sakīna*), the Dome of the Chain (*qubbat al-silsila*), and the stopping place of the Kaʿba, in addition to shrines that cannot be counted and merits that cannot be hidden.[59]

This introduction goes on to extol the natural resources, specialties, and salubrious conditions of the region, as well as its well-known cities and the qualities of its people, all in a sophisticated, poetic Arabic style best described as "rhyming prose" (*sajʿ*). This is one of al-Muqaddasī's longest introductions, possibly because he was a native of Syria and thus well positioned to enumerate its many merits, most of which have to do with the traces left on its territory, both urban and rural, by the prophetic past. However, he begins every chapter in a similar style, emphasizing a region's association with sacred history, extolling its natural and human resources, and, usually briefly at the end, admitting some shortcoming of the land or people, a gesture toward *adab* conventions of debate.[60] Then he switches to standard prose as he embarks upon the enumeration and organization of the territorial "building blocks" that make up each region.

Al-Muqaddasī clearly intends his introduction to fulfill a different purpose than the rest of the chapter, especially since most of its allusions get repeated and explained later on, either in the city-by-city enumeration that follows the introduction, where he describes mosques or other loci of devotion, or in the final sections that systematically address topics such as climate, coinage, tax revenue, agricultural and industrial products, weights and measures, manners and physiognomy, systems of Qurʾānic recitation, and schools of Islamic jurisprudence. One clue to his intention for these opening sections can be found in the introduction to the work as a whole, where he describes his approach to writing:

> We have used in [this work] some degree of obscure and figurative language so that it will be dignified and elevated. We have supplied evidence as confirmation and stories as clarification; we have included rhyming prose (*sajʿ*) to show elegance and religious reports (*akhbār*) to obtain blessing. But we have simplified most of [the work] so that the general public (*ʿawamm*) will be able to understand it if they reflect upon it.[61]

This returns to the question of the audience whose expectations and needs shaped al-Muqaddasī's composition of the *Aḥsan al-taqāsīm fī-ma'rifat al-aqālīm.* On the one hand, he hopes to gain respect and blessing because of the erudition and piety of his work; and on the other, he hopes to render the geographical knowledge he is producing and ordering accessible and comprehensible to a "general public" (*'awāmm*). He intends his maps to contribute to the accessibility of the work, and he indicates here that he sees his writing as another way to achieve the goal of reaching nonspecialists. However, he is also concerned with reaching more specialist audiences, audiences for whom he is self-consciously performing feats of verbal sophistication and religious devotion in his writing. Whereas for Ibn Ḥawqal it was the kind of information about a region that determined the audience—geographical, political, and economic information for the elite, and cultural, religious, and social information for everyone else—it is the way in which the information about a region is presented that determines the audience for al-Muqaddasī. Thus, al-Muqaddasī crafts his regional introductions with their rhyming prose, *adab* conventions, Qur'ānic allusions, and pious formulas for particular groups, whereas others can get the same information in a more readily accessible format later in the chapter. The introductions act simultaneously as proofs of his linguistic agility, the currency of exchange with the *udabā'*, and of his religious authority, the currency of exchange with the *'ulamā'* and, ultimately, God, from whom he hopes to "obtain a blessing." They are truly invocations, addressed to both the lettered and the divine, in the hopes of receiving worldly and otherworldly benefits. And as invocations, they are performative.

Sometimes these performances might be particularly politically charged, as in the following introduction to the region of Egypt:

> This is the region in which Pharaoh gloried over humankind and which provided for the people of the world by the hand of Joseph. In it are the traces of the prophets, the Tīh and Mount Sinai, the shrines of Joseph, and the wonders of Moses. Thither fled Mary with Jesus. God has mentioned it repeatedly in the Qur'ān and has shown its virtue to creation. It is one of the two wings of the world, and its glories are inestimable. Its metropolis (*miṣr*) is the apogee of Islam and its river is the most magnificent of rivers. The Ḥijāz thrives on its bounties; the season of the hajj is made joyful by its people. Its righteousness spreads to east and to west, as God situated it between the two seas and raised its reputation in both east and west. Suffice it to say that Syria, with its majesty, is but one of its rural areas (*rustāq*), and the Ḥijāz, with its inhabitants, is but one of its dependents. It is said to be the high ground (*al-rabwa*), and its river flows with honey in paradise. The presence of the Commander of the Believers has returned to it, and it has abrogated Baghdad until Judgment Day. Its metropolis has become the greatest pride of the

> Muslims. Even so, there has been drought there for seven consecutive years; grapes and figs there are expensive; the customs of the Copts prevail; and disaster befalls its people regularly.[62]

This introduction, quoted here in its entirety, compares Egypt explicitly with two other regional entities, Syria and the Ḥijāz, which are described as its dependents. In fact, what the introduction does is to evoke Egypt as a greater region that contains, or has the capacity to contain, both Syria and the Ḥijāz, a regionalism at odds with the division of the *Mamlakat al-Islām* to which the work is dedicated. This introduction actually lays claim to several of the meritorious sites associated with Syria in the previous introduction, as if Egypt was in the process of absorbing Syria: the *rabwa*, or "high ground" on which Jesus and Mary sought refuge in Qurʾān 23:50; the "rock of Moses," a reference to Mount Sinai; and the "meeting point of the two seas," a reference to the Mediterranean Sea and Indian Ocean and to Qurʾān 55:19–20.[63] Moreover, Egypt is portrayed as "abrogating Baghdad until the Day of Judgment" because of the "presence of the Commander of the Believers," meaning the Fatimid caliph, whose rule was a direct challenge to the legitimacy of the Abbasid caliph in Baghdad. Al-Muqaddasī's introduction to his chapter on Egypt, therefore, constructs the region as a flexible and potentially expansive—even expansionist—territorial category of belonging and in so doing invokes a particular audience, the Fatimid dynasty, its supporters, and Ismāʿīlī Shiites in general, with a statement of political and religious loyalty.[64]

Al-Iṣṭakhrī and Ibn Ḥawqal do not craft introductions the same way that al-Muqaddasī does, though Ibn Ḥawqal inserts what could be considered political invocations, albeit without any stylistic flourishes, after the opening description of the frontiers of the regions of the Arabian Peninsula, Egypt, and Transoxiana and before the enumeration of their cities. These passages celebrate the rulers and administrative practices, past and present, that could be boasted by these regions.[65] Significantly, the Arabian Peninsula is associated with the current and sometimes controversial dynasties reigning in southern and eastern Arabia, especially the Qarmatians of Bahrain, rather than with the lifetime of the Prophet or his immediate successors in Medina, substantiating an interpretation of these passages as an invocation aimed at a contemporary political audience sympathetic to Ismāʿīlī Shiism.[66] As for Egypt, Ibn Ḥawqal represents its past association with pharaonic rule as a virtue, superimposing on its territory a tradition of strong political and administrative leadership that was highly successful in bringing prosperity to the country.[67] However, while Ibn Ḥawqal makes clear an allegiance to the Ismāʿīlī Fatimid dynasty in his chapter on the Maghrib, he does not consider Fatimid rule to have been an economic boon to the territory of Egypt.[68] This ambivalence about contemporary conditions in Egypt is perhaps why he is concerned with representing the region as a past symbol of strength and prosperity, rather than as a present symbol of Fatimid prestige.

On the other hand, the beginning of Ibn Ḥawqal's notably lengthy chapter on Transoxiana represents the region as a current exemplar of political and administrative success. He begins by praising the land for its fertility and resilience and the people for their generosity, piety, and martial skills.[69] He also celebrates Transoxiana as a bulwark against the infidel and its people as the most zealous of warriors.[70] Like al-Muqaddasī in his introduction to Egypt, Ibn Ḥawqal highlights the region's close relationship to the Arabian Peninsula, declaring that "despite the distance of their abode, they are the first to arrive for hajj ... and no one has entered the [Arabian] desert in the same numbers."[71] He then moves seamlessly from this praise to point out that even with this devotion to the cradle of Islam, the people of Transoxiana are no less devoted to their political rulers, an observation that seems to acknowledge and reject the assumption that there might be tension between universal loyalty to Islam and loyalty to territorially particular political authority. Ibn Ḥawqal devotes the rest of the introduction, before embarking on his usual enumeration of cities and routes, to eulogizing the Samanid dynasty of the region for its political stability and justice and its rationalized and consistent administrative practices. Many other chapters contain such information about ruling dynasties, administrative practices, and religious and cultural virtues, but when Ibn Ḥawqal presents it en masse at the beginning of the chapter it accomplishes something similar to al-Muqaddasī's introductions: it uses the idea of a bounded region, its boundedness sketched in both word and map immediately previous to the presentation of this information, as a platform from which to invoke an audience with a statement of political loyalty or religious belonging superimposed upon a plot of land as a whole, before breaking it down in terms of its constituent cities and other territorial "building blocks."

The performative nature of these invocation-introductions anticipates interaction, whether between al-Muqaddasī or Ibn Ḥawqal and his audience or between one audience and another audience. The performances of the political and religious meanings of regions in the introductions to chapters could be useful in the same way information about itineraries, tax revenue, or coinage in a region would be useful to a traveler, merchant, or administrator. They are, in fact, mini-*faḍāʾil* treatises on regions, which might function as scripts for others who wish to celebrate territory as an object of loyalty and a category for belonging.[72] It is important that these geographers imagine regions as both bounded and connected. Without boundedness there would be no way of containing, limiting, and thereby making distinctive the merits that could be intoned for blessings or accolades. For instance, boundedness makes conspicuous the rival claims to Mount Sinai of Egypt and Syria in al-Muqaddasī's work. And without connectivity there would be no way to claim belonging in or loyalty to these regions without also claiming particular ties, such as residence or birthright. For instance, connectivity is what allows al-Muqaddasī, a native of Syria, to claim belonging in Egypt by virtue of his political and religious allegiances. Thus, regions were both closed and open—closed vessels for the enumeration of *faḍāʾil* as well as for the organization of territorial "building blocks," and open categories of identification, attachment, and belonging among Muslims. They were imagined as capacious catchment areas that "caught" meanings and made possible multiple modes of belonging.

The claims of any one region to religious or political meaning in the context of these works were meant, therefore, to be understood by and relevant to anyone anywhere in the *Mamlakat al-Islām*. This is what makes the regionalism conveyed by the discourse of place so effective in lodging contentious or even controversial political claims; the claims of the Fatimid caliph in Egypt are expressed in terms particular to Egypt but were also intended to inspire loyalty across the *Mamlakat al-Islām*, just as Egypt is portrayed as taking the place of Baghdad as a universal category of religious and political belonging. The association of these claims with a region rather than a city gave them greater weight and acted as a kind of textual performance of expansionism in the name of a political ruler. By opening his chapter on the Arabian Peninsula with a description of Qarmatian rule in Bahrain, Ibn Ḥawqal emphasizes an interconnectivity between that eastern subregion and the better-known western subregion of the Ḥijāz and its cities of Mecca and Medina, despite the fact that the Qarmatians were notorious among their many detractors for attacking the hajj caravans going to and from Mecca. Moreover, he forges a mental link between the political pretensions of the Qarmatians and all the routes and waterways connecting the Arabian Peninsula to the rest of the *Mamlakat al-Islām*, especially southern Iraq and Baghdad, which are pictured on the regional map accompanying the chapter. Regions were thus products of the geographical imagination that were useful and actionable in terms of making particular claims to political legitimacy and religious belonging, even those that might be considered marginal or objectionable to mainstream sensibilities, universally legible and territorially expansive.

The Politics of Regions

World geographies can be distinguished from other works in the discourse of place primarily by their focus on multiple cities and regions, an effect of a basic concern with dividing the world. Other works, such as *faḍāʾil* treatises and topographical histories, are devoted to the representation of a single city, albeit sometimes with an eye to a greater regional context, as in the case of Isfahan or

Damascus.[73] To a lesser extent, the discourse of place includes works devoted in whole or large part to the representation of a single region—a textual practice that might be termed monography to contrast it with the multiregional scope of geography.[74] One question that arises regarding these subcategories of the discourse of place is: what differentiates the works devoted to a single region from those discussed previously as embedding a city in a regional context? This is a subtle difference and primarily a matter of emphasis, a matter made even more difficult by the use in some cases of the same toponym for both city and region.[75] One way of approaching the problem is to compare the amount of space that is occupied with naming and locating a city, assembling its foundation or conquest narrative, and describing its built environment with the amount of space that is occupied with sketching the contours of the region, describing its constituent parts and nonurban areas, and locating it in the context of neighboring regions or other subdivisions of the world. Another way of approaching the problem is to ask whether the region in question is clearly dominated by or associated with the representation of a single city. The clearest examples of works that privilege a city and only secondarily set it in a regional context are those that do not portray any competition for the role of dominant city in that context. Works that privilege the representation of the region often portray more than one city occupying a meaningful position therein. Using these approaches, it is possible to identify three plots of land to which surviving texts are devoted entirely or in large part to representing at the regional scale: Egypt, Yemen, and Andalusia.[76]

For the ninth through eleventh centuries, only one region, Egypt, is the subject of multiple extant works. The earliest surviving monographic representation of Egypt as a region comes from one of a group of conquest chronicles and biographical dictionaries of the Islamic west that lavish significant attention on the territory itself.[77] While these works generally cluster most of the material related to the topography and *faḍāʾil* of the regions in a short introduction before shifting to a chronological or prosopographical ordering mechanism, the *Futūḥ Miṣr* (Conquest of Egypt) by Abū l-Qāsim ʿAbd al-Raḥmān b. ʿAbd Allāh b. ʿAbd al-Ḥakam (d. 257/871) maintains a focus on the territory itself, conceived at a regional scale, for approximately two-thirds of the work.[78] A century later, two *faḍāʾil* treatises reproduce material from the *Futūḥ Miṣr* and also clearly address Egypt as a regional entity.[79] Ibn al-Kindī (fl. 355/966), the son of the better-known historian Abū ʿUmar Muḥammad al-Kindī (d. 350/961), compiled his *Faḍāʾil Miṣr* (Merits of Egypt) at the behest of the then governor of Egypt, the former slave of the founder of the Ikhshidid dynasty, Abū l-Misk Kāfūr. The other *Faḍāʾil Miṣr*, very similar in content to that of Ibn al-Kindī but much more systematically organized, was composed by Abū Muḥammad al-Ḥasan b. Zūlāq (d. 387/997), a younger contemporary of Ibn al-Kindī and a student of his father's. Ibn Zūlāq's heavy emphasis on the members of the family of ʿAlī associated with the region also reflects the new circumstances following the Fatimid conquest of Egypt in 359/969–970 and acts as an explicit statement of political and religious allegiance to the new regime.

Three themes elaborated in all of these works make it clear that the territory they are evoking is imagined first and foremost as a region: the importance of agricultural wealth, prompting multiple descriptions of nonurban areas; the focus on the region's constituent parts, especially the fabled "eighty districts (*kuwar*)"; and the absence of a clearly dominant city that might function as a stand-in for the region as a whole. Moreover, Ibn ʿAbd al-Ḥakam opens the *Futuḥ Miṣr* with a version of the tradition quoted above on the authority of ʿAbd Allāh b. ʿAmr b. al-ʿĀṣ in which the world is created in the form of a bird, with Mecca, Medina, and Yemen as the head, Egypt and Syria as the chest, Iraq and al-Sind as the wings, and the Maghrib as the tail.[80] This tradition immediately situates Egypt in the context of the world as a whole and establishes its place in a hierarchy of regional subdivisions, a privileged place that it shares with Syria, second only to the Arabian Peninsula. Moving into a foundation narrative, Ibn ʿAbd al-Ḥakam describes the Biblical Noah's assumption of control over a region stretching "from 'Two Trees' beyond al-ʿArīsh to Aswān in length and from Barqa to Ayla in width," which he then divides into four parts and bequeaths to his sons.[81] This corresponds with the site of "Two Trees" identified by al-Yaʿqūbī, a contemporary of Ibn ʿAbd al-Ḥakam, as the border between Egypt and Syria, suggesting a consistency in understandings of the boundedness of the two regions. This foundation narrative establishes Egypt as a region, comparable to yet clearly separable from neighboring regions, boasting ample land, and occupying a privileged place in world geography and sacred history.

It is initially in Egypt's association with sacred history that all three works emphasize its agricultural wealth and nonurban areas. Ibn Zūlāq quotes Adam invoking God to make Egypt's land flourish, and other traditions compare its verdant landscape, flowing river, and fertile soil to paradise.[82] The pre-Islamic prophet Joseph is particularly associated with the agricultural wealth of the region, and the story of his appointment by the pharaoh to control Egypt's vast storehouses suggests the importance of rightly guided leadership to tap the land's God-given fertility.[83] While the pharaohs might be characterized as enemies of God in other kinds of writing, texts from the discourse of place tend to portray them as capable rulers and generous stewards of the country's riches, which reinforces the sense that a focus on land accommodated or neutralized what might be considered strikingly unorthodox claims in other contexts.[84] Ibn ʿAbd al-Ḥakam quotes a tradition that cites as evidence of the effectiveness of pharaonic rule the great extent of land and natural resources they controlled and their mastery of the agricultural potential of the Nile River.[85] Joseph too harnessed the Nile for Egypt's benefit, digging a canal to bring water and thus prosperity to the town of al-Fayyūm.[86] This emphasis on the methods by which the ancients capitalized on the Nile appears in Ibn Ḥawqal's chapter on Egypt and is reinforced by passages calculating the revenue generated by the region's agricultural base from the days of the pharaohs forward.[87] Indeed, it is the very worldliness of this wealth that makes possible Egypt's otherworldly merits. Ibn al-Kindī opens his work by distinguishing Egypt among the countries of the world for excellence in both religious and secular spheres. For example, by producing a surplus of food Egypt feeds the holy cities of Mecca and Medina, which, in effect, enables Muslims all over the world to perform the hajj.[88] When both tenth-century *faḍāʾil* treatises quote the Torah describing Egypt as the *khizānat al-arḍ* ("treasure house of the earth"), they are representing its bounty as an earthly sign of divine favor over the *longue durée* of sacred history.[89]

Egypt's agricultural wealth is also expressed in terms of the constituent parts that together construct its territory as a region. The second half of each *faḍāʾil* treatise is occupied with a survey of the eighty administrative districts, or *kuwar*, of Egypt and the distinguishing characteristics of some of the most prominent of them. In the following passage, Ibn al-Kindī suggests that within the scope of the eighty *kuwar* of Egypt can be found a whole world:

> There is not a single district (*kūra*) that does not have curiosities and marvels among the varieties of terrain, buildings, production, drink, food, fruit, and all of that from which people benefit and which kings store away. Every species can be recognized from its district, and every appearance can be traced to its district. Upper Egypt is Ḥijāzī land (*arḍ*), its heat like the heat of the Ḥijāz. The date palm, the acacia, the trefoil, the jujube tree, and the milkweed grow there. Lower Egypt is Syrian, its rains the rain of Syria. The plants of Syria grow there, such as grapevines, figs, bananas, walnuts, and the rest of the fruits, as well as vegetables and herbs, and snow falls there.[90]

The explicit comparison of the climate, trees, and plants of Egypt with those of the Arabian desert and Mediterranean Syria evokes a territory notable for both its extent and its variety, a territory imagined at a regional scale that could boast the physical extremes of neighboring regions, as well as, it is implied, everything in between. By emphasizing highlands and lowlands, natural resources, and agricultural produce, Ibn al-Kindī minimizes the importance of urban areas to Egypt's division into constituent parts. Although he explains that each of the eighty districts contains a city, and many clearly take their names from an urban focal point, no city dominates the region as a whole in either of the tenth-century *faḍāʾil* treatises. Even Ibn ʿAbd al-Ḥakam's earlier description of the parcels of land (*khiṭaṭ*) assigned to members of ʿAmr b. al-ʿĀṣ's conquering army at al-Fusṭāṭ and Giza, the twin garrisons that would become Islamic Egypt's largest urban area, is counterbalanced by the attention paid to Alexandria and especially to its foundation by Alexander the Great and its famous lighthouse.[91] It is particularly striking that Ibn Zūlāq never mentions Cairo, despite the fact that its foundation as the new Fatimid capital at a site near al-Fusṭāṭ predated the composition of his work and he elsewhere indicates his support for the regime.[92]

Moreover, these monographs all dedicate separate sections to the Nile and to the way its size and path, rather than any city or cities, provide a focal point and organizing mechanism for the region.[93] Ibn ʿAbd al-Ḥakam uses a description of the Nile and an enumeration of its merits as a prelude to ʿAmr b. al-ʿĀṣ's conquest of upper Egypt, moving up the river in the text just as the famous Muslim general sent his armies south and west on the ground.[94] Ibn al-Kindī and Ibn Zūlāq quote an early Islamic source calculating the number of people it took to dig canals, construct bridges and irrigation channels, and clear brush and trees from its banks, essential prerequisites to making use of the river for industry, agriculture, and transportation: 70,000 people in upper (or southern) Egypt and 50,000 in lower (or northern) Egypt.[95] Ibn Zūlāq organizes his enumeration of Egypt's districts in terms of the Nile's bisection of the region into two sides, east and west.[96] In these sections it is the Nile itself, rather than any central city or urban network, that determines the division of the region into constituent parts.

Why did Egypt receive treatment at the regional level in the discourse of place between the ninth and eleventh centuries, while other regions were evoked primarily as one of many in world geographies or as a setting for a central or significant city? One possible answer has to do with its ancient association with the Copts. All three works dedicate apologias to Coptic Christians, consisting primarily of traditions in which the Prophet Muḥammad designates them as recipients of protection (*al-dhimma*) and calls upon Muslims to treat them with respect and justice during the conquests. They also highlight the prophetic link to the Copts by marriage, especially through the figures of Hagar and Maria, wives of Abraham and Muḥammad, respectively.[97] However, other regions were associated with specific peoples, such as Fārs and Isfahan with the Persians, and while this association emerges in the discourse of place, it does not produce the same privileging of a territory conceived at the regional scale over its constituent or central cities, at least in extant texts. Another reason that Egypt might have received particular attention as a region is its association with an ancient and continuing tradition of strong and independent political leadership from the time of the pharaohs through the tenth century, when the *faḍāʾil* treatises were composed under dynastic regimes that operated independently from Baghdad and that even, in the case of the Fatimids, openly challenged the Abbasid claim to the caliphate.

All three works conspicuously interpret Egypt's pharaonic past as a virtue of the region. The first section of Ibn Zūlāq's *faḍāʾil* treatise is dedicated to an enumeration of the Qurʾānic verses that refer to Egypt, either by including the toponym "Miṣr" itself or another allusion to the territory, including the term "pharaoh."[98] One way of looking at this is to suggest that the mere fact that the word "pharaoh" is mentioned in the Qurʾān, regardless of context, made it possible for participants in the discourse of place to associate Egypt with God's revelation. This dynamic was at work in *faḍāʾil* treatises that interpret the Qurʾānic allusion to Iram, the ancient city that was destroyed for its sins, as a reference to, and therefore a merit of, Damascus.[99] However, the monographs on Egypt go further than this, including material explicitly celebrating the political acumen of the pharaohs. Ibn ʿAbd al-Ḥakam praises their mastery of the Nile and the wisdom of the pharaoh of Joseph who put him in charge of the storehouses of the country. Even the pharaoh of Moses, the most reviled of the pharaohs, is rehabilitated at the hands of Ibn al-Kindī and Ibn Zūlāq. Ibn Zūlāq includes a divine tradition in which God explains to Moses why he had spared the pharaoh, despite his pretension to be a god: "I have granted him a respite in spite of his weakness. Verily, I like it that he is just and generous, and I reserved for him your education."[100] Quoting the Qurʾānic verses 26:34–37, in which the pharaoh responds to Moses's message of the one true God by convening a council of notables to advise him, Ibn al-Kindī asks: "Has there been in the world an assembly of rulers superior in intelligence and more moderate in influence than they were?"[101] Then he compares the treatment Moses received at the hands of the pharaoh in this incident favorably to the brutal fate hastily decreed for Abraham at the hands of Nimrod, the king of Mesopotamia. These authors thus focus attention on the positive aspects of the political heritage of Egypt and make a case for an appreciation of the role played by Egypt and its rulers, especially in comparison to Iraq, in sacred history.

Egypt's tenth-century rivalry with the Abbasid Empire and its successor states in the east for the leadership of the Islamic world finds an outlet in these works through their insistence on the illustrious individuals, especially political figures, associated with Egypt over the centuries. Ibn Zūlāq, to a much greater extent than his predecessors, systematically lists such figures, including the prophets before Muḥammad born in or summoned to Egypt, the rulers and conquerors of Egypt, from Alexander the Great and the pharaohs up to the great general ʿAmr b. al-ʿĀṣ, who claimed the region for Islam, and the governors assigned to the region under the early years of Muslim rule. Ibn Zūlāq's *faḍāʾil* also acts as a more direct challenge to the political dominance of Iraq in the Islamic world than do the other works because of its legitimization of the Shiite Fatimid regime under which it was composed. In addition to the requisite sections listing the Companions of the Prophet and prominent early *ʿulamāʾ* who had traveled, lived, or died in Egypt, Ibn Zūlāq includes a section entitled "Caliphs who entered Egypt before al-Muʿizz" and explains that with the entry of this Fatimid ruler into the region Egypt went from being a *Dār al-Imāra* (Abode of Governorship) to being a *Dār al-Khilāfa* (Abode of the Caliphate), thus endorsing the legitimacy of his claim to the caliphate.[102] Moreover, he asserts Egypt's long-standing association with the family of ʿAlī in a lengthy section that represents the region as a *Dār Tashīʿ* (Abode of Shiism) by virtue of the 2,200 Alids who had trod on, and were sometimes buried in, its soil, a number that exceeded even that of Iraq.[103] Ibn Zūlāq's *faḍāʾil* treatise, therefore, reflects an Egypt that was no longer content to be a satellite state of the Abbasid Empire. In claiming the title of caliph, the Fatimid rulers were asserting their leadership of the entire Islamic world, and Ibn Zūlāq's representation of Egypt can be seen as an expression of that claim as the natural patrimony of a region defined by such an esteemed history of leadership.

Although Egypt's association with an ancient and ongoing tradition of political independence may have been an important factor in its consistent representation at the regional scale before the eleventh century, it is certainly not a sufficient explanation for its nearly unique treatment in this regard. Other territories could be associated with longstanding claims to political autonomy and ethno-cultural particularism, but it is unclear that they were imagined first and foremost as regions in monographs from the discourse of place in this period.[104] Moreover, other regimes were closely associated with territory, most notably the Abbasids, but their representation in the discourse of place occurs primarily through representations of the cities in which they invested, such as Baghdad, Samarra, and Mecca, rather than through representations of the regions of Iraq or the Sawād. The closest comparison to Egypt's regionalism in the discourse of place from this period comes from an early-tenth-century work representing the region of the Arabian Peninsula and its subregion of Yemen, territories lying at what might be considered the periphery of the Islamic world at that time, and certainly territories that did not present a serious challenge to the up-and-coming Fatimids or even to the languishing Abbasids.

Like the representations of Egypt, the *Ṣifat Jazīrat al-ʿArab* (Attributes of the Arabian Peninsula) by al-Ḥasan b. Aḥmad al-Hamdānī (d. 334/945) situates the Arabian Peninsula in terms of its relationship to the other subdivisions of the world as a whole and is not dominated by a city or urban network.[105] Also like Egypt, its contours and internal divisions are determined by natural features of the landscape, the Sarāt mountain range running north-south in western Arabia playing a similar role to that of the Nile in this evocation of regionalism.[106] However, al-Hamdānī clearly considered himself to be composing a work of geography in the strict sense of the term, and his obvious familiarity with Ptolemy's oeuvre and concern with calculations of longitude and latitude differentiate his work from those on Egypt. Despite this preoccupation with systems of dividing the world as a whole, al-Hamdānī dedicates the vast majority of the work to a subregion of the Arabian Peninsula, Yemen.[107] Thus, the *Ṣifat Jazīrat al-ʿArab* can be seen as a representation of a region within a region within the world as a whole. As the epicenter of this nested regionalism, Yemen functions in much the same way that the city of Isfahan functions in other texts; it is the smaller but more symbolically charged plot of land to which is tied any discussion of its regional context, only, in this case, the smaller plot of land is represented as a region rather than as a city. Strikingly, the cities of Mecca and Medina, and even their broader region of the Ḥijāz, are not privileged in the representation of the Arabian Peninsula.[108] Instead, he chooses the mountains and valleys of his native Yemen, a territory that loosely conforms to the territory of present-day Yemen but that tends to expand under al-Hamdānī's pen, as does the territory of the Arabian Peninsula as a whole, to encompass surrounding lands.

This expansive Yemen set within an expansive Arabian Peninsula needs an equally expansive setting, which al-Hamdānī is more than capable of providing due to his deep engagement with the fields of mathematical geography and astronomy. The introductory sections of the *Ṣifat Jazīrat al-ʿArab* are devoted to a description of the Ptolemaic clime system, even to the point of a division of the world into twenty-some latitudinal parallels calculated on the basis of the longest day, which seems to substantiate the existence of a faithful Arabic translation of Ptolemy's *Geography* to which al-Hamdānī had direct access.[109] Like the earlier Ptolemaic scholars al-Khwārazmī and Suhrāb, he also describes the conventional seven parallel climes, furnishing latitude and longitude for the center point (*wasaṭ*) of each of them.[110] In addition, he sketches the boundaries (*ḥudūd*) of what appear to be seven circular climes and identifies each of them with one or more toponyms.[111] Finally, he includes a discussion of astrology and climatic determinism based on a division of the world into northeastern, northwestern, southeastern, and southwestern quadrants similar to, though much more complex than, that of his contemporary al-Masʿūdī.[112] These introductory sections touch upon most of the methods of dividing the world in the discourse of place, and they seem intended primarily as a display of citational authority, since they do not appear to substantiate the premise laid out in the opening passages that the Arabian Peninsula is the most privileged plot of land on earth.[113] Far from revealing a clash between universalist Greek geography and particularist Arabian monography, these introductory sections are consistent with the way in which many authors accumulated intellectual capital by reference to earlier authorities and then deployed it to construct a particular territorial category of belonging. Al-Hamdānī is establishing the credentials with which to construct the Arabian Peninsula and Yemen as regional entities among the regions of the world.

But the regionalism was expansive, even expansionist. The opening passages of the work sketch boundaries of the Arabian Peninsula that encompass parts of Egypt, Syria, and Iraq, not unlike the maps of that region designed by al-Iṣṭakhrī and Ibn Ḥawqal.[114] In the mini-*faḍāʾil* treatise appended in rhyming prose to these opening passages, the holy sites of Mecca, Medina, Jerusalem, Hebron, and Mount Sinai are associated with the Arabian Peninsula, suggesting a conception of its territory that stretched into areas claimed in other texts by Syria and Egypt.[115] Moreover, his focus on the Sarāt mountain range as a definitive feature of the Arabian landscape, not unlike the Nile in Egypt, tends to extend his representation northward, following the line of summits until they reach the Gulf of Aqaba. This sense is reinforced later in the work when he describes hajj routes originating from Iraq, Sanaa, Aden, and the Ḥadramawt, suggesting an equivalency between the three plots of land and their spatial relationships with Mecca.[116] Similarly, although al-Hamdānī sets out the borders (*ḥudūd*) of Yemen with great care, the description of its constituent parts, including a series of plots of land referred to as *mikhlāf* (plural: *makhālīf*), a pre-Islamic designation for district or tribal lands, seems to extend beyond the borders to parts of the Ḥadramawt in southeastern Arabia and to the northwestern Ḥijāz.[117] While it could be argued that Yemen's borders were always a matter of theory over practice, especially considering the nomadic groups in the area whose routes took them hundreds of miles to the north or south, east or west, depending on the season, al-Hamdānī's emphasis on the place of the Arabian Peninsula in the world, while focusing particularly on its interior region of Yemen, seems to promote a certain slippage between the Arabian Peninsula and Yemen, akin to that between certain cities and their regional contexts elsewhere in the discourse of place.

There are no clear clues as to why al-Hamdānī chooses to represent Yemen at the regional level. Why not consign a monograph to the city of Sanaa, al-Hamdānī's hometown, as Aḥmad b. ʿAbd Allāh al-Rāzī (d. 460/1068) does a century later? One possible explanation is that al-Hamdānī was actually attempting a world geography with this work, the rest of which has been lost.[118] This explanation interprets the introductory sections on divisions of the world as a necessary prelude to a more comprehensive treatment of that world. Another possible explanation is that al-Hamdānī wanted to evoke the land of Yemen as a paean to the Himyarite regime similar to that which he accomplishes in his multivolume work *al-Iklīl* (The Crown).[119] This would explain the de-emphasis on the Islamic symbolism of the Arabian Peninsula and the focus on Yemen, but a near absence of direct references to the Himyarites, certainly in comparison to the references to the pharaohs or even the Copts in the works on Egypt, makes this hypothesis difficult to sustain.

Finally, the marked lexicographical bent of this work, noticed by all who have worked on editing and interpreting it, seems to suggest that al-Hamdānī saw in the land of the Arabian Peninsula a rapidly fading language that he hoped to recover for his generation. This is not unlike what Yāqūt expresses two centuries later as one of the motivations for the compilation of his landmark geographical gazetteer.[120] In al-Hamdānī's case, he has to address territory at a regional scale in order to encompass the range of vocabulary it has inspired over the centuries; the same task would be too circumscribed with a city and too overwhelming with the world as a whole (though this is exactly what Yāqūt undertakes). One also suspects that al-Hamdānī was just not as interested in other places or their vocabulary. It was the Arabian Peninsula, the Yemen, of the poets that he was attempting to recapture, and his emphasis on the arcane signifiers for its natural landscape, the contours of its earth, and its flora and fauna speak not so much of antiquarianism as of familiarity and fondness.[121] At the same time, the essentially didactic function of lexicography opens up what might seem a particularly provincial regionalism and addresses it to a broad audience. Al-Hamdānī's performance of lexicography is intended to render the vocabulary of southern Arabia accessible and comprehensible well beyond the confines of the peninsula. In translating the idiom of a particular plot of land into a more universal language, he creates a regional category of belonging that is intentionally both bounded and connective.

Like Yemen, the region of Andalusia was located on the periphery of the Islamic world—if not also of the known world more generally—in this period, and it, like Yemen, is represented in the discourse of place by stressing its geographical connectivity to more centrally located lands, even as it is distinguished by its remoteness. Monographic treatments of Andalusia seem to have been produced between the ninth and eleventh centuries, though the surviving works from this period are known only through quotes in later works and are often in fragmentary form.[122] However, it is worth glancing at one of them, since Andalusian regionalism would constitute a flourishing segment of the discourse of place in the centuries to come. A *faḍāʾil* treatise on Andalusia by the famed eleventh-century Cordoban litterateur Ibn Ḥazm is reproduced seemingly in its entirety in Aḥmad b. Muḥammad al-Maqqarī's seventeenth-century compilation *Nafḥ al-ṭīb min ghuṣn al-Andalus al-raṭīb* (The perfumed breeze from the verdant branches of Andalusia), itself a rich and complex contribution to the later discourse of place devoted to a performance of Andalusian regionalism by, in large part, recalling earlier such performances.[123]

In this treatise, Ibn Ḥazm takes a defensive stance in response to a letter criticizing Andalusians for their failure to commemorate in writing what heritage of learning they possessed. Thus, the region is explicitly represented in terms of its human intellectual capital rather than in terms of its topography or urban areas. In order for a region to lay claim to human intellectual capital, however, some determination has to be made as to what constitutes belonging to and in the region. Residence, Ibn Ḥazm writes, rather than birthplace, is what connects a person to a region: "When someone emigrates from another country (*bilād*) to us, we are the most entitled to him ... And if someone emigrates from us to somewhere else, we have no share in him, while the place (*makān*) that he chooses profits from him."[124] The preference for residence over birthright in establishing belonging recalls the flexibility of the idea of homeland and privileges a direct physical connection with the land itself over a genealogical or emotional connection. The vast majority of the treatise is then taken up with the enumeration of scholars in each category of learning upon whom Andalusians might lay valid claim according to this principle. Therefore, Ibn Ḥazm inscribes upon the land of Andalusia the names of those thinkers whose life and death occurred there and whose works vouchsafe its reputation and, by inference, his own.

This *faḍāʾil* treatise has a notable eastward orientation, explicitly setting Andalusia in competition with what might be considered the Islamic heartlands rather than with its more immediate, and similarly geographically peripheral, rival, the region of the Maghrib to its south.[125] Accordingly, Ibn Ḥazm takes care to kowtow to Baghdad as the supreme center of learning in the Islamic world, while at the same time insisting:

> Despite our country's (*baladnā*) distance from the source of knowledge and its remoteness from the dwelling of the *ʿulamāʾ*, we have mentioned among the works of its people such that if one sought their equivalent in Fārs and al-Ahwāz, in the Diyār Muḍar and the Diyār Rabīʿa, in Yemen and in Syria, their existence would be found lacking, despite the short distance of these countries (*bilād*) from Iraq, the destination of immigration for intelligence and those who possess it and the desired vantage point for learning and those who have gained it.[126]

Ibn Ḥazm thus represents Andalusia by its remoteness, its intellectual merits all the more meritorious than those of other regions because of this handicap. At the same time, the explicit comparison of Andalusia with regions that might be considered more geographically central acts itself as a performance of Andalusia's centrality, reinforced by Ibn Ḥazm's silence on the topic of its immediate neighbors. This *faḍāʾil* treatise constructs regionalism by establishing a textual rivalry in which Andalusia's human intellectual capital is pitted against that of a group of geographically central regions with which, it is implied, it has more in common than with other geographically remote regions on the periphery of the Islamic world. Ibn Ḥazm's resulting regional category of belonging is simultaneously connective, welcoming as it does any emigrant to Andalusia as one of its own, and bounded, its very distance and separation from other regions, both near and far, rendering it distinctive in the discourse of place.

The interplay between the bounded and connective natures of regions in all of these texts makes their representation in the discourse of place a political one.

Even when regions were not associated as explicitly with political regimes as was Egypt, their evocation in texts rested on a division of the world that separated peoples and polities as much as it did territories. The resulting regionalism lent itself particularly well to the promotion of one people or polity, even those considered marginal or heterodox, over another. However, the category of the region tends to privilege connectivity, or at least to complicate persistently any notion of absolute boundedness. A case in point might be how few regional monographs survive from the ninth to the eleventh centuries, so that the predominant format for the textual performance of the region in this period is the world geography, which by its very nature highlights the connectivity between regions. Even the few surviving monographs on single regions embed their territories within a vision of the world as a whole and its interconnected parts, if sometimes to establish rivalry or competition. That said, regions were not fuzzy areas brought into focus only when necessary for the promotion of a political regime or a particular lexicon. But neither were they persistently isolated from each other in texts. Instead of perceiving the connectivity between regions in the discourse of place as a failure to understand the concept of area or to employ "real borderlines," it should be seen as a product of the success of the cultural and linguistic unity of territories stretching from the Iberian Peninsula to the Oxus and Indus river valleys, even into the eleventh century. The reality of political fragmentation, which by the end of the period under study had rendered the unifying project of the Abbasid Caliphate a thing of the past, had not yet transformed regionalism into an exercise in exclusion.

Conclusion: Looking Forward

The simultaneously connective and bounded nature of regions in the discourse of place can be generalized to the categories of home and city as well. All three land-based categories of belonging were bounded by their necessary relationship to real plots of land, specifically imagined as places on the ground, destinations for visitation and immigration, goals for conquest, and sites for the erection of monumental architecture. But they became profoundly connective in the process of being imagined and textualized as part of the discourse of place. They had to be recognizable and legible; they were intended to communicate with an audience. Their representation in texts entailed an assembly of literary material from the pre-Islamic and Islamic periods, from interlocutors both Christian and Jewish, male and female, from Arabian nomads and Persian viziers, from prophets, caliphs, poets, and *ʿulamāʾ*. Homesickness was expressed equally by the bedouin and the city-based literati. Cities were erected in the geographical imagination from the rubble of sacred history, its prophets—like the land upon which they walked and the structures they built—touched by the human and the divine, impermanent, striving toward salvation, but stumbling—and crumbling—along the way. Cities were not inviolable sanctuaries, and homes once lost could always be found, or made, anew. Regions too were bounded but not impermeable, identifiable and coherent but not reified and isolated. The discourse of place was not a discourse of exclusion, even if—or especially because—its language was often the language of negotiation, contestation, restoration.

***

The analysis of the discourse of place in this book contributes to scholarship on the history of the Islamic world between the ninth and the eleventh centuries in three main ways. First, it offers an interpretive and methodological approach to sources from this period by reading them as purposefully crafted textual performances interacting with an audience. This approach reveals the multivalent and complex nature of texts and proposes a way to think about their influence in the culture at large, even in the absence of substantial evidence for circulation or reception. Related to this, considering a wide range of written and graphic texts in terms of a shared thematic focus rather than a shared genre or field illuminates patterns in form and content among a critical mass of sources. Second, in identifying land as the shared thematic focus of a wide range of texts, its importance among early Muslims and the many ways in which it was associated with claims to authority and belonging stand in sharp relief. In a period normally understood as politically and religiously fragmented, texts representing territories of different shapes and scales communicated an overwhelming sense of connectivity and accommodated heterogeneous peoples, pasts, and agendas. Third, by tracing the contours of the discourse of place in the earliest period of intensive written production among Muslims, this book lays the groundwork for further research on the geographical imagination and attachment to land up to the present day.

The discourse of place reached a fever pitch in many parts of the Islamic world in the centuries following the period covered in this book. The twelfth century witnessed the composition and circulation of Ibn ʿAsākir's landmark biographical dictionary the *Taʾrīkh madīnat Dimashq* (History of the city of Damascus), which bequeathed to posterity a fully developed statement of Syrian regionalism and an up-to-date topography of its principal city of Damascus. While Ibn ʿAsākir's Syria is crafted from some intentionally exclusionary textual strategies, marginalizing material used in earlier representations of the region that might seem to legitimize the claims of Christian Crusaders to Syrian territory, his Damascus reflects the same polyphony of sources that made cities in the earlier discourse of place symbols of continuity with the past and connectivity with the present.[1] A century later, Ibn Shaddād refined Ibn ʿAsākir's vision of Syrian regionalism, bringing Damascus into dialogue with the city of Aleppo to the north and fleshing out its nonurban areas in a paean to the stability and unity that Mamluk rule had brought to the region.[2]

Other areas too developed distinctive branches of the discourse of place punctuated by prominent texts and shaped by local contexts. Fifteenth-century Egypt gave birth to one of the most vivid commemorations of times past in a city in Arabic literature, al-Maqrīzī's historical topography of Cairo, known simply as the *Khiṭaṭ* (Delineation).[3] In Andalusia, the beginning of a flourishing regional discourse of place, articulated in the elegiac register, was linked to the realities of territorial loss and mass displacement in the centuries of the *Reconquista*.[4] In Ṭabaristān, Khurāsān, and Transoxiana over the next few centuries, the discourse of place was translated into and transformed by the newly widespread literary and chancellery languages of Persian and Turkish.[5] The increasingly energetic copying and circulation during the fourteenth and fifteenth centuries of earlier texts from the discourse of place in multiple centers of manuscript production in the Islamic world went hand in hand with new contributions and trends, as the burst of enthusiasm for composing *faḍāʾil* literature on Mecca and Medina in fifteenth-century Egypt attests.[6]

At the same time that more particularist and local manifestations of the discourse of place were emerging, a new turn to the universal, exemplified in geographical works by al-Idrīsī (d. 560/1165) and Yāqūt (d. 626/1229), celebrated connectivity. Al-Idrīsī's world geography, *Nuzhat al-mushtāq fīʾkhtirāq al-āfāq* (Pleasant strolls across distant lands), launched a new mapping tradition in the Islamic world—indeed in the world as a whole, as it was commissioned and executed at the Norman court of Roger II in Sicily and represented one of the earliest efforts anywhere to put Ptolemy's cartographic vision of the globe to practical and systematic application.[7] In addition to composing a lengthy written text on lands and peoples, al-Idrīsī designed seventy rectangular sectional maps, based on a gridlike division of the inhabited world by longitude and latitude. These sectional maps were intended explicitly to fit together to make an enormous world map. This cartographic project, which did not differentiate between the "Realm of Islam" and the rest of the inhabited world and which understood regions as mathematically determined segments of territory rather than bounded but connective "realms," was vigorously universalist. Despite al-Idrīsī's universalism and what might be thought of as the technical accomplishments on display in his cartographic project, the regional maps of the "Balkhī school" geographies continued to be copied concurrently with those of al-Idrīsī. Indeed, the thirty-some extant copies, abridgements, and Persian translations of al-Iṣṭakhrī's work, in most cases complete with a full set of maps, outnumber those of al-Idrīsī three to one and date from as late as the nineteenth century, four hundred years later than the most recent copy of the *Nuzhat al-mushtāq*. The lingering popularity of the "Balkhī school" map forms, even in the face of more universalist mapping traditions and new technologies, suggests the resonance of their bounded but connective performance of regionalism among the peoples of the *Mamlakat al-Islām* until very recently.

Yāqūt's voluminous geographical dictionary of the Islamic world, the *Muʿjam al-buldān* (Compendium of countries), represents a veritable archive of the discourse of place as it had developed up to the thirteenth century. It preserves fragments of a huge number of works that have otherwise been lost. Yāqūt's introduction can be seen as a manifesto to the production, reproduction, and preservation of knowledge about land in the Islamic world:

> This is a book on the names of countries; on mountains, valleys, and plains; on villages, post-houses, and dwellings; on seas, rivers, and lakes; on idols, graven images, and objects of heathen worship. I have not undertaken to write this book, nor dedicated myself to composing it, in a spirit of frolic or diversion. Nor have I been impelled to do so

> by dread or desire; nor moved by longing for my native land (*waṭan*); nor prompted by yearning for one who is loving and compassionate. Rather, I considered it my duty to address myself to this task, and, being capable of performing it, I regarded responding to its challenge as an inescapable obligation.[8]

For Yāqūt, participation in the discourse of place sprang from a self-consciously universalist position. It was not an exercise in local pride or nostalgia. It was a duty that related to his belief in God's command: "Journey through the land and behold the manner in which the disbelievers have met their end" (Qurʾān 6:11).[9] To reinforce this message, Yāqūt also quotes a tradition attributed to Jesus: "The world is a place of visitation and an abode of transition. Be you then travelers in it, and take warning from what remains of the traces (*āthār*) of the early ones."[10] For Yāqūt, land was the portal between the sacred past and the sacred future, and it was essential for Muslims to learn to read the land, to comprehend the cautionary tales it had to tell, and thus to prepare for God's salvation. Yāqūt intended his gazetteer as an act of restoration and preservation of the polyphonous heritage of the discourse of place in the present. He quotes from a great variety of sources and organizes his material under the relevant toponym, in alphabetical order, thus privileging among the many textual acts in the discourse of place that of naming the land. Yāqūt attributes his ability to name and interpret the land for his fellow Muslims to his tireless traveling, by which he means traveling on the ground, but he is equally, if not more, qualified for the task by virtue of his extensive travels in texts, his citational authority, and his mastery of the discourse of place.

Other medieval Muslim travelers on the ground, Ibn Jubayr and ʿAlī al-Harawī in the thirteenth, Ibn Baṭṭūṭa in the fourteenth, and Leo Africanus in the sixteenth centuries, were also travelers in texts. They inherited the bounded and connective understanding of territory bequeathed to them by the discourse of place and reproduced many of its tropes in the context of "firsthand" observations of the world around them.[11] They, like al-Muqaddasī centuries earlier, flaunted their credentials as travelers but revealed themselves to be as thoroughly steeped in the textual heritage of the discourse of place as their armchair counterparts. The world around them was, therefore, mediated by the texts that came before, which had established a genealogy of attachment to land and shaped certain territorial categories of belonging, just as it was by their own personalities, backgrounds, and experiences. Later, the Ottoman Empire would inspire in its subjects—urban flaneurs and long-distance travelers alike—new assertions of self in relation to both land and sea, even as its ateliers became key centers for the preservation of the early discourse of place.[12]

In the modern era, Middle Eastern intellectuals and political leaders would draw from the discourse of place to make authoritative and attractive expressions of territorial nationalism. The categories of belonging explored in this book—home, city, and region—would be put to the tasks of evoking and elaborating the linked categories of nation and peoplehood.[13] One of the goals of this book has been to deepen scholarly engagement with nationalist discourses in Middle East history, as the use of vocabulary, source material, and methodologies in these discourses must be compared not only to their European counterparts but also to the earlier discourse of place to comprehend their richness, allusiveness, and multivalence.[14] At the same time, this comparison reveals the transformation of the categories of belonging shaped by the early discourse of place into more exclusive and exclusionary identities. The language of the *waṭan* in particular has marked the intellectual production of nationalist movements in Turkey, Iran, and the Arab world as well as of diasporic communities of Arabic speakers all over the globe. In the period after the eleventh century, the politics of the *waṭan* overlapped increasingly with those of the region to generate an indigenous genealogy for Middle Eastern territorial nationalism, so that it need not be seen solely as a borrowing or import from more "rooted," i.e., European, civilizations.[15] However, encounters with Europeans also transformed the concept of *waṭan* as a category of belonging in new—and newly exclusionary—ways; its articulation in the context of nationalist resistance to imperialism, for instance, has established bases for belonging that are bounded and gendered at an unprecedented level of rigidity.[16]

The prolific production in the Middle East over the past century of critical editions of texts from the discourse of place, many of which include impassioned and nationalistic introductions by their editors, testifies to the ongoing relevance of these early expressions of attachment to land in the Islamic world.[17] Such a phenomenon brings the act of interpretation performed in this book full circle. The texts analyzed here have, in many cases, been made available, and thus mediated, by contemporary interest among Middle Easterners in their own history of attachment to land. This interest stands in sharp contrast to the tendency, particularly pronounced in Europe and North America, to underestimate the role played by land in conceptions of community and polity among Arabs and Muslims and to overdetermine the roles played by kinship and religion. This tendency has been compounded in recent years by views of globalization as a uniquely deterritorializing process. Thus, globalization has been seen as heralding the end of the nation-state, or at least loosening territorial attachments in its constant flows of information, capital, and people. Moreover, political rhetoric about the global dimensions of the "War on Terror" is dominated by the threatening figure of the "Muslim terrorist," loyal only to a worldwide network of like-minded Muslims committed to otherworldly and utopian (or dystopian) goals rather than local, national, or geopolitical agendas. These assumptions have distracted from the modes in which territories, imagined in new ways and deployed in new forms of discourse, have retained wide relevance in the geographical imagination as well as on the ground in the late twentieth and twenty-first centuries—not just among Muslims or in the Middle East, but everywhere.[18] At a time when tensions between the local and the global inspire new notions of rootedness, it is more vital than ever to examine the changing ways in which people have looked to the land to declare loyalty and claim belonging over the centuries—the many ways in which they have expressed the power of place.

NOTES

Introduction

1. Ibn Ḥawqal, *Kitāb ṣūrat al-arḍ,* 329–330. I have taken the liberty of filling in some details based on other information about Ibn Ḥawqal's life and the probable context of this kind of encounter. See the introduction to J. H. Kramers' French translation of the work, Ibn Ḥawqal, *La Configuration de la Terre,* ix–xvii; see also Miquel, 1:299–309.
2. This differs from André Miquel's approach in his masterful four-volume *La géographie humaine du monde musulman.* The first volume of this work traces a genealogy of Arabic geographical writing that culminates in what he calls the "*masālik wa-l-mamālik*" genre, a series of works produced between the mid-tenth and mid-eleventh century that offered "a veritable human geography" of the Islamic world. He regards historical writing as too backward-looking and particularist to belong in this category; see Miquel, 1:28–33, 239–241, 253–257. In the second, third, and fourth volumes of the work, Miquel changes tack and treats his corpus of geographical writing as an archive for evidence of geographical reality and attitudes toward that reality through the eleventh century. This approach not surprisingly tends to privilege those works, primarily from the "*al-masālik wa-l-mamālik*" genre, that appear to document this reality most transparently. For a critique of the "circularity" of this approach, see Bray, 79–80. For a related critique, see Montgomery, "Serendipity, Resistance, and Multivalency."
3. See LaCapra, 250.
4. On the ways in which writing and speech are performative, see Austen, *How to Do Things with Words*; Pratt, *Toward a Speech Act Theory*; Butler, *Excitable Speech.* For a relevant application of this theory, see Smith, *Religion, Culture, and Sacred Space.*
5. This departs from Samer Ali's conceptualization of performance as limited to its extratextual dimensions, defining it as an oral act before an audience; see Ali, *Arabic Literary Salons.*
6. This use of "serendipity" comes from Montgomery, "Serendipity, Resistance, and Multivalency."
7. On approaching surviving manuscript copies and printed critical editions of a particular work as stages in a "reception history," rather than as authorial redactions, see Zadeh, *Mapping Frontiers,* especially chapters 6–7.
8. Although this book's chronological focus is the same as Miquel's, it does not share his characterization of geographical writing after the mid-eleventh century as a casualty of disappearance of unity in the Islamic world, increasingly produced in "a climate of prudence and short-sightedness"; see Miquel, 1:ix–xx.
9. On "strategies of compilation," see Donner, "ʿUthmān and the Rāshidūn Caliphs."
10. For one such study, see Zadeh, *Mapping Frontiers.*

Chapter 1

1. On the complexities of defining *adab* in this period, see *EI*[2]: "Adab"; Malti-Douglas, *Structures of Avarice*, 5–28; Bonebakker, "*Adab* and the Concept of *Belles-Lettres*"; Kilpatrick and Leder, "Classical Arabic Prose Literature"; Heinrichs, "The Classification of the Sciences"; Sadan, "*Hārūn al-Rashīd and the Brewer*."
2. On the *adab* anthology, see Thomas, "The Concept of *Muḥāḍara*." On contrastive enumeration, see Geries, *Un genre littéraire*. On the oral performance of the kinds of material collected in *adab* anthologies, see Ali, *Arabic Literary Salons*.
3. While it has been argued that the world of *adab* was a secular world that could be contrasted with the world of *dīn* (religion) or *ʿilm* (religious knowledge), this contrast is overstated for the period under study. It is clear that the methods for analyzing Ḥadīth, for instance, were articulated as an area of specialist inquiry among the *ʿulamāʾ* by the tenth century. However, it is unclear that ninth- to eleventh-century Muslims considered *adab* anthologies devoid of religious significance or at odds with the culture that produced more specialized scholarship on the Qurʾān or Ḥadīth, especially since so many *ʿulamāʾ* authored works that might be categorized as *adab*; on this question, see Malti-Douglas, "Playing with the Sacred."
4. al-Jāḥiẓ [attr.], *al-Ḥanīn*, 3–4. Other extant anthologies that will be considered in this chapter include the fifth section of *al-Muntahā fī l-kamāl*, published independently as Ibn al-Marzubān, *Kitāb al-ḥanīn ilā l-awṭān*; al-Bayhaqī, "Maḥāsin al-ḥanīn ilā l-awṭān" and "Masāwiʾ man kariha al-waṭan," in *al-Maḥāsin wa-l-masāwiʾ*, 1:487–506; al-Jāḥiẓ [attr.], "Maḥāsin ḥubb al-waṭan" and "Ḍidduhu," in *al-Maḥāsin wa-l-aḍdād*, 118–127; al-Rāghib al-Iṣfahānī, "wa-Mimmā jāʾa fī l-ḥanīn ilā l-awṭān," in *Muḥāḍarāt al-udabāʾ*, 2:652–655; al-Ḥuṣrī al-Qayrawānī, "al-Ḥanīn ilā l-waṭan," in *Zahr al-ādāb*, 2:681–689; Ibn ʿAbd al-Barr, "Bāb al-bukāʾ ʿalā mā maḍā min al-azmān wa-l-talahhuf ʿalā ṣāliḥ al-ikhwān, wa-l-ḥanīn ilā l-awṭān," in *Bahjat al-majālis*, 1:795–807. Although the parameters of this study are the ninth to the eleventh centuries, this chapter also includes citations to later anthologies on the same topic: al-Zamakhsharī, "Bāb al-bilād wa-l-diyār wa-l-abniya wa-mā yattaṣilu bihā min dhikr al-ʿimāra wa-l-kharāb wa-ḥubb al-waṭan," in *Rabīʿ al-abrār*, 1:169–211; idem, "Bāb al-shawq wa-l-ḥanīn ilā l-awṭān ... ," in *Rabīʿ al-abrār*, 2:331–333; Ibn al-ʿArabī, "Fī l-waṭan," "Khabar ẓarīf fī l-ḥanīn ilā l-waṭan," "wa-Min bāb ḥubb al-waṭan," and "wa-Min bāb al-ghurba wa-dhikr al-waṭan," in *Kitāb muḥāḍarat al-abrār*, 2:20, 69–70, 409–412, 431–433; al-Ghuzūlī, "Fī I-ḥanīn ilā l-awṭān wa-tadhakkur man bihā min al-quṭṭān," in *Maṭāliʿ al-budūr*, 611–623.
5. See, for examples, Arazi, "*al-Ḥanīn ilā al-awṭān*," 300–305, 319–325; al-Qadi, 19–23; al-Jubūrī, 51–133. For a similar assessment focusing on a single poet's oeuvre, see Granara, "Remaking Muslim Sicily."
6. Thus, while the very interesting tenth-century *adab* anthology *Kitāb al-ghurabāʾ* attributed to Abū l-Faraj al-Iṣfahānī is a collection of graffiti on the experience of alienation, it does not primarily or even substantially evoke a sense of territoriality. Although many of its entries were left by travelers, Patricia Crone and Shmuel Moreh, in their English translation and study of the work, argue that "it is their family, friends, and lovers that they hanker for, never physical surroundings such as landscape, cityscape, vegetation, or climate, let alone social, political, or religious institutions"; see al-Iṣfahānī [attr.], 10.
7. Haarmann, *al-Umma wa-l-waṭan*; *EI*[2]: "Waṭan." See also Ghomi, "The Land of Love."
8. On "strategies of compilation," see Donner, 47. For the significance of titles and subheadings in *adab* anthologies, see Thomas, "The Concept of *Muḥāḍara*."
9. Ibn al-Marzubān, *Kitāb al-ḥanīn*, 36.
10. The attribution of the earliest extant anthology on *al-ḥanīn ilā l-awṭān* to al-Jāḥiẓ dates back to the twelfth century; see Pellat, "Nouvel essai," 138. However, this attribution has been disputed, as the title does not appear under the list of works by al-Jāḥiẓ in the well-known tenth-century bio-bibliography: Ibn al-Nadīm, *al-Fihrist*, 344–351; idem, *The Fihrist*, trans. Dodge, 397–409. Jalīl al-ʿAṭiyya makes a convincing case that this anthology was actually authored by the lesser-known Mūsā b. ʿĪsā al-Kisrawī, who probably died several decades later than al-Jāḥiẓ and was the major source for Ibn al-Marzubān's tenth-century anthology on the same topic; see Ibn al-Marzubān, *Kitāb al-ḥanīn*, 10–12. Nonetheless, the anthology continues to be published in collections of the essays of al-Jāḥiẓ, including the following English translation:

al-Jāḥiẓ, "Homesickness," trans. Hutchins, 123–137. The attribution of the longer work of contrastive enumeration, *al-Maḥāsin wa-l-aḍdād*, to al-Jāḥiẓ dates back to the eleventh century, but this attribution has been refuted definitively; see Pellat, 147. The real author remains unknown. For a discussion of the significance of such "forgeries," with special mention of this latter work, see Kilito, 64–66, 73–75. For a partially extant essay on cities and regions, including a small selection of material on *al-ḥanīn ilā l-awṭān*, that was more likely authored by al-Jāḥiẓ himself, see al-Jāḥiẓ, *Kitāb al-buldān*.

11. For a list of the anthologies from this period, including those that are no longer extant, see Ibn al-Marzubān, *Kitāb al-ḥanīn*, 9–10; al-Jubūrī, *al-Ḥanīn wa-l-ghurba*, 14–16.
12. My analysis in the rest of this chapter was greatly eased by Kathrin Müller's meticulous taxonomy of motifs and corresponding textual units found in the four earliest of these anthologies; see Müller, "*al-Ḥanīn ilā l-awṭān*."
13. Arazi, "*al-Ḥanīn ilā al-awṭān*," 294–295, 296–298.
14. Ibn Marzubān, *Kitāb al-ḥanīn*, 87, 93, 101.
15. al-Jāḥiẓ [attr.], *al-Ḥanīn*, 4.
16. See Arazi, "*al-Ḥanīn ilā al-awṭān*," 293, 296; al-Qadi, 10–11; al-Jubūrī, 159–162. For examples, see al-Jāḥiẓ, *Kitāb al-buldān*, 465–466; al-Jāḥiẓ [attr.], *al-Ḥanīn*, 4, 6, 7, 9, 10–11, 23; Ibn al-Marzubān, *Kitāb al-ḥanīn*, 66, 101; al-Bayhaqī, 1:490, 493, 506; al-Jāḥiẓ [attr.], *al-Maḥāsin*, 120; al-Ḥuṣrī al-Qayrawānī, 2:681; al-Zamakhsharī, 2:332–333; Ibn al-ʿArabī, 2:411; al-Ghuzūlī, 622.
17. al-Jāḥiz [attr.], *al-Ḥanīn*, 10; Ibn al-Marzubān, *Kitāb al-ḥanīn*, 41; al-Bayhaqī, 1:487; al-Jāḥiẓ [attr.], *al-Maḥāsin*, 118; al-Rāghib al-Iṣfahānī, 2:653. See also al-Jāḥiz [attr.], *al-Ḥanīn*, 14–16; Ibn al-Marzubān, *Kitāb al-ḥanīn*, 41; al-Bayhaqī, 1:488–489; al-Jāḥiẓ [attr.], *al-Maḥāsin*, 119.
18. Ibn al-Marzubān, *Kitāb al-ḥanīn*, 43; al-Bayhaqī, 1:490. While the verses appear anonymously in these two anthologies, elsewhere they are attributed to Hārūn al-Rashīd's sister ʿUlayya bint al-Mahdī; see al-Iṣfahānī [attr.], 47–48; Usāma b. Munqidh, 208–209; al-Ghuzūlī, 615. They also appear in the entry for "Marj al-Qalʿa" in the well-known thirteenth-century gazetteer: Yāqūt, *Muʿjam al-buldān*, 5:101. For Hippocrates and Galen, see al-Jāḥiẓ [attr.], *al-Ḥanīn*, 7–8; Ibn al-Marzubān, *Kitāb al-ḥanīn*, 40; al-Bayhaqī, 1:487; al-Jāḥiẓ [attr.], *al-Maḥāsin*, 118; Ibn al-ʿArabī, 2:410. A ninth-century geographer cites Hippocrates in a subsection entitled "Dhikr ḥubb al-awṭān" in the section devoted to his birthplace, Hamadan; see Ibn al-Faqīh, *Mukhtaṣar kitāb al-buldān*, 5:238. A tenth-century historian and encyclopedist cites Hippocrates and Galen; see al-Masʿūdī, *Murūj al-dhahab*, 2:72. On beliefs about the healing properties of the water or soil of the homeland expressed by a variety of characters, see al-Jāḥiẓ [attr.], *al-Ḥanīn*, 12–13 (bedouin), 33–34 (ancient Persian royalty), 35 (Barmakids); al-Rāghib al-Iṣfahānī, 2:653 (bedouin and ancient Persian royalty); al-Zamakhsharī, 1:198 (bedouin), 208 (ancient Persian royalty and Barmakids); al-Ghuzūlī, 611 (bedouin, ancient Persian royalty, and Barmakids).
19. al-Jāḥiẓ [attr.], *al-Ḥanīn*, 34–35; al-Zamakhsharī, 1:208; al-Ghuzūlī, 611.
20. al-Jāḥiẓ [attr.], *al-Ḥanīn*, 6, 6–7; Ibn al-Marzubān, *Kitāb al-ḥanīn*, 66; al-Bayhaqī, 1:490, 495; al-Jāḥiẓ [attr.], *al-Maḥāsin*, 118–119, 120. For variants focusing on the concept of *ghidhāʾ* ("nourishment"), see al-Jāḥiẓ [attr.], *al-Ḥanīn*, 6; al-Bayhaqī, 1:495; al-Jāḥiẓ [attr.], *al-Mahāsin*, 119; al-Rāghib al-Iṣfahānī, 2:653; al-Zamakhsharī, 1:198; Ibn al-Faqīh, *Mukhtaṣar kitāb al-buldān*, 238; al-Masʿūdī, *Murūj al-dhahab*, 2:71.
21. al-Jāḥiẓ [attr.], *al-Ḥanīn*, 11; al-Ḥuṣrī al-Qayrawānī, 2:681; al-Zamakhsharī, 1:198, 2:331; al-Ghuzūlī, 611.
22. al-Jāḥiẓ [attr.], *al-Ḥanīn*, 6, 11; al-Zamakhsharī, 1:197; Ibn al-ʿArabī, 2:411.
23. *EI*²: "Raḍāʿ or Riḍāʿ."
24. al-Jāḥiẓ [attr.], *al-Ḥanīn*, 6; al-Zamakhsharī, 1:198; al-Masʿūdī, *Murūj al-dhahab*, 2:71.
25. See Musallam, 39–59.
26. al-Jāḥiẓ [attr.], *al-Ḥanīn*, 11; Ibn al-Marzubān, *Kitāb al-ḥanīn*, 65; al-Bayhaqī, 1:490; al-Jāḥiẓ [attr.], *al-Maḥāsin*, 120; Ibn al-ʿArabī, 2:411.
27. al-Jāḥiẓ [attr.], *al-Ḥanīn*, 22; Ibn al-ʿArabī, 2:432. For other material about women missing their homelands after leaving for marriage, see al-Jāḥiẓ [attr.], *al-Ḥanīn*, 12; Ibn al-ʿArabī, 2:70, 411, 432–433.
28. For more, see sections on women, al-Jubūrī, 101–102; Arazi, "*al-Ḥanīn ilā al-awṭān*," 306; Ḥuwwar, 167–187. A study of gender and law in the seventeenth and eighteenth centuries

mentions *fatāwā* (legal opinions) limiting the distance a man could insist his wife live away from her hometown or family; see Tucker, 63–64.

29. Ibn ʿAbd al-Barr, 1:804–805. A variation on this anecdote and these verses appear in Ibn al-ʿArabī, 2:69–70; and in the entry for "al-Uqḥuwāna," a site near Mecca, in Yāqūt, *Muʿjam al-buldān*, 1:234.
30. One anthology includes a subsection devoted entirely to the idea of homeland as site of social belonging entitled "Longing for places because of their people"; see Ibn al-Marzubān, *Kitāb al-ḥanīn*, 45.
31. al-Rāghib al-Iṣfahānī, 2:652; al-Ḥuṣrī al-Qayrawānī, 2:681; Ibn ʿAbd al-Barr, 1:795; Ibn al-ʿArabī, 2:410; al-Ghuzūlī, 611; Ibn al-Faqīh, *Mukhtaṣar kitāb al-buldān*, 238; al-Masʿūdī, *Murūj al-dhahab*, 2:71. For variants, see al-Jāḥiẓ [attr.], *al-Ḥanīn*, 9–10; Ibn al-Marzubān, *Kitāb al-ḥanīn*, 40; Ibn ʿAbd al-Barr, 1:795.
32. al-Rāghib al-Iṣfahānī, 2:653; al-Ḥuṣrī al-Qayrawānī, 2:682; al-Zamakhsharī, 1:206; Ibn al-ʿArabī, 2:69; al-Ghuzūlī, 614; Usāma b. Munqidh, 222. These verses appear as the sole entry under the subheading "What has been said about love of homelands (*awṭān*)" along with the curious commentary that Ibn al-Rūmī was "the first to elucidate the reason for love of homeland (*waṭan*)" in a fourteenth-century *adab* encyclopedia; see al-Nuwayrī, 1:415.
33. al-Jāḥiẓ [attr.], *al-Ḥanīn*, 21–22; Ibn al-Marzubān, *Kitāb al-ḥanīn*, 42–43. These verses appear in several variations in the anthologies, each of which features place names from the Arabian Peninsula, in this case Ṣāra, a mountain near the settlement of Taymāʾ, and the tribal lands of the Banū Ghaṭafān. For the variants, see al-Rāghib al-Iṣfahānī, 2:653; al-Ḥuṣrī al-Qayrawānī, 2:682; Ibn ʿAbd al-Barr, 1:802; Ibn al-ʿArabī, 2:431; Usāma b. Munqidh, 268–269.
34. For more on Ḥammād b. Isḥaq al-Mawṣilī, see Ibn al-Nadīm, *al-Fihrist*, 270–274; idem, *The Fihrist*, trans. Dodge, 307–312. Ṭayyiʾ was the name of a tribal group and a region in the northeastern Arabian Peninsula.
35. See Ali, *Arabic Literary Salons*.
36. Other variations on these verses identify as a rite of passage the unfastening of the amulets at adolescence, marked by the sprouting of the mustache in many examples, but also with the onset of intellectual maturity, applicable to both boys and girls. See al-Jāḥiẓ [attr.], *al-Ḥanīn*, 4–5; Ibn al-Marzubān, *Kitāb al-ḥanīn*, 43–44, 47; al-Bayhaqī, 1:491; al-Jāḥiẓ [attr.], *al-Maḥāsin*, 120–121; al-Ḥuṣrī al-Qayrawānī, 2:684, 685; Ibn ʿAbd al-Barr, 1:802; Ibn al-ʿArabī, 2:20, 432.
37. Arazi, "*al-Ḥanīn ilā al-awṭān*," 307; Stetkevych, *The Zephyrs of Najd*, 50ff.
38. al-Ḥuṣrī al-Qayrawānī, 2:681.
39. Stetkevych, *The Zephyrs of Najd*; idem, "Toward an Arabic Elegiac Lexicon"; Enderwitz, "Homesickness and Love in Arabic Poetry"; El Tayib, "Pre-Islamic Poetry"; *EI²*: "Nasīb."
40. al-Jāḥiẓ [attr.], *al-Ḥanīn*, 5; Ibn al-Marzubān, *Kitāb al-ḥanīn*, 36; Usāma b. Munqidh, 267–268. A variant on the verses that omits the image of Sulaymā can be found in Ibn al-ʿArabī, 2:20.
41. Stetkevych, *The Zephyrs of Najd*, 81; Kilito, 55–56.
42. Ibn al-Marzubān, *Kitāb al-ḥanīn*, 48. The same verses with a slight variant are recited by Abū al-Naṣr al-Asadī in al-Jāḥiẓ [attr.], *al-Ḥanīn*, 21. See also Usāma b. Munqidh, 351; Ibn al-ʿArabī, 2:431. For other verses expressing a similar sentiment recited by a member of the Banū Hudhayl, an Arabian tribe, see al-Jāḥiẓ [attr.], *al-Ḥanīn*, 23–24; Ibn al-Marzubān, *Kitāb al-ḥanīn*, 48; and by the early eight-century poet Dhū l-Rumma, see al-Jāḥiẓ [attr.], *al-Ḥanīn*, 29–30; Ibn al-Marzubān, *Kitāb al-ḥanīn*, 49.
43. al-Bayhaqī, 1:491; al-Jāḥiẓ [attr.], *al-Mahāsin*, 121; Ibn al-Marzubān, *Kitāb al-ḥanīn*, 43; al-Jāḥiẓ [attr.], *al-Ḥanīn*, 24.
44. These verses are recited by Ibn al-Rūmī in al-Ḥuṣrī al-Qayrawānī, 2:684.
45. This is the analysis of several important studies of modern nationalist discourse gendering the nation (*waṭan*) female and the citizen who owes the nation loyalty or love male; see Massad, "Conceiving the Masculine"; Baron, *Egypt as a Woman*; Najmabadi, *Women with Mustaches*.
46. Arazi, "*al-Ḥanīn ilā al-awṭān*," 294–299.
47. It may also account for the fact that many of the larger *adab* collections considered here include anthologies on travel or displacement, often placed alongside the anthologies on *al-ḥanīn ilā l-awṭān*. For examples, see al-Rāghib al-Iṣfahānī, "wa-Mimmā jāʾa fī l-tagharrub,"

in *Muḥāḍarāt al-udabāʾ*, 2:642–652; al-Bayhaqī, "Maḥāsin al-duʿāʾ li-l-musāfir" and "Masāwiʾ al-duʿāʾ li-l-musāfir," in *al-Maḥāsin wa-l-masāwiʾ*, 1:507–510; Ibn al-Marzubān, "Bāb al-duʿāʾ li-l-musāfir" and "Bāb al-duʿāʾ ʿalā l-musāfir" in *al-Muntahā fī l-kamāl*, published independently as *Kitāb al-shawq wa-l-firāq*, 47–49, 64–67; Ibn ʿAbd al-Barr, "Bāb al-safar wa-l-ightirāb," in *Bahjat al-Majālis*, 1:221–237; al-Ḥuṣrī al-Qayrawānī, "al-Bāʿith ʿalā l-raḥīl" and "al-Waṣāyā fī l-safar," in *Zahr al-Ādāb*, 1:383–387.

48. Ibn ʿAbd al-Barr, 1:221–237, 238–245.
49. Ibn al-Marzubān, *Kitāb al-ḥanīn*, 53, 57; al-Rāghib al-Iṣfahānī, 2:644, 645 ("wa-Mimmā jāʾa fī l-tagharrub"). See also al-Bayhaqī, 1:490.
50. For more on this ambivalence toward the figure of the bedouin, see Sadan, "An Admirable and Ridiculous Hero." See also Müller, 42–43; Arazi, "*al-Ḥanīn ilā al-awṭān*," 307.
51. al-Bayhaqī, 1:492; al-Jāḥiẓ [attr.], *al-Maḥāsin*, 125; al-Rāghib al-Iṣfahānī, 2:644 ("wa-Mimmā jāʾa fī l-tagharrub").
52. Attributed to ʿUmar by Ibn al-Marzubān, *Kitāb al-ḥanīn*, 40; al-Bayhaqī, 1:487; al-Jāḥiẓ [attr.], *al-Maḥāsin*, 118. Attributed to Muḥammad by al-Rāghib al-Iṣfahānī, 2:652. Anonymous saying in al-Jāḥiẓ [attr.], *al-Ḥanīn*, 9; Ibn al-ʿArabī, 2:410; al-Ghuzūlī, 622. For related sayings, see al-Jāḥiẓ, *Kitāb al-buldān*, 463–464; al-Jāḥiẓ [attr.], *al-Ḥanīn*, 7, 8, 9; Ibn al-Marzubān, *Kitāb al-ḥanīn*, 36, 40, 55; al-Bayhaqī, 1:487, 490; al-Jāḥiẓ [attr.], *al-Maḥāsin*, 118, 119–120; al-Rāghib al-Iṣfahānī, 2:645 ("wa-Mimmā jāʾa fī l-tagharrub"), 652; al-Zamakhsharī, 1:176; al-Ghuzūlī, 611; al-Masʿūdī, *Murūj al-dhahab*, 2:71. See also the following eleventh-century work of contrastive enumeration, which does not include an anthology on *al-ḥanīn ilā l-awṭān*, al-Thaʿālibī, *al-Laṭāʾif wa-l-ẓarāʾif*, 230 ("Bāb dhamm al-ghurba").
53. See the discussion of "pro-alienation literature," in al-Qadi, 13–18.
54. al-Rāghib al-Iṣfahānī, 2:644 ("wa-Mimmā jāʾa fī l-tagharrub"). See also Ibn al-Faqīh, *Mukhtaṣar kitāb al-buldān*, 49 ("Bāb fī madḥ al-ghurba wa-l-ightirāb"). For a variant, see Ibn al-Marzubān, *Kitāb al-ḥanīn*, 60. For related sayings, see al-Bayhaqī, 1:493; al-Jāḥiẓ [attr.], *al-Maḥāsin*, 125. For a variant of this saying attributed to ʿAlī b. Abī Ṭālib, see al-Jubūrī, *al-Ḥanīn wa-l-ghurba*, 17.
55. Ibn al-Marzubān, *Kitāb al-ḥanīn*, 60; al-Thaʿālibī, *al-Laṭāʾif wa-l-ẓarāʾif*, 229 ("Bāb madḥ al-ghurba").
56. Ibn al-Marzubān, *Kitāb al-ḥanīn*, 59; al-Bayhaqī, 1:493; al-Jāḥiẓ [attr.], *al-Maḥāsin*, 125–126; Ibn ʿAbd al-Barr, 1:244; al-Thaʿālibī, *al-Laṭāʾif wa-l-ẓarāʾif*, 229 ("Bāb madḥ al-ghurba"); Ibn al-Faqīh, *Mukhtaṣar kitāb al-buldān*, 48 ("Bāb fī madḥ al-ghurba wa-l-ightirāb"). A variant of the second verse is attributed to Abū Dulaf in al-Rāghib al-Iṣfahānī, 2:652.
57. al-Rāghib al-Iṣfahānī, 2:645 ("wa-Mimmā jāʾa fī l-tagharrub"). These verses are quoted anonymously in Ibn al-Marzubān, *Kitāb al-ḥanīn*, 59; al-Thaʿālibī, *al-Laṭāʾif wa-l-ẓarāʾif*, 229 ("Bāb madḥ al-ghurba").
58. Ibn ʿAbd al-Barr, 1:238.
59. Ibid., 240.
60. Ibid., 238.
61. For more on the "brigand poets" and Mālik b. al-Rayb, see Arazi, "*al-Ḥanīn ilā al-awṭān*," 303, note 52.
62. Ibn ʿAbd al-Barr, 1:243–244.
63. al-Bayhaqī, 1:496–498.
64. Ibid., 498–501.
65. Ibn ʿAbd al-Barr, 1:805–807.
66. See also the anecdote about an Abbasid caliph who married a bedouin woman, built her a palace on the banks of the Tigris near Samarra complete with camel and goats to remind her of home, but who ultimately allowed her to return to her family in the desert because of some verses she recited expressing her homesickness; Ibn al-ʿArabī, 2:70, 432–433.
67. On the use of poetry recitation as an effective method of making requests of a patron, see Ali, *Arabic Literary Salons*, 75–116.
68. al-Bayhaqī, 1:492; al-Jāḥiẓ [attr.], *al-Maḥāsin*, 125; Ibn al-Faqīh, *Mukhtaṣar kitāb al-buldān*, 48 ("Bāb fī madḥ al-ghurba wa-l-ightirāb"). A similar saying is attributed to the Prophet Muḥammad in al-Rāghib al-Iṣfahānī, 2:242 ("wa-Mimmā jāʾa fī l-tagharrub").

69. Ibn al-Marzubān, *Kitāb al-ḥanīn*, 61. See also al-Rāghib al-Iṣfahānī, 2:642 ("wa-Mimmā jā'a fī l-tagharrub"); al-Tha'ālibī, *al-Laṭā'if wa-l-ẓarā'if*, 224 ("Bāb madḥ al-safar"); Ibn al-Faqīh, *Mukhtaṣar kitāb al-buldān*, 47 ("Bāb fī madḥ al-ghurba wa-l-ightirāb"). The related verses, Qur'ān 73:20 and 62:10, are quoted in al-Jāḥiẓ, *Kitāb al-buldān*, 465.
70. al-Jāḥiẓ, *Kitāb al-buldān*, 464; al-Jāḥiẓ [attr.], *al-Ḥanīn*, 9; Ibn al-Marzubān, *Kitāb al-ḥanīn*, 39; al-Bayhaqī, 1:487; al-Jāḥiẓ [attr.], *al-Maḥāsin*, 120; Ibn al-'Arabī, 2:410.
71. Ibn 'Abd al-Barr, 1:802–807.
72. al-Zamakhsharī, 2:331; al-Ghuzūlī, 611, 623.
73. Arazi, "*al-Ḥanīn ilā al-awṭān*," 305–319. For more on the *Shu'ūbiyya*, see Norris, "*Shu'ūbiyyah* in Arabic Literature"; Mottahedeh, "The Shu'ūbīyah Controversy."
74. al-Jāḥiẓ [attr.], *al-Ḥanīn*, 4.
75. Ibid., 9.
76. Among the features of bedouin life that might have inspired mockery in this anthology are their bizarre culinary preferences, as in the bedouin abroad who hungered for "a one-eyed, impotent male lizard" (ibid., 10), and irrational beliefs, as in "they deem the [fertile] countryside unhealthy" (ibid., 8). For more on the complexity of bedouin heroism in Abbasid literary circles, see Sadan, "An Admirable and Ridiculous Hero."
77. An early twelfth-century *adab* compendium embeds material on *al-ḥanīn ilā l-awṭān* in an anthology that also includes descriptions of cities from North Africa to Central Asia and the urban built environment from public baths to palaces; see al-Zamakhsharī, 1:169–211 ("Bāb al-bilād wa-l-diyār wa-l-abniya wa-mā yattaṣilu bihā min dhikr al-'imāra wa-l-kharāb wa-ḥubb al-waṭan"). While the Arabian Peninsula still appears in some of the anthologized material, the cities of Mecca and Medina receiving particular attention, bedouin interlocutors are few and far between in this anthology.
78. al-Bayhaqī, 1:501–501. Al-Ahwāz refers to a town situated in the southwestern corner of what is today Iran. For a work dedicated to a collection of such graffiti, see al-Iṣfahānī [attr.], *The Book of Strangers*.
79. Ibn al-Marzubān, *Kitāb al-ḥanīn*, 67.
80. Ibid., 79; al-Rāghib al-Iṣfahānī, 2:647 ("wa-Mimmā jā'a fī l-tagharrub"); Ibn al-Faqīh, *Mukhtaṣar kitāb al-buldān*, 51 ("Bāb fī madḥ al-ghurba wa-l-ightirāb"). These verses are also cited in the introduction to al-Mas'ūdī, *Kitāb al-tanbīh*, 7. Al-Raqqatayn refers to the "sister-cities" of al-Raqqa and al-Rāfiqa in what is today northeastern Syria, and al-Fusṭāṭ refers to the garrison city founded in the seventh century just to the south of what would become the site of Cairo in the tenth century. For more on al-Khiḍr, see *EI*[2]: "*Khaḍir*."
81. al-Rāghib al-Iṣfahānī, 2:652.
82. al-Ḥuṣrī al-Qayrawānī, 2:682–683; al-Ghuzūlī, 614.
83. For examples of references to the *al-ḥanīn ilā l-awṭān* tradition outside of *adab* anthologies in the discourse of place, see al-Māfarrūkhī, 52, 61–64; al-Rāzī, 181–184; 'Umar b. Shabba, 283–299. For a similar assessment focusing on a single poet's oeuvre, see Granara, "Remaking Muslim Sicily."
84. al-Khaṭīb al-Baghdādī, 1:46.
85. Ibn 'Abd Rabbih, 29:75.

Chapter 2

1. Franz Rosenthal tentatively characterizes these as "a truncated form of theological local historiography," which is far too narrow a characterization; see Rosenthal, *A History of Muslim Historiography*, 149. Certainly, *faḍā'il* treatises on the Qur'ān, the Prophet, ritual devotions, or religiously significant cities like Mecca, Medina, or Jerusalem were undertaken with attention to the sources and methods of religious scholarship; for examples, see the sections devoted to Medina in the following well-known compendia of Ḥadīth from the eighth and ninth centuries: Muslim, 9:134–171 ("Kitāb al-ḥajj"); al-Bukhārī, 3:271–286 ("Kitāb al-ḥajj," nos. 1680–1703); Mālik, 1: 884–897 (Book 45, "Kitāb al-Jāmi'," nos. 1–26); al-San'ānī, 9:260–269 (nos. 17145–17172). For a discussion of such "merits" literature in the context of the development of the Ḥadīth, see Afsaruddin, "In Praise of the Caliphs." However, there is nothing particular to the format of *faḍā'il* treatises that required either a pious topic or the expertise of the

ʿulamāʾ, and "merits" literature on cities often bears distinct similarities to *adab* anthologies, which themselves did not exclude religious material; for an example, see chapter ten (entitled "Khaṣāʾiṣ al-buldān wa-dhikr maḥāsinihā wa-masāwīhā") in al-Thaʿālibī, *Laṭāʾif al-maʿārif*, 152–239. On the use of religious sources in *adab* works, see Malti-Douglas, "Playing with the Sacred." For more on the origins of and sensibilities apparent in *faḍāʾil* literature in general, see *EI*²: "Faḍīla"; Gruber, *Verdienst und Rang*; Arazi, "Matériaux pour l'étude du conflit."

2. While a large number of topographical histories, *faḍāʾil* treatises, and other works featuring city names in their titles were composed before the eleventh century, only a few have survived to the present day and are thus available for analysis as participants in the discourse of place. For lists of the works that are no longer extant, see Rosenthal, *A History of Muslim Historiography*, 130–149, 381–408; Brockelmann, *Geschichte der arabischen Literatur*, 1:137–138, 329–341; ibid., suppl., 1:209–211, 562–581; Sezgin, *Geschichte des arabischen Schrifttums*, 1:339–364.
3. Examples include al-Khaṭīb al-Baghdādī, *Taʾrīkh Baghdād*; Abū Nuʿaym, *Kitāb dhikr akhbār Iṣbahān*; al-Rāzī, *Kitāb taʾrīkh madīnat Ṣanʿāʾ*; Baḥshal, *Taʾrīkh Wāsiṭ*; ʿUmar b. Shabba, *Kitāb taʾrīkh al-Madīna al-Munawwara*. For a discussion of the relationship between the introduction to city-based biographical dictionaries and the discourse of place in a slightly later period, see Antrim, "Ibn ʿAsakir's Representations."
4. This is Wittgenstein's phrase, quoted in Eickelman, 313–314.
5. For examples of studies that propose a prototypical "Islamic city" organized around a Friday mosque, a public bath, and a market, see Brunschvig, "Urbanisme médiéval"; le Tourneau, *Fès*; von Grunebaum, "Structure of the Muslim Town"; Marçais, "L'islamisme et la vie urbaine." For critiques of this idea, see Kennedy, "How to Found an Islamic City"; Abu-Lughod, "The Islamic City"; Raymond, "Islamic City, Arab City"; AlSayyad, *Cities and Caliphs*; the essays in Lapidus, ed., *Middle Eastern Cities*; the essays in Hourani and Stern, eds., *The Islamic City*; and the essays in Jayyusi et al., eds., *The City in the Islamic World*.
6. The tenth-century geographer al-Muqaddasī attempted to systematize the use of these terms, though he admits their continuing ambiguity in general usage and in fact is unable himself to use them consistently throughout his work; see al-Muqaddasī, *Kitāb aḥsan al-taqāsīm*, 47, 156, 270–271. For more on these terms, see Miquel, 4:138–140, 210–211; Wheatley, 74–84. For the equivalent Persian terms and their use, see Piacentini, "*Madīna/Shahr, Qarya/Deh, Nāḥiya/Rustāq*."
7. A maxim about the virtues implied by a multiplicity of names among the bedouin from a fourteenth-century work on Mecca is quoted in Arazi, "Matériaux pour l'étude du conflit," 218.
8. This is Richard Frye's English translation from a twelfth-century Persian redaction of the original Arabic in al-Narshakhī, 21.
9. Ibid., 22.
10. al-Hamdānī, *al-Iklīl*, 3–5, 10–21; idem, *Ṣifat*, 82; al-Rāzī, 14–15, 18–28, 180–184. See also Ibn Rustih, *Kitāb al-aʿlāq al-nafīsa*, 110. On the symbolism of Ghumdān, see Khoury, "The Dome of the Rock, the Kaʿba, and Ghumdan."
11. Ibn al-Faqīh, *Mukhtaṣar kitāb al-buldān*, 217. This is actually an abridgement of the original ninth-century work prepared by ʿAlī al-Shayzarī in 413/1022. Miquel argues that this abridgement faithfully reflects the original spirit and eighty-one percent of the original text of Ibn al-Faqīh's *Kitāb al-buldān*; see Miquel, 1:153–160. A second abridgement of Ibn al-Faqīh's work was discovered in the 1920s in Mashhad and is commonly referred to as the "Mashhad MS," which has been published in facsimile in Sezgin, ed., *Majmūʿ fī l-Jughrāfiyā*. It dates to the thirteenth century and contains material on the towns of Iraq that is lacking in al-Shayzarī's abridgement. Its sections on Baghdad have been published as Ibn al-Faqīh, *Baghdād*; and its sections on al-Sawād, al-Ahwāz, and the Turks have been published as Ibn al-Faqīh, *Nuṣūṣ*. For more information on the "Mashhad MS," see Van Laer, "Ibn al-Faqīh."
12. Ibn al-Faqīh, *Baghdād*, 27–28; al-Khaṭīb al-Baghdādī, 1:58–62; Ibn Rustih, *Kitāb al-aʿlāq al-nafīsa*, 108; al-Bakrī, *Muʿjam mā istaʿjama*, 1:240–241. See also Cooperson, "Baghdad," 102.
13. ʿUmar b. Shabba, 1:162–163. Compare with the traditions reported in Ibn Rustih, *Kitāb al-aʿlāq al-nafīsa*, 78. For variants on these lists of ten names, see al-Muqaddasī, *Kitāb aḥsan al-taqāsīm*, 30; Ibn al-Faqīh, *Mukhtaṣar kitāb al-buldān*, 23; al-Bakrī *Muʿjam mā istaʿjama*,

4:75; al-Bakrī, *al-Masālik wa-l-mamālik*, 1:320. For "Ṭayba" as a name for Medina, see also al-Jāḥiẓ, *Kitāb al-buldān*, 485–488; al-Thaʿālibi, *Laṭāʾif al-maʿārif*, 155; al-Yaʿqūbī, *Kitāb al-buldān*, 312.

14. Similarly, one of the names listed for Sanaa in several works—Azāl—is cited on the authority of the Torah in an eleventh-century topographical history of the city; see al-Rāzī, 14–15. Compare with al-Hamdānī, *al-Iklīl*, 21–22; idem, *Ṣifat*, 81.
15. ʿUmar b. Shabba, 1:164–165; al-Janadī, 26; Muslim, 9:155–156. For an instance of the use of "Yathrib" to denigrate the city of Medina in al-Fākihī's partially extant ninth-century work on Mecca, see Arazi, "Matériaux pour l'étude du conflit," 229–230.
16. Qurʾān 33:13 ("Yathrib"); Qurʾān 9:101, 33:60, 63:8 ("al-Madīna"). Some argue that it is not clear whether "al-Madīna" is being used in these verses as a proper name or merely as the noun "al-madīna," meaning "the city"; see *EI*[2]: "al-Madīna."
17. See the traditions likening Medina to a furnace that renders its contents "pure" (*ṭayyib*): al-Janadī, 27; Muslim, 9:153–156.
18. al-Rabaʿī, 20 (no. 36), 21 (no. 38). See also Ibn Khurradādhbih, 76; al-Bakrī, *Muʿjam mā istaʿjama*, 1:131. For a discussion of this idea, see Cobb, 46.
19. See, for examples, Ibn ʿAbd al-Ḥakam, 61; Ibn al-Kindī, 16, 31; Ibn Zūlāq, 4, 63; al-Hamdānī, *al-Iklīl*, 33; idem, *Ṣifat*, 7; al-Muqaddasī, *Kitāb aḥsan al-taqāsīm*, 87; al-Masʿūdī, *Murūj al-dhahab*, 1:384; al-Bakrī, *al-Masālik wa-l-mamālik*, 2:160–161.
20. On these terms, see Hawting, 36–38.
21. al-Azraqī, 1:390.
22. Ibid., 391 (no. 354), 393–394 (no. 362), 394 (no. 364), 395 (no. 365). See also Ibn al-Faqīh, *Mukhtaṣar kitāb al-buldān*, 16–17; al-Bakrī, *Muʿjam mā istaʿjama*, 1:245–246.
23. al-Azraqī, 1:392 (no. 357), 392–393 (no. 359), 393 (no. 361), 395 (no. 366). See also Ibn al-Faqīh, *Mukhtaṣar kitāb al-buldān*, 17; al-Bakrī, *Muʿjam mā istaʿjama*, 1:246–247; al-Jāḥiẓ, *Kitāb al-buldān*, 481–484. "Al-Bayt al-ʿAtīq" also occurs in Qurʾān 22:29.
24. al-Azraqī, 1:67 (no. 3). See also al-Ḥasan al-Baṣrī, 19. For a related commentary, see al-Jāḥiẓ, *Kitāb al-buldān*, 463.
25. al-Muqaddasī, *Kitāb aḥsan al-taqāsīm*, 47; Miquel, 4:217–219, 229; Wheatley, 74–84. It should be noted that a variant of his name is al-Maqdisī.
26. These two works both preface Isfahan-based biographical dictionaries with *faḍāʾil* treatises dedicated to the city, though the first reflects the sensibilities and emphases of the world of *adab* while the second reflects the methods and sources of the field of Ḥadīth studies: al-Māfarrūkhī, 54–58, 64–68; Abū Nuʿaym, 1:14–17, 31–43. On these works, see Paul, "The Histories of Isfahan." Abū Nuʿaym follows earlier geographers by identifying Isfahan as made up of two cities side by side, on the east "Jayy," "Shahristān," or simply "al-Madīna" and on the west "al-Yahūdiyya," named after Jewish immigrants fleeing Nebuchadnezzar settled in the area, whereas al-Māfarrūkhī only mentions "Jayy"; see Ibn al-Faqih, *Mukhtaṣar kitāb al-buldān*, 267; Ibn Ḥawqal, *Kitāb ṣūrat al-arḍ*, 362, 366–367; al-Yaʿqūbī, *Kitāb al-buldān*, 274. An early tenth-century Isfahan-resident describes Isfahan as a district (*kūra*) made up of twenty rural areas (*rasātīq*) with "Jayy" as its capital (*qasaba*); see Ibn Rustih, *Kitāb al-aʿlāq al-nafīsa*, 152. In another tenth-century work, Isfahan is described as a district (*kūra*), with "al-Yahūdiyya" as its capital (*qaṣaba*); see al-Muqaddasī, *Kitāb aḥsan al-taqāsīm*, 385, 388–389. The city of Qom is similarly associated with a set of dependent rural areas, which were broken off from those administered by Isfahan in 189/804–805, according to a late tenth-century topographical history of the city; see Qummī, 39–82. This work has not survived in its original Arabic, but only in this early fifteenth-century partial Persian translation by Tāj al-Dīn Ḥasan Khaṭīb b. Bahāʾ al-Dīn ʿAlī b. Ḥasan b. ʿAbd al-Malik Qummī. See Lambton, "An Account of the *Tārīkhi Qumm*." On the relationship of Qom and Isfahan, see Ibn Rustih, *Kitāb al-aʿlāq al-nafīsa*, 152. For more on all of these territorial divisions, see Piacentini, 88–93; Golombek, "Urban Patterns in Pre-Safavid Isfahan."
27. al-Māfarrūkhī, 56.
28. Ibid., 72. On Salmān and "Jayy," see also al-Yaʿqūbī, *Kitāb al-buldān*, 274. Although Abū Nuʿaym opens his introductory *faḍāʾil* treatise with a series of *ḥadīth*s that celebrates Salmān's Persian identity, it is not until the biographical entry for Salmān that he is associated explicitly with Isfahan and "Jayy"; see Abū Nuʿaym, 1:49.

29. al-Māfarrūkhī, 62–64.
30. al-Raba'ī, 17–19 (nos. 28–33), 21 (no. 39), 22–23 (nos. 41–45), 26 (no. 49), 53–55 (no. 89), 60 (no. 94).
31. On Wāsiṭ, see Baḥshal, 43; al-Ya'qūbī, *Kitāb al-buldān*, 322. On Mosul, see Ibn al-Faqīh, *Mukhtaṣar kitāb al-buldān*, 128.
32. Baḥshal, 45.
33. See Qur'ān 9:19–22.
34. al-Ya'qūbī, *Kitāb al-buldān*, 234. The region of "al-Sind" corresponds roughly to present-day Pakistan and "al-Daylam" to the territory just south of the Caspian Sea. On "the Turks," a group of peoples inhabiting the Central Asian steppe, and "the Khazars," a people and territory north of the Caucasus in the Volga River valley, see Miquel, 2:203–255, 286–300.
35. Ibn al-Faqīh, *Baghdād*, 86–87. There are no extant manuscripts of any work authored by Yazdajird al-Kisrawī, but he is reported to have lived around the turn of the tenth century and to have composed at least one book in praise of the city of Baghdad, from which Ibn al-Faqīh drew. For more on his identity, see the editor's introduction to Ibn al-Faqīh, *Baghdād*, 5–25; Tskitishvili, "Yazddjard." For more on images of Baghdad's centrality, see Cooperson, "Baghdad"; Antrim, "Connectivity and Creativity."
36. For Baghdad, see al-Khaṭīb al-Baghdādī, 1:23 (*wasaṭ al-arḍ*); al-Ya'qūbī, *Kitāb al-buldān*, 233 (*wasaṭ al-dunyā, surrat al-arḍ*); al-Tha'ālibī, *Laṭā'if al-ma'ārif*, 170 (*wāsiṭat al-dunyā*). For Jerusalem, see Abū l-Ma'ālī, 147 (no. 184) (*surrat al-arḍ*), 241 (no. 361) (*wasaṭ al-dunyā*), 262 (no. 399) (*surrat al-arḍ*); Ibn al-Faqīh, *Mukhtaṣar kitāb al-buldān*, 94 (*surrat al-arḍ*); Muqātil, 2:513 (*surrat al-araḍīn*). For more on the concept of the "navel of the earth" in conjunction with cities in the Islamic world, see von Grunebaum, "The Sacred Character of Islamic Cities." See also, Wensinck, 590. Though both von Grunebaum and Wensinck refer to Mecca in Islamic cosmology as the "navel of the earth," I have not found the epithets *surrat al-arḍ* or *surrat al-dunyā* for Mecca in the works I have examined through the eleventh century. However, Isfahan is called *surrat al-arḍ* in al-Māfarrūkhī, 53.
37. See, for examples, Abū l-Ma'ālī, 102–103 (nos. 105, 106), 106 (no. 112), 264 (no. 399); al-Wāsiṭī, 68 (no. 110), 78 (no. 128); Ibn al-Faqīh, *Mukhtaṣar kitāb al-buldān*, 95; al-Bakrī, *al-Masālik wa-l-mamālik*, 2:41. Mountains were often portrayed as points of proximity if not junction between heaven and earth; see, for examples, Abū l-Ma'ālī, 233 (no. 345); al-Wāsiṭī, 56–57 (nos. 85–86). Several traditions even specify the distance between the Rock and heaven as eighteen miles; see Abū l-Ma'ālī, 108 (nos. 118–119); Muqātil, 2:513.
38. Abū l-Ma'ālī, 106 (no. 113), 108 (no. 119), 109–110 (no. 122); al-Wāsiṭī, 69 (no. 111), 71 (no. 116); Ibn al-Faqīh, *Mukhtaṣar kitāb al-buldān*, 97. See also Abū l-Ma'ālī, 108–109 (nos. 120–121), 110–111 (no. 123), 119–120 (no. 142), 121–122 (no. 144), 124–126 (nos. 150, 151), 127 (no. 155), 264 (no. 399); al-Wāsiṭī, 70 (nos. 114–115), 72–75 (nos. 117–121), 94–96 (no. 155).
39. al-Azraqī, 1:91 (no. 36); see also ibid., 2:675 (no. 762), 676–677 (nos. 766, 767). For the Torah reference explaining the obscure name *al-Ḍurāḥ* as a synonym for *al-Bayt al-Ma'mūr*, see ibid., 1:91 (no. 35); see also ibid., 1:90–93 (nos. 34, 37–40). For similar traditions relating both Jerusalem's Rock and the Ka'ba to structures in heaven, see Abū l-Ma'ālī, 103 (no. 107), 166 (no. 227); al-Wāsiṭī, 43 (no. 59). See also Wensinck, 590.
40. For the Ka'ba's centrality in creation, see al-Azraqī, 1:66–68 (nos. 1–4); al-Ḥasan al-Baṣrī, 19. For Jerusalem's role on Judgment Day, the material is copious; see, for examples, Abū l-Ma'ālī, 104 (nos. 108–109), 109 (no. 121), 111 (nos. 124, 125), 211–213 (nos. 305–310), 254 (no. 387), 261 (no. 399); al-Wāsiṭī, 40 (no. 55), 70–71 (no. 115), 88 (no. 143) 92–93 (nos. 150–153); Ibn al-Faqīh, *Mukhtaṣar kitāb al-buldān*, 94; al-Bakrī, *al-Masālik wa-l-mamālik*, 2:41–42; Muqātil, 2:514. See also Livne-Kafri, "Jerusalem in Early Islam." Works on Mecca also associate it with Judgment Day, but not with as much frequency; for examples, see al-Ḥasan al-Baṣrī, 21–22, 23–24; al-Azraqī, 1:430–431 (no. 388), 446–447 (nos. 418–419), 449 (no. 426), 450 (no. 427), 455 (no. 441).
41. On Mecca, see Ibn al-Faqīh, *Mukhtaṣar kitāb al-buldān*, 21–22; Ibn Ḥawqal, *Kitāb ṣūrat al-arḍ*, 28; al-Azraqī, 2:686–687. On Jerusalem, see al-Muqaddasī, *Kitāb aḥsan al-taqāsīm*, 173; Abū al-Ma'ālī, 115 (no. 136); al-Wāsiṭī, 41 (no. 56).

42. Ibn ʿAbd Rabbih, 29:74 (Isfahan); al-Māfarrūkhī, 55 (Isfahan); Abū Nuʿaym, 1:41 (Isfahan); al-Jāḥiẓ, *Kitāb al-buldān*, 498 (Basra); al-Thaʿālibī, *Laṭāʾif al-maʿārif*, 191 (Nishapur); al-Hamdānī, *Ṣifat*, 81 (Sanaa); Ibn Khurradādhbih, 5 (Baghdad). For this concept, see Miquel, 4:215–217. Nishapur is located in the northeastern corner of present-day Iran.
43. al-Muqaddasī, *Kitāb aḥsan al-taqāsīm*, 84, 298–299. Merv is located in present-day Turkmenistan. Zabīd is a town in Yemen.
44. See Elinson, 34–35.
45. Ibn Ḥazm, "Risāla," 174. See the discussion of this and later *faḍāʾil* treatises on Andalusia in Elinson, 117–150.
46. The maps that accompany different manuscripts, even of the same work, are not identical, and some of them portray cities more centrally than others. For Hamadan, see Miller, plates 40–42; for Shiraz, see ibid., plates 28–30. For Shiraz, see also Figures 5.5 and 5.6 in this book. For a map of Sicily in which the city of Palermo is portrayed as strikingly central, see *Kitāb gharāʾib al-funūn*, fol. 32b–33a.
47. See Savage-Smith, "Memory and Maps."
48. For more on this work, see the remarkable online reproduction of the manuscript from The Bodleian Library, accompanied by an Arabic critical edition and English translation: Emilie Savage-Smith and Yossef Rapoport, eds., *The Book of Curiosities: A Critical Edition*, March 2007 (http://cosmos.bodley.ox.ac.uk/hms/home.php). See also Johns and Savage-Smith, "*The Book of Curiosities*"; Rapoport and Savage-Smith, "Medieval Islamic View of the Cosmos."
49. In *Space and Muslim Urban Life*, Simon O'Meara presents city foundation narratives for Fez, Kairouan, Baghdad, and Samarra as culminating in "an inviolable enclave, or *ḥaram*: a space politically, religiously, and communally elevated from the region around it, over which it seeks dominion" (67). While my analysis builds on O'Meara's insights, his argument that these narratives tend to conclude with the "reversal of a prior state" (60) does not seem applicable to representations of cities in the discourse of place from the ninth to eleventh centuries. The only example of a full "reversal" that I have found in this period is the foundation narrative for the city of Kairouan, which O'Meara analyzes in a fourteenth-century work, but which also appears in an eleventh-century work; see al-Mālikī, 1:10–13.
50. See Abū Nuʿaym, 1:19–30. Similar is the conquest narrative for Bukhara in al-Narshakhī, 37–48. The foundation narrative for Qom also reflects contestation; see Qummī, 83–99. On these, see Pourshariati, "Local Histories," 57–64; Pourshariati, "Local Historiography," 133–140.
51. Another good case study for the way narratives of foundation, in particular, represented cities as sites of continuity and accommodation would be Cairo, founded in 359/969 as a capital city for the Shiite Fatimid Caliphate, rival to the Abbasid Caliphate. However, to my knowledge, no text devoted in whole or substantial part to the representation of Cairo as a city, comparable to the texts devoted to Mecca, Jerusalem, and Baghdad, survives from the ninth to the eleventh centuries, though brief treatments of Cairo do occur in world geographies and itineraries from the period. In Nāṣir-i Khusraw's eleventh-century travelogue, for instance, he discusses the foundation of Cairo as a garrison city for the conquering Fatimid army purposefully kept separate from the neighboring "old city" of al-Fusṭāṭ so as not to harm or displace its preexisting inhabitants, even though most of them were not Shiite and many were not even Muslims. He then proceeds to describe the two cities, both the old and the new, and their heterogeneous inhabitants as symbols of Fatimid power, prosperity, and inclusivity; see Nāṣir-i Khusraw, 56–74.
52. For more on these topics, see Tottoli, "Origin and Use of the term *Isrāʾīliyyāt*"; de Prémare, "Wahb b. Munabbih"; Pregill, "Isrāʾīliyyāt, Myth, and Pseudepigraphy."
53. This outcome of this process, not at all inevitable, was that the Ḥadīth, particularly as mediated by a specialized group of *ʿulamāʾ*, attained the status of the second most important guide, after the Qurʾān, to right belief and practice among Muslims. See Goldziher, 2:126–144; Juynboll, 134–160.
54. For a historical analysis of the pre-Islamic origins and significance of the Kaʿba, see Rubin, "The Kaʿba"; Hawting, 23–47.
55. This follows O'Meara's argument that Islamic city foundation narratives reproduced topoi from the *sīra* tradition in order to present "their founders, their medinas, and by extension

their inhabitants as cast of Prophetic mold"; O'Meara, 67. The crystallization of the *sīra* tradition is often dated to the early ninth century, when the *Sīrat Rasūl Allāh* or *al-Sīra al-Nabawiyya* by Muḥammad b. Isḥāq (d. 150/767) was prepared in a single edition by ʿAbd al-Malik b. Hishām (d. 218/834). For more on the *sīra* tradition, see *EI*²: "Sīra"; Kister, "The Sīrah Literature." On the development and themes of the *sīra* tradition, see Newby, *The Making of the Last Prophet*; Rubin, *The Eye of the Beholder*.

56. al-Azraqī, 1:66–68.
57. Ibid., 66 (no. 1). See also al-Ḥasan al-Baṣrī, 19.
58. See Qurʾān 24:36–37 on the meaning of *bayt* as "house of worship."
59. al-Azraqī, 1:72–82. See also al-Ḥasan al-Baṣrī, 19–20; Ibn al-Faqīh, *Mukhtaṣar kitāb al-buldān*, 19. An early-tenth-century work also contains a foundation narrative for Mecca drawn largely from al-Azraqī's work; see Ibn Rustih, *Kitāb al-aʿlāq al-nafīsa*, 24–25.
60. For Islamic cosmological theories about the levels of heaven and earth, see Karamustafa, "Cosmographical Diagrams"; *EI*²: "Samāʾ."
61. Compare, for example, al-Azraqī, 1:72–74, 95–96 (nos. 11, 47) and 1:77–78, 93–94 (nos. 15, 41–44).
62. One tradition makes explicit that the foundations on which Abraham built are the same as those that Adam used in al-Azraqī, 1:107–108 (no. 62); see also Ibn Rustih, *Kitāb al-aʿlāq al-nafīsa*, 25–26. In general, however, there is ambiguity here, which is why I use the term "(re)built"; see Wensinck, 589.
63. al-Azraqī, 1:96 (no. 48).
64. Ibid., 97–98 (nos. 49, 50). See also Ibn Rustih, *Kitāb al-aʿlāq al-nafīsa*, 26–27.
65. al-Azraqī, 1:100–101 (nos. 52, 53, 54). See also Ibn Rustih, *Kitāb al-aʿlāq al-nafīsa*, 27–28.
66. Ibn Hishām, 1:155–167.
67. al-Azraqī, 1:98–100 (no. 51). See also Ibn Rustih, *Kitāb al-aʿlāq al-nafīsa*, 40. For more on the spring of Zamzam, see *EI*²: "Zamzam."
68. al-Azraqī, 1:106–118 (nos. 57, 58, 59, 60, 61, 63, 64, 69, 73, 75, 76, 77). See also Ibn Rustih, *Kitāb al-aʿlāq al-nafīsa*, 28.
69. al-Azraqī, 1:133–136 (nos. 110–119); Ibn al-Faqīh, *Mukhtaṣar kitāb al-buldān*, 17. See also Qurʾān 14:37, 28:57, 106:3–4.
70. al-Azraqī, 1:108–109 (no. 63), 115–116 (no. 73). See also Ibn Rustih, *Kitāb al-aʿlāq al-nafīsa*, 28–29.
71. al-Azraqī, 1:239 (no. 174), 243 (no. 177), 255 (no. 191). See Rubin, "The Kaʿba," 101–102. The use of skilled labor from the Byzantine Empire for the erection or renovation of Islamic monumental architecture recurs in the discourse of place; see, for examples, Ibn Rustih, *Kitāb al-aʿlāq al-nafīsa*, 69 (on the Prophet's Mosque of Medina); al-Muqaddasī, *Kitāb aḥsan al-taqāsīm*, 158 (on the Great Mosque of Damascus).
72. al-Azraqī, 1:139 (no. 125); for variants, see ibid., 136–138 (nos. 120–124), 261 (no. 202). *Ḥanīfs* were believed to be those who worshipped the God of Abraham before the revelation of Islam; see *EI*²: "Ḥanīf."
73. al-Azraqī, 1:137 (no. 121), 139 (no. 125). See also Hawting, 39.
74. See, for an example from the Great Mosque in Damascus, al-Rabaʿī, 21–22 (no. 40), 34–35 (no. 62). On an "eyewitness" account of the ninth-century discovery of one such ancient and difficult-to-decipher inscription at the Kaʿba, see Kister, "Maqām Ibrāhīm."
75. al-Azraqī, 1:241 (no. 176), 247 (no. 177), 254–255 (no. 190), 258–259 (nos. 197, 198), 260–261 (no. 201), 303 (no. 227). Ibn Hishām, 1:192–199.
76. See, for examples, al-Azraqī, 1:443–456. See also Rubin, "The Kaʿba," 118–120.
77. See, for examples, al-Azraqī, 1:116–117 (no. 73), 292 (no. 221), 313 (no. 240), 314 (no. 241), 317 (no. 251). See also al-Bakrī, *al-Masālik wa-l-mamālik*, 1:301. For details of the war, see al-Azraqī, 1:289–298.
78. al-Azraqī, 1:298–320.
79. Ibid., 1:300–301 (no. 227); see also ibid., 255–256 (no. 193), 256–257 (no. 194), 309 (no. 230), 309–310 (no. 231), 318–319 (no. 253), 428–429 (no. 384). For other traditions that describe the reduction of the size of the structure by the Quraysh, see ibid., 1:240 (nos. 174, 175), 246 (no. 177), 256–258 (nos. 194–196), 403, 430 (no. 386), 435 (no. 398).
80. See al-Azraqī, 1:256–257 (no. 194).

81. For examples, see Muslim, 9:88–96 ("Kitāb al-ḥajj"); al-Bukhārī, 3:118–120 ("Kitāb al-ḥajj," nos. 1431–1434); Mālik, 1:363–364 (Book 20, "Kitāb al-ḥajj," no. 104). See also al-Muqaddasī, *Kitāb aḥsan al-taqāsīm*, 74.
82. See, for examples, al-Azraqī, 1:298–299 (no. 226), 310 (no. 232). The description of fear at the prospect of demolishing a locus of devotion, even of incorrect or superseded devotion, such as the Qurayshī Kaʿba, also occurs in descriptions of the Umayyad Caliph al-Walīd I's demolition of the Church of St. John in Damascus to make room for the Great Mosque; see al-Rabaʿī, 41 (no. 71); Ibn al-Faqīh, *Mukhtaṣar kitāb al-buldān*, 106.
83. al-Azraqī, 1:305–307 (no. 227). See also ibid., 1:255–256 (no. 193), 319–320 (no. 255), 429 (no. 384); al-Muqaddasī, *Kitāb aḥsan al-taqāsīm*, 74–75. The extant portions of another late ninth-century history of Mecca contain a narrative of the war between Ibn al-Zubayr and the Umayyads, including numerous accounts of Ibn al-Zubayr's defeat at the hands of al-Ḥajjāj, but they do not discuss the rebuilding of the Kaʿba; see al-Fākihī, *Kitāb al-muntaqā*, 18–30; idem, "Min kitāb taʾrīkh Makka," 42–54.
84. Ibn ʿAbd Rabbih, 29:92–93; Ibn Ḥawqal, *Kitāb ṣūrat al-arḍ*, 28; al-Muqaddasī, *Kitāb aḥsan al-taqāsīm*, 72; Ibn Rustih, *Kitāb al-aʿlāq al-nafīsa*, 29–30; al-Bakrī, *al-Masālik wa-l-mamālik*, 1:302. For a description of the location and proportion of the *Ḥijr* during his lifetime, see al-Azraqī, 1:440–443; see also Ibn Rustih, *Kitāb al-aʿlāq al-nafīsa*, 37–38. For ambiguities about the term *Ḥijr* and its location vis-à-vis the Kaʿba, see Rubin, "The Kaʿba." For later beautification and renovation projects, see Grabar, "Upon Reading al-Azraqī."
85. Even his destruction of idols in the Kaʿba after the conquest of Mecca is represented as subject to accommodation and negotiation, as he is reported to have allowed an image of Mary and Jesus to be preserved; see al-Azraqī, 1:248–249 (no. 177), 251 (no. 181), 253 (nos. 185, 187).
86. Suleiman Mourad has reconstructed a much earlier *faḍāʾil* treatise on Jerusalem by Abū l-ʿAbbās al-Walīd b. Hammād al-Ramlī al-Zayyāt (d. ca. 300/912) from the material quoted in these two eleventh-century works; see Mourad, "A Note on the Origin of *Faḍāʾil Bayt al-Maqdis* Compilations"; idem, "The Symbolism of Jerusalem." Mourad's reconstruction has clear significance for the dating of the origins of the discourse of place on Jerusalem, a question that, among others, has raised debate in the considerable body of secondary scholarship on Jerusalem's importance in early Islam; see, for examples, Hasson, "The Muslim View of Jerusalem"; idem, "Muslim Literature in Praise of Jerusalem"; Elad, *Medieval Jerusalem*, especially 1–22; al-ʿAsalī, *Makhṭūṭāt faḍāʾil Bayt al-Maqdis*; Sivan, "The Beginnings of the *Faḍāʾil al-Quds* Literature." Two other extant works before the eleventh century, one on geography and one on Qurʾānic exegesis, include relatively substantial sections that follow the format of a *faḍāʾil* treatise on Jerusalem: 1) Ibn al-Faqīh, *Mukhtaṣar kitāb al-buldān*, 93–101; and 2) a section of the *Tafsīr* of Muqātil b. Sulaymān (d. 150/767) on traditions in praise of Jerusalem, a variation of which is also quoted in Abū l-Maʿālī, 259–264 (no. 399); see Muqātil, 2:513–515; see also an English translation in Hasson, "The Muslim View of Jerusalem," 383–385.
87. Al-Wāsiṭī's work presents the component parts of this narrative in shorter textual units peppered throughout the work, and Ibn al-Faqīh and Muqātil present it in brief. Thus, this discussion will follow Abū l-Maʿālī's text with citations to the same material as presented by al-Wāsiṭī, Ibn al-Faqīh, and Muqātil.
88. Abū l-Maʿālī, 8 (no. 1); al-Azraqī, 1:583 (nos. 705, 706).
89. Some scholars argue that early exegesis associated "al-Masjid al-Aqṣā" with heaven rather than Jerusalem. For diverging views, see *EI*[2]: "Miʿrādj," "al-Ḳuds"; Busse, "Jerusalem in the Story of Muḥammad's Night Journey"; El-Khatib, "Jerusalem in the Qurʾān"; Rubin, "Muḥammad's Night Journey."
90. Abū l-Maʿālī, 10 (no. 2); al-Wāsiṭī, 16 (no. 18).
91. Abū l-Maʿālī, 11 (no. 3).
92. For traditions asserting Mecca's status as the first *bayt* established on earth, as in Qurʾān 3:96, see al-Azraqī, 1:131–132.
93. Abū l-Maʿālī, 15 (no. 6). See also Abū l-Maʿālī, 12–14 (nos. 4–5), 15–16 (nos. 7, 8); al-Wāsiṭī, 6–8 (nos. 5, 6), 9–11 (nos. 8–10); Ibn al-Faqīh, *Mukhtaṣar kitāb al-buldān*, 98. For the Biblical references in this story, see Mourad, "The Symbolism of Jerusalem," 91–92; for more on David and Jerusalem in Islamic belief, see Busse, "The Tower of David."

94. See Qur'ān 21:82, 34:12, 38:37–38.
95. Abū l-Ma'ālī, 20 (no. 13). It is interesting to note that the way in which the *jinn* advise Solomon to accomplish the filling of the foundations, which stretched down through all the layers of earth to a well of bottomless water, was by throwing into the water a stone upon which had been inscribed the same words that were on Solomon's seal: "There is no god but God alone; he has no partner; and Muḥammad is his servant and messenger." Thus, this episode acts both as superhuman guidance and a prophecy of Muḥammad's coming projected back to the time of Solomon.
96. Ibid., 21 (no. 13).
97. Ibid., 25–26 (no. 19).
98. Mourad has pointed to a similar continuity between traditions about "the blessing of Solomon" (*da'wa Sulaymān*) in these works and Islamic-era practice. See Mourad, "The Symbolism of Jerusalem," 92; see also Busse, "*Bāb Ḥiṭṭa*," especially 8–12.
99. Abū l-Ma'ālī, 21–22 (no. 13), 90 (no. 82), 91 (no. 85), 92 (no. 87), 93 (nos. 88–89), 94 (no. 90), 96 (no. 93), 261 (no. 399), 263 (no. 399), 268 (no. 407); al-Wāsiṭī, 11 (no. 10), 23 (no. 29), 28 (no. 38), 29 (no. 39), 75 (no. 120); Ibn al-Faqīh, *Mukhtaṣar kitāb al-buldān*, 99–100; al-Bakrī, *al-Masālik wa-l-mamālik*, 2:41; Muqātil, 2:514. In one variant of the traditions relating to the "Blessing of Solomon," God refuses Solomon's request that the Temple be a site of absolution; see Abū l-Ma'ālī, 129 (158); al-Wāsiṭī, 17 (no. 19). This has been interpreted as a sign that God was waiting for the coming of Islam to grant such absolution; for this interpretation, see Lassner, "Muslims on the Sanctity of Jerusalem," 190–191; for a related interpretation, see Busse, "*Bāb al-Ḥiṭṭa*," 12–15. Mecca is also associated with the absolution of sins in the discourse of place (and even in the two eleventh-century treatises on Jerusalem), but without the same emphasis on continuities from the pre-Islamic era; see, for examples, Abū l-Ma'ālī, 92 (no. 86), 161 (no. 215); al-Ḥasan al-Baṣrī, 29, 30.
100. al-Azraqī, 1:248–254. Other references to the conquest contextualize material presented in later sections, such as the description of Muḥammad's first prayer in the Ka'ba (ibid., 1:370–385) and the oft-quoted *ḥadīth* in which the Prophet renounces violence of any kind, even the cutting down of trees, in the Meccan sanctuary (ibid., 2:669–685).
101. These are the dates given in al-Wāsiṭī, 67 (nos. 105, 106); see also Busse, "'Omar's Image."
102. The parallel with Mecca here are the traditions compiled by al-Azraqī, many of which also occur in the canonical collections of Ḥadīth, in which the Prophet explains that his conquest of the city was, by divine dispensation, a one-time exception to the rule that forbids violence in the Meccan sanctuary; see al-Azraqī, 2:669–685.
103. Abū l-Ma'ālī, 44 (no. 35). In fact it is significant that 'Umar himself is portrayed as leaving his headquarters in Medina specifically to assume control of the conquest of Jerusalem from his generals, so much so that the episode is given the epithet "'Umar's conquest" in Abū l-Ma'ālī, 54 (no. 40). For a discussion of this significance, see Busse, "'Omar's Image."
104. Abū l-Ma'ālī, 44 (no. 35), 45–50 (no. 36), 54 (no. 40), 55–57 (no. 44). See also al-Bakrī, *al-Masālik wa-l-mamālik*, 2:39.
105. For the generosity of the Jerusalem settlement, see Abū l-Ma'ālī, 44 (no. 35). For Damascus, see al-Raba'ī, 40–42 (no. 71).
106. Abū l-Ma'ālī, 51 (no. 37); see also, ibid., 55 (no. 42).
107. Ibid., 45 (no. 36); al-Wāsiṭī, 66 (no. 104). The location of the *Miḥrāb Dāwūd* is a matter of some debate; see Busse, "'Omar's Image," 165–167; idem, "The Tower of David," 154–156. On the form of the *miḥrāb* in the pre-Islamic and early Islamic periods, see Khoury, "The Mihrab"; idem, "The Dome of the Rock, the Ka'ba, and Ghumdan."
108. Abū l-Ma'ālī, 54 (no. 41); al-Wāsiṭī, 78–79 (nos. 129, 132).
109. Abū l-Ma'ālī, 52–53 (no. 39). See also al-Bakrī, *al-Masālik wa-l-mamālik*, 2:39. A similar tradition relates the same story, but does not include any reason for 'Umar's disagreement with Ka'b or his criticism of Ka'b for imitating Judaism; see al-Wāsiṭī, 45–46 (no. 63).
110. Abū l-Ma'ālī, 96–101 (nos. 94–103a); al-Wāsiṭī, 49–52 (nos. 74–78). The point of amassing these traditions in the context of these works seems to have been to portray Jerusalem's status as the first *qibla* as evidence of the city's sanctity for Muslims, even though in so doing they are also associating prayer toward Jerusalem with the disobedience or ignorance of Jews and Christians. In one tradition, the problem of the two *qibla*s is depicted as not having occurred

until Muḥammad had fled to Medina because in Mecca it was possible to pray toward the Kaʿba without turning one's back on Jerusalem; see Abū l-Maʿālī, 101 (no. 103a). See also Rubin, "Between Arabia and the Holy Land"; Neuwirth, 309–312; Kister, "Sanctity Joint and Divided," especially 52–60.

111. See Abū l-Maʿālī, 249 (no. 374), 253 (no. 383), 265 (no. 401); al-Wāsiṭī, 21 (no. 24), 44 (no. 61); Ibn al-Faqīh, *Mukhtaṣar kitāb al-buldān*, 96.

112. On the Jews, in addition to the section on Nebuchadnezzar mentioned above, see Abū l-Maʿālī 216–217 (no. 317), 230 (no. 340); al-Wāsiṭī, 60 (no. 95), 62–63 (no. 100), 67 (no. 107).

113. Although this is the interpretation suggested by these two eleventh-century works, the historical question of the reason for the construction of the Dome of the Rock has attracted considerable debate in the secondary scholarship; see, for examples, Goldziher, 2:44–46; Goitein, "The Sanctity of Jerusalem"; Grabar, "The Umayyad Dome of the Rock"; idem, "The Meaning of the Dome of the Rock"; Blair, "What is the Date of the Dome of the Rock?"; Rabbat, "The Meaning of the Umayyad Dome of the Rock"; idem, "The Dome of the Rock Revisited"; Elad, 158–163.

114. Abū l-Maʿālī, 58–59 (no. 47); al-Wāsiṭī, 81–82 (no. 136).

115. See Rabbat, "The Dome of the Rock Revisited," 70.

116. Abū l-Maʿālī, 60 (no. 47); al-Wāsiṭī, 83 (no. 136).

117. Abū l-Maʿālī, 59–60 (no. 47); al-Wāsiṭī, 82–83 (no. 136). See also al-Bakrī, *al-Masālik wa-l-mamālik*, 2:42.

118. Abū l-Maʿālī, 63–64 (no. 50). See also al-Wāsiṭī, 86 (no. 138); this variant specifies that the scripture from which Kaʿb recited was the Torah and omits the second half of the prophecy. Both of these eleventh-century works are, as Nasser Rabbat has observed, conspicuously silent on the Qurʾānic verses inscribed inside the Dome, among which were those that affirmed the unity of God against those who would associate him with partners, i.e., Christians. This silence also downplays any characterization of Muslim sovereignty in Jerusalem as a rejection of Christian sovereignty there. See Rabbat, "The Dome of the Rock Revisited," 70; Grabar, *The Dome of the Rock*, 90–96.

119. Representations of Baghdad nod to pre-Islamic history in discussions of the derivation of the name "Baghdād" from ancient languages, such as Persian and Chinese. Moreover, traditions on the authority of Kaʿb al-Aḥbār that number the Tigris and Euphrates Rivers among the rivers of paradise were clearly in circulation between the ninth and eleventh centuries, lending the city's site cosmological significance in the discourse of place. For examples, see Ibn al-Faqīh, *Baghdād*, 27–28, 116–117; al-Khaṭīb al-Baghdādī, 1:54–62; Ibn Rustih, *Kitāb al-aʿlāq al-nafīsa*, 108.

120. In one formulation, the land of the Sawād is said to have stretched from Mosul to Abadan; see al-Khaṭīb al-Baghdādī, 1:11–12.

121. Ibid., 4–22.

122. Questions of the conquest-era legal status of cities or city sites recur in the discourse of place as a means of legitimating the creation or transformation of urban spaces. The status of Damascus as having been acquired at least partially by force allows the Umayyad Caliph al-Walīd I to legitimate his demolition of the Church of St. John to make way for the Great Mosque; see al-Rabaʿī, 24–25 (no. 47), 40–42 (no. 71). Moreover, the question of the legitimate purchase of land for a city occurs in the Jerusalem foundation narrative as, in one tradition, God denies David the opportunity to build the Temple because he had not legally purchased the site from its owner; see Abū l-Maʿālī, 12 (no. 4); al-Wāsiṭī, 6–7 (no. 5). See also Mourad, "The Symbolism of Jerusalem," 91. The question of the legitimate purchase of the site for the Temple is also invoked in reference to an anecdote about the acquisition of land for ʿUmar's enlargement of the Prophet's Mosque in Medina; see al-Janadī, 38.

123. For more on al-Khaṭīb al-Baghdādī's falling out with the Ḥanbalī *madhhab*, see Malti-Douglas, "Controversy and its Effect"; *EI*[2]: "al-*Khaṭ*īb al-Ba*gh*dādī." *Dīnār* was the generic term for a gold coin during the Islamic period, and its weight varied from place to place and from mint to mint.

124. al-Khaṭīb al-Baghdādī, 1:27–44. Recent scholarship has shown that Ḥadīth scholars in this period did subject the content of traditions to analysis, though they almost always tied their

findings to a discussion of the chain of transmission; see Brown, "How We Know Early Ḥadīth Critics Did *Matn* Criticism."

125. al-Khaṭīb al-Baghdādī, 1:43.
126. Ibn al-Faqīh, *Baghdād*, 31–32. See also al-Yaʿqūbī, *Kitāb al-buldān*, 237–238; al-Muqaddasī, *Kitāb aḥsan al-taqāsīm*, 119–120.
127. al-Khaṭīb al-Baghdādī, 1:63–66.
128. Ibid., 66; Ibn al-Faqīh, *Baghdād*, 33–35. Al-Yaʿqūbī's foundation narrative has al-Manṣūr's father utter the prophecy that his son would found Baghdad as a political capital for him and his descendants; see al-Yaʿqūbī, *Kitāb al-buldān*, 237–238. This episode has been interpreted as a "ritual re-enactment" of the prediction by the monk Bāḥirā that the young Muḥammad would be a prophet, which serves to associate al-Manṣūr and the city he founds with the Islamic model of prophethood; see O'Meara, 61. See also Wendell, 111–113. O'Meara also points out al-Yaʿqūbī's inclusion of a similar prophecy issued by a Christian monk to the Abbasid Caliph al-Muʿtaṣim predicting the foundation of the city of Samarra by a "magnificent king"; see O'Meara, 62. For the prophecy, see al-Yaʿqūbī, *Kitāb al-buldān*, 257.
129. Ibn al-Faqīh, *Baghdād*, 30.
130. For "al-Zawrāʾ," see al-Khaṭīb al-Baghdādī, 1:77; al-Bakrī, *al-Masālik wa-l-mamālik*, 2:15. For parallels with the foundation of Wāsiṭ, see Wendell, 111–116; Lassner, *The Topography of Baghdad*, 134–136.
131. Lassner, *The Topography of Baghdad*, 124–126.
132. al-Khaṭīb al-Baghdādī, 1:66–67; Ibn al-Faqīh, *Baghdād*, 31, 32; al-Yaʿqūbī, *Kitāb al-buldān*, 238. See also al-Muqaddasī, *Kitāb aḥsan al-taqāsīm*, 121; al-Bakrī, *al-Masālik wa-l-mamālik*, 2:14. This is very similar to al-Yaʿqūbī's account of the foundation of Samarra, in which Caliph al-Muʿtaṣim calls on artisans from far and near to contribute to the construction of the city, and they end up settling there with their families, emphasizing the connective role of the new Abbasid capital; see al-Yaʿqūbī, *Kitāb al-buldān*, 264.
133. al-Khaṭīb al-Baghdādī, 1:67; al-Yaʿqūbī, *Kitāb al-buldān*, 238. Both Charles Wendell and Jacob Lassner cite evidence of earlier circular cities, particularly among the Persians, as an indication that al-Manṣūr may have been self-consciously employing an urban form recognizable to the people of the region as befitting an imperial capital and the symbolism of absolute kingship; see Wendell, 103–106; Lassner, *The Topography of Baghdad*, 128–137. Ibn Rustih claims that Alexander the Great founded the city of Isfahan as "perfectly circular"; Ibn Rustih, *Kitāb al-aʿlāq al-nafīsa*, 160. Emulating the great monarchs of old may have been al-Manṣūr's motivation in choosing a circular shape for his capital city, but there is no indication of that in these foundation narratives, which use descriptions of Baghdad's shape to communicate the unprecedented and unique character of the city.
134. al-Khaṭīb al-Baghdādī, 1:72; Ibn al-Faqīh, *Baghdād*, 35. This resonates with al-Masʿūdī's claim that "the monarchs of old used to say that a great king is the center of the circle of his kingdom, so that his distance from its circumference is the same everywhere"; al-Masʿūdī, *Kitāb al-tanbīh*, 36.
135. al-Khaṭīb al-Baghdādī, 1:78–79, 80; Ibn al-Faqīh, *Baghdād*, 37–38. See also al-Bakrī, *al-Masālik wa-l-mamālik*, 2:15. On the question of whether al-Karkh formed part of the city of Baghdad or was considered administratively its own municipality, see Lassner, *The Topography of Baghdad*, 178–183.
136. al-Yaʿqūbī, *Kitāb al-buldān*, 234–235, 237–238. The aforementioned description of its circular shape as unprecedented reinforces this image of Baghdad's site as providing a political clean slate. Al-Yaʿqūbī's account of the foundation of Samarra also describes the site as a kind of clean slate—deserted, unbuilt, and uninhabited—before the construction of the Abbasid capital began; al-Yaʿqūbī, *Kitāb al-buldān*, 255, 257. O'Meara sees this description as emphasizing an "undomesticated" and "ruin[ed]" prior state that would be reversed by the foundation of the city; O'Meara, 62.
137. al-Khaṭīb al-Baghdādī, 1:130–131; Ibn al-Faqīh, *Baghdād*, 36–37. On these accounts, see Wendell, 123–128; Lassner, *The Topography of Baghdad*, 128–129; Savant, "Forgetting Iran's Pre-Islamic Past." The version in the *Taʾrīkh Baghdād* comes as part of a curious postscript to the introductory *faḍāʾil*-cum-historical-topography in which the Madāʾin Kisrā, one of the chief metropolitan areas of the defunct Persian Empire and the site of *Īwān Kisrā*, is described

as "so close to [Baghdad] that it is like a continuation of it"; see al-Khaṭīb al-Baghdādī, 1:127. This highlights the association of cities not only with the legacies of the pre-Islamic past, but also, more generally, with their hinterlands in the discourse of place and has the practical value of allowing al-Khaṭīb al-Baghdādī to claim the illuminati of a broader area for his Baghdad-centric biographical dictionary.

138. This is similar to al-Narshakhī's report that gates from the villas of the pre-Islamic aristocracy, each of which was adorned with an image of the family idol, were used to construct the Great Mosque of Bukhara at the beginning of the eighth century, although the faces of the idols were effaced; see al-Narshakhī, 49.

Chapter 3

1. Recent scholarship on early and medieval Islamic urban architecture is so voluminous that it must suffice here to mention the prolific publications of Oleg Grabar. Other works are noted as relevant in the notes to this chapter.
2. For ways in which historical narratives from this period invoke the visual, see Cooperson, "Images without Illustrations."
3. Kevin Lynch's *The Image of the City* proposed "legibility" as a concept that would help American urban planners design functionally and aesthetically successful cities; see Lynch, 2–3.
4. In *The Places Where Men Pray Together*, Paul Wheatley argues of the tenth-century geographer al-Muqaddasī that "it is implicit in his descriptions that he regarded a congregational mosque (*masjid jāmiʿ*) and a permanent market (*sūq*) as essential attributes of the mature urban form." "Indeed," Wheatley continues, "this was the customary practice of medieval Muslim topographers" (75). Whether or not the presence of a congregational mosque was determinant of urban status on the ground, it is not clear that its description or even mention was essential to the legibility of cities in the discourse of place. Other aspects of the built environment associated with security, administration, and access to water were enumerated as frequently as mosques and markets in works that considered multiple cities, even in that of al-Muqaddasī. See, for examples, al-Muqaddasī, *Kitāb aḥsan al-taqāsīm*, 163 (Acre's maritime fortifications), 168 (Jerusalem's water distribution system), 288 (riverworks in al-Jurjāniyya), 440 (advice to the builders of Shiraz). See also the attention to infrastructure for industry in the representation of the Nile Delta island-city of Tinnīs in the *Kitāb gharāʾib al-funūn*, fol. 34b–36a. However, the preoccupation with monumental architecture in most representations of cities made detailed descriptions of any kind of modest or practical structure, including mosques, comparatively rare.
5. In the accompanying text, the author focuses mainly on the foundation of the city by the Fatimid Caliph al-Mahdī in 297/910 and the miraculous events that persuaded the populace to quit nearby al-Raqqāda, former seat of Aghlabid authority, and take up residence in al-Mahdiyya. See *Kitāb gharāʾib al-funūn*, fol. 33b–34a.
6. To my knowledge, only a handful of iconographic representations of cities are constituent parts of works participating in the discourse of place in this period, notably the images of Palermo, al-Mahdiyya, and Tinnīs from this anonymous eleventh-century world geography. On these images, see Johns and Savage-Smith, "*The Book of Curiosities*"; Rapoport and Savage-Smith, "Medieval Islamic View of the Cosmos." Others images of cities appear in later works or in such different contexts that they merit separate analysis, though they might, of course, have similar political and religious resonance. On the depictions of cities in the mosaics of the Great Mosque of Damascus, see Rabbat, "The Dialogic Dimension." On depictions of Mecca, Medina, and Jerusalem in medieval pilgrim's certificates, see Aksoy and Milstein, "A Collection"; Roxburgh, "Pilgrimage City." On the thirteenth-century depictions of urban scenes accompanying manuscripts of the *Maqāmāt* stories, see Grabar, "The Illustrated *Maqamat* of the Thirteenth Century"; Guthrie, *Arab Social Life*. In a thirteenth-century manuscript of al-Iṣṭakhrī's tenth-century world geography, cities are depicted on regional maps not by circles or other geometric shapes, as was the convention in these maps, but by small images of ornate buildings; see Kamal, 3:595–599.
7. According to Martyn Smith, in al-Azraqī's work "stories are harnessed to explain the landscape of the hajj"; Smith, 144. See also Grabar, "Upon Reading al-Azraqī," 3.

8. On this "hierarchical ordering of space," see Smith, 141.
9. al-Azraqī, 2:764–811. Here, the key distinction is between the yearly hajj, which takes place between the eighth and the twelfth day of the lunar month Dhū l-Ḥijja and consists of a series of ritual activities in the village of Minā and on the plain of ʿArafa (or ʿArafāt), about fifteen miles outside of Mecca, and the *ʿumra*, often translated as "lesser pilgrimage," which may take place at any time of the year and consists of circumambulation of the Kaʿba and other ritual activity within the bounds of the Meccan sanctuary. See Qurʾān 2:196, which makes the distinction between hajj and *ʿumra*, as well as the distinction between full-time residents of Mecca and everyone else; see also *EI*²: "Ḥ*adjdj*". For the way in which medieval hajj certificates privilege the iconographic depiction of ʿArafa, see Aksoy and Milstein, "A Collection"; Roxburgh, "Pilgrimage City."
10. al-Azraqī, 1:415–423, 432–433, 437–438, 579–580, 593–612, 2:757–763. See also Grabar, "On Reading al-Azraqī," 4–5. Arazi argues that the Abbasid-era transformations of the Meccan built environment described by al-Azraqī were part of a concerted Abbasid effort to appropriate, supersede, or outdo Umayyad-era works—and the Umayyad presence—in the city; see Arazi, "Matériaux pour l'étude du conflit," 206–212.
11. For the destruction of his ancestral home, see al-Azraqī, 1:603, 2:878–880. Al-Muqaddasī describes Meccan families as more reluctant to sacrifice their homes to these building projects than does al-Azraqī; see al-Muqaddasī, *Kitāb aḥsan al-taqāsīm*, 75. For anecdotes about the destruction of adjacent homes for the enlargement of the Prophet's Mosque in Medina, see Ibn Rustih, *Kitāb al-aʿlāq al-nafīsa*, 67–73; al-Janadī, 38.
12. For examples, see al-Azraqī, 1:404–414, 424–428, 440–443, 481–482, 543–544, 580–582, 612–639, 2:640–647, 665–668, 781–797. For a lengthy section added by al-Khuzāʿī, see ibid., 2:649–656.
13. Ibid., 1:623–624. Al-Ṣafā is one of the two small hills between which pilgrims are supposed to run imitating Hagar in her frantic search for water for the young Ishmael, and al-Masʿā refers to the path between the two hills. On the cubit, approximately two feet, as a unit of measure, see *EI*²: "al-*Dh*irāʿ".
14. See Grabar, "Upon Reading al-Azraqī," 3–4. Whether this description was intended to guide or influence the design of other monumental structures, as Jonathan Bloom has suggested might have been the case for descriptions of the Great Mosques of Damascus and Cordoba, is impossible to know, though it was certainly detailed enough to act as such a guide; see Bloom, "On the Transmission of Designs."
15. Grabar, "Upon Reading al-Azraqī," 5.
16. Abū l-Maʿālī, 64–81. See also Elad, 68–77.
17. Abū l-Maʿālī's six-part pilgrimage guide is supplemented later in the work by another series of sections on the merits of the various sites within the sanctuary and in the environs of Jerusalem. These sections follow a much more conventional *faḍāʾil* format, listing under each heading relevant traditions prefaced by full chains of transmission, most of which also occur in al-Wāsiṭī's earlier work. The separate placement of this six-part pilgrimage guide within Abū l-Maʿālī's work, in addition to the different configuration of material therein, functions to emphasize not only the overall representation of Jerusalem's built environment as a ritual topography, but also the uniqueness of the format of this textual interlude. See, for examples, Abū l-Maʿālī, 123–131 (nos. 148–163), 133–139 (nos. 166–172); al-Wāsiṭī, 14–16 (nos. 14–17), 17 (no. 19), 20 (no. 23), 45–46 (no. 63), 73–76 (nos. 119–123), 78 (no. 130), 90 (no. 147).
18. Abū l-Maʿālī, 64–65 (no. 52).
19. For more information about the location and meaning of these sites, among others, see Elad, 47–50.
20. For maps of this itinerary, see Elad, maps 2, 2a.
21. Abū al-Maʿālī, 78–79 (no. 67). For more information about the location and meaning of the sites mentioned in this passage, see Elad, 82–117. For more about the *Miḥrāb Maryam* as a raised, enclosed structure, see Khoury, "The Dome of the Rock, the Kaʿba, and Ghumdan," 58.
22. See, in particular, Qurʾān 19:16–34.
23. al-Muqaddasī, *Kitāb aḥsan al-taqāsīm*, 43–45. On al-Muqaddasī, see also Miquel, 1:313–330. Miquel credits the ninth-century geographer al-Yaʿqūbī with introducing the importance of *ʿiyān* as a source for geographical writing; see Miquel, 1:285–292.

24. Ibn ʿAbd Rabbih, 29: 74–107. The description of these three structures as iconic "stand-ins" for the cities, and all the sites therein, visited on pilgrimage have a striking parallel in "pilgrimage certificates" from the medieval Islamic world, which represent Mecca, Medina, and Jerusalem through highly stylized depictions of *al-Masjid al-Ḥarām*, the Prophet's Mosque, and the Dome of the Rock; see Şule Aksoy and Rachel Milstein, "A Collection"; Roxburgh, "Pilgrimage City."
25. On these accounts, see Shafīʿ, "A Description of the Two Sanctuaries of Islam." Nuha Khoury argues that these passages were inserted by a later redactor of the work, as there is no record of Ibn ʿAbd Rabbih having traveled to the Arabian Peninsula and as the description of the Prophet's Mosque in Medina exhibits striking similarities to the Great Mosque of Cordoba as expanded and renovated after Ibn ʿAbd Rabbih's death. Khoury calls this description "a critical instrument of iconographic transfer that conflated two monuments in order to re-create one as an image of the other"; see Khoury, "The Meaning of the Great Mosque of Cordoba," 90. Whatever the intended goal for the descriptions, whether an "instrument of iconographic transfer" or a pious documentation of pilgrimage experience, their authority in the context of the work as a whole rests on their presentation as knowledge produced by the physical visitation of cities.
26. Nāṣir-i Khusraw, 89–103 (for specific mention of his status as *mujāwir*, see 78, 92, 102).
27. This is Wheeler Thackston's English translation in ibid., 30.
28. This is Thackston's English translation in ibid., 43.
29. This is Thackston's English translation in ibid., 33.
30. Ibid., 56–74. Paula Sanders has argued that the Fatimids created "an Ismaʿili ritual city" in Cairo that was noteworthy for, among other things, its inclusivity of the non-Ismāʿīlī and non-Muslim populations; see Sanders, 39–40.
31. Nāṣir-i Khusraw, 61–66. On these inundation ceremonies, see Sanders, 99–119.
32. For his relationship with Ismāʿīlī Shiism, see Nāṣir-i Khusraw, xi–xiii.
33. Ibid., 73–74.
34. When he notes that these structures are all owned by the caliph and then rented out or made available freely to the urban population, he is in effect saying that the city itself is an extension of the caliph's authority; see ibid., 57–58.
35. Unfortunately portions of the beginning of this work, in which ʿUmar b. Shabba's representation of Medina occurs, are missing, so it is difficult to assess the space occupied or the role played by the representation of the city in relation to the work as a whole. As it stands, the vast majority of the first volume of the published edition of this work is dedicated to a topographical description of Medina, with episodes from Muḥammad's life largely harnessed to aspects of its topography, and to *faḍāʾil*-type material; see ʿUmar b. Shabba, 1:3–310. After this, the episodes from Muḥammad's life assume the more chronological organization of political history and biography, and this organization and emphasis continues in the following sections on ʿUmar and ʿUthmān.
36. Ibid., 229–268.
37. Ibid., 256–260.
38. Ibid., 251.
39. al-Azraqī, 2:857–908.
40. For examples of such primary documents, see ʿUmar b. Shabba, 1:225–228, 238–239.
41. A very similar effect is produced by a delineation (*khiṭaṭ*) of the mosques of Jurjān in the introduction to Ḥamza b. Yūsuf al-Sahmī's eleventh-century city-based biographical dictionary, known as the *Taʾrīkh Jurjān* or the *Kitāb maʿrifat ʿulamāʾ ahl Jurjān*. In this section, which concludes an extended conquest history focusing on the settlement of the city by Companions and Successors to the Prophet, the author lists the mosques founded within the city and its immediate suburbs during the Umayyad period, but he includes up-to-date information about their locations and their names. While he provides the original name of the mosque, in almost every case he adds "it is now called _____" and gives its location vis-à-vis contemporary landmarks. In this way, he links the topography of the city during his lifetime to the foundational period of its Islamization in the early eighth century. See al-Sahmī, 16–17; see also Pourshariati, "Local Histories," 53–57.
42. The consensus has been that the surviving manuscripts of this work represent only the seventh part of a multivolume *adab*-style compilation, though some have taken issue with this consensus; see Montgomery, "Ibn Rusta's Lack of 'Eloquence.'"

43. Ibn Rustih, *Kitāb al-aʿlāq al-nafīsa*, 73–78.
44. Ibid., 30–40, 44–57.
45. The possibility that he did not in fact make it to Mecca, and would have taken credit for a description of Mecca if he could have, is suggested by the introduction to the section on his hometown of Isfahan in which he celebrates his firsthand access to information: "In mentioning other countries in my book, I only recorded reports, some of which were sound and some of which were flimsy, and stories from sources upon whom I had to rely because they were the only sources I could find ... However, what I am going to say about Isfahan comes from direct experience (*ʿiyān*) or from stories whose authority it is impossible to better because I never worked from only one source"; ibid., 151.
46. Miquel, 1:198–202. See also Montgomery, "Ibn Rusta's Lack of 'Eloquence.'"
47. Melani McAlister uses the term "citational" to describe knowledge production in Europe about the Islamic world as criticized by Edward Said in *Orientalism*; see McAlister, 9. Said uses the term "textual" to describe this form of knowledge production; see Said, 92–94. Since all knowledge production in the discourse of place was "textual," the term "citational" is useful for distinguishing textual strategies that depend on the citation of previous authorities from those that depend on knowledge produced by the lived experience of the author of the text.
48. See Miquel, 1:153–189.
49. Ibn al-Faqīh, *Mukhtaṣar kitāb al-buldān*, 100.
50. This use of "virtual" was inspired by Cobb, "Virtual Sacrality." A striking parallel can be seen in the practice, documented by a cache of "pilgrimage certificates" from eleventh- and twelfth-century Syria, of individuals commissioning a "substitute pilgrim" to perform the rituals of the hajj or the *ʿumra* in their stead, with the spiritual benefits accruing to them rather than to the "substitute." These legal documents describe in some detail the rituals undertaken at various sites in Mecca for the benefit of the commissioner and therefore can be seen as "virtual pilgrimages." See Sourdel and Sourdel-Thomine, "Une collection."
51. A similar effect can be seen in descriptions of cemeteries as part of the urban built environment. Even if the material assembled to describe the cemeteries is mediated by earlier authorities rather than reported from firsthand experience, tombs of prophets, ascetics, or other figures of religious authority, like monumental mosques or shrines (and sometimes such tombs are located within monumental mosques or shrines, as in Muḥammad's tomb in the Prophet's Mosque of Medina), are usually associated with pious visitation. This association makes their description a form of the recognition and commemoration of the sacred past in the discourse of place, a textual act of pilgrimage, if not also a documentation of a physical one. For examples, see ʿUmar b. Shabba, 1:86–132; al-Khaṭīb al-Baghdādī, 1:120–127.
52. al-Muqaddasī, *Kitāb aḥsan al-taqāsīm*, 171.
53. Extremely relevant here is the discussion of the relationship between the twelfth-century traveler Ibn Jubayr's account of his trip to Mecca and al-Azraqī's *Akhbār Makka* in Smith, 115–152.
54. On this, see Lassner, *The Topography of Baghdad*, 31–34, 40–42.
55. al-Yaʿqūbī, *Kitāb al-buldān*, 254.
56. Ibid., 254, 255–268. It is worth noting that the only other detailed topographical information he furnishes is on the land grants and construction projects ordered by ʿUmar b. al-Khaṭṭāb immediately after the foundation of the garrison city of Kufa in Iraq; ibid., 310–311. Similarly, works from the discourse of place devoted to cities that did not enjoy the same level of direct caliphal intervention in shaping their built environments as Baghdad and Samarra tend to focus on the role of representatives of the Abbasid caliph, especially governors, in shaping their built environments and, particularly, in building and adorning congregational mosques; for examples, see al-Rāzī, 85–88 (on Sanaa); Abū Nuʿaym, 1: 16–17, 38 (on Isfahan); Qummī, 100–125 (on Qom); al-Narshakhī, 48–52 (on Bukhara, including material added by later redactors of al-Narshakhī's tenth-century original). On this idea, see also Kennedy, "How to Found an Islamic City."
57. On Muḥammad b. Khalaf as a source for al-Khaṭīb al-Baghdādī, see Lassner, *The Topography of Baghdad*, 29–30.
58. al-Khaṭīb al-Baghdādī, 1:87. See also the translation and annotation of this passage in Lassner, *The Topography of Baghdad*, 70.

59. Lassner, *The Topography of Baghdad,* 255, note 35.
60. al-Khaṭīb al-Baghdādī, 1:100–105.
61. Ibid., 101–102.
62. Another anecdote included in the introduction to the *Taʾrīkh Baghdād* mentions an illustration (*ṣūra*) of Baghdad's "land, markets, streets, palaces, and waterways of both the east and west side" that was made for a Byzantine emperor. Supposedly, when the Byzantine emperor drank, he would pull out this illustration and declare, "I have never seen an illustration of a built environment (*abniya*) more handsome than [Baghdad's]"; ibid., 94. Representatives of the Byzantine Empire praising Islamic cities constitutes something of a topos in the discourse of place and recurs in the introduction to the *Tāʾrīkh Baghdād*; for another example, see ibid., 91–92.
63. Ibid., 117–118. Compare with the somewhat more sober figures given for the same period in al-Yaʿqūbī, *Kitāb al-buldān,* 250, 254.
64. al-Khaṭīb al-Baghdādī, 1:118. A very good parallel can be found in the statistics quoted in al-Rāzī's eleventh-century topographical history of Sanaa. He reports that the city reached its height during the reign of Abbasid Caliph Hārūn al-Rashīd at the end of the eighth century, boasting 10,000 mosques and 120,000 houses, including the spacious residence of the Barmakid family, which sported "large columned gates"; al-Rāzī, 105–106, 111. He then quotes different sources on the greatly decreased number of houses in the city in the early tenth century, after a period of political instability, totaling anywhere from 30,000 to 52,000; ibid., 110, 113. Finally, he provides a set of figures from the mid-tenth century tracking the decline in the city's population to a low of 1,040 houses in the year 381/991; ibid., 114.
65. Ibn al-Faqīh quotes Yazdajird al-Kisrawī disputing a rumored 200,000 baths in ninth-century Baghdad with, in his estimation, the more realistic figure of 60,000. He then submits this figure to various calculations involving the number of attendants at each bath and the number of households served to arrive at the wildly implausible figure of 96,000,000 for the total population of the city at this time; Ibn al-Faqīh, *Baghdād,* 90–108. In his eleventh-century topographical history of Sanaa, al-Rāzī quotes the seemingly exaggerated figure of 109,000 mosques for, of all places, the city of Basra on the authority of the prominent judge Yaḥyā b. Aktham (d. 242/857); al-Rāzī, 116. Coming as it does at the end of a set of statistics for the decreasing number of homes in Sanaa during the ninth and tenth centuries, the figures al-Rāzī quotes for Basra seem intended more as a foil for Sanaa's decline than as a faithful representation of the size of the Iraqi city.
66. On Ibn al-Faqīh's *Kitāb al-buldān,* and in particular his treatment of Baghdad, as a kind of "mythic geography," see Khalidov, "Myth and Reality."
67. al-Khaṭīb al-Baghdādī, 1:119.
68. George Makdisi detects a similar nostalgia in the fragmentary topographical description of Baghdad by Abū l-Wafāʾ b. ʿAqīl (d. 513/1119) preserved in a work entitled *Manāqib Baghdād* attributed to Abū l-Faraj b. al-Jawzī (d. 597/1200). In this fragment, Ibn ʿAqīl reminisces about the Baghdad of his childhood before Seljuk rule resulted in the deterioration of the city's built environment and a general population exodus; see Makdisi, "The Topography of Eleventh Century Baġdād." On nostalgia as a topos in descriptions of Baghdad from the ninth century to the present, see Cooperson, "Baghdad."
69. For similar conclusions based on a different selection of sources, see Micheau, "Baghdad in the Abbasid Era." For a different approach to similar sources, see Antrim, "Connectivity and Creativity."
70. On the politics of the panegyric, see Stetkevych, *The Poetics of Islamic Legitimacy*; Ali, *Arabic Literary Salons,* 75–116. On the elegy, see al-Ḥillī, *al-Rithāʾ fī l-shiʿr al-ʿArabī.*
71. While panegyrics for cities do not seem to have been a discrete genre of poetry, panegyrics for rulers sometimes included descriptions of their palaces or the monumental architecture with which they were associated to emphasize their power; on this phenomenon in Persian poetry, see Meisami, "Palaces and Paradises."
72. al-Ṭabarī, *Taʾrīkh al-rusul wa-l-mulūk,* 11 (3d ser., vol. 2), 874 (year 197). I have been guided in my English translation of these verses by Michael Fishbein in al-Ṭabarī, *The War between Brothers,* 142. See also the discussion and translation of passages from this poem in Elinson, 20–24; and the discussion of this and other elegies for Baghdad in al-Ḥillī, 230–256.

73. On pathways, districts, and landmarks, see Lynch, *The Image of the City*.
74. Along with the idea of protection go the frequent images in elegies for cities of women formerly protected by the walls of the built environment now exposed in their ruins. All three of the poems discussed here include lines referring to the women enclosed within the intact urban built environment. On the gendered significance of urban walls, see O'Meara, 54–56; on images of the violation of women in poetry elegizing the fall of Baghdad to the Mongols in 1258, see Hassan, 40–45.
75. This is A. J. Arberry's English translation in Arberry, 66–69. For the Arabic, see also Ibn al-Rūmī, 424. For a discussion of this poem, see al-Ḥillī, 257–265.
76. This is Alexander Elinson's English translation in Elinson, 40, 161–162. For the Arabic, see also Ibn Shuhayd, 109–111. For more on Andalusian elegies for cities, see al-Zayyāt, *Rithāʾ al-mudun*; Ruggles, "Arabic Poetry and Architectural Memory"; Robinson, "*Ubi Sunt*."
77. Elinson, 46–47. See also Christys, "The Meaning of Topography."
78. Elinson argues that Ibn Shuhayd saw it as "his job as a poet, and the audience's job as mourners, to perpetuate Cordoba's life in the only way available to them—by 'sing[ing its] praises (*nafkharu*)'" (47–48).
79. See, in particular, Stetkevych, *The Zephyrs of Nejd*.
80. Other interpretations of nostalgia for places as active and political include Meisami, "Places in the Past"; Elinson, *Looking Back at al-Andalus*.
81. The most obvious example of this is the debate between the two early garrison cities of Iraq, Kufa and Basra, a debate that probably has its origins in the real political and religious rivalry between Kufan factions backing the claim of ʿAlī and his descendants to the leadership of the Islamic world and Basran factions backing the claims of ʿAlī's various opponents in the seventh and eighth centuries. The recurrent allusions to, if not full performances of, this debate in the discourse of place may have been intended to reproduce these sympathies and antipathies, but clearly they were also useful as widely understood platforms for the display of linguistic agility. For examples, see the famous defense of Basra against the insults of Kufans and other Iraqis in al-Jāḥiẓ, *Kitāb al-buldān*, 497–505; see also the reproduction of a debate between the representatives of Kufa and Basra set in the presence of an Abbasid caliph in Ibn al-Faqīh, *Mukhtaṣar kitāb al-buldān*, 163–173. Other debates that reflect an *adab* sensibility, especially the vogue for contrastive enumeration as a test of wit, are the many lists of cities in terms of their good and bad qualities; see, for example, al-Thaʿālibī, *Laṭāʾif al-maʿārif*, 233–239. For more on these *adab*-inspired lists, see Miquel, 4:128–131.
82. The secondary literature on this rivalry is abundant. See, for examples, Rubin, "Between Arabia and the Holy Land"; Kister, "Sanctity Joint and Divided"; Arazi, "Matériaux pour l'étude du conflit"; von Grunebaum, "The Sacred Character of Islamic Cities"; Neuwirth, 309–312. For a recent discussion of such texts focusing on Syria, see Khalek, *Damascus after the Conquest*, especially chapter 4.
83. Kister, "'You shall only set out for three mosques.'"
84. al-Ḥasan al-Baṣrī, 22.
85. Ibid., 20, 21, 23, 24, 29, 30.
86. Abū al-Maʿālī, 239 (no. 356). See also al-Wāsiṭī, 92 (no. 151). Recall that an *ʿumra* consisted of the visitation of *al-Masjid al-Ḥarām* without the attendant visitation of ʿArafa and Minā associated with the hajj.
87. For examples of Jerusalem's implied precedence over Mecca on Judgment Day, see Ibn al-Faqīh, *Mukhtaṣar kitāb al-buldān*, 94; al-Muqaddasī, *Kitāb aḥsan al-taqāsīm*, 166–167; Abū al-Maʿālī, 211–213 (nos. 305–310); al-Wāsiṭī, 40 (no. 55), 92–93 (nos. 150–153). Even al-Azraqī devotes a chapter to proving that Mecca, not Jerusalem, was the first "house [of worship]" (*bayt*) on earth, indicating that champions of Mecca's preeminence still found it necessary to dismiss other claimants; see al-Azraqī, 1:131–132 (nos. 105–109).
88. al-Janadī, 18–20.
89. al-Rabaʿī, 36–37 (no. 64).
90. Ibid., 37 (no. 65).
91. See, for examples, Ibn al-Faqīh, *Mukhtaṣar kitāb al-buldān*, 173–174; Abū l-Maʿālī, 11 (no. 3). See also discussions in Livne-Kafri, "The Early Šīʿa and Jerusalem"; Kister, "'You shall only set out for three mosques,'" 188–191.

92. For example, see the separate section devoted to the merits of Hebron (*faḍāʾil al-Khalīl*), which focuses on the virtue of prayer at the tombs of Abraham, Isaac, and Jacob located there, in Abū l-Maʿālī, 329–358.
93. See, for example, the sections on "shrines" (*mashāhid*) and "marvels" (*ʿajāʾib*) at the end of each chapter in al-Muqaddasī, *Kitāb aḥsan al-taqāsīm*. On the concept of *ʿajāʾib* in relation to geographical writing, see Miquel, 4:51–54, 95–122. See also Zadeh, *Mapping Frontiers*; idem, "The Wiles of Creation"; von Hees, "The Astonishing"; Mottahedeh, "*ʿAjāʾib*."
94. al-Muqaddasī, *Kitāb aḥsan al-taqāsīm*, 166–167.
95. See Arazi, "Matériaux pour l'étude du conflit."
96. In his late-nineteenth-century work *Muhammedanische Studien*, Ignaz Goldziher argued that the fabrication and circulation of traditions praising Jerusalem should be seen as propaganda linked directly to the Umayyad Caliph ʿAbd al-Malik's construction of the Dome of the Rock in a bid to upstage his rival Ibn al-Zubayr by proposing pilgrimage to Jerusalem as an alternative to or even substitute for pilgrimage to Mecca; see Goldziher, 2:44–46. S. D. Goitein later rejected this argument in his essay "The Sanctity of Jerusalem and Palestine in Early Islam" and insisted that the motivation for ʿAbd al-Malik's erection of the Dome of the Rock was the desire to upstage not a Muslim competitor but the Christian community in Jerusalem and the splendor of its holy architecture. He attributes Goldziher's argument to a "Shiʿite fable" spun by the ninth-century scholar al-Yaʿqūbī and finds no basis for it in other works. Furthermore, Goitein states that the circulation of the traditions in question testifies to an early and ongoing debate among religious scholars within Islam about the sanctity of Jerusalem, and thus the transmission and collection of *faḍāʾil* material on Jerusalem arose from religious concerns relevant to all Muslims rather than an Umayyad political agenda. Since then, scholars have generally accepted some combination of universal religious and partisan political motivations for the emergence of traditions related to the merits of Jerusalem and affirm the dating of the circulation of this material and its preservation in written form as having occurred as early as the late seventh century.
97. Abū Nuʿaym, 1:1–14.
98. A similar effect is produced by Ibn Rustih's early-tenth-century representation of Isfahan, which concludes with a notice about the virtues of the people of Isfahan after a lengthy discussion of the city's associations with both the Abbasid regime and pre-Islamic Persian monarchs; see Ibn Rustih, *Kitāb al-aʿlāq al-nafīsa*, 151–163. For further discussions of the relationship between pre-Islamic Persian identity and local history, see Paul, "The Histories of Isfahan"; Pourshariati, "Local Historiography"; Savant, *The New Muslims of Post-Conquest Iran*.

Chapter 4

1. On "human geography," see Miquel, 1:35–112.
2. On Islamic cosmology and astronomy, see Nasr, *An Introduction*; Savage-Smith, "Celestial Mapping"; Karamustafa, "Cosmographical Diagrams."
3. See King, *World Maps*.
4. See Gutas, *Greek Thought, Arabic Culture*; Zadeh, *Mapping Frontiers*.
5. Ptolemy never sets out his criteria for the regional divisions he uses, and some of them are clearly unrelated to known administrative practices; see Berggren and Jones, 84–85.
6. Ibid., 40–41.
7. On the contents of "al-Ṣūra al-Maʾmūniyya," its relationship with Ptolemy's *Geography* and al-Khwārazmī's *Ṣūrat al-arḍ*, see the contrasting views in Sezgin, *Mathematical Geography*, 1:71–137; Tibbetts, "The Beginnings of a Cartographic Tradition"; Hopkins, 303–306; *EI*[2]: "Iḳlīm".
8. For a critical edition from the earliest surviving manuscript of this work (dated 428/1037), see al-Khwārazmī, *Kitāb ṣūrat al-arḍ*. This edition also includes reproductions of four maps that accompany the manuscript, one a model for drawing the contours of a coastline, one of "Jewel Island" ("Jazīrat al-Jawhar") in "the Dark Sea" ("al-Baḥr al-Muẓlim"), one of the Nile River, and one of the Sea of Azov. The maps of the Nile and "Jewel Island" each portray the line of the equator, and the map of the Nile also portrays latitudinal lines for the first through

third climes. For color images of the maps from this manuscript, see Sezgin, *Mathematical Geography*, 3:8–10 (maps 1f–i); Harley and Woodward, plates 4–5. On these maps, see also Tibbetts, "The Beginnings of a Cartographic Tradition," 105–106; Sezgin, *Mathematical Geography*, 1:121–123.

9. Suhrāb, 8. He is also known as Ibn Sarābiyūn or Ibn Serapion.
10. Ibid., 23.
11. Ibid., 23–31; see also al-Khwārazmī, 15–23.
12. Tibbetts, "The Beginnings of a Cartographic Tradition," 93–94. For more on the idea and land of Īrānshahr from the pre-Islamic through the early Islamic periods, see Christensen, *The Decline of Iranshahr*.
13. For published reproductions of this diagram, see al-Bīrūnī, *Taḥdīd*, 107 (fig. 23); idem, *The Determination*, 102 (fig. 23); idem, *Ṣifat al-maʿmūra*, 61; Levtzion and Hopkins, xix (fig. 1). See also Nasr, 143–147.
14. This is Jamil Ali's English translation in al-Bīrūnī, *The Determination*, 101–102. For the Arabic, see idem, *Taḥdīd*, 106–107.
15. Levtzion and Hopkins, xv-xviii; *EI*[2]: "Iḳlīm".
16. al-Masʿūdī, *Kitāb al-tanbīh*, 31–32. On the *farsakh*, a unit of measure derived from the ancient Persian indicating the distance a mounted rider could cover in an hour, estimated at about 6km in the Islamic period, see *EI*[2]: "*Dhirā*ʿ," "Farsa*kh*." On Gog and Magog, designations for legendary peoples or their lands located at the end of the earth, see Miquel, 2:483–513; *EI*[2]: "*Yādjūdj* wa-*Mādjūdj*"; Zadeh, *Mapping Frontiers*. On the toponym "Yawamārīs," compare with Ibn al-Faqīh, *Mukhtaṣar kitāb al-buldān*, 5 (note h). "Ifrīqiyya" is generally considered to have referred to the central portion of North Africa corresponding roughly to present-day Tunisia and parts of neighboring Libya and Algeria.
17. In al-Masʿūdī's longer work *Murūj al-dhahab*, of which the *Kitāb al-tanbīh wa-l-ishrāf* was said to be an abridgement, he numbers the seven climes differently (and never describes them explicitly as a circular formation); thus, Babylon is first, then India, then the Ḥijāz, then Egypt, then Byzantium and Syria, then the lands of the Turks, and then finally China. See al-Masʿūdī, *Murūj al-dhahab*, 1:85–87; see also Ali, "Some Geographical Ideas of al-Masʿūdī." Miquel has mapped al-Masʿūdī's climes and contrasted them with a map of the seven latitudinal climes as described by al-Muqaddasī; see Miquel, 2:58–59 (fig. 14).
18. al-Masʿūdī, *Kitāb al-tanbīh*, 33. It is also possible that *qiṭaʿ al-arḍ* ("sections of the earth") is an error and that it should read *ṣūrat al-arḍ* ("depiction of the earth"); see Sezgin, *Mathematical Geography*, 1:79 (note 1).
19. al-Masʿūdī, *Kitāb al-tanbīh*, 35. Al-Masʿūdī is quite specific about setting the limits or borders (*ḥudūd*) of each of his climes. For the fourth clime, he writes: "[Its] limit is [first] at al-Thaʿlabiyya (on the pilgrimage route from Kufa), second in the middle of the Oxus River, third twelve *farsakhs* behind Naṣībīn in the direction of Sinjār (in upper Mesopotamia), fourth six *farsakhs* beyond al-Daybul on the coast of al-Manṣūra in the country of al-Sind"; see al-Masʿūdī, *Kitāb al-tanbīh*, 32. These borders situate al-Masʿūdī's fourth clime strikingly eastward, with a north-eastern limit at the Oxus River, which runs along the border between present-day Turkmenistan and Uzbekistan, and a southeastern limit on the coast of what is today Pakistan. Its western limits extend only to the border area between Turkey, Syria, and Iraq to the northwest of Mosul and along the pilgrimage route running southwest from Kufa to a site in the northeast of what is today Saudi Arabia, which hardly makes the region of Iraq centrally situated within the territory of the fourth clime, despite al-Masʿūdī's statements to the contrary.
20. al-Masʿūdī, *Kitāb al-tanbīh*, 35–36. This territory comprises much of present-day Iraq south of the city of Mosul.
21. Miquel's distinction between Greek technical influences and Persian geopolitical influences on early Arabic geography is overstated, despite al-Bīrūnī's endorsement of just such a distinction; see Miquel, 1:70–72, 82–83.
22. For more on this, see Zadeh, *Mapping Frontiers*, chapter 4.
23. See Alavi, "Al-Masʿūdī's Conception."
24. al-Masʿūdī, *Kitāb al-tanbīh*, 22–24.
25. This discussion of climatic determinism is similar to Ibn Rustih's, though he does not differentiate between east and west; see Ibn Rustih, *Kitāb al-aʿlāq al-nafīsa*, 101–103. Compare with

the much more complex discussion of astrology and climatic determinism in al-Hamdānī, *Ṣifat*, 37–53. See also Miquel, 2:33–56.

26. For a discussion of the association of the "peoples" (*shuʿūb*) in this Qurʾānic verse with particular territories among proponents of the *Shuʿūbiyya* movement, see Mottahedeh, "The Shuʿūbīyah Controversy."
27. *Kitāb gharāʾib al-funūn*, fol. 24b–25a. Similarly, one of the two seven-clime systems proposed by the eleventh-century Andalusian geographer al-Bakrī has Egypt, North Africa, and Andalusia occupying the fourth and central clime; the other has his own city of Cordoba listed in the fourth clime, while Baghdad languishes in the third. See al-Bakrī, *al-Masālik wa-l-mamālik*, 1:129–137. Ibn Rustih also locates Baghdad in the third clime, while his hometown of Isfahan is situated in the fourth; see Ibn Rustih, *Kitāb al-aʿlāq al-nafīsa*, 97.
28. Ibn al-Faqīh, *Mukhtaṣar kitāb al-buldān*, 3. "Wāq-Wāq" and "Manshak and Māshak" refer to legendary peoples or territories on the edge of the earth; see Miquel, 2:483–513; *EI*²: "Wāḳwāḳ." "Dhāt al-Ḥumām" is a site just to the west of Alexandria on the North African coast. "Al-Maghrib" is a regional toponym often used to designate northwest Africa, including much of present-day Algeria and Morocco. A variation on this tradition, also on the authority of ʿAbd Allāh b. ʿAmr b. al-ʿĀṣ, has Mecca, Medina, and Yemen as the head of the bird, Syria and Egypt the chest, Iraq the right wing, al-Sind the left, and the Maghrib, again, as the "worst part of a bird, the tail"; see Ibn ʿAbd al-Ḥakam, 19; Ibn Zūlāq, 12. Some attribute the origins of the world-as-bird metaphor to ancient Indian or Persian traditions. That it may indeed have had one or both of these origins is certainly likely, but the participants in the discourse of place do not so attribute it.
29. al-Rabaʿī, 4 (no. 2). See also the version quoted by Ibn Ḥawqal, which has Syria as the head, al-Jazīra as the chest, Yemen the tail, and Basra and Egypt as the two wings; Ibn Ḥawqal, *Kitāb ṣūrat al-arḍ*, 209. Ibn Ḥawqal is critical of this method of dividing the world, both because it excludes many territories and because it can be altered based on the agenda of its interlocutor. A very different version of this metaphor has Isfahan as the head of the bird and Fārs and Azerbaijan as its two wings; see al-Māfarrūkhī, 55.
30. al-Masʿūdī, *Murūj al-dhahab*, 2:66–69; compare with idem, *Les prairies d'or*, 3:123–130. "Khūzistān" refers to a region traversing the southerly border between present-day Iraq and Iran. "Al-Jazīra" refers to upper Mesopotamia, including territory located today in northern Iraq and northern Syria.
31. al-Masʿūdī, *Murūj al-dhahab*, 2:67; compare with idem, *Les prairies d'or*, 3:124–125. See also Ziadeh, "Diyār al-Shām."
32. al-Masʿūdī, *Murūj al-dhahab*, 2:67, 69; compare with idem, *Les prairies d'or*, 3:126, 129. "Al-Tahāʾim" is a plural form of the toponym "al-Tihāma," which refers to the territory along the southwest Red Sea coast of the Arabian Peninsula.
33. al-Masʿūdī, *Murūj al-dhahab*, 2:69; compare with idem, *Les prairies d'or*, 3:130.
34. This is the same way that al-Muqaddasī justifies his exclusion of territories outside of the "Realm of Islam" from his world geography; see al-Muqaddasī, *Kitāb aḥsan al-taqāsīm*, 9.
35. al-Jāḥiẓ, *Kitāb al-buldān*, 463.
36. Similarly, the tenth-century geographers al-Iṣṭakhrī and Ibn Ḥawqal call it the "Diyār al-ʿArab," a toponym that highlights its association with a particular people, and describe it as "the country and homelands (*awṭān*) of the Arabs, a residence that they do not share with anyone else"; al-Iṣṭakhrī, *al-Masālik*, ed. al-Ḥīnī, 20; Ibn Ḥawqal, *Kitāb ṣūrat al-arḍ*, 18.
37. See King and Lorch, "Qibla Charts"; King, *World Maps*.
38. Ibn Khurradādhbih, 5. See a reconstruction of this four-part schema in the form of a *qibla* chart in King and Lorch, 190 (fig. 9.1).
39. al-Iṣṭakhrī, *al-Masālik*, ed. al-Ḥīnī, 15–19; Ibn Ḥawqal, *Kitāb ṣūrat al-arḍ*, 9–17; al-Muqaddasī, *Kitāb aḥsan al-taqāsīm*, 62–66. Although al-Iṣṭakhrī and Ibn Ḥawqal define it explicitly in relation to the earlier "Empires of China, Persia, and Rūm," they also use the less overtly political category "country/territory/land of Islam" (*bilād al-Islām*) to refer to the entity then subdivided in the rest of the work.
40. By contrast, Miquel has described the idea of the *Mamlakat al-Islām* in these works as a "fiction" at odds with the reality of political decentralization on the ground in the mid-tenth century; Miquel, 1:273.

41. al-Muqaddasī, *Kitāb aḥsan al-taqāsīm*, 9.
42. In reference to Ibn Ḥawqal, see Miquel, 1:299–309.
43. Measurements for its length and width are also provided, which characterize it as a bounded regional entity and thus, it is implied, separable from the rest of the inhabited world; see al-Iṣṭakhrī, *al-Masālik*, ed. al-Ḥīnī, 19; Ibn Hawqal, *Kitāb ṣūrat al-arḍ*, 16–17; al-Muqaddasī, *Kitāb aḥsan al-taqāsīm*, 65–66.
44. For examples of these maps from various manuscripts, see Miller, vol. 6; Kamal, 3:584–663.
45. al-Muqaddasī, *The Best Divisions*, 54, 407 (Map III).
46. This is one of Miquel's major arguments; see Miquel, 1:274.
47. al-Muqaddasī, *Kitāb aḥsan al-taqāsīm*, 9.
48. For a statement of the "urban bias" of this literature, see Brauer, "Geography in the Medieval Muslim World," 77–78. See also the "urban systems" in Wheatley, *Places Where Men Pray*.
49. See Miquel, 1:87–92, 102–104.
50. Ibn al-Nadīm indicates that he held this post for the region of al-Jibāl, but nowhere is it specified for which Abbasid caliph he was so employed or to whom the book was dedicated. Ibn al-Nadīm does remark that Ibn Khurradādhbih was a boon companion of Caliph al-Muʿtamid, and since the version of the *Kitāb al-masālik wa-l-mamālik* under study here was composed during his reign it seems likely that the work was intended for him; see Ibn al-Nadīm, *al-Fihrist*, 283; idem, *The Fihrist*, trans. Dodge, 326. On the two versions of the work and the issues of patronage and reception, see Montgomery, "Serendipity, Resistance, and Multivalency"; Zadeh, *Mapping Frontiers*. Compare with Miquel, 1:87–92.
51. al-Yaʿqūbī, *Kitāb al-buldān*, 268.
52. See Zadeh, *Mapping Frontiers*, 17.
53. Ibn Khurradādhbih, 5. For a similar description, see Ibn Rustih, *Kitāb al-aʿlāq al-nafīsa*, 104.
54. Ibn Khurradādhbih, 6. See also Ibn al-Faqīh, *Nuṣūṣ*, 57. The exact derivation of the term *kūra* (pl. *kuwar*) is unclear; both Persian and Greek origins have been suggested. On these terms see also Piacentini, "*Madīna/Shahr, Qarya/Deh, Nāḥiya/Rustāq*."
55. Ibn Khurradādhbih, 6–14. Compare with Ibn al-Faqīh, *Nuṣūṣ*, 63–76.
56. Ibn Khurradādhbih, 20. Compare with the enumeration of the rural areas (*rasātīq*) of Isfahan, which starts with "the rural area of Jayy, in which is the city," in al-Yaʿqūbī, *Kitāb al-buldān*, 275. A dirham was a silver coin worth some fraction of the gold *dīnār*.
57. Ralph Brauer argues that reporting length and breadth as two separate numbers, rather than multiplying them together and reporting the result, constitutes a neglect of the concept of area in Arabo-Islamic geography; see Brauer, *Boundaries and Frontiers*, 36. While mathematically speaking this may be true, reporting length and breadth still conjures an image of an expanse of land rather than a network of urban nodes.
58. Examples include al-Māfarrūkhī, *Maḥāsin Iṣfahān*; al-Rabaʿī, *Faḍāʾil al-Shām wa-Dimashq*; and the introduction to al-Khaṭīb al-Baghdādī, *Taʾrīkh Baghdād*.
59. Qudāma b. Jaʿfar's early-tenth-century *Kitāb al-kharāj* reproduces Ibn Khurradādhbih's division of the Sawād into provinces and districts, but then makes a point of demonstrating its anachronism. Qudāma's more contemporary al-Sawād is smaller, many of the districts mentioned by Ibn Khurradādhbih having been attached to surrounding regions. He also furnishes tax revenue for the region from a particular year in the Islamic era (204/819–820). See Qudāma, *Kitāb al-kharāj*, 235–239. For more on this, see Miquel, 1:95–101; Zadeh, *Mapping Frontiers*, chapter 1; Heck, *The Construction of Knowledge*, chapter 3.
60. What exactly constituted an "Arab" and a "non-Arab" is a question of considerable magnitude and complexity for the period under study.
61. al-Yaʿqūbī, *Kitāb al-buldān*, 348, 350, 354–355. On the origins of the *ajnād* of Damascus, Jordan, Homs, and Qinnasrīn, which doubled as names for the administrative subdivisions of Syria during the Umayyad period, see Shahid, "The Jund System"; Haldon, "Seventh-Century Continuities." Al-Yaʿqūbī may have been the first participant in the discourse of place to use the term *jund* for these subdivisions of Syria, which would become a convention in later works on Syria. Compare, for example, with Ibn Khurradādhbih, who uses the terms *kuwar* and *aqālīm* for the subdivisions of Syria; Ibn Khurradādhbih, 75–79.
62. al-Yaʿqūbī, *Kitāb al-buldān*, 270. "Al-Jabal" is a variant of the regional toponym "al-Jibāl," located in the west-central part of present-day Iran.

63. Ibid., 282–286, 295–308. Sijistān refers to territory located today in southeastern Iran and southwestern Afghanistan and Pakistan.
64. Ibid., 347–352.
65. Ibid., 347.
66. Ibid., 348. The mile (*mīl*) in this context was the equivalent of approximately two kilometers, or 1.24 contemporary miles; for more on measurements, see *EI*²: "*Dhirā*ʿ."
67. al-Yaʿqūbī, *Kitāb al-buldān*, 349–351.
68. Ibid., 351–352.
69. In less meticulous ways, al-Yaʿqūbī accomplishes something similar with the lands ruled by the Rustamid dynasty from Tāhart, located in present-day Algeria, and the Idrisid dynasty from Fez, in present-day Morocco, neither of which were even nominally under the authority of the Abbasid Caliphate; see al-Yaʿqūbī, *Kitāb al-buldān*, 352–353, 355–359.
70. Ibid., 317–319, 324–329.
71. Ibid., 330. On the obscure toponym "Two Trees," see Maspero and Wiet, 111.
72. For a contrast with Qudāma b. Jaʿfar's approach to geography from an overwhelmingly administrative perspective, see Heck, *The Construction of Knowledge*, especially chapter 3.
73. al-Bakrī, *al-Masālik wa-l-mamālik*, 2:193–194.

Chapter 5

1. On the "Balkhī school," see Tibbetts, "The Balkhī School"; Hopkins, "Geographical and Navigational Literature"; *EI*²: "*Djughrāfiyā*." Some scholars use other names to describe the intellectual relationship between al-Iṣṭakhrī, Ibn Ḥawqal, and al-Muqaddasī and their contribution to geographical thought, such as the "classical" school (I. I. Kratchkovsky), the "*masālik wa-l-mamālik*" genre (André Miquel), or the "Atlas of Islam" school (Konrad Miller). Karen Pinto rejects the "Balkhī school" sobriquet and coins instead the phrase "KMMS mapping tradition"; for an explanation, see Pinto, "Ways of Seeing," 11–16.
2. Because of this, Miquel has called al-Iṣṭakhrī, Ibn Ḥawqal, and al-Muqaddasī the first (and last) representatives of "a veritable human geography" of the Islamic world (he also includes al-Yaʿqūbī and al-Muhallabī in this group); see Miquel, 1:267–330. See also *EI*²: "*Kharīṭa*," "*Djughrāfiyā*."
3. This is one of the reasons why Miquel gives these geographies such a privileged place in his *La géographie humaine du monde musulman*, which establishes an intellectual genealogy of geographical literature in the first volume and then moves to a reconstruction of geographical reality in the second through fourth volumes.
4. Miquel devotes only one paragraph to an analysis of their regional maps; see Miquel, 2:18–20. (Elsewhere he uses traced and transcribed reproductions of maps attributed to Ibn Ḥawqal as illustrations, but not as objects of analysis; see Miquel, 2:81, 131–133, 365–368, 405–411.) Indeed, for Miquel, it is a mark of the maturation of the genre that Ibn Ḥawqal and al-Muqaddasī wrested themselves more fully "free from the spirit of cartography" than had al-Iṣṭakhrī; Miquel, 1:298. Thus, Miquel regards maps not simply as secondary to written texts, but as an impediment to the realization of "a veritable human geography" because of their association with prevailing "technical"—and, it is implied, "foreign"—influences in the field, such as the measuring of longitude and latitude and its application in cartographic projects like the "Ṣūra al-Maʾmūniyya." Even in his one-paragraph analysis of the maps themselves, he attributes their use of geometrical shapes and simplified, familiar forms to ancient Greek and Persian influence. On the other hand, some scholars have overlooked these maps for not contributing enough to the technical and scientific history of cartography; see Sezgin, *Mathematical Geography*. For a pathbreaking study that challenges such dismissals and approaches these maps as culturally meaningful and historically contingent representations of space, see Savage-Smith, "Memory and Maps."
5. See the description of al-Balkhī's atlas and al-Iṣṭakhrī's relationship to it in al-Muqaddasī, *Kitāb aḥsan al-taqāsīm*, 4–5.
6. Ibn Ḥawqal, *Kitāb ṣūrat al-arḍ*, 329–330. This is the encounter that I describe in the opening of the Introduction to this book.

7. On the relationship between al-Iṣṭakhrī and al-Balkhī, see de Goeje, "Die Istachri-Balchi-Frage." On the relationship between al-Iṣṭakhrī and Ibn Ḥawqal, see Miquel, 1:302–304, 367–390 (Appendix I).
8. In his *Mappae Arabicae*, Konrad Miller argued that three anonymous manuscripts, attributed by later scholars to al-Iṣṭakhrī, actually represent the original atlas authored by al-Balkhī. J. H. Kramers disagreed and attributed them to al-Iṣṭakhrī, and later scholars have followed him; see Kramers, "La question Balḫī-Iṣṭaḫrī-Ibn Ḥawḳal."
9. See al-Muqaddasī, *The Best Divisions*, xv–xxx.
10. See della Dora, "Performative Atlases"; Cosgrove, "Introduction."
11. For a list of the extant manuscripts, the earliest of which is attributed to Ibn Ḥawqal and dated 479/1086, see Tibbetts, "The Balkhī School," 130–135 (Appendix 5.1). For published photographic reproductions of many of the maps from these manuscripts, see Miller, vols. 2–5 (including sketch versions with the writing transliterated into the Latin alphabet); Kamal, vol. 3 (fascs. 2–3). In addition, Kramers includes a full set of maps, most of which are reproduced from the earliest manuscript of the work, in his edition of Ibn Ḥawqal, *Kitāb ṣūrat al-arḍ*, and sketch versions of the maps with the writing transliterated and, where applicable, translated into French in Ibn Ḥawqal, *La Configuration de la Terre*. Basil Collins includes a full set of maps reproduced from the Berlin and Istanbul manuscripts, as well as sketch versions of the maps with the writing transliterated, in al-Muqaddasī, *The Best Divisions*. Muḥammad al-Ḥīnī includes maps taken from a set of Cairo manuscripts of the work in his edition of al-Iṣṭakhrī, *al-Masālik wa-l-mamālik*.
12. Scholars have put considerable work into identifying lines of filiation and broad trends in this mapping tradition and classifying related manuscripts under common rubrics, such as "al-Iṣṭakhrī I and II," "Ibn Ḥawqal I, II, and III," and "al-Muqaddasī." These rubrics, it has been argued, organize the map forms and commentaries found in the manuscripts chronologically, from those that reflect the form of the earliest versions prepared by al-Balkhī and al-Iṣṭakhrī ("al-Iṣṭakhrī I and II") to those that reflect the form of later versions by Ibn Ḥawqal and al-Muqaddasī. This is not necessarily the same as a chronological organization of the manuscripts themselves; some later manuscripts actually preserve earlier map forms and versions of the commentaries than earlier manuscripts. See Kramers, "La question Balḫī-Iṣṭaḫrī-Ibn Ḥawḳal"; Tibbetts, "The Balkhī School." A similar classification scheme using the rubrics "Iṣṭakhrian" and "Ḥawqalian" is developed in Kahlaoui, 97–113. These classifications are in contrast to Miller's approach in *Mappae Arabicae*, which was to assign the collective sobriquet "Atlas of Islam" to all the maps found in all the manuscripts coming out of the "Balkhī school" and differentiate them from the mapping tradition associated with the twelfth-century geographer al-Idrīsī. They are also in contrast to Pinto's approach, which is to treat the maps as representative of the era of the extant manuscript in which they appear—if a map appears in a fifteenth-century manuscript, it should be discussed as a fifteenth-century map; see Pinto, "'Surat Bahr al-Rum'"; idem, "The Maps Are the Message"; idem, "Ways of Seeing." Some scholars have compared maps and written texts to determine whether alterations have been made to maps by later copyists; see, for examples, Kaplony, "Comparing al-Kāshgharī's Map to his Text"; Kahlaoui, 86–97. However, the copying of maps was not necessarily any less stable than the copying of written texts (if anything, it may have been more so; see Kahlaoui, 101), and if the written texts can be seen as products of three different tenth-century authors, or even as authorial traditions originating in the tenth century, then the maps should too.
13. One of the most obvious ways that maps from later manuscripts differ from the tenth-century originals is in the use of color and iconography. For iconography that clearly would not have appeared in the tenth century, such as mermaids and sea monsters, see the following manuscripts copied in the nineteenth century: al-Iṣṭakhrī [attr. al-Jayhānī], *Ashkāl al-ʿalam*, Ms. Or. 1587; ibid., Ms. Add. 23542. For a discussion of such works, see Tibbetts, "The Balkhī School," 125–127, figs. 5.23, 5.24. Analysis of individual manuscripts sometimes reveals that new coats of paint may have been overlaid well after the maps were first copied, perhaps to "touch up" the manuscript for potential buyers. However, in these cases the basic map forms underneath the paint and ornamentation stay more or less constant. Nonetheless, some outliers, like the maps in a Persian abridgement of al-Iṣṭakhrī attributed to Nāṣir al-Dīn al-Ṭūsī

(d. 672/1274), clearly bear so little resemblance to the map forms in the majority of the other manuscripts of the work that they will not be considered here; see Mžik, *al-Iṣṭaḫrī*.

14. A later abridgement of Ibn Ḥawqal's work also includes a map of the source of the Nile including latitudinal clime lines similar to that found in an eleventh-century copy of al-Khwārazmī's *Kitāb ṣūrat al-arḍ*; see Kamal, 3:809; Miller, plate 10; Tibbetts, "Later Cartographic Developments," 137–138. For al-Khwārazmī's map, see al-Khwārazmī, plate 3; Harley and Woodward, plate 4; Sezgin, *Mathematical Geography*, 3:8 (map 1f). For an earlier version of Ibn Ḥawqal's work that includes the same map without the latitudinal clime lines, see Ibn Ḥawqal, *Kitāb ʿajāʾib al-dunyā*, Ms. Ayasofya 2934, 26.
15. After Iraq they proceed to its southeast from Khūzistān in the west through Fārs and Kirmān to al-Sind in the east and then double back and proceed to the northeast of Iraq from Armenia and Azerbaijan in the west through al-Jibāl, al-Daylam and Ṭabaristān, the Caspian Sea, the Persian Desert, Sijistān, and Khurāsān to Transoxiana in the east.
16. al-Muqaddasī, *Kitāb aḥsan al-taqāsīm*, 9.
17. This difference raises the question of whether bodies of water were considered regions in the same sense as the other plots of land described and mapped in the geographies. On this question, see Pinto, "'Surat Bahr al-Rum'"; Rapoport, "The *Book of Curiosities*"; Kahlaoui, "The Depiction of the Mediterranean." Ibn Ḥawqal's work contains the longest commentaries on sea maps, and his approach to them resembles his approach to terrestrial regions. However, both al-Iṣṭakhrī's and al-Muqaddasī's commentaries on seas and deserts are shorter in comparison to the other regions and suggest they were imagined differently.
18. Al-Iṣṭakhrī is similar to al-Muqaddasī in his treatment of the west, but to Ibn Ḥawqal in his treatment of the east.
19. These toponyms can also be found in the anonymous tenth-century Persian *Ḥudūd al-ʿālam*, which addresses eighteen regions (*nāḥiyat*) that are roughly the same as those treated by al-Iṣṭakhrī, Ibn Ḥawqal, and al-Muqaddasī: Khurāsān, the Khurāsānian borderlands (=al-Iṣṭakhrī's and Ibn Ḥawqal's Sijistān), Transoxiana, the Transoxianan borderlands (included in al-Iṣṭakhrī's and Ibn Ḥawqal's treatment of Transoxiana), Sind, Kirmān, Pārs (Fārs in Arabic), Khūzistān, Jibāl, Daylam, Iraq, Jazīra, Azerbaijan and Armenia, the Arabian Peninsula, Syria, Egypt, Maghrib, and Andalusia. The big difference, however, is that the *Ḥudūd al-ʿālam* also includes regions lying outside of the *Mamlakat al-Islām* and does not include any maps, though it seems clear that the author had access to some version of al-Iṣṭakhrī's work. See Minorsky, lii–liii, 15–23.
20. Ibn Ḥawqal, *Kitāb ṣūrat al-arḍ*, 2; al-Iṣṭakhrī, *al-Masālik*, ed. al-Ḥīnī, 15; al-Muqaddasī, *Kitāb aḥsan al-taqāsīm*, 3–4 (where he dismisses the seven-clime system as described in a no longer extant work by al-Jayhānī), 58–61 (where he describes the seven-clime system as something propagated by "everyone who has written on this topic").
21. Ibn Ḥawqal, *Kitāb ṣūrat al-arḍ*, 2–3; compare with al-Iṣṭakhrī, *al-Masālik*, ed. al-Ḥīnī, 15.
22. It is not clear what this map was, but Ibn Ḥawqal's allusion to it suggests that the seven-clime system continued to be interpreted cartographically over a century after the era of the "Ṣūra al-Maʾmūniyya." "Al-Quwādhiyān" probably refers to a town located just northeast of Balkh on the eastern side of the Oxus River in what is today Tajikistan.
23. Ibn Ḥawqal, *Kitāb ṣūrat al-arḍ*, 2.
24. Ibid., 3. This is from what Kramers posits is the second version of the work; see the "Preface" to Ibn Ḥawqal, *Kitāb ṣūrat al-arḍ*, vi.
25. The anonymous author of the *Ḥudūd al-ʿālam*, who also dedicates his work to a prince, makes a similar point when he writes: "One country (*nāḥiyat*) differs (*judhā*) from another in four respects (*rūy*). First, by the difference of water, air, soil, and temperature (*garmā-va-sarmā*). Secondly, by the difference of religion, law (*sharīʿat*), and beliefs (*kīsh*). Thirdly, by the difference of words (*lughāt*) and languages. Fourthly, by the difference of kingdoms (*padhshāʾi-hā*)"; this is V. Minorsky's English translation in Minorsky, 82.
26. Ibn Ḥawqal, *Kitāb ṣūrat al-arḍ*, 3–4. He reprises much of this when he describes his encounter with al-Iṣṭakhrī later in the book; see ibid., 329–330.
27. al-Muqaddasī, *Kitāb aḥsan al-taqāsīm*, 3–6. Ibn Ḥawqal too refers to the work of Ptolemy, al-Jayhānī, Qudāma b. Jaʿfar, and al-Iṣṭakhrī; see Ibn Ḥawqal, *Kitāb ṣūrat al-arḍ*, 13, 329. Abū ʿAbd Allāh al-Jayhānī was an author of Persian descent who is believed to have written a work by the title *Kitāb al-masālik wa-l-mamālik*.

28. Miquel has called this a savvy strategy for legitimizing what was actually the brand-new genre of human geography by associating it with earlier genres of technical, administrative, and *adab*-style geography; Miquel, 1:285.
29. He does, however, indicate his knowledge of these local nomenclatures; for Yemen's *mikhlāf*, see al-Muqaddasī, *Kitāb aḥsan al-taqāsīm*, 88–89.
30. Ibid., 9.
31. Ibn Ḥawqal, *Kitāb ṣūrat al-arḍ*, 18; al-Iṣṭakhrī, *al-Masālik*, ed. al-Ḥīnī, 20; al-Muqaddasī, *Kitāb aḥsan al-taqāsīm*, 67.
32. The reader may compare Figures 5.1 and 5.2 with those published in Miller, plates 19–21. See also al-Iṣṭakhrī, *Kitāb aqālīm al-arḍ*, Ms. Ayasofya 2971, fol. 6a.
33. For more overlap, compare their maps of Syria, al-Jazīra, and Iraq in Miller, plates 11–18.
34. This map, portrayed in Figure 5.3, comes from the earliest extant manuscript of Ibn Ḥawqal's work, dated 479/1086, and was drawn in two sections, the easternmost shores of the Mediterranean occupying one half of the folio page facing the written text that introduces it and the rest of the region occupying the two half-folio pages immediately following it. A reader would have to flip the page to go from the eastern part to the central and western parts. However, the map is given a single title and is clearly conceived as a single artistic unit representing contiguous space. A passage inserted in another version of the work suggests that Ibn Ḥawqal decided to separate the Iberian Peninsula (*jazīrat al-Andalus*) from the Byzantine Empire (*balad al-Rūm*) by designing two different maps; see Ibn Ḥawqal, *Kitāb ṣūrat al-arḍ*, 60. However, since the extant manuscripts of this version do not include maps, it is impossible to determine what exactly came of this decision. A third version of the work includes for the Maghrib a single map spread over two half-folio pages. It differs from the map in Figure 5.3 by its smaller size, its exaggeration of waterways, and its minimization of details like toponyms and captions on both northern and southern shores of the Mediterranean; for examples of this map, see Ibn Ḥawqal, *Kitāb ʿajāʾib al-dunyā*, Ms. Ayasofya 2934, 19; Kamal, 3:807. This map is similar to the one for the Mediterranean in a later abridgement of the work; see Kamal, 3:815; Miller, plate 2. In one manuscript, which is attributed to al-Balkhī but which reproduces much of Ibn Ḥawqal's written commentary, a map of the Maghrib omits territory on the northern and eastern shores of the Mediterranean entirely; see Ibn Ḥawqal [attr. al-Balkhī], *Kitāb aqālīm al-buldān*, Ms. Ayasofya 2577M, 40; Kamal, 3:662.
35. By contrast, al-Muqaddasī's chapter on "al-Mashriq" includes two maps, one for Khurāsān and one for Transoxiana; in this case, it is the written text that connects and the graphic text that separates.
36. See Beckingham, "Ibn Hauqal's Map of Italy"; Miquel, 2:365–368. Ibn Ḥawqal's Mediterranean map from the earliest extant manuscript of his work actually lavishes greater attention on the Byzantine territories of the Anatolian Peninsula than on North Africa, perhaps because North Africa had been covered in greater detail on the Maghrib map; see Ibn Ḥawqal, *Ṣūrat al-arḍ*, Ms. III. Ahmed 3346, fol. 58b.
37. During the early Abbasid period, as incursions into Byzantine territory yielded more and more land for the Islamic polity, the phrase *al-ʿawāṣim wa-l-thughūr* (literally "strongholds and frontier fortresses") was applied to the territory along the frontier with Byzantium in northern Syria and southern Anatolia and was sometimes described as the sixth *jund*, or military district, of Syria. Thus, "al-Thughūr" should be seen here as a regional toponym assigned to frontier territory within the *Mamlakat al-Islām*. For more on the emergence of this frontier zone, see Bonner, *Aristocratic Violence*.
38. Sezgin defines the term *ḥudūd* as it is used in the tables of coordinates compiled by al-Khwārazmī and Suhrāb as "reference points," or points to be plotted on a map within the contours of regions (*buldān*)—possibly even acting as "approximate centres" for each region. On this see Sezgin, *Mathematical Geography*, 1:116–118. For the lists of *ḥudūd*, see al-Khwārazmī, 101–105; Suhrāb, 46–50.
39. Miquel, 1:308.
40. Ibn Ḥawqal, *Kitāb ṣūrat al-arḍ*, 97. See also his chapter on Transoxiana for a similarly lively trade with Central Asia; ibid., 464–465.
41. Ibid., 92, 109. Ancient Ghana was the center of a kingdom located on the southern "shores" of the Sahara, in present-day Mali and Mauritania, not in present-day Ghana.

42. His section on the Caspian Sea (*Baḥr al-Khazar*) is very similar to al-Iṣṭakhrī's (as are the accompanying maps), but his chapters on the Indian Ocean and the Mediterranean include more extensive commentaries on the non-Muslim peoples and polities bordering these seas than do al-Iṣṭakhrī's. In the case of the Indian Ocean, Ibn Ḥawqal's description of the Būja people of east Africa is what makes his account of this body of water lengthier than al-Iṣṭakhrī's (he also discusses them in his commentary on Egypt). Some of Ibn Ḥawqal's maps also feature inscribed writing about non-Muslim peoples, effectively merging the written and graphic evocations of connectivity; see, for examples, his maps of Egypt and the Mediterranean Sea in Ibn Ḥawqal, *Ṣūrat al-arḍ*, Ms. III. Ahmed 3346, fols. 46b-47a, 58b; idem, *Kitāb ʿajāʾib al-dunyā*, Ms. Ayasofya 2934, 23; Kamal, 3:658–659, 808. For more on the presence of the Būja on maps, see Pinto, "Capturing Imagination."
43. That is, far from acting as natural barriers or boundaries, bodies of water serve a connective function in Ibn Ḥawqal's cartography and, to a lesser extent, in that of al-Iṣṭakhrī and al-Muqaddasī. A similar point can be made about deserts, which are portrayed graphically in these works (the Persian desert in all three and the Arabian desert in al-Muqaddasī's work) in terms of the routes that cross them to connect the cities and regions arrayed along their "shores." This is in strong contrast to the argument that bodies of water acted as the only definitive borders between regions in the medieval Islamic world; see Brauer, *Boundaries and Frontiers*, 33–34. Similarly, the anonymous author of the tenth-century *Ḥudūd al-ʿālam* recognizes frontiers between countries only when they can be seen to follow the contours of the natural landscape, such as mountain ranges, rivers, and deserts; see Minorsky, 82.
44. It is relevant here that al-Muqaddasī is the only geographer who explicitly excludes seas and oceans from the category of region (*iqlīm*).
45. The map of Arabia portrayed in Figure 5.4 is from a nineteenth-century manuscript copied at the request of M. J. de Goeje from a thirteenth-century manuscript housed in Istanbul in preparation of his critical edition of al-Muqaddasī's text; see Witkam, 3:26–27. This can be compared to a slightly different version of the Arabia map—equally circumscribed—in the Berlin manuscript, which has been reproduced in Miller, plate 20.
46. Moreover, since he does not include a separate map for Sijistān, but absorbs it into the map of (and commentary for) Khurāsān, he avoids the major overlap that these two regional maps produce in al-Iṣṭakhrī's and Ibn Ḥawqal's works. However, generally his maps for regions east of Iraq are very similar to those of his predecessors, and actually include the same overlapping territory between al-Jibāl and al-Daylam.
47. He does inscribe the toponyms "Ghalijashkash" (land of Jacá) and "Ifranjī" (land of the Francs) within the map in territory bordering the Iberian Peninsula, but all other references to frontier territory are outside the frame; see al-Muqaddasī, *Kitāb aḥsan al-taqāsīm*, Ms. Or. 1013, f. 232. On Ghalijashkash, see Minorsky, 424–425. Al-Iṣṭakhrī's map of the Maghrib is very similar to al-Muqaddasī's, despite the great difference between their maps of the Arabian Peninsula, Iraq, Syria, and al-Jazīra; see Miller, plates 5–7; Kamal, 3:589, 592, 597, 602, 608, 622 (al-Iṣṭakhrī), 673, 677 (al-Muqaddasī).
48. This is also true of al-Iṣṭakhrī's and Ibn Ḥawqal's maps in general, but they do not put the same emphasis in their written commentaries on hierarchically ordered plots of land. Some maps in all three works depict a city occupying a very central location in the region, as in the maps of Fārs or al-Jibāl, but this cannot be considered part of a deliberate plan by al-Muqaddasī to use his maps to distinguish metropolises from other cities, since the vast majority show no clearly central or dominant city.
49. Maps for regions east of Iraq from all three works resemble each other much more consistently than those for the rest of the regions. In general, maps in manuscripts attributed to al-Iṣṭakhrī and al-Muqaddasī display similar forms for the Maghrib and Egypt, while those in manuscripts attributed to Ibn Ḥawqal are different. Maps in manuscripts attributed to al-Iṣṭakhrī and Ibn Ḥawqal display similar forms for Syria, al-Jazīra, Iraq, and the Arabian Peninsula, while those in manuscripts attributed to al-Muqaddasī are different.
50. The reader may compare Figures 5.5 and 5.6 with those published in Miller, plates 28–30. See also al-Iṣṭakhrī, *Kitāb aqālīm al-arḍ*, Ms. Ayasofya 2971, fol. 33a. Al-Muqaddasī's maps also overwhelmingly display labeled borders; for good examples, see his maps of Egypt, Iraq, Fārs, Kirmān, al-Sind, and Khurāsān in Miller, plates 8, 10, 18, 30, 33, 36.

51. Notice that one of these borders is with Isfahan, a toponym that does not represent its own *iqlīm* in these works (the city of Isfahan is portrayed on the maps of the region of al-Jibāl). This labeled border may represent a recognition of the existence of certain city-centered subregions, in this case at the frontier between Fārs and al-Jibāl. A similar city-centered subregion may be indicated by the term *ḥadd Bukhārā* portrayed just north of the Oxus River on some of the maps of Khurāsān; see Miller, plates 55–58.
52. The reader may compare Figure 5.7 with the maps published in Miller, plates 31–33. See also al-Iṣṭakhrī, *Kitāb aqālīm al-arḍ*, Ms. Ayasofya 2971, fol. 45b; idem, *al-Masālik wa-l-mamālik*, Ms. Ayasofya 2613, p. 82/fol. 41b. This has also been noticed by Tibbetts, "The Balkhī School," 115–116.
53. Flipping between the maps of Khurāsān and the maps of Transoxiana in al-Iṣṭakhrī's work, a similar communication is evoked iconographically through the distinctive shape of the Oxus River forming the border that separates, just as it visually connects, the two regions. See, for examples, Miller, plates 55–62. Another way of evoking this connectivity is by including overlapping territory on the edges of multiple maps, as al-Iṣṭakhrī and Ibn Ḥawqal do with the Arabian Peninsula, Syria, and Iraq. Significant overlapping territory is noticeable also between their maps of Syria, al-Jazīra, and Iraq, as well as on the maps of al-Jibāl and al-Daylam (the cities of al-Rayy and Qom appear on each of them) and on the maps of Sijistān and Khurāsān (Khurāsān containing most of Sijistān).
54. For the clearest statement of this, see Brauer, *Boundaries and Frontiers*, 3.
55. I would argue that this concern with establishing whether or not "real borderlines" have existed between polities historically, both in the Islamic world and beyond, is a reflection of the modern fetishization of the nation-state as the ultimate expression of political and territorial belonging. On these questions, see Kashani-Sabet, *Frontier Fictions*; Thongchai, *Mapping Siam*, especially chapter 3; Anderson, *Imagined Communities*, especially chapter 10. See also the essays in Diener and Hagen, eds., *Borderlines and Borderlands*; Power and Standen, eds., *Frontiers in Question*.
56. Not all of the maps in the "Balkhī school" manuscripts include these labeled borders, but enough of them do to suggest that it was the labeled borders that were in the original design while their omission is due to the decisions or mistakes of later copyists.
57. Thus, the fact that the late-eleventh-century geographer al-Bakrī pays much more systematic attention to names of and borders between regions than Ibn Khurradādhbih and al-Yaʿqūbī had two centuries earlier may be due to the influence of the tenth-century "Balkhī school" geographies and their bounded regionalism in the discourse of place.
58. al-Iṣṭakhrī, *al-Masālik*, ed. al-Ḥīnī, 43. Ibn Ḥawqal adds the phrase "formerly known as *Thughūr al-Jazīra*" to describe the toponym "al-Thughūr" and uses the first person singular as opposed to the first person plural in the final sentence; see Ibn Ḥawqal, *Kitāb ṣūrat al-arḍ*, 165. The toponym "al-Tīh" refers to the Sinai desert, and "al-Hārūniyya" refers to a city founded by the Abbasid Caliph Hārūn al-Rashīd in present-day Turkey.
59. al-Muqaddasī, *Kitāb aḥsan al-taqāsīm*, 151; for detailed annotation that identifies most of the sites referred to in this passage, see idem, *Aḥsan at-taqāsīm*, trans. Miquel, 145–152.
60. His introductions to the eastern regions contain fewer references to sacred history, and he tends to praise the piety and the religious authority of the people of the region instead. Some regions have virtually no references to religion whatsoever, such as Fārs, al-Sind, and Kirmān.
61. al-Muqqadasī, *Kitāb aḥsan al-taqāsīm*, 7–8.
62. Ibid., 193.
63. See also Ibn al-Kindī, 8, 48; Ibn Zūlāq, 3, 73.
64. The end of the introductory invocation, which criticizes Egypt's high prices and conspicuous Coptic traditions, may be read as subverting or qualifying his endorsement of Fatimid rule. However, many of his introductions conclude with a short list of negative attributes of the region, acting as a performance of the *adab*-style convention of contrastive enumeration. Nonetheless, as Miquel has noted, al-Muqaddasī's political preferences seem to have been overwhelmingly in favor of the Samanid dynasty in Khurāsān (not that such a preference necessarily conflicts with loyalty to the Fatimids), and, indeed, the introduction to his region of al-Mashriq, and to its subregion of Khurāsān, are noteworthy for dispensing with any critique. See al-Muqaddasī, *Kitāb aḥsan al-taqāsīm*, 260, 293–294; Miquel, 1:316–320.

65. Ibn Ḥawqal includes after the description of Iraq's frontiers a very short passage praising the region, its people, and its past prosperity, but concludes by bemoaning the sharp decline of that prosperity; Ibn Ḥawqal, *Kitāb ṣūrat al-arḍ*, 234–235. Similarly, al-Muqaddasī's introduction to Iraq concludes with a very strong critique focusing on its decline and the oppression of its people; al-Muqaddasī, *Kitāb aḥsan al-taqāsīm*, 113.
66. Ibn Ḥawqal, *Kitāb ṣūrat al-arḍ*, 23–25. For Ibn Ḥawqal's Shiite sympathies, see Miquel, 1:300–302. On the Qarmatians, see *EI*²: "Ḳarmaṭī." See also the mini-biographical dictionary inserted by al-Iṣṭakhrī and continued by Ibn Ḥawqal in the chapter on Fārs including notable Qarmatians in al-Iṣṭakhrī, *al-Masālik*, ed. al-Ḥīnī, 84–90; Ibn Ḥawqal, *Kitāb ṣūrat al-arḍ*, 292–297. This textual interlude is the lengthiest association of a region and a political and religious meaning provided by al-Iṣṭakhrī, possibly because, as his name suggests, he was a native of Fārs. It starts out with a catalogue of pre-Islamic Persian rulers and moves through the Islamic period, a political history that Ibn Ḥawqal discards in favor of adding to al-Iṣṭakhrī's biographical entries for contemporary figures from the region associated with Ismāʿīlī Shiism. It is worth speculating that if Ibn Ḥawqal were not following al-Iṣṭakhrī's written text so closely he might have moved this association between a region and its political and religious meanings to the beginning of the chapter so that it would function the way his openings to the chapters on the Arabian Peninsula or Transoxiana functioned.
67. Ibn Ḥawqal, *Kitāb ṣūrat al-arḍ*, 136–137.
68. Ibid., 143, 153.
69. Ibid., 463–467.
70. Al-Muqaddasī does this too in the introduction to "al-Mashriq"; see al-Muqaddasī, *Kitāb aḥsan al-taqāsīm*, 260.
71. Ibn Ḥawqal, *Kitāb ṣūrat al-arḍ*, 468.
72. They also communicate intertextually with other *faḍāʾil* treatises past and future; what al-Muqaddasī includes in terms of the merits of Syria, for instance, can be compared and contrasted with what al-Rabaʿī includes in his *faḍāʾil* treatise a century later.
73. See, for examples, al-Māfarrūkhī, *Maḥāsin Iṣfahān*; al-Rabaʿī, *Faḍāʾil al-Shām wa-Dimashq*.
74. This is Miquel's practice, preferring monography over "chorography," the Ptolemaic term for a regional geography; see Miquel, 1:70.
75. Examples include "Miṣr" vs. "al-Fusṭāṭ" and later "al-Qāhira"; "al-Shām" vs. "Dimashq"; as well as many examples from Persian-speaking areas, such as Isfahan, Sijistān/Sīstān, and Nishapur, in which the pre-Islamic Persian practice of using *shahr* as a word for both city and region still held sway; see Piacentini, "*Madīna/Shahr, Qarya/Deh, Nāḥiya/Rustāq*." The late eleventh-century anonymous *Tārīkh-i Sīstān* is an example of a local history in Persian that chronicles events taking place across a regional entity, but that also focuses considerable attention on its central city of Zaranj, which is referred to as "Sīstān." For other examples in which a regional name is the same as one of its cities, see the tables of longitude and latitude from the voluminous *al-Qānūn al-Masʿūdī* in al-Bīrūnī, *Ṣifat al-maʿmūra*, 9–53.
76. Many works composed in this period that are no longer extant are mentioned by title in other works from the discourse of place. Even when the title includes a toponym, it is difficult to tell whether the work was devoted in whole or large part to a representation of a plot of land and, if so, whether that plot of land was conceived primarily as a city or a region. However, those with titles that include toponyms that were associated primarily with regions rather than cities, such as Khurāsān and Ṭabaristān, may have been regional monographs; see Rosenthal, *A History of Muslim Historiography*, 130–149, 381–408; Brockelmann, *Geschichte der arabischen Literatur*, 1:137–138, 329–341; 1 [suppl.]:209–211, 562–581; Sezgin, *Geschichte des arabischen Schrifttums*, 1:339–364.
77. The introductions to two tenth-century biographical dictionaries on Ifrīqiyya include short *faḍāʾil* treatises on the region, though the introduction to al-Mālikī's focuses mostly on the city of Kairouan; see al-Qayrawānī, 43–64; al-Mālikī, 1:5–13. For the way in which descriptions of the region's landscape in chronologically organized histories of Andalusia communicated particular political and religious messages, see Safran, *The Second Umayyad Caliphate*, chapter 5. Safran's analysis illuminates the way material from the discourse of place was interwoven in other kinds of works, such as chronological histories, to evoke particular meanings aimed at particular audiences.

78. On this work and similar works on North Africa from the period, see Brunschvig, "Ibn ʿAbdalhʾakam."
79. To this list might be added al-Bakrī's treatment of Egypt, which draws substantially from Ibn ʿAbd al-Ḥakam's *Futūḥ Miṣr* and forms a large part of his late-eleventh-century geography, *al-Masālik wa-l-mamālik*. Although this work includes representations of all the regions of the Islamic world, the sections on Egypt, North Africa (Ifrīqiyya and the Maghrib), and Andalusia are far longer and more detailed than those for all the other regions combined. On Egypt, see al-Bakrī, *al-Masālik wa-l-mamālik*, 2:65–173.
80. Ibn ʿAbd al-Ḥakam, 19; Ibn Zūlāq, 12.
81. Ibn ʿAbd al-Ḥakam, 29. See also Ibn Zūlāq, 10; al-Bakrī, *al-Masālik wa-l-mamālik*, 2:78.
82. Ibn Zūlāq, 9, 11; Ibn ʿAbd al-Ḥakam, 24; Ibn al-Kindī, 39.
83. Ibn ʿAbd al-Ḥakam, 33–34; Ibn al-Kindī, 27; Ibn Zūlāq, 4. On this, see Qurʾān 12:54–56.
84. On the positive image of the pharaoh in Arabic writing, see Daly, *Egyptology*, chapter 9. On the ambiguous image of the pharoah in Arabic writing, see Haarmann, "Regional Sentiment"; idem, "Medieval Muslim Perceptions." See also Hirschler, "The 'Pharaoh' Anecdote."
85. Ibn ʿAbd al-Ḥakam, 25–26.
86. Ibid., 35–36; Ibn Zūlāq, 55; al-Bakrī, *al-Masālik wa-l-mamālik*, 2:127.
87. Ibn al-Kindī, 36–38; Ibn Zūlāq, 86–94.
88. Ibn al-Kindī, 6–7.
89. Ibid., 29; Ibn Zūlāq, 11.
90. Ibn al-Kindī, 29–30.
91. Ibn ʿAbd al-Ḥakam, 58–65 (on the foundation of Alexandria), 115–165 (*khiṭaṭ*, mostly on al-Fusṭāṭ and Giza, but some on Alexandria as well). Al-Bakrī reproduces material from Ibn ʿAbd al-Ḥakam's *khiṭaṭ* of al-Fusṭāṭ; see al-Bakrī, *al-Masālik wa-l-mamālik*, 2:139–144. On Alexandria, see also Ibn al-Kindī, 31–33; Ibn Zūlāq, 60–63; al-Bakrī, *al-Masālik wa-l-mamālik*, 2:160–163 (on the city), 163–173 (on the lighthouse).
92. Cairo is only mentioned once at the very end of the section on al-Fusṭāṭ in al-Bakrī, *al-Masālik wa-l-mamālik*, 145.
93. The emphasis on the Nile is linked to another emphasis in the representation of Egypt in the discourse of place—Egypt as a region of marvels (*ʿajāʾib*), both marvels of the natural world, like the Nile, and marvels of the ancient and/or supernatural worlds, such as the pyramids. See, for examples, al-Bakrī, *al-Masālik wa-l-mamālik*, 2:65–85; Ibn al-Kindī, 46–52; Ibn Zūlāq, 69–73. The dominance of Egypt in a catalog of the world's marvels can be seen in a cosmographical work that may have come from the period under study, the *Mukhtaṣar ʿajāʾib al-dunyā*. This work has been described as the abridgement of a work by the well-known tenth-century scholar al-Masʿūdī (and, indeed, much of the material on Egypt that is included in the *Mukhtaṣar* also appears in al-Masʿūdī's *Murūj al-dhahab*) and has been attributed to the relatively obscure Ibn Waṣīf Shāh, thought to have lived somewhere between the tenth and the thirteenth centuries. See Ibn Waṣīf Shāh, 11–13; Miquel, 1:xxxv; Sezgin, *Geschichte des arabischen Schrifttums*, 15:43–51.
94. Ibn ʿAbd al-Ḥakam, 175–177.
95. Ibn al-Kindī, 41; Ibn Zūlāq, 75–76.
96. Ibn Zūlāq, 63, 67.
97. Ibn ʿAbd al-Ḥakam, 19–23; Ibn al-Kindī, 9, 12, 14; Ibn Zūlāq, 6–8, 15.
98. Ibn Zūlāq, 3–5, 22. See also Ibn al-Kindī, 7–9, 12–14.
99. See, for instance, al-Rabaʿī, 20 (no. 36), 21 (no. 38). See also Cobb, 46.
100. Ibn Zūlāq, 21.
101. Ibn al-Kindī, 13.
102. Ibn Zūlāq, 26.
103. Ibid., 43, 46.
104. Possible exceptions include local histories from the Persian-speaking world, such as the *Tārīkh-i Sīstān*, though to the extent that many of them focus on territory in and of itself rather than as a backdrop for annalistic history, it is often at the scale of the city; see Bosworth, "Sistan"; Pourshariati, "Local Historiography"; Fragner, *Die "Persophonie."* Another possible exception is the tenth-century work of Ibn Waḥshiyya on the Nabataeans of al-Sawād, which stresses ethnocultural particularism and strong ties to land; see Hämeen-Anttila,

"Mesopotamian National Identity." For a study on the regional territory associated with the Kurds in world geographies from this period, see James, "Le 'territoire tribal des Kurdes.'"

105. Sanaa is assigned only a short chapter, and other Yemeni cities are mentioned in a list of longitudes and latitudes; al-Hamdānī, *Ṣifat*, 70–81 (other cities), 81–99 (Sanaa).
106. Ibid., 99–167.
107. For a calculation of the relative space assigned to Yemen and the rest of the Arabian Peninsula in the work, see Miquel, 1:247–248, note 6.
108. These cities, along with Jerusalem, Hebron, and Mount Sinai, are invoked in rhymed prose in the mini-*faḍā'il* treatise on the Arabian Peninsula that opens the book, but are, to use Miquel's words, "nearly absent" for the rest of the work; see al-Hamdānī, *Ṣifat*, 6–7; Miquel, 1:248, note 1. A notable contrast is furnished by al-Bakrī's short introduction to his geographical gazetteer. This introduction is devoted to a representation of the Arabian Peninsula, including a careful accounting of its borders and its territorial divisions, but is clearly meant to celebrate the Ḥijāz as the most important subregion; see al-Bakrī, *Muʿjam mā istaʿjama*, 1:7–20.
109. al-Hamdānī, *Ṣifat*, 16–32. On this, see Miquel, 1:249.
110. al-Hamdānī, *Ṣifat*, 11–15.
111. Ibid., 9–10.
112. Ibid., 34–53. See also Miquel, 2:33–56. Travis Zadeh argues that here al-Hamdānī was drawing on another of Ptolemy's works, the shorter *Tetrabiblos*, which was definitely translated into Arabic and which may have been a more direct influence on the divisions of the world favored by other participants in the discourse of place than was Ptolemy's *Geography*; see Zadeh, *Mapping Frontiers*, 90–91.
113. al-Hamdānī, *Ṣifat*, 3–7. Miquel interprets the apparent disconnect between these general introductory sections and the overwhelming focus in the rest of the work on the attributes of one part of the world as a fundamental clash between the universalist methods of Greek technical geography and the particularism of a monolithic "Arab" milieu; see Miquel, 1:252–253.
114. al-Hamdānī, *Ṣifat*, 3–5, 64–65.
115. Ibid., 6–7.
116. Ibid., 335–344.
117. Ibid., 65–68 (borders of Yemen), 167–264 (constituent parts). For more on the borders of Yemen in the pre-Islamic and early Islamic periods, see al-Madʿaj, 4–6, maps 1 and 2; see also *EI*[2]: "Mikhlāf."
118. See al-Hamdānī's eleventh-century biographer, al-Qiftī, 1:283 (cited in *EI*[2]: "al-Hamdānī").
119. Only four parts of this ten-part work on the pre-Islamic history of Yemen under the Himyarites have been found. The eighth part, which includes a substantial representation of the city of Sanaa, is described as "on the memory of the castles of the Ḥimyar, their cities and inscriptions, and what has been preserved of the poetry, elegies, and transmissions of ʿAlqama"; al-Hamdāni, *al-Iklīl*, 2.
120. Yāqūt, *Muʿjam al-buldān*, 1:8–9. This is also cited as the reason al-Bakrī composed his late-eleventh-century gazetteer, which supplies alphabetical entries for toponyms from the entire Islamic world but devotes the most space to explicating obscure toponyms from the Arabian Peninsula, particularly those associated with the life of Muḥammad; see al-Bakrī, *Muʿjam mā istaʿjama*, 1:3–7.
121. al-Hamdānī, *Ṣifat*, 265–323. The extended poetic quotations that conclude the work also bear out this thesis.
122. One of the best examples of this is a topographical description of Andalusia by the tenth-century historian Aḥmad b. Muḥammad al-Rāzī that seems to have acted as an introduction to a longer conquest chronicle by the same author. It was used by later Andalusian scholars, most notably al-Bakrī, as a blueprint for their descriptions of the region; see al-Bakrī, *al-Masālik wa-l-mamālik*, 2:378–400. See also Lévi-Provençal, "La 'Description de l'Espagne'"; Muʾnis, 56–80.
123. al-Maqqarī, *Nafḥ al-ṭīb*, 3:156–179. For an edition of this letter in isolation, see Ibn Ḥazm, "Risāla," 171–188.
124. Ibn Ḥazm, "Risāla," 176.
125. See Elinson, 123–130.

126. Ibn Ḥazm, "Risāla," 187. "Diyār Muḍar" and "Diyār Rabīʿa" refer to areas located in upper Mesopotamia or "al-Jazīra."

Conclusion

1. See Antrim, "Ibn ʿAsakir's Representations."
2. See Antrim, "Making Syria Mamluk"; and idem, "*Waṭan* before *Waṭaniyya*."
3. See Rabbat, "Al-Maqrizi's *Khitat*."
4. See Elinson, *Looking Back at al-Andalus.*
5. See, for examples, Kaplony, "Comparing al-Kāshgharī's Map to his Text"; Pourshariati, "Local Historiography"; Bosworth, "Sistan"; Paul, "The Histories of Herat"; Melville, "The Caspian Provinces."
6. See Arazi, "Matériaux pour l'étude du conflit."
7. See Ahmed, "Cartography of al-Sharīf al-Idrīsī."
8. This is Wadie Jwaideh's English translation in Yāqūt, *The Introductory Chapters,* 1. For the Arabic, see idem, *Muʿjam al-buldān,* 1:7.
9. This is Jwaideh's English translation in Yāqūt, *The Introductory Chapters,* 2. For the Arabic, see idem, *Muʿjam al-buldān,* 1:7.
10. This is Jwaideh's English translation in Yāqūt, *The Introductory Chapters,* 2. For the Arabic, see idem, *Muʿjam al-buldān,* 1:8.
11. See Smith, *Religion, Culture, and Sacred Space,* especially chapter 4 on Ibn Jubayr. For a slightly contrasting view on Ibn Baṭṭūṭa, which places more emphasis on his use of firsthand observation, see Euben, 63–89. On Leo Africanus, see Davis, *Trickster Travels.*
12. See Sajdi, "Ibn Kannān"; Brummett, "Visions of the Mediterranean"; idem, "Imagining the Early Modern Ottoman Space"; Gerber, "'Palestine' and Other Territorial Concepts"; Rooke, "Writing the Boundary"; Dankoff, *An Ottoman Mentality*; Casale, *The Ottoman Age of Exploration.* For the prominence of Ottoman ateliers in the copying of "Balkhī school" maps, see Pinto, "The Maps are the Message."
13. The literature on Middle Eastern nationalism is too copious to encompass here. See, for relevant examples, Kashani-Sabet, *Frontier Fictions*; Tavakoli-Targhi, *Refashioning Iran*; Gershoni and Jankowski, *Egypt, Islam, and the Arabs*; idem, *Redefining the Egyptian Nation*; Philipp and Schumann, eds., *From the Syrian Land*; Zachs, *The Making of a Syrian Identity*; Gelvin, *Divided Loyalties.*
14. A pioneering comparative approach to premodern and modern notions of space has been demonstrated by Thongchai Winichakul in *Siam Mapped,* though his analysis focuses mainly on transformations in the nineteenth century and devotes only one chapter to the premodern period. Firoozeh Kashani-Sabet's *Frontier Fictions* also explores the relationship between premodern conceptions of Iranian territory and the role these conceptions played in the development of modern Iranian nationalism.
15. See Antrim, "*Waṭan* after *Waṭaniyya*."
16. See, for examples, Najmabadi, *Women with Mustaches*; Baron, *Egypt as a Woman*; Massad, "Conceiving the Masculine."
17. See, for example, Sami Dahhan's introductions to his critical editions of portions of Ibn Shaddād's thirteenth-century historical topography of Syria: Ibn Shaddād, *al-Aʿlāq al-khaṭīra fī dhikr umarāʾ al-Shām wa-l-Jazīra: Taʾrīkh Madīnat Dimashq,* 9m–12m; idem, *al-Aʿlāq al-khaṭīra fī dhikr umarāʾ al-Shām wa-l-Jazīra: Taʾrīkh Lubnān wa-l-Urdunn wa-Filasṭīn,* 11m–16m.
18. See Elden, *Terror and Territory.*

BIBLIOGRAPHY

Abbreviation

EI[2] = *Encyclopaedia of Islam*. 13 vols. Edited by H. A. R. Gibb et al. New ed./2d ed. Leiden: E. J. Brill, 1960–2009. CD-ROM Edition *Encyclopaedia of Islam*. Edited by P. J. Bearman, Th. Bianquis, C. E. Bosworth, E. van Donzel, and W. P. Heinrichs. New ed./2nd ed. Leiden: E. J. Brill, 2004. (All citations in the notes refer to entries from the CD-ROM edition of this work.)

Manuscripts

Ibn Ḥawqal, Abū l-Qāsim Muḥammad al-Naṣībī. *Kitāb al-masālik wa-l-mamālik*. Arabic. Ms. Or. 314. Leiden University Library.

———. *Kitāb ʿajāʾib al-dunyā*. Arabic. Ms. Ayasofya 2934. Süleymaniye Kütüphanesi.

——— [attr. al-Balkhī]. *Kitāb aqālīm al-buldān*. Arabic. Ms. Ayasofya 2577M. Süleymaniye Kütüphanesi.

———. *Ṣūrat al-arḍ*. Arabic. Ms. III. Ahmed 3346. Topkapı Sarayı Müzesi Kütüphanesi.

al-Iṣṭakhrī, Abū Isḥāq Ibrāhīm b. Muḥammad al-Fārisī. *Kitāb ashkāl al-bilād*. Arabic. Ms. 3521. Biblioteca Universitaria di Bologna.

———. *Ṣuwar al-buldān*. Persian. Ms. Ouseley 373. Dept. of Oriental Collections, The Bodleian Library, Oxford University.

——— [attr. al-Jayhānī]. *Ashkāl al-ʿālam*. Persian. Ms. Or. 1587. British Library.

——— [attr. al-Jayhānī]. *Ashkāl al-ʿālam*. Persian. Ms. Add. 23542. British Library.

———. *Kitāb ṣuwar al-aʿlām*. Arabic. Ms. Or. 5305. British Library.

———. *Tarjumat al-masālik wa-l-mamālik*. Persian. Ms. IO Islamic 1026 (Ethé 707). British Library.

———. *Kitāb aqālīm al-arḍ ʿalā I-mamālik al-islāmiyya*. Arabic. Ms. Ayasofya 2971. Süleymaniye Kütüphanesi.

———. *al-Masālik wa-l-mamālik*. Arabic. Ms. Ayasofya 2613. Süleymaniye Kütüphanesi.

———. *Tarjumat al-masālik wa-l-mamālik*. Persian. Ms. Ayasofya 3156. Süleymaniye Kütüphanesi.

Kitāb gharāʾib al-funūn wa-mulāḥ al-ʿuyūn. Arabic. Ms. Arab. c. 90. Dept. of Oriental Collections, The Bodleian Library, University of Oxford. Online: *The Book of Curiosities: A Critical Edition*. Edited by Emilie Savage-Smith and Yossef Rapoport. http://cosmos.bodley.ox.ac.uk/hms/home.php. March 2007.

al-Muqaddasī, Abū ʿAbd Allāh Shams al-Dīn Muḥammad b. Aḥmad. *Kitāb aḥsan al-taqāsīm fī maʿrifat al-aqālīm*. Arabic. Ms. Or. 1013. Leiden University Library.

———. *Kitāb aḥsan al-taqāsīm fī maʿrifat al-aqālīm*. Arabic. Ms. Ayasofya 2971M. Süleymaniye Kütüphanesi.

Published Sources

Abu-Lughod, Janet L. "The Islamic City—Historic Myth, Islamic Essence, and Contemporary Relevance." *International Journal of Middle East Studies* 19 (1987): 155–176.

Abū l-Maʿālī al-Musharraf b. al-Murajjā b. Ibrāhīm al-Maqdisī. *Faḍāʾil Bayt al-Maqdis wa-l-Khalīl wa-faḍāʾil al-Shām.* Edited by Ofer Livne-Kafri. Shafā ʿAmr, Israel: Dār al-Mashriq li-l-Tarjama wa-l-Ṭibāʿa wa-l-Nashr, 1995.

Abū Nuʿaym Aḥmad b. ʿAbd Allāh. *Kitāb dhikr akhbār Iṣbahān.* 2 vols. Edited by Sven Dedering. Leiden: E. J. Brill, 1931–1934.

Afsaruddin, Asma. "In Praise of the Caliphs: Recreating History from the *Manāqib* Literature." *International Journal of Middle East Studies* 31 (1999): 329–350.

Ahmed, S. Maqbul. "Cartography of al-Sharīf al-Idrīsī." In *The History of Cartography*, vol. 2, bk. 1, edited by J. B. Harley and David Woodward, 156–174. Chicago: University of Chicago Press, 1992.

Aksoy, Şule, and Rachel Milstein. "A Collection of Thirteenth-Century Illustrated Hajj Certificates." In *M. Uğur Derman Armağanı/M. Uğur Derman Festschrift*, edited by İrvin Cemil Schick, 101–134. Istanbul: Sabancı Universitesi, 2000.

Alavi, S. M. Ziauddin. "Al-Masʿūdī's Conception of the Relationship between Man and Environment." In *Al-Masʿūdī Millenary Commemoration Volume*, edited by S. Maqbul Ahmad and A. Rahman, 93–96. Kolkata: The Indian Society for the History of Science and the Institute of Islamic Studies, Aligarh Muslim University, 1960.

Ali, S. M. "Some Geographical ideas of al-Masʿūdī." In *Al-Masʿūdī Millenary Commemoration Volume*, edited by S. Maqbul Ahmad and A. Rahman, 84–92. Kolkata: The Indian Society for the History of Science and the Institute of Islamic Studies, Aligarh Muslim University, 1960.

Ali, Samer. *Arabic Literary Salons in the Islamic Middle Ages: Poetry, Public Performance, and the Presentation of the Past.* Notre Dame, IN: Notre Dame University Press, 2010.

AlSayyad, Nezar. *Cities and Caliphs: On the Genesis of Arab Muslim Urbanism.* New York: Greenwood Press, 1991.

Anderson, Benedict. *Imagined Communities.* Rev. ed. London and New York: Verso, 1991.

Antrim, Zayde. "Connectivity and Creativity: Representations of Baghdad's Centrality, 3rd/9th to 5th/11th Centuries." In *İslam Medeniyetinde Bağdat (Medînetü's-Selâm) Uluslararası Sempozyum/International Symposium on Baghdad (Madinat al-Salam) in the Islamic Civilization*, edited by İsmail Safa Üstün, 55–74. Istanbul: Marmara Üniversitesi, İlâhiyat Fakültesi, İslâm Tarihi ve Sanatları Bölümü & İslâm Konferansı Teşkilatı, İslâm Tarih, Sanat ve Kültür Araştırma Merkezi (IRCICA), 2011.

———. "Ibn ʿAsakir's Representations of Syria and Damascus in the Introduction to the *Taʾrikh Madinat Dimashq*." *International Journal of Middle East Studies* 38, 1 (2006): 109–129.

———. "Making Syria Mamluk: Ibn Shaddād's *al-Aʿlāq al-Khaṭīrah*." *Mamlūk Studies Review* 11, 1 (2007): 1–18.

———. "*Waṭan* before *Waṭaniyya*: Loyalty to Land in Ayyūbid and Mamlūk Syria." *Al-Masāq: Islam and the Medieval Mediterranean* 22, 2 (2010): 173–190.

Arazi, Albert. "*Al-Ḥanīn ilā al-awṭān*: Entre la Ǧāhiliyya et l'Islam: Le Bédouin et le citadin reconciliés." *Zeitschrift der Deutschen Morgenländischen Gesellschaft* 143, 2 (1993): 287–327.

———. "Matériaux pour l'étude du conflit de préséance entre la Mekke et Médine." *Jerusalem Studies in Arabic and Islam* 5 (1984): 177–235.

Arberry, A. J. *Arabic Poetry: A Primer for Students.* Cambridge, UK: Cambridge University Press, 1965.

al-ʿAsalī, Kāmil Jamīl. *Makhṭūṭāt faḍāʾil Bayt al-Maqdis.* Amman: Dār al-Bashīr, 1984.

Austin, J. L. *How to Do Things with Words.* Cambridge, MA: Harvard University Press, 1975.

al-Azraqī, Abū l-Walid Muḥammad b. ʿAbd Allāh. *Akhbār Makka wa-mā jāʾa fīhā min al-āthār.* 2 vols. Edited by ʿAbd al-Malik b. ʿAbd Allāh b. Duhaysh. Mecca: Maktabat al-Asadī, 2003.

Baḥshal, Aslam b. Sahl. *Taʾrīkh Wāsiṭ.* Edited by Kūrkīs ʿAwwād. Baghdad: Maṭbaʿat al-Maʿārif, 1967.

al-Bakrī, Abū ʿUbayd ʿAbd Allāh b. ʿAbd al-ʿAzīz. *al-Masālik wa-l-mamālik.* 2 vols. Edited by Jamāl Ṭulba. Beirut: Dār al-Kutub al-ʿIlmiyya, 2003. Partial French translation: *Description de l'Afrique Septentrionale*. Translated by William Mac Guckin de Slane. Rev. ed. Algiers: Typographie Adolphe Jourdan, 1913.

———. *Muʿjam mā istaʿjama min asmāʾ al-bilādwa-l-mawāḍiʿ*. 5 vols. in 3. Edited by Jamāl Ṭulba. Beirut: Dār al-Kutub al-ʿIlmiyya, 1998.

Baron, Beth. *Egypt as a Woman: Nationalism, Gender, and Politics*. Berkeley and Los Angeles: University of California Press, 2005.

al-Bayhaqī, Ibrāhīm b. Muḥammad. *al-Maḥāsin wa-l-masāwiʾ*. 2 vols. Edited by Muḥammad Abū l-Faḍl Ibrāhīm. Cairo: Maktabat Nahḍat Miṣr, 1961.

Beckingham, C. F. "Ibn Hauqal's Map of Italy." In *Iran and Islam*, edited by C. E. Bosworth, 73–78. Edinburgh: Edinburgh University Press, 1971.

Berggren, J. Lennart, and Alexander Jones. *Ptolemy's* Geography*: An Annotated Translation of the Theoretical Chapters*. Princeton: Princeton University Press, 2000.

al-Bīrūnī, Abū Rayḥān Muḥammad b. Aḥmad. *Ṣifat al-maʿmūra ʿala I-Bīrūnī/Bīrūnī's Picture of the World*. Edited by A. Zeki Validi Togan. 1934. Reprint, New Delhi: The Director General, Archaeological Survey of India, 1999.

———. *Taḥdīd nihāyat al-amākin li-taṣḥīḥ masāfat al-masākin*. Edited by Muḥammad b. Tāwīt al-Ṭanjī. Ankara: Doğus Ltd., 1962. English translation: *The Determination of the Coordinates of Positions for the Correction of Distances between Cities*. Translated by Jamil Ali. Beirut: American University of Beirut, 1967.

Blair, Sheila. "What is the Date of the Dome of the Rock?" In *Bayt al-Maqdis: ʿAbd al-Malik's Jerusalem*, pt. 1, edited by Julian Raby and Jeremy Johns, 59–87. Oxford: Oxford University Press, 1992.

Bloom, Jonathan. "On the Transmission of Designs in Early Islamic Architecture." *Muqarnas* 10 (1993): 21–28.

Bonebakker, S. A. "*Adab* and the Concept of *Belles-Lettres*." In *ʿAbbasid Belles-Lettres*, edited by Julia Ashtiany, T. M. Johnstone, J. D. Latham, R. B. Serjeant, and G. Rex Smith, 16–30. Cambridge, UK: Cambridge University Press, 1990.

Bonner, Michael. *Aristocratic Violence and Holy War: Studies in the Jihad and the Arab-Byzantine Frontier*. New Haven: American Oriental Society, 1996.

Bosworth, C. Edmund. "Sistan and Its Local Histories." *Iranian Studies* 33, 1–2 (2000): 31–43.

Brauer, Ralph W. *Boundaries and Frontiers in Medieval Muslim Geography*. Philadelphia: The American Philosophical Society, 1995.

———. "Geography in the Medieval Muslim World: Seeking a Basis for Comparison of the Development of the Natural Sciences in Different Cultures." *Comparative Civilizations Review* 26 (1992): 73–110.

Bray, Julia Ashtiany. "Figures in a Landscape: The Inhabitants of the Silver Village." In *Story-Telling in the Framework of Non-Fictional Arabic Literature*, edited by Stefan Leder, 79–93. Wiesbaden: Harrassowitz Verlag, 1998.

Brockelmann, Carl. *Geschichte der arabischen Literatur*. 2 vols. Weimar and Berlin: Emil Felber, 1898–1902. Supplement, 3 vols., Leiden: E. J. Brill, 1937–1942.

Brown, Jonathan A. C. "How We Know Early Ḥadīth Critics Did *Matn* Criticism and Why It's So Hard to Find." *Islamic Law and Society* 15 (2008): 143–184.

Brummett, Palmira. "Imagining the Early Modern Ottoman Space, from World History to Piri Reis." In *The Early Modern Ottomans: Remapping the Empire*, edited by Virginia H. Aksan and Daniel Goffman, 15–58. Cambridge, UK: Cambridge University Press, 2007.

———. "Visions of the Mediterranean: A Classification." *Journal of Medieval and Early Modern Studies* 37, 1 (2007): 9–55.

Brunschvig, Robert. "Ibn ʿAbdalhʾakam et la conquête de l'Afrique du Nord par les Arabes." In *Etudes sur l'Islam classique et l'Afrique du Nord*, edited by Abdel-Magid Turki, 108–155 (XI). London: Variorum Reprints, 1986.

———. "Urbanisme médiéval et droit musulman." *Revue des études islamiques* 15 (1947): 127–155.

al-Bukhārī, Muḥammad b. Ismāʿīl. *Ṣaḥīḥ al-Bukhārī*. 11 vols. Edited by Muḥammad Tawfīq ʿUwayda. [Cairo]: al-Jumhuriyya al-ʿArabiyya al-Muttaḥida, al-Majlis al-Aʿlā li-l-Shuʾūn al-Islāmiyya, Lajnat Iḥyāʾ Kutub al-Sunna, 1388/[1968].

Busse, Heribert. "*Bāb Ḥiṭṭa*: Qur'ān 2:58 and the Entry into Jerusalem." *Jerusalem Studies in Arabic and Islam* 22 (1998): 1–17.

———. "Jerusalem in the Story of Muḥammad's Night Journey and Ascension." *Jerusalem Studies in Arabic and Islam* 14 (1991): 1–40.

———. "'Omar's Image as the Conqueror of Jerusalem." *Jerusalem Studies in Arabic and Islam* 8 (1986): 149–168.

———. "The Tower of David/Miḥrāb Dāwūd: Remarks on the History of a Sanctuary in Jerusalem in Christian and Islamic Times." *Jerusalem Studies in Arabic and Islam* 17 (1994): 142–165.

Butler, Judith. *Excitable Speech: A Politics of the Performative*. New York and London: Routledge, 1997.

Casale, Giancarlo. *The Ottoman Age of Exploration*. New York: Oxford University Press, 2010.

Christensen, Peter. *The Decline of Iranshahr*. Copenhagen: Museum Tusculanum Press, 1993.

Christys, Ann. "The Meaning of Topography in Umayyad Córdoba." In *Cities, Texts and Social Networks, 400–1500: Experiences and Perceptions of Medieval Urban Space*, edited by Caroline Goodson, Anne E. Lester, and Carol Symes, 103–123. Surrey, UK: Ashgate, 2010.

Cobb, Paul. "Virtual Sacrality: Making Muslim Syria Sacred before the Crusades." *Medieval Encounters: Jewish, Christian and Muslim Culture in Confluence and Dialogue* 8, 1 (2002): 35–55.

Cooperson, Michael. "Baghdad in Rhetoric and Narrative." *Muqarnas* 13 (1996): 99–113.

———. "Images Without Illustrations: The Visual Imagination in Classical Arabic Biography." In *Islamic Art and Literature*, edited by Oleg Grabar and Cynthia Robinson, 7–20. Princeton: Markus Wiener, 2001.

Cornu, Georgette. *Atlas du monde arabo-islamique à l'époque classique, IXe–Xe siècles*. Leiden: E. J. Brill, 1985.

Cosgrove, Denis. "Introduction: Mapping Meaning." In *Mappings*, edited by Denis Cosgrove, 1–23. London: Reaktion Books, 1999.

Creswell, Tim. *Place: A Short Introduction*. Oxford: Blackwell Publishing, 2004.

Daly, Okasha. *Egyptology: The Missing Millennium*. London: UCL Press, 2005.

Dankoff, Robert. *An Ottoman Mentality: The World of Evliya Çelebi*. Rev. ed. Leiden: Brill, 2006.

Davis, Natalie Zemon. *Trickster Travels: A Sixteenth-Century Muslim between Worlds*. New York: Hill and Wang, 2007.

Diener, Alexander C. and Joshua Hagen, eds. *Borderlines and Borderlands: Political Oddities at the Edge of the Nation-State*. Lanham, MD: Rowman & Littlefield, 2010.

Donner, Fred M. "'Uthmān and the Rāshidūn Caliphs in Ibn 'Asākir's *Ta'rīkh madīnat Dimashq*: a Study in Strategies of Compilation." In *Ibn 'Asākir and Early Islamic History*, edited by James E. Lindsay, 44–61. Princeton: The Darwin Press, Inc., 2001.

della Dora, Veronica. "Performative Atlases: Memory, Materiality, and (Co-) Authorship." *Cartographica* 44, 4 (2009): 240–255.

Duncan, James, and David Ley, eds. *Place/Culture/Representation*. London: Routledge, 1993.

Eickelman, Dale. "The Comparative Studies of 'Islamic' City." In *Urbanism in Islam: Proceedings of the Second International Conference on Urbanism in Islam (ICUIT II), November 27–29, 1990*, edited by Tadeshi Yukuwa, 309–319. Tokyo: Research Project "Urbanism in Islam" and Middle Eastern Culture Center in Japan, 1994.

Elad, Amikam. *Medieval Jerusalem and Islamic Worship*. Leiden: E. J. Brill, 1995.

Elden, Stuart. *Terror and Territory: The Spatial Effects of Sovereignty*. Minneapolis: University of Minnesota Press, 2009.

Elinson, Alexander. *Looking Back at al-Andalus: The Poetics of Loss and Nostalgia in Medieval Arabic and Hebrew Literature*. Leiden: Brill, 2009.

Enderwitz, Susanne. "Homesickness and Love in Arabic Poetry." In *Myths, Historical Archetypes and Symbolic Figures in Arabic Literature: Towards a New Hermeneutic Approach (Proceedings of the International Symposium in Beirut, June 25th–June 30th, 1996)*, edited by Angelika Neuwirth, Birgit Embaló, Sebastian Günther, and Maher Jarrar, 59–70. Beirut: Orient-Institut der Deutschen Morgenländischen Gesellschaft, and Stuttgart: Franz Steiner Verlag, 1999.

Euben, Roxanne L. *Journeys to the Other Shore: Muslim and Western Travelers in Search of Knowledge.* Princeton: Princeton University Press, 2006.

al-Fākihī, Abū ʿAbd Allāh Muḥammad b. Isḥāq. *Kitāb al-muntaqā fī akhbār Umm al-Qurā.* Vol. 2 of *Auszüge aus den Geschichtsbüchern der Stadt Mekka,* edited by Ferdinand Wüstenfeld. 1859. Reprint, Beirut: Khayats, 1964.

———. "Min kitāb taʾrīkh Makka." In *al-Muntaqā fī akhbār Umm al-Qurā,* edited by Muḥammad ʿAbd Allāh Malībārī. Mecca: Maṭābiʿ al-Ṣafā, 1985.

Fragner, Bert. *Die "Persophonie": Regionalität, Identität und Sprachkontakt in der Geschichte Asiens.* Berlin: Das Arabische Buch, 1999.

Frye, Richard N. "City Chronicles of Central Asia and Khurasan: A History of Nasaf?" In *Mélanges Fuad Köprülü,* 165–168. Istanbul: Osman Yalçın Matbaası, 1953.

Frye, Richard N., ed. *The Histories of Nishapur.* Cambridge, MA: Harvard University Press, 1965.

Gelvin, James. *Divided Loyalties: Nationalism and Mass Politics in Syria at the Close of Empire.* Berkeley and Los Angeles: University of California Press, 1998.

Gerber, Haim. "'Palestine' and Other Territorial Concepts in the 17th Century." *International Journal of Middle East Studies* 30 (1998): 563–572.

Geries, Ibrahim. *Un genre littéraire arabe: al-maḥāsin wa-l-masāwī.* Paris: Maisonneuve et Larose, 1977.

Gershoni, Israel, and James Jankowski. *Egypt, Islam, and the Arabs: The Search for Egyptian Nationhood.* New York: Oxford University Press, 1986.

———. *Redefining the Egyptian Nation, 1930–1945.* Cambridge, UK: Cambridge University Press, 1995.

Ghomi, Haideh. "The Land of Love: Rumi's Concept of 'Territory' in Islam." In *The Concept of Territory in Islamic Law and Thought,* edited by Yanagihashi Hiroyuki, 69–85. London: Kegan Paul International, 2000.

al-Ghuzūlī, ʿAlāʾ al-Dīn ʿAlī b. ʿAbd Allāh al-Bahāʾī. *Maṭāliʿ al-budūr fī manāzil al-surūr.* Cairo: Maktabat al-Thaqāfa al-Dīniyya, 2000.

de Goeje, M. J. "Die Istachri-Balchi-Frage." *Zeitschrift der Deutschen Morgenländischen Gesellschaft* 25 (1871): 42–58.

Goitein, S. D. "The Sanctity of Jerusalem and Palestine in Early Islam." In *Studies in Islamic History and Institutions,* 135–148. Leiden: E. J. Brill, 1968.

Goldziher, Ignaz. *Muslim Studies.* 2 vols. Edited and translated by C. R. Barber and S. M. Stern. Albany: State University of New York Press, 1966–1971.

Golombek, Lisa. "Urban Patterns in Pre-Safavid Isfahan." *Iranian Studies* 7, 1 (1974): 18–44.

Grabar, Oleg. *The Dome of the Rock.* Cambridge, MA: The Belknap Press, 2006.

———. "The Illustrated *Maqamat* of the Thirteenth Century: The Bourgeoisie and the Arts." In *The Islamic City: A Colloquium,* edited by Albert Habib Hourani and S. M. Stern, 207–222. Philadelphia: University of Pennsylvania Press, 1970.

———. "The Meaning of the Dome of the Rock." In *The Medieval Mediterranean,* edited by Marilyn J. Chiat and Kathryn L. Reyerson, 1–10. St. Cloud, MN: North Star Press, 1988.

———. "Upon Reading al-Azraqī." *Muqarnas* 3 (1986): 1–7.

———. "The Umayyad Dome of the Rock." *Ars Orientalis* 3 (1959): 33–62.

Granara, William. "Remaking Muslim Sicily: Ibn Ḥamdīs and the Poetics of Exile." *Edebiyât* 9, 2 (1998): 167–198.

Gruber, Ernst August. *Verdienst und Rang: Die Fada'il als literarisches und gesellschaftliches Problem in Islam.* Freiburg: Klaus Schwarz Verlag, 1975.

von Grunebaum, Gustave E. "The Sacred Character of Islamic Cities." In *Ilā Ṭāhā Ḥusayn fī ʿid mīlādihi al-sabʿīn: dirāsāt muhadāh min aṣdiqāʾihi wa-talāmīdhih/Mélanges Taha Huṣain: offerts par ses amis à l'occasion de son 70ième anniversaire,* edited by ʿAbd al-Raḥmān Badawī, 25–37. [Cairo]: Dār al-Maʿārif, 1962.

———. "The Structure of the Muslim Town." In *Islam: Essays in the Nature and Growth of a Cultural Tradition,* 141–158. 2d ed. London: Routledge and Kegan Paul Ltd., 1961.

Gutas, Dimitri. *Greek Thought, Arabic Culture: The Graeco-Arabic Translation Movement in Baghdad and Early ʿAbbāsid Society (2nd–4th/8th–10th Centuries)*. London: Routledge, 1998.
Guthrie, Shirley. *Arab Social Life in the Middle Ages*. London: Saqi Books, 1995.
Haarmann, Ulrich. "Medieval Muslim Perceptions of Pharaonic Egypt." In *Ancient Egyptian Literature: History and Forms*, edited by Antonio Loprieno, 605–627. Leiden: E. J. Brill, 1996.
———. "Regional Sentiment in Medieval Islamic Egypt." *Bulletin of the School of Oriental and African Studies* 43, 1 (1980): 55–66.
———. *al-Umma wa-l-waṭan fī l-fikr al-Islāmī wa-l-Masīḥī fī l-ʿuṣūr al-wusṭā: muḥāḍara*. Jerusalem: al-Jamʿiyya al-Filasṭīniyya al-Akādīmiyya li-l-Shuʾūn al-Dawliyya, 1989.
Haldon, John. "Seventh-Century Continuities: the *Ajnād* and the 'Thematic Myth.'" In *The Byzantine and Early Islamic Near East*, vol. 3, *States, Resources and Armies*, edited by Averil Cameron, 379–423. Princeton: The Darwin Press, 1995.
al-Hamdānī, al-Ḥasan b. Aḥmad. *al-Iklīl*. Pt. 8. Edited by Nabīh Amīn Fāris. Princeton: Princeton University Press, 1940. English translation: *The Antiquities of South Arabia, Being a Translation from the Arabic with Linguistic, Geographic, and Historic Notes of the Eighth Book of al-Hamdānī's al-Iklīl*. Translated by Nabīh Amīn Fāris. Princeton: Princeton University Press, 1938.
———. *Ṣifat Jazīrat al-ʿArab*. Edited by Muḥammad b. ʿAlī al-Akwaʿ al-Ḥawālī. Riyadh: Dāral-Yamāma li-l-Baḥth wa-l-Tarjama wa-l-Nashr, 1974.
Hämeen-Anttila, Jaakko. "Building an Identity: Place as an Image of Self in Classical Arabic Literature." *Quaderni di Studi Arabi* 3 (2008): 25–38.
———. "Mesopotamian National Identity in Early Arabic Sources." *Wiener Zeitschrift für die Kunde des Morgenlandes* 92 (2002): 53–79.
Harley, J. B. *The New Nature of Maps*. Edited by Paul Laxton. Baltimore: Johns Hopkins University Press, 2001.
Harley, J. B., and David Woodward, eds. *Cartography in the Traditional Islamic and South Asian Societies*. Vol. 2, bk. 1 of *The History of Cartography*. Chicago: University of Chicago Press, 1992.
al-Ḥasan al-Baṣrī, Abū Saʿīd Yasār. *Faḍāʾil Makka wa-l-sakan fīhā*. Edited by Sāmī Makkī al-ʿĀnī. Kuwait: Maktabat al-Falāḥ, 1980.
Hassan, Mona. "Loss of Caliphate: Trauma and Aftermath of 1258 and 1924." PhD diss., Princeton University, 2009.
Hasson, Izhak. "Muslim Literature in Praise of Jerusalem: Faḍāʾil Bayt al-Maqdis." In *The Jerusalem Cathedra*, vol. 1, edited by Lee I. Levine, 168–184. Jerusalem: Yad Izhak Ben-Zvi, 1981.
———. "The Muslim View of Jerusalem: The Qurʾān and Hadīth." In *The History of Jerusalem: The Early Muslim Period, 638–1099*, edited by Joshua Prawer and Haggai Ben-Shammai, 349–385. Jerusalem: Yad Izhak Ben-Zvi, 1996.
Hawting, G. R. "The Origins of the the Muslim Sanctuary at Mecca." In *Studies on the First Century of Islamic Society*, edited by G. H. A. Juynboll. Carbondale and Edwardsville: Southern Illinois University Press, 1982.
Heck, Paul L. *The Construction of Knowledge in Islamic Civilization: Qudāma b. Jaʿfar and his* Kitāb al-kharāj wa-ṣināʿat al-kitāba. Leiden: Brill, 2002.
von Hees, Syrinx. "The Astonishing: A Critique and Re-reading of ʿAjāʾib-literature." *Middle Eastern Literatures* 8, 2 (2005): 101–120.
Heinrichs, Wolfhart. "The Classification of the Sciences and the Consolidation of Philology in Classical Islam." In *Centres of Learning: Learning and Location in Pre-Modern Europe and the Near East*, edited by Jan Willem Drijvers and Alasdair A. MacDonald, 119–139. Leiden: E. J. Brill, 1995.
al-Ḥillī, ʿAbd al-Ḥusayn ʿAbbās. *al-Rithāʾ fī l-shiʿr al-ʿArabī: al-ʿaṣr al-ʿabbāsī ḥattā nihāyat al-qarn al-thālith al-hijrī*. Beirut: Dār al-Kitāb al-ʿArabī, 2008.
Hirschler, Konrad. *Medieval Arabic Historiography: Authors as Actors*. London: Routledge, 2006.
———. "The 'Pharaoh' Anecdote in Pre-Modern Arabic Historiography." *Journal of Arabic and Islamic Studies* 10, 3 (2010): 45–74.

Hopkins, J. F. P. "Geographical and Navigational Literature." In *Religion, Learning, and Science in the ʿAbbasid Period*, edited by M. J. L. Young, J. D. Latham, and R. B. Serjeant, 301–327. Cambridge, UK: Cambridge University Press, 1990.

Hourani, Albert Habib, and S. M. Stern, eds. *The Islamic City: A Colloquium*. Philadelphia: University of Pennsylvania Press, 1970.

Hoyland, Robert. "History, Fiction and Authorship in the First Centuries of Islam." In *Writing and Representation in Medieval Islam*, edited by Julia Bray, 16–46. London: Routledge, 2006.

al-Ḥuṣrī al-Qayrawānī, Ibrāhīm b. ʿAlī. *Zahr al-ādāb wa-thamar al-albāb*. 2 vols. Edited by ʿAlī Muḥammad al-Bajāwī. 2d ed. [Cairo]: Dār Iḥyāʾ al-Kutub al-ʿArabiyya, 1969–1970.

Ḥuwwar, Muḥammad Ibrāhīm. *al-Ḥanīn ilā l-waṭan fī l-adab al-ʿarabī ḥattā nihāyat al-ʿaṣr al-Umawī*. [Cairo]: Dār Nahḍat Miṣr, 1973.

Ibn ʿAbd al-Barr, Yūsuf b. ʿAbd Allāh. *Bahjat al-majālis wa-uns al-mujālis wa-shaḥdh al-dhāhin wa-l-hājis*. 2 vols. Edited by Muḥammad Mursī al-Khūlī and ʿAbd al-Qādir al-Quṭṭ. Cairo: al-Dār al-Miṣriyya li-l-Taʾlīf wa-l-Tarjama and Dār al-Kātib al-ʿArabī li-l-Ṭibāʿa wa-l-Nashr, 1967–1970.

Ibn ʿAbd al-Ḥakam, Abū l-Qāsim ʿAbd al-Raḥmān b. ʿAbd Allāh. *Futūḥ Miṣr wa-l-Maghrib*. Edited by ʿAlī Muḥammad ʿUmar. Cairo: Maktabat al-Thaqāfa al-Dīniyya, 1995.

Ibn ʿAbd Rabbih, Aḥmad b. Muḥammad. *al-ʿIqd al-farīd*. 31 vols. in 8. Edited by Karam al-Bustānī. Beirut: Maktabat Ṣādir, 1951–1953.

Ibn al-ʿArabī, Muḥyī l-Dīn. *Kitāb muḥāḍarat al-abrār wa-musāmarat al-akhyār fī l-adabiyyāt wa-l-nawādir wa-l-akhbār*. 2 vols. [Damascus]: Dār al-Yaqẓa al-ʿArabiyya, [1968].

Ibn al-Faqīh, Aḥmad b. Muḥammad al-Hamadhānī. *Baghdād, Madīnat al-Salām*. Edited by Ṣāliḥ Aḥmad al-ʿAlī. [Baghdad]: Wizārat al-Iʿlām, 1977.

———. *Mukhtaṣar kitāb al-buldān*. Edited by M. J. de Goeje. Vol. 5 of *Bibliotheca Geographorum Arabicorum*, edited by M. J. de Goeje. 2d ed. Leiden: E. J. Brill, 1967. French translation: *Abrégé du livre des pays*. Translated by Henri Massé. Damascus: Institut Français de Damas, 1973.

———. *Nuṣūṣ lam tuḥaqqaq min* Kitāb akhbār al-buldān: *al-Sawād, al-Ahwāz, al-Turk*. Edited by Ḍayf Allāh Yaḥyā al-Zahrānī and Murayzin Saʿīd ʿAsīrī. Mecca: Jāmiʿat Umm al-Qurā, 1997.

Ibn Ḥawqal, Abū l-Qāsim Muḥammad al-Naṣībī. *Kitāb ṣūrat al-arḍ*. Edited by J. H. Kramers. Vol. 2 of *Bibliotheca Geographorum Arabicorum*, edited by M. J. de Goeje. 3d ed. Leiden: E. J. Brill, 1967. French translation: *La Configuration de la Terre*. 2 vols. Translated by J. H. Kramers and G. Wiet. Paris: Maisonneuve et Larose, 2001.

Ibn Ḥazm, Abū Muḥammad ʿAlī. "Risāla fī faḍl al-Andalus wa-dhikr rijālihā." In *Rasāʾil Ibn Ḥazm al-Andalusī*, vol. 2, edited by Iḥsān ʿAbbās, 171–188. 2d ed. Beirut: al-Muʾassasa al-ʿArabiyya li-l-Dirasāt wa-l-Nashr, 1987. French translation: "Ibn Ḥazm, bibliographe et apologiste de l'Espagne musulmane." Edited and translated by Charles Pellat. *Al-Andalus* 19, 1 (1954): 53–102.

Ibn Hishām, ʿAbd al-Malik. *al-Sīra al-Nabawiyya*. 2 vols. Edited by Muṣṭafā al-Saqqā, Ibrāhīm al-Ibyārī, and ʿAbd al-Ḥafīẓ Shalabī. 2d ed. [Cairo]: Maktabat wa-Maṭbaʿat Muṣṭafā al-Bābī al-Ḥalabī, 1955.

Ibn Isḥāq, Muḥammad. See Ibn Hishām, ʿAbd al-Malik.

Ibn Khurradādhbih, Abū l-Qāsim ʿUbayd Allāh b. ʿAbd Allāh. *Kitāb al-masālik wa-l-mamālik*. Edited by M. J. de Goeje. Vol. 6 of *Bibliotheca Geographorum Arabicorum*, edited by M. J. de Goeje. 2d ed. Leiden: E. J. Brill, 1967. (This edition also includes a French translation of the Arabic text. All page citations in the notes refer to the Arabic.)

Ibn al-Kindī, ʿUmar b. Muḥammad. *Faḍāʾil Miṣr*. Edited by ʿAlī Muḥammad ʿUmar. Cairo: Maktabat al-Khānjī, 1997.

Ibn al-Marzubān, Muḥammad b. Sahl. *Kitāb al-ḥanīn ilā l-awṭān*. Edited by Jalīl al-ʿAṭiyya. Beirut: ʿĀlam al-Kutub, 1987.

———. *Kitāb al-shawq wa-l-firāq*. Edited by Jalīl al-ʿAṭiyya. Beirut: Dār al-Gharb al-Islāmī, 1988.

Ibn al-Nadīm, Abū l-Faraj Muḥammad b. Isḥāq. *al-Fihrist li-Ibn al-Nadīm*. Edited by Nāhid ʿAbbās ʿUthmān. Doha: Dār Qaṭarī Ibn al-Fujāʾa, 1985. English translation: *The Fihrist: A 10th*

Century AD Survey of Islamic Culture. Edited and translated by Bayard Dodge. 2 vols. New York: Columbia University Press, 1970. Reprint (2 vols. in 1), Chicago: Kazi Publications, 1998. (All page citations in the notes refer to the reprint edition.)

Ibn al-Rūmī, Abū l-Ḥasan ʿAlī b. al-ʿAbbās. *Dīwān Ibn al-Rūmī*. Edited by Kāmil Kīlānī. [Cairo]: Maṭbaʿat al-Tawfīq, 1924.

Ibn Rustih, Abū ʿAlī Aḥmad b. ʿUmar. *Kitāb al-aʿlāq al-nafīsa*. Pt. 7. Edited by M. J. de Goeje. Vol. 7 of *Bibliotheca Geographorum Arabicorum*, edited by M. J. de Goeje. 2d ed. Leiden: E. J. Brill, 1967. French translation: *Les atours précieux*. Translated by Gaston Wiet. Cairo: La Société de Géographie d'Egypte, 1955.

Ibn Shaddād, ʿIzz al-Dīn. *al-Aʿlāq al-khaṭīra fī dhikr umarāʾ al-Shām wa-l-Jazīra: Taʾrīkh madīnat Dimashq*. Edited by Sāmī al-Dahhān. Damascus: Institut Français de Damas, 1956.

———. *al-Aʿlāq al-khaṭīra fī dhikr umarāʾ al-Shām wa-l-Jazīra: Tairīkh Lubnān wa-l-Urdunn wa-Filasṭīn*. Edited by Sāmī al-Dahhān. Damascus: Institut Français de Damas, 1963.

Ibn Shuhayd, Abū ʿĀmir Aḥmad b. Abī Marwān ʿAbd al-Malik. *Dīwān Ibn Shuhayd al-Andalusī*. Edited by Yaʿqūb Zakī. Cairo: Dār al-Kitāb al-ʿArabī li-l-Ṭibāʿa wa-l-Nashr, [1969].

Ibn Waṣīf Shāh, Ibrāhīm. *Mukhtaṣar ʿajāʾib al-dunyā*. Edited by Sayyid Kisrawī Ḥasan. Beirut: Dār al-Kutub al-ʿIlmiyya, 2001.

Ibn Zūlāq, Abū Muḥammad al-Ḥasan. *Faḍāʾil Miṣr*. Edited by ʿAlī Muḥammad ʿUmar. Cairo: Maktabat al-Khānjī, 2000.

al-Iṣfahānī, Abū l-Faraj [attr.]. *The Book of Strangers: Medieval Arabic Graffiti on the Theme of Nostalgia*. Edited and translated by Patricia Crone and Shmuel Moreh. Princeton: Markus Wiener, 2000.

al-Iṣṭakhrī, Abū Isḥāq Ibrāhīm b. Muḥammad al-Fārisī. *al-Masālik wa-l-mamālik*. Edited by Muḥammad Jābir ʿAbd al-ʿĀl al-Ḥīnī. Cairo: Dār al-Qalam, 1961.

———. *Kitāb al-masālik wa-l-mamālik*. Edited by M. J. de Goeje. Vol. 1 of *Bibliotheca Geographorum Arabicorum*, edited by M. J. de Goeje. 3d ed. Leiden: E. J. Brill, 1967.

al-Jāḥiẓ, Abū ʿUthmān ʿAmr b. Baḥr [attr.]. *al-Ḥanīn ilā l-awṭān*. Edited by Ṭāhir al-Jazāʾirī. [Cairo]: Maṭbaʿat al-Manār, 1333/[1915]. English translation: "Homesickness." In *Nine Essays of al-Jahiz*, translated by William M. Hutchins, 123–137. New York: Peter Lang, 1989.

———. *Kitāb al-buldān*. Edited by Ṣāliḥ Aḥmad al-ʿAlī. Baghdad: Maṭbaʿat al-Ḥukūma, 1970.

——— [attr.]. *al-Maḥāsin wa-l-aḍdād*. Edited by Gerlof van Vloten. Leiden: E. J. Brill, 1898.

James, Boris. "Le 'territoire tribal des Kurdes' et l'aire iraqienne (Xe–XIIIe siècles): Esquisse des recompositions spatiales." *Revue des mondes musulmans et de la Méditerranée* 117–118 (2007): 101–126.

al-Janadī, Abū Saʿīd al-Mufaḍḍal b. Muḥammad. *Faḍāʾil al-Madīna*. Edited by Muḥammad Muṭīʿ al-Ḥāfiẓ and Ghazwa Budayr. Damascus: Dār al-Fikr, 1985.

Jayyusi, Salma K., Renata Holod, Attilio Petruccioli, and André Raymond, eds. *The City in the Islamic World*. 2 vols. Leiden: Brill, 2008.

al-Jubūrī, Yaḥyā. *al-Ḥanīn wa-l-ghurba fī l-shiʿr al-ʿarabī: al-ḥanīn ilā l-awṭān*. Amman: Dār Majdalāwī, 2008.

Juynboll, G. H. A. *Muslim Tradition*. Cambridge, UK: Cambridge University Press, 1983.

Kahlaoui, Tarek. "The Depiction of the Mediterranean in Islamic Cartography (11th to 16th Centuries)." PhD diss., University of Pennsylvania, 2008.

Kamal, Youssouf, ed. *Monumenta Cartographica Africae et Aegypti*. 5 vols. [Cairo]: n.p., 1926–1951.

Kaplony, Andreas. "Comparing al-Kāshgharī's Map to his Text: On the Visual Language, Purpose, and Transmission of Arabic-Islamic Maps." In *The Journey of Maps and Images on the Silk Road*, edited by Philippe Forêt and Andreas Kaplony, 137–153. Leiden: Brill, 2008.

Karamustafa, Ahmet T. "Cosmographical Diagrams." In *The History of Cartography*, vol. 2, bk. 1, edited by J. B. Harley and David Woodward, 71–89. Chicago: University of Chicago Press, 1992.

Kashani-Sabet, Firoozeh. *Frontier Fictions: Shaping the Iranian Nation, 1804–1946*. Princeton: Princeton University Press, 1999.

Keaney, Heather. "Confronting the Caliph: ʿUthmān b. ʿAffān in Three ʿAbbasid Chronicles." *Studia Islamica, nouvelle édition/new series* 1 (2011): 37–65.

Kennedy, Hugh. "How to Found an Islamic City." In *Cities, Texts and Social Networks, 400–1500: Experiences and Perceptions of Medieval Urban Space*, edited by Caroline Goodson, Anne E. Lester, and Carol Symes, 45–63. Surrey, UK: Ashgate, 2010.

Khalek, Nancy. *Damascus after the Muslim Conquest: Text and Image in Early Islam*. New York: Oxford University Press, 2011.

Khalidov, Anas B. "Myth and Reality in the K. Akhbār al-Buldān by Ibn al-Faqīh." In *Myths, Historical Archetypes and Symbolic Figures in Arabic Literature: Towards a New Hermeneutic Approach (Proceedings of the International Symposium in Beirut, June 25th–June 30th, 1996)*, edited by Angelika Neuwirth, Birgit Embaló, Sebastian Günther, and Maher Jarrar, 481–489. Beirut: Orient-Institut der Deutschen Morgenländischen Gesellschaft, and Stuttgart: Franz Steiner Verlag, 1999.

El-Khatib, Abdallah. "Jerusalem in the Qurʾān." *British Journal of Middle Eastern Studies* 28, 1 (2001): 25–53.

al-Khaṭīb al-Baghdādī, Abū Bakr b. Thābit. *Taʾrīkh Baghdād*. 14 vols. Cairo: Maktabat al-Khānjī, 1931. Reprint, Beirut: Dār al-Kitāb al-ʿArabī, [1966]. (All page citations in the notes refer to the reprint edition.)

al-Khawlānī, ʿAbd al-Jabbār. *Taʾrīkh Dārayyā*. Edited by Saʿīd al-Afghānī. Damascus: Maṭbaʿat al-Turqī, 1950.

Khoury, Nuha N. N. "The Dome of the Rock, the Kaʿba, and Ghumdan: Arab Myths and Umayyad Monuments." *Muqarnas* 10 (1993): 57–66.

———. "The Meaning of the Great Mosque of Cordoba in the Tenth Century." *Muqarnas* 13 (1996): 80–98.

———. "The Mihrab: From Text to Form." *International Journal of Middle East Studies* 30, 1 (1998): 1–27.

al-Khwārazmī, Abū Jaʿfar Muḥammad b. Mūsā. *Kitāb ṣūrat al-arḍ*. Edited by Hans von Mžik. Leipzig: Otto Harrassowitz, 1926.

Kilito, Abdelfattah. *The Author & His Doubles: Essays on Classical Arabic Culture*. Translated by Michael Cooperson. Syracuse: Syracuse University Press, 2001.

Kilpatrick, Hilary, and Stefan Leder. "Classical Arabic Prose Literature: A Researchers' Sketch Map." *Journal of Arabic Literature* 23, 1 (1992): 2–26.

King, David A. *World Maps for Finding the Direction and Distance to Mecca: Innovation and Tradition in Islamic Science*. Leiden: Brill, 1999.

King, David A., and Richard P. Lorch. "Qibla Charts, Qibla Maps, and Related Instruments." In *The History of Cartography*, vol. 2, bk. 1, edited by J. B. Harley and David Woodward, 189–205. Chicago: University of Chicago Press, 1992.

Kister, M. J. "Maqām Ibrāhīm: A Stone with an Inscription." *Le Muséon* 84 (1971): 477–491.

———. "Sanctity Joint and Divided: On Holy Places in the Islamic Tradition." *Jerusalem Studies in Arabic and Islam* 20 (1996): 18–65.

———. "The Sīrah Literature." In *Arabic Literature to the End of the Umayyad Period*, ed. A. F. L. Beeston, T. M. Johnstone, R. B. Serjeant, and G. R. Smith, 352–367. Cambridge, UK: Cambridge University Press, 1983.

———. "'You Shall Only Set Out for Three Mosques': A Study of an Early Tradition." *Le Muséon* 82 (1969): 173–196.

Kramers, J. H. "La question Balḫī-Iṣṭaḫrī-Ibn Ḥawḳal et l'Atlas de l'Islam." *Acta Orientalia* 10, 1 (1931): 9–30.

Kratchkovsky, I. I. *Taʾrīkh al-adab al-jughrāfī al-ʿarabī*. 2 vols. Translated by Ṣalāḥ al-Dīn ʿUthmān Hāshim. [Cairo]: al-Idāra al-Thaqāfiyya fī Jāmiʿat al-Duwal al-ʿArabiyya, 1963–1965.

LaCapra, Dominick. "Rethinking Intellectual History and Reading Texts." *History and Theory* 19, 3 (1980): 245–276.

Lambton, Ann K. S. "An Account of the *Tārīkhi Qumm*." *Bulletin of the School of Oriental and African Studies* 12, 3/4 (1948): 586–596.

Lapidus, Ira M., ed. *Middle Eastern Cities: A Symposium on Ancient, Islamic, and Contemporary Middle Eastern Urbanism*. Berkeley and Los Angeles: University of California Press, 1969.

Lassner, Jacob. "Muslims on the Sanctity of Jerusalem: Preliminary Thoughts on the Search for a Conceptual Framework." *Jerusalem Studies on Arabic and Islam* 31 (2006): 164–195.

———. *The Topography of Baghdad in the Early Middle Ages: Text and Studies*. Detroit: Wayne State University Press, 1970.

Lévi-Provençal, E., ed. and trans. "La 'Description de l'Espagne' d'Aḥmad al-Rāzī." *Al-Andalus* 18, 1 (1953): 51–108.

Levtzion, N., and J. F. P. Hopkins, eds. *Corpus of Early Arabic Sources for West African History*. Princeton: Markus Wiener, 2000.

Lilley, Keith D. *City and Cosmos: The Medieval World in Urban Form*. London: Reaktion Books, 2009.

Livne-Kafri, Ofer. "The Early Šīʿa and Jerusalem." *Arabica* 48 (2001): 112–120.

———. "Jerusalem in Early Islam: The Eschatological Aspect." *Arabica* 53, 3 (2006): 382–403.

Lynch, Kevin. *The Image of the City*. Cambridge, MA: The M.I.T. Press, 1960.

al-Madʿaj, ʿAbd al-Muhsin Madʿaj M. *The Yemen in Early Islam, 9–233/630–847*. London: The Ithaca Press, 1988.

al-Māfarrūkhī, Mufaḍḍal b. Saʿd. *Maḥāsin Iṣfahān*. Edited by ʿĀrif Aḥmad ʿAbd al-Ghanī. Damascus: Dār Kinān, 2010.

Makdisi, George. "The Topography of Eleventh Century Baġdād: Materials and Notes (I and II)," *Arabica* 6, 2–3 (1959): 178–197, 281–309.

Mālik b. Anas. *al-Muwaṭṭaʾ*. 2 vols. Edited by Muḥammad Fuʾād ʿAbd al-Bāqī. [Cairo]: Dār Iḥyāʾ al-Kutub al-ʿArabiyya, 1951.

al-Mālikī, Abū Bakr ʿAbd Allāh b. Muḥammad. *Riyāḍ al-nufūs fī ṭabaqāt ʿulamāʾ al-Qayrawān wa-Ifrīqiyya*. 3 vols. Edited by Bashīr al-Bakkūsh and Muḥammad al-ʿArūsī al-Maṭwī. Beirut: Dār al-Gharb al-Islāmī, 1981–1984.

Malti-Douglas, Fedwa. "Controversy and its Effects in the Biographical Tradition of al-Khaṭīb al-Baghdādī." *Studia Islamica* 46 (1977): 115–132.

———. "Playing with the Sacred: Religious Intertext in *Adab* Discourse." In *Humanism, Culture, and Language in the Near East*, edited by Asma Afsaruddin and A. H. Mathias Zahniser, 51–59. Winona Lake, IN: Eisenbrauns, 1997.

———. *Structures of Avarice: The Bukhalāʾ in Medieval Arabic Literature*. Leiden: E. J. Brill, 1985.

al-Maqqarī, Aḥmad b. Muḥammad. *Nafḥ al-ṭīb min ghuṣn al-Andalus al-raṭīb*. 8 vols. Edited by Iḥsān ʿAbbās. Beirut: Dār Ṣādir, 1968. Partial English translation: *The History of the Mohammedan Dynasties in Spain*. 2 vols. Edited and translated by Pascual de Gayangos. 1840–1843. Reprint, London: RoutledgeCurzon, 2002.

Marçais, William. "L'islamisme et la vie urbaine." In *Articles et Conférences*, 59–67. Paris: Adrien-Maisonneuve, 1961.

Marin, Manuela. "Historical Images of al-Andalus and of Andalusians." In *Myths, Historical Archetypes and Symbolic Figures in Arabic Literature: Towards a New Hermeneutic Approach (Proceedings of the International Symposium in Beirut, June 25th–June 30th, 1996)*, edited by Angelika Neuwirth, Birgit Embaló, Sebastian Günther, and Maher Jarrar, 409–421. Beirut: Orient-Institut der Deutschen Morgenländischen Gesellschaft, and Stuttgart: Franz Steiner Verlag, 1999.

Maspero, Jean and Gaston Wiet. *Matériaux pour server à la géographie de l'Egypte*. Volume 36 of *Mémoires publiés par les members de l'Institut Français d'Archéologie Orientale du Caire*. Cairo: Imprimerie de l'Institut Français d'Archéologie Orientale, 1919.

Massad, Joseph. "Conceiving the Masculine: Gender and Palestinian Nationalism." *Middle East Journal* 49, 3 (1995): 467–483.

al-Masʿūdī, ʿAlī b. al-Ḥusayn. *Kitāb al-tanbīh wa-l-ishrāf*. Edited by M. J. de Goeje. Vol. 8 of *Bibliotheca Geographorum Arabicorum*, edited by M. J. de Goeje. 2d ed. Leiden: E. J. Brill, 1967. French translation: *Le livre de l'avertissement et de la revision*. Translated by B. Carra de Vaux. Paris: Imprimerie Nationale, 1896.

———. *Murūj al-dhahab wa-maʿādin al-jawhar*. 4 vols. Edited by Mufīd Muḥammad Qumayḥa. Beirut: Dār al-Kutub al-ʿIlmiyya, [1985]. French translation: *Les prairies d'or*. 9 vols. Translated by C. Barbier de Meynard and A. Pavet de Courteille. Paris: Imprimerie Impériale and Imprimerie Nationale, 1861–1874.

McAlister, Melani. *Epic Encounters: Culture, Media, and U.S. Interests in the Middle East since 1945*. Berkeley and Los Angeles: University of California Press, 2005.

Meisami, Julie Scott. "Palaces and Paradises: Palace Description in Medieval Persian Poetry." In *Islamic Art and Literature*, edited by Oleg Grabar and Cynthia Robinson, 21–54. Princeton: Markus Wiener, 2001.

———. "Places in the Past: The Poetics/Politics of Nostalgia." *Edebiyât* 8, 1 (1998): 63–106.

Melville, Charles. "The Caspian Provinces: A World Apart: Three Local Histories of Mazandaran." *Iranian Studies* 33, 1–2 (2000): 45–91.

Micheau, Françoise. "Baghdad in the Abbasid Era: A Cosmopolitan and Multi-Confessional Capital." In *The City in the Islamic World*, vol. 1, edited by Salma K. Jayyusi, Renata Holod, Attilio Petruccioli, and André Raymond, 221–245. Leiden: Brill, 2008.

Milich, Stephan. *Poetik der Fremdheit: Palästinensische und irakische Lyrik des Exils*. Wiesbaden: Reichert Verlag, 2010.

Miller, Konrad, ed. *Mappae Arabicae*. 6 vols. Stuttgart: Selbstverlag des Herausgebers, 1926–1931.

Minorsky, V., trans. *Ḥudūd al-ʿĀlam*. 2d ed., with a preface by V. V. Barthold and edited by C. E. Bosworth. London: Luzac & Company, 1970.

Miquel, André. *La géographie humaine du monde musulman jusqu'au milieu du 11ᵉ siècle*. 4 vols. Paris: Mouton & Co. and Editions de l'Ecole des Hautes Etudes en Sciences Sociales, 1967–1988. Reprint, vols. 1–2, Paris: Editions de l'Ecole des Hautes Etudes en Sciences Sociales, 2001. (All page citations in the notes for volumes 1 and 2 refer to the reprint editions.)

Montgomery, James E. "Ibn Rusta's Lack of 'Eloquence,' the Rūs, and Samanid Cosmography." *Edebiyât* 12 (2001): 73–93.

———. "Serendipity, Resistance, and Multivalency: Ibn Khurradādhbih and his *Kitāb al-Masālik wa-l-mamālik*." In *On Fiction and* Adab *in Medieval Arabic Literature*, edited by Philip F. Kennedy, 177–232. Wiesbaden: Harrassowitz Verlag, 2005.

Mottahedeh, Roy P. "*ʿAjāʾib* in *The Thousand and One Nights*." In *The Thousand and One Nights in Arabic Literature*, edited by Richard Hovannisian and Georges Sabagh, 29–39. Cambridge, UK: Cambridge University Press, 1997.

———. "The Shuʿūbīyah Controversy and the Social History of Early Islamic Iran." *International Journal of Middle East Studies* 7 (1976): 161–182.

Mourad, Suleiman Ali. "A Note on the Origin of *Faḍāʾil Bayt al-Maqdis* Compilations." *al-Abḥāth* 44 (1996): 31–48.

———. "The Symbolism of Jerusalem in Early Islam." In *Jerusalem: Idea and Reality*, edited by Tamar Meyer and Suleiman Ali Mourad, 86–102. London: Routledge, 2008.

Müller, Kathrin. "al-Ḥanīn ilā l-awṭān in Early Adab Literature." In *Myths, Historical Archetypes and Symbolic Figures in Arabic Literature: Towards a New Hermeneutic Approach (Proceedings of the International Symposium in Beirut, June 25th–June 30th, 1996)*, edited by Angelika Neuwirth, Birgit Embaló, Sebastian Günther, and Maher Jarrar, 33–58. Beirut: Orient-Institut der Deutschen Morgenländischen Gesellschaft, and Stuttgart: Franz Steiner Verlag, 1999.

Muʾnis, Ḥusayn. *Taʾrīkh al-jughrāfiyya wa-l-jughrāfiyyīn fī l-Andalus*. Madrid: Maṭbaʿat al-Dirāsāt al-Islāmiyya, 1967.

al-Muqaddasī, Abū ʿAbd Allāh Shams al-Dīn Muḥammad b. Aḥmad. *Kitāb aḥsan al-taqāsīm fī maʿrifat al-aqālīm*. Edited by M. J. de Goeje. Vol. 3 of *Bibliotheca Geographorum Arabicorum*, edited by M. J. de Goeje. 3d ed. Leiden: E. J. Brill, 1967. French translation: *Aḥsan at-taqāsīm fī maʿrifat al-aqālīm (La meilleure répartition pour la conaissance des provinces)*. Edited and translated by André Miquel. Damascus: Institut Français de Damas, 1963. English translation: *The Best Divisions for Knowledge of the Regions: Aḥsan al-Taqāsīm fī Maʿrifat al-Aqālīm*. Translated by Basil Collins. Reading, UK: Garnet Publishing, 2001.

Muqātil b. Sulaymān al-Balkhī. *Tafsīr Muqātil b. Sulaymān*. 5 vols. Edited by ʿAbd Allāh Maḥmūd Shiḥāta. [Cairo]: al-Hayʾa al-Miṣriyya al-ʿĀmma li-l-Kitāb, 1979–1989.

Murād, Ẓarīf Ramaḍān. *Dirāsa fī l-turāth al-jughrāfī al-ʿarabī: Ibn Ḥawqal wa-manhajihi al-jughrāfī*. Cairo: Maktabat al-Anjulū al-Miṣriyya, 2004.

Musallam, B. F. *Sex and Society in Islam: Birth Control before the Nineteenth Century*. Cambridge, UK: Cambridge University Press, 1983.

Muslim b. al-Ḥajjāj al-Qurashī. *Saḥīḥ Muslim bi-sharḥ al-Nawawī*. 18 vols. Cairo: n.p., 1349/ [1930].

Mžik, Hans, ed. *al-Iṣṭaḫrī und seine Landkarten im Buch "Ṣuwar al-aḳālīm."* Vienna: Georg Prachner Verlag, 1965.

Najmabadi, Afsaneh. *Women with Mustaches and Men without Beards: Gender and Sexual Anxieties of Iranian Modernity*. Berkeley and Los Angeles: University of California Press, 2005.

al-Narshakhī, Abū Bakr b. Jaʿfar. *The History of Bukhara: Translated from a Persian Abridgement of the Arabic Original by Narshakhī*. Edited and translated by Richard N. Frye. Cambridge, MA: The Mediaeval Academy of America, 1954.

Nāṣir-i Khusraw. *Nasir-i Khusraw's Book of Travels: A Parallel Persian and English Text*. Edited and translated by Wheeler M. Thackston. Costa Mesa, CA: Mazda, 2001.

Nasr, Seyyed Hossein. *An Introduction to Islamic Cosmological Doctrines*. Rev. ed. Boulder, CO: Shambhala, 1978.

Neuwirth, Angelika. "Geography." In *Encyclopaedia of the Qurʾān*, vol. 2, edited by Jane Dammen McAuliffe, 293–313. Leiden: Brill, 2001–2006.

Newby, Gordon Darnell. *The Making of the Last Prophet: A Reconstruction of the Earliest Biography of Muhammad*. Columbia: University of South Carolina Press, 1989.

Nicolet, Claude. *Space, Geography, and Politics in the Early Roman Empire*. Ann Arbor: University of Michigan Press, 1991.

Norris, H. T. "*Shuʿūbiyyah* in Arabic Literature." In *ʿAbbasid Belles-Lettres*, edited by Julia Ashtiany, T. M. Johnstone, J. D. Latham, R. B. Serjeant, and G. Rex Smith, 31–47. Cambridge, UK: Cambridge University Press, 1990.

al-Nuwayrī, Shihāb al-Dīn Aḥmad b. ʿAbd al-Wahhāb. *Nihāyat al-arab fī funūn al-adab*. 18 vols. Cairo: Maṭbaʿat Dār al-Kutub al-Miṣriyya, 1923–1955.

O'Meara, Simon. *Space and Muslim Urban Life: At the Limits of the Labyrinth of Fez*. London: Routledge, 2007.

Paul, Jürgen. "The Histories of Herat." *Iranian Studies* 33, 1–2 (2000): 93–115.

———. "The Histories of Isfahan: Mafarrukhi's *Kitāb mahāsin Iṣfahān*." *Iranian Studies* 33, 1–2 (2000): 117–132.

Pellat, Charles. "Nouvel essai d'inventaire de l'oeuvre Ǧāḥiẓienne." *Arabica* 31, 2 (1984): 117–164.

Philipp, Thomas, and Christoph Schumann, eds. *From the Syrian Land to the States of Syria and Lebanon*. Beirut: Orient-Institut der Deutschen Morgenländischen Gesellschaft, and Würzburg: Ergon Verlag, 2004.

Piacentini, Valeria Fiorani. "*Madīna/Shahr, Qarya/Deh, Nāḥiya/Rustāq*: The City as Political Administrative Institution: The Continuity of a Sasanian Model." *Jerusalem Studies in Arabic and Islam* 17 (1994): 85–107.

Pinto, Karen. "Capturing Imagination: The Buja and Medieval Islamic Mappa Mundi." In *Views from the Edge: Essays in Honor of Richard W. Bulliet*, edited by Neguin Yavari, Lawrence G. Potter, and Jean-Marc Ran Oppenheim, 154–183. New York: Columbia University Press, 2004.

———. "The Maps Are the Message: Mehmet II's Patronage of an 'Ottoman Cluster.'" *Imago Mundi* 63, 2 (2011): 155–179.

———. "'Surat Bahr al-Rum' (Picture of the Sea of Byzantium): Possible Meanings Underlying the Forms." In *Eastern Mediterranean Cartographies*, edited by George Tolias and Dimitris Loupis, 223–241. Athens: Institute for Neohellenic Research and National Hellenic Research Foundation, 2004.

———. "Ways of Seeing. 3: Scenarios of the World in the Medieval Islamic Imagination." PhD diss., Columbia University, 2001.

Pourshariati, Parvaneh. "Local Histories of Khurāsān and the Pattern of Arab Settlement." *Studia Iranica* 27 (1998): 41–81.

———. "Local Historiography in Early Medieval Iran and the Tārīkh-i Bayhaq." *Iranian Studies* 33, 1–2 (2000): 133–164.

Power, Daniel and Naomi Standen, eds. *Frontiers in Question: Eurasian Borderlands, 700–1700*. New York: St. Martin's Press, 1999.

Pratt, Mary Louis. *Toward a Speech Act Theory of Literary Discourse*. Bloomington: Indiana University Press, 1977.

Pregill, Michael. "Isrā'īliyyāt, Myth, and Pseudepigraphy: Wahb b. Munabbih and the Early Islamic Versions of the Fall of Adam and Eve." *Jerusalem Studies on Arabic and Islam* 34 (2008): 215–284.

de Prémare, Alfred-Louis. "Wahb b. Munabbih, une figure singulière du premier Islam." *Annales* 60, 3 (2005): 531–549.

al-Qadi, Wadad. "Dislocation and nostalgia: al-ḥanīn ilā l-awṭān." In *Myths, Historical Archetypes and Symbolic Figures in Arabic Literature: Towards a New Hermeneutic Approach (Proceedings of the International Symposium in Beirut, June 25th–June 30th, 1996)*, edited by Angelika Neuwirth, Birgit Embaló, Sebastian Günther, and Maher Jarrar, 3–31. Beirut: Orient-Institut der Deutschen Morgenländischen Gesellschaft, and Stuttgart: Franz Steiner Verlag, 1999.

al-Qayrawānī, Abū l-ʿArab Muḥammad b. Aḥmad b. Tamīm. *Ṭabaqāt ʿulamāʾ Ifrīqiyya wa-Tūnis*. Edited by ʿAlī al-Shābbī and Naʿīm Ḥasan al-Yāfī. Tunis: Dār al-Tūnisiyya li-l-Nashr, 1985.

al-Qifṭī, ʿAlī b. Yūsuf. *Inbāh al-ruwāh ʿalā anbāh al-nuḥāh*. 4 vols. Edited by Muḥammad Abū l-Faḍl Ibrāhīm. Cairo: Maṭbaʿat Dār al-Kutub al-Miṣriyya, 1950–1973.

Qudāma b. Jaʿfar, Abū l-Faraj. *Kitāb al-kharāj* (excerpts). Edited by M. J. de Goeje. Vol. 6 of *Bibliotheca Geographorum Arabicorum*, ed. M. J. de Goeje. 2d ed. Leiden: E. J. Brill, 1967. (This edition also includes a French translation of the Arabic text. All page citations in the notes refer to the Arabic.)

Qummī, Ḥasan b. Muḥammad. *Tārīkh-i Qum*. Persian translation by Tāj al-Dīn Ḥasan Khaṭīb b. Bahāʾ al-Dīn ʿAlī b. Ḥasan b. ʿAbd al-Malik Qummī. Edited by Muḥammad Riḍā Anṣārī Qummī. Tehran: Marashi Library, 2006.

al-Qushayrī, Muḥammad b. Saʿīd. *Taʾrīkh al-Raqqa*. Edited by Ibrāhīm Ṣāliḥ. Damascus: Dār al-Bashāʾir, 1998.

al-Rabaʿī, Abū l-Ḥasan ʿAlī b. Muḥammad. *Faḍāʾil al-Shām wa-Dimashq*. Edited by Ṣalāḥ al-Dīn al-Munajjid. Damascus: Maṭbaʿat al-Turqī, 1950.

Rabbat, Nasser. "The Dialogic Dimension of Umayyad Art." *Res* 43 (2003): 79–94.

———. "The Dome of the Rock Revisited: Some Remarks on al-Wasiti's Accounts." *Muqarnas* 10 (1993): 67–75.

———. "Al-Maqrizi's *Khitat*, an Egyptian *Lieu de Mémoire*." In *The Cairo Heritage: Essays in Honor of Laila Ali Ibrahim*, edited by Doris Behrens-Abouseif, 17–30. Cairo: American University in Cairo Press, 2000.

———. "The Meaning of the Umayyad Dome of the Rock." *Muqarnas* 6 (1989): 12–21.

al-Rāghib al-Iṣfahānī, al-Ḥusayn b. Muḥammad. *Muḥāḍarāt al-ʿudabāʾ wa-muḥāwarāt al-shuʿarāʾ wa-l-bulaghāʾ*. 2 vols. Edited by ʿUmar al-Ṭabbāʿ. Beirut: Dār al-Arqam, 1999.

Rapoport, Yossef. "The *Book of Curiosities*: A Medieval Islamic View of the East." In *The Journey of Maps and Images on the Silk Road*, edited by Philippe Forêt and Andreas Kaplony, 155–171. Leiden: Brill, 2008.

Raymond, André. "Islamic City, Arab City: Orientalist Myths and Recent Views." *British Journal of Middle Eastern Studies* 21, 1 (1994): 3–18.

———. "The Spatial Organization of the City." In *The City in the Islamic World*, vol. 1, edited by Salma K. Jayyusi, Renata Holod, Attilio Petruccioli, and André Raymond, 47–70. Leiden: Brill, 2008.

al-Rāzī, Aḥmad b. ʿAbd Allāh. *Kitāb taʾrīkh madīnat Ṣanʿāʾ*. Edited by Ḥusayn ʿAbd Allāh al-ʿAmrī and ʿAbd al-Jabbār Zakkār. Sanaa: n.p., 1974.

Robinson, Cynthia. "*Ubi Sunt*: Memory and Nostalgia in Taifa Court Culture." *Muqarnas* 15 (1998): 20–31.

Rooke, Tetz. "Writing the Boundary: *Khiṭaṭ al-Shām* by Muhammad Kurd ʿAli." In *The Concept of Territory in Islamic Law and Thought*, edited by Yanagihashi Hiroyuki, 165–186. London: Kegan Paul International, 2000.

Rosenthal, Franz. *A History of Muslim Historiography*. Leiden: E. J. Brill, 1952.

———. "The Stranger in Medieval Islam." *Arabica* 44 (1997): 35–75.

Roxburgh, David J. "Pilgrimage City." In *The City in the Islamic World*, vol. 2, edited by Salma K. Jayyusi, Renata Holod, Attilio Petruccioli, and André Raymond, 753–774. Leiden: Brill, 2008.

Rubin, Uri. "Between Arabia and the Holy Land: A Mecca-Jerusalem Axis of Sanctity." *Jerusalem Studies in Arabic and Islam* 34 (2008): 345–362.

———. *The Eye of the Beholder: The Life of Muḥammad as Viewed by the Early Muslims*. Princeton: The Darwin Press, 1995.

———. "The Kaʿba: Aspects of its ritual functions and position in pre-Islamic and early Islamic times." *Jerusalem Studies in Arabic and Islam* 8 (1986): 97–131.

———. "Muḥammad's Night Journey (*isrāʾ*) to al-Masjid al-Aqṣā: Aspects of the Earliest Origins of the Islamic Sanctity of Jerusalem." *Al-Qanṭara* 29 (2008): 147–165.

Ruggles, D. F. "Arabic Poetry and Architectural Memory in al-Andalus." *Ars Orientalis* 23 (1993): 171–178.

Sadan, Joseph. "An Admirable and Ridiculous Hero: Some Notes on the Bedouin in Medieval Arabic Belles Lettres, on a Chapter of *Adab* by al-Rāghib al-Iṣfahānī, and on a Literary Model in Which Admiration and Mockery Coexist." *Poetics Today* 10, 3 (1989): 471–492.

———. "*Hārūn al-Rashīd and the Brewer*: Preliminary Remarks on the *Adab* of the Elite Versus *Ḥikāyāt*." In *Studies in Canonical and Popular Arabic Literature*, edited by S. Ballas and R. Snir, 1–22. Toronto: York Press Ltd., 1998.

Safran, Janina. *The Second Umayyad Caliphate: The Articulation of Caliphal Legitimacy in al-Andalus*. Cambridge, MA: Harvard University Press, 2000.

al-Sahmī, Ḥamza b. Yūsuf. *Ta'rīkh Jurjān*. Hyderabad-Deccan: Osmania Oriental Publications Bureau, 1950.

Said, Edward. *Orientalism*. New York: Vintage Books, 1979.

Sajdi, Dana. "Ibn Kannān." In *Historians of the Ottoman Empire*, edited by C. Kafadar, H. Karateke, and C. Fleischer. Online: http://www.ottomanhistorians.com/database/html/ibnkannan_en.html. November 2009.

al-Sanʿānī, ʿAbd al-Razzāq b. Ḥammām. *al-Muṣannaf*. 11 vols. Edited by Ḥabīb al-Raḥmān al-Aʿẓamī. N.p.: al-Majlis al-ʿIlmī, and Beirut: al-Maktab al-Islāmī, 1970–1972.

Sanders, Paula. *Ritual, Politics, and the City in Fatimid Cairo*. Albany: State University of New York Press, 1994.

Savage-Smith, Emilie. "Celestial Mapping." In *The History of Cartography*, vol. 2, bk. 1, edited by J. B. Harley and David Woodward, 12–70. Chicago: University of Chicago Press, 1992.

———. "Memory and Maps." In *Culture and Memory in Medieval Islam: Essays in Honor of Wilferd Madelung*, edited by Farhad Daftary, 109–127. London: I. B. Tauris, 2003.

Savage-Smith, Emilie, and Jeremy Johns. "*The Book of Curiosities*: A Newly Discovered Series of Islamic Maps." *Imago Mundi* 55 (2003): 7–24.

Savage-Smith, Emilie, and Yossef Rapoport. "Medieval Islamic View of the Cosmos: The Newly Discovered *Book of Curiosities*." *The Cartographic Journal* 41, 3 (2004): 253–259.

Savant, Sarah Bowen. "Forgetting Iran's Pre-Islamic Past, ca. 800–1100 CE." In *History and Identity in the Late Antique Near East*, edited by Philip Wood. Oxford: Oxford University Press, forthcoming.

———. *The New Muslims of Post-Conquest Iran: Tradition, Memory, and Conversion*. Cambridge, UK: Cambridge University Press, forthcoming.

Sezgin, Fuat. *Geschichte des arabischen Schrifttums*. 15 vols. Vols. 1–9, Leiden: E. J. Brill, 1967–1984. Vols. 10–15, Frankfurt am Main: Institut für Geschichte der Arabisch-Islamischen Wissenschaften an der Johann Wolfgang Goethe-Universität, 2000–2010.

———. *Mathematical Geography and Cartography in Islam and their Continuation in the Occident.* 3 vols. Translated by Guy Moore and Geoff Sammon. Frankfurt am Main: Institut für Geschichte der Arabisch-Islamischen Wissenschaften an der Johann Wolfgang Goethe-Universität, 2000–2007.

Sezgin, Fuat, ed. *Majmūʿ fī l-Jughrāfiyā.* Frankfurt am Main: Institut für Geschichte der Arabisch-Islamischen Wissenschaften an der Johann Wolfgang Goethe-Universität, 1987.

Shafīʿ, Muḥammad. "A Description of the Two Sanctuaries of Islam by Ibn ʿAbd Rabbihi (d. 940)." In *The Great Mosque of the Prophet in Medina (al-Ḥaram al-Madanī): Texts and Studies*, vol. 1 of *Islamic Architecture*, edited by Fuat Sezgin, 10–32. Frankfurt am Main: Institut für Geschichte der Arabisch-Islamischen Wissenschaften an der Johann Wolfgang Goethe-Universität, 2007.

Shahid, Irfan. "The Jund System in Bilād al-Shām: Its Origin." In *Bilād al-Shām fī I-ʿahd al-Bīzanṭī*, vol. 2, edited by Muḥammad ʿAdnān al-Bakhīt and Muḥammad ʿAṣfūr, 45–52. Amman: University of Jordan and Yarmouk University, 1986.

Sivan, Emmanuel. "The Beginnings of the *Faḍāʾil al-Quds* Literature." *Israel Oriental Studies* 1 (1971): 263–271.

Smith, Martyn. *Religion, Culture, and Sacred Space.* New York: Palgrave Macmillan, 2008.

Sourdel, Dominique, and Janine Sourdel-Thomine, eds. and trans. "Une collection médiévale de certificats de pèlerinage à la Mekke conservés à Istanbul." In *Etudes médiévales et patrimoine turc: Volume publié à l'occasion du centième anniversaire de la naissance de Kemal Atatürk*, edited by Janine Sourdel-Thomine, 167–273. Paris: Editions du Centre National de la Recherche Scientifique, 1983.

Spellberg, Denise. *Politics, Gender, and the Islamic Past: The Legacy of ʿAʾisha bint Abi Bakr.* New York: Columbia University Press, 1996.

Stetkevych, Jaroslav. "Toward an Arabic Elegiac Lexicon: The Seven Words of the *Nasīb*." In *Reorientations/Arabic and Persian Poetry*, edited by Suzanne Pinckney Stetkevych, 58–129. Bloomington and Indianapolis: Indiana University Press, 1994.

———. *The Zephyrs of Najd: The Poetics of Nostalgia in the Classical Arabic* Nasīb. Chicago: University of Chicago Press, 1993.

Stetkevych, Suzanne Pinckney. *The Poetics of Islamic Legitimacy: Myth, Gender, and Ceremony in the Classical Arabic Ode.* Bloomington: Indiana University Press, 2002.

Suhrāb. *Kitāb ʿajāʾib al-sabʿa ilā nihāyat al-ʿimāra.* Edited by Hans von Mžik. Leipzig: Otto Harrassowitz, 1930.

al-Ṭabarī, Muḥammad b. Jarīr. *Taʾrīkh al-rusul wa-l-mulūk.* 15 vols. Edited by M. J. de Goeje et al. 1879–1901. Reprint, Leiden: E. J. Brill, 1964–1965. Partial English translation: *The War between Brothers.* Edited and translated by Michael Fishbein. Vol. 31 of *The History of al-Ṭabarī (Taʾrīkh al-rusul waʾl-mulūk)*, edited by Ehsan Yar-Shater et al. Albany: State University of New York Press, 1992.

Tārīkh-i Sīstān. Edited by Malik al-Shuʿarā Bahār. Tehran: Khāvar, 1314/[1935]. English translation: *The Tārīkh-i Sīstān.* Translated by Milton Gold. Rome: Istituto italiano per il Medio ed Estremo Oriente, 1976.

Tavakoli-Targhi, Mohamad. *Refashioning Iran: Orientalism, Occidentalism and Historiography.* Basingstoke, UK: Palgrave, 2001.

El Tayib, Abdulla. "Pre-Islamic Poetry." In *Arabic Literature to the End of the Umayyad Period*, ed. A. F. L. Beeston, T. M. Johnstone, R. B. Serjeant, and G. R. Smith, 27–113. Cambridge, UK: Cambridge University Press, 1983.

al-Thaʿālibī, Abū Manṣūr ʿAbd al-Malik b. Muḥammad. *Laṭāʾif al-maʿārif.* Edited by Ibrāhīm al-Ibyārī and Ḥasan Kāmil al-Ṣayrafī. [Cairo]: Dār Iḥyāʾ al-Kutub al-ʿArabiyya, 1960. English translation: *The* Laṭāʾif al-maʿārif *of Thaʿālibī: The Book of Curious and Entertaining Information.* Edited and translated by C. E. Bosworth. Edinburgh: The University Press, 1968.

———. *al-Laṭāʾif wa-l-ẓarāʾif.* Beirut: Dār al-Manāhil, 1992.

Thomas, Stephanie. "The Concept of *Muḥāḍara* in the Adab Anthology with Special Reference to al-Rāghib al-Iṣfahānī's *Muḥāḍarāt al-udabāʾ*." PhD diss., Harvard University, 2000.

Thongchai Winichakul. *Siam Mapped: A History of the Geo-Body of a Nation*. Honolulu: University of Hawaii Press, 1994.

Tibbetts, Gerald R. "The Balkhī School of Geographers." In *The History of Cartography*, vol. 2, bk. 1, edited by J. B. Harley and David Woodward, 108–129. Chicago: University of Chicago Press, 1992.

———. "The Beginnings of a Cartographic Tradition." In *The History of Cartography*, vol. 2, bk. 1, edited by J. B. Harley and David Woodward, 90–107. Chicago: University of Chicago Press, 1992.

———. "Later Cartographic Developments." In *The History of Cartography*, vol. 2, bk. 1, edited by J. B. Harley and David Woodward, 137–155. Chicago: University of Chicago Press, 1992.

Tomasch, Sylvia, and Sealy Gilles, eds. *Text and Territory: The Geographical Imagination in the European Middle Ages*. Philadelphia: University of Pennsylvania Press, 1998.

Tottoli, Roberto. "Origin and Use of the Term *Isrāʾīliyyāt* in Muslim Literature." *Arabica* 46 (1999): 193–210.

le Tourneau, Roger. *Fès avant le protectorat: étude économique et sociale d'une ville de l'occident musulman*. Casablanca: Société Marocaine de Librairie et d'Edition, 1949.

Tskitishvili, Otar. "Yazd*dj*ard b. Bahandā*dh* al-Kisrawī and Some Questions of the Inner Structure of Madīnat al-Manṣūr." *Studia Islamica* 64 (1989): 167–175.

Tucker, Judith E. *In the House of the Law: Gender and Islamic Law in Ottoman Syria and Palestine*. Berkeley and Los Angeles: University of California Press, 1998.

ʿUmar b. Shabba, Abū Zayd al-Baṣrī. *Kitāb taʾrīkh al-Madīna al-Munawwara*. 4 vols. Edited by Fahīm Muḥammad Shaltūt. [Mecca]: Ḥabīb Maḥmūd Aḥmad, [1979].

Usāma b. Munqidh. *Kitāb al-manāzil wa-l-diyār*. Edited by Muṣṭafā Ḥijāzī. Cairo: Dār Suʿād al-Ṣabbāḥ, 1992.

Van Laer, Zacharias. "Ibn al-Faqīh et le Livre des Pays." *Arabica* 31, 1 (1984): 69–79.

Waldman, Marilyn Robinson. *Toward a Theory of Historical Narrative: A Case Study in Perso-Islamicate Historiography*. Columbus: Ohio State University Press, 1980.

al-Wāsiṭī, Abū Bakr Muḥammad b. Aḥmad. *Faḍāʾil al-Bayt al-Muqaddas*. Edited by Isaac Hasson. Jerusalem: The Magnes Press, 1979.

Wendell, Charles. "Baghdād: *Imago Mundi*, and Other Foundation-Lore." *International Journal of Middle Eastern Studies* 2 (1971): 99–128.

Wensinck, A. J. "Kaʿba." In *E. J. Brill's First Encyclopaedia of Islam, 1913–1936*, vol. 4, edited by M. Th. Houtsma et al., 584–592. Reprint, Leiden: E. J. Brill, 1987.

Wheatley, Paul. *The Places Where Men Pray Together*. Chicago: University of Chicago Press, 2001.

Witkam, Jan Just. *Inventory of the Oriental Manuscripts of the Library of the University of Leiden*. 25 vols. Online: http://www.islamicmanuscripts.info/inventories/leiden/. Leiden: Ter Lugt Press, 2006–2008.

al-Yaʿqūbī, Aḥmad b. Abī Yaʿqūb. *Kitāb al-buldān*. Edited by M. J. de Goeje. Vol. 7 of *Bibliotheca Geographorum Arabicorum*, edited by M. J. de Goeje. 2d ed. Leiden: E. J. Brill, 1967. French translation: *Les Pays*. Translated by Gaston Wiet. Cairo: Institut Français d'Archéologie Orientale, 1937.

Yāqūt b. ʿAbd Allāh al-Ḥamawī al-Rūmī. *Muʿjam al-buldān*. 7 vols. Beirut: Dār Ṣādir, 1995. Partial English translation: *The Introductory Chapters of Yāqūt's Muʿjam al-Buldān*. Edited and translated by Wadie Jwaideh. Leiden: E. J. Brill, 1959.

Zachs, Fruma. *The Making of a Syrian Identity: Intellectuals and Merchants in Nineteenth-Century Beirut*. Leiden: Brill, 2005.

Zadeh, Travis. *Mapping Frontiers Across Medieval Islam: Geography, Translation, and the ʿAbbāsid Empire*. London: I. B. Tauris, 2012.

———. "The Wiles of Creation: Philosophy, Fiction, and the *ʿAjāʾib* Tradition." *Middle Eastern Literatures* 13, 1 (2010): 21–48.

al-Zamakhsharī, Maḥmūd b. ʿUmar. *Rabīʿ al-abrār wa-fuṣūṣ al-akhbār*. 2 vols. Vol. 1, edited by ʿAbd al-Majīd Diyāb and Ramaḍān ʿAbd al-Tawwāb. [Cairo]: al-Hayʾa al-Miṣriyya al-ʿĀmma li-l-Kitāb,

1992. Vol. 2, edited by Muhammad ʿAlī Qurna and Ramaḍān ʿAbd al-Tawwāb. Cairo: Dār al-Kutub wa-l-Wathāʾiq al-Qawmiyya, 2001.

al-Zayyāt, ʿAbd Allāh Muḥammad. *Rithāʾ al-mudun fī l-shiʿr al-Andalusī*. Benghazi: Jāmiʿat Qāriyūnis, 1990.

Ziadeh, Nicola A. "Diyār al-Shām according to al-Masʿūdī." In *Al-Masʿūdī Millenary Commemoration Volume*, edited by S. Maqbul Ahmad and A. Rahman, 20–24. Kolkata: The Indian Society for the History of Science and the Institute of Islamic Studies, Aligarh Muslim University, 1960.

INDEX

Abbasid Caliphate: in *adab* anthologies, 17, 25, 153n66; administrative needs of, 88–89, 102; Baghdad as capital of, 33, 35, 43, 55–60, 79, 89, 163n128, 163n133; challenges to, 59, 82, 96, 129, 135, 137; claims to power and legitimacy, 58–59, 95; fragmentation of, 7, 34, 83, 100, 142, 144; patronage of building, 59, 63, 65, 70, 137, 167n56; patronage of scholars, 88–89; in relation to Baghdad's built environment, 72–76; representatives of, 105; Samarra as capital of, 163n132, 163n136; territories of, 28, 102, 105. *See also under specific caliphs*
ʿAbd al-Malik, Umayyad Caliph, 48–49, 54–55, 58, 170n96
Abraham: and Egypt, 135; and Hebron, 81; and Iraq, 136; and Mecca, 44–46, 50, 58, 63, 80; and Syria, 45, 126
Abrahamic tradition, 46–47, 49, 55. *See also* Christianity/Christians; Judaism/Jews; prophets
Abū l-Maʿālī, 49–55, 65–66, 78, 80, 82
Abū Nuʿaym, 82–83, 156n26
Abū Tammām, 21, 23, 27, 29
adab: and citational practices, 70–71; and debate/contrastive enumeration, 12, 34, 79, 82, 97, 127, 169n81, 179n64. *See also* Ifrīqiyya; al-Maghrib
Africa, sub-Saharan, 119
Aghlabids, 105, 106
agriculture. *See* regions, in relation to rural areas
al-Ahwāz, 27, 97, 141
ʿĀʾisha, 47–48
ʿajāʾib (wonders, marvels), 6, 81, 181n93
Aleppo, 112, 144
Alexander the Great, 17, 38, 44, 91, 135, 136
Alexandria, 37, 135
Ali, Samer, 149n5
ʿAlī b. Abī Ṭālib: and Egypt, 133, 137; and Kufa, 29, 80, 169n81; on Medina, 36; and the *waṭan*, 29, 153n54
America, North, 147
al-Amīn, Abbasid Caliph, 73–75
Amīr al-Muʾminīn (Commander of the Believers), 57, 97, 100, 128–129
ʿAmr b. al-ʿĀṣ, 134–135, 136
Andalusia/al-Andalus: and al-Bakrī, 107, 172n27, 181n79; as a division of the world, 110, 119; and Ibn ʿAbd Rabbih, 67; in local histories, 180n77; maps of, 117, 176n19; in regional monographs, 132, 140–141, 144, 182n122; in relation to eastern lands, 41; and the *waṭan*, 24
anthologies: as a genre, 2, 33, 67, 154n1; in relation to the culture of *adab*, 12–13; subheadings in, 15, 17, 22; on the topic of homesickness/*al-ḥanīn ilā l-awṭān*, 6, 11–29
Aqṣā Mosque. *See* al-Masjid al-Aqṣā
Arab: in geographies, 98–99, 104, 110, 172n36; in modern usage, 7, 147
Arabian Peninsula: as a division of the world, 88, 92, 97, 100, 110, 114, 133, 176n19; maps of, 115–117 (incl. Figs. 5.1, 5.2), 119–121 (incl. Fig. 5.4), 138, 178n43, 178n45, 178n49, 179n53; in regional monographs, 137–140, 182n108; in relation to the *waṭan*, 16–17, 19–20, 22, 26–27, 152n33, 154n77; in relation to Egypt, 134; in relation to Transoxiana, 130; in relation to Yemen and Bahrain, 129, 131
Arabic: as a language, 2, 3, 7; as a literary heritage, 13, 14, 20, 27
Arabicization: of city names, 35–36; of populations, 43
ʿArafa/ʿArafāt, 63